COMMUNICATING
U N R E A L I T Y

COMMUNICATING UNREALITY

Modern
Media
and the
Reconstruction
of Reality

GABRIEL WEIMANN

Sage Publications, Inc.
International Educational and Professional Publisher
Thousand Oaks ▪ London ▪ New Delhi

For information:

Sage Publications, Inc.
2455 Teller Road
Thousand Oaks, California 91320
E-mail: order@sagepub.com

Sage Publications Ltd.
6 Bonhill Street
London EC2A 4PU
United Kingdom

Sage Publications India Pvt. Ltd.
M-32 Market
Greater Kailash I
New Delhi 110 048 India

Printed in the United States of America

Library of Congress Cataloging-in-Publication Data

Weimann, Gabriel, 1950-
   Communicating unreality: Modern media and the reconstruction of reality /
by Gabriel Weimann.
      p. cm.
   Includes bibliographical references (p.) and index.
   ISBN 0-7619-1985-6
   ISBN 0-7619-1986-4
   1. Mass media—Influence. 2. Mass media—United States.
   3. Mass media—Social aspects. 4. Mass media—Psychological aspects.
   5. Reality. I. Title.
   P94 .W45 2000
   302.23—dc21   99-6520

00   01   02   03   04   05   06   7   6   5   4   3   2   1

Acquiring Editor:	Margaret H. Seawell
Editorial Assistant:	Renée Piernot
Production Editor:	Astrid Virding
Editorial Assistant:	Karen Wiley
Typesetter/Designer:	Marion Warren
Cover Designer:	Candice Harman

Contents

PART III Conclusions

Preface

Long before the introduction of mass media, before communication scholars started to realize the power of mass media in shaping our perceptions of reality, the Greek philosopher Plato presented the notion of reconstructed reality in his famous Allegory of the Cave. "Imagine," said Plato, "the condition of men who had always lived deep within a dark cave. There is a fire burning in the cave, and it glows so strongly that it casts shadows on the opposite wall. The people in the cave are chained so they face the wall and the shadows. They cannot see the actual figures moving in the cave but only the puppet show of shadows on the wall." Plato added sound effects to his shadow show. "Suppose," he said, "that the people moving in the cave talked freely, but the chained men could hear only the echoes from the walls and imagine that these were the original voices." Plato's lesson was simple: The chained men in the cave, exposed only to shadows and echoes, would believe that these reflections were reality. Sooner or later, they would develop shared interpretations of the shadows, give them names and meanings, and hate or like some of them, but always accept them as the real things, not their distorted reflections. The sounds, images, and movements reflected on their wall shaped their perception of reality.

Suppose that one of them was set free and he could see it all: the wall, the true figures, the real movements, the reality. He could learn how distorted his former perceptions were and recognize the true reality. "But then," asks Plato, "what will happen if we bring him back to the chained men, still facing the shadows on the wall? What will happen when he will try to explain to his former companions that what they were all seeing was not reality at all?" Plato was convinced that the chained men would laugh at him and reject his ideas of the "real" reality out there.

The wall in the cave was replaced by the screens of television, movies, and computers, by pictures and text in newspapers and magazines, by the sounds of recorded and transmitted voices and sounds on radio sets. We may not be chained, but nevertheless these media "walls" are our main source of information about the world out there.

This book attempts to break away from the cave, to gather and analyze the findings of numerous studies about mass-mediated realities, and then to return to the cave with the evidence. Equipped with data from various research areas in many societies, cultures, and domains there is, I hope, no real threat that the "return to the cave" will end as Plato predicted: According to him, the returning man, trying to convince the others that they were not seeing true reality, would eventually be killed by them.

In Chapter 1, we look at the nature of a mediated environment and the early recognition by Walter Lippmann that the media shape "the pictures in our heads" of the "world out there." We examine the growing dependence on the mass-mediated presentations and interpretations of events, processes, and occurrences, especially in the "global village" we live in, where the technology of modern communication systems has made the world shrink and national or cultural boundaries collapse. In Chapter 2, we examine the lingering debate about the power of media and their impact on our attitudes, values, emotions, and opinions. We examine the evolution of research in the area of media effects. First, we consider what *media effects* means, then, we briefly trace the evolution in scholars' perspectives on media effects, and finally, we examine selected processes and theories by which media effects are thought to occur. Chapter 3 is devoted to the notion of cultivation and the related concept of mainstreaming. We examine the nature of these processes, the methodology used to study them, and the differences between them and other media effects. In this part, we also learn about the "debate over cultivation": Cultivation studies have been criticized on conceptual and methodological grounds, including response biases and problems with the measuring instruments. Finally, this chapter looks at cultivation studies after two decades: It has been over 20 years since the first cultivation findings were published. Since then, many studies have explored, enhanced, critiqued, dismissed, or defended the conceptual assumptions and methodological procedures of cultivation analysis. Where is cultivation theory?

Chapter 4 looks at the psychology of cultivation: What are the various psychological processes that lead us to accept media realities? Who are more vulnerable to the media's cultivation? The chapter reviews the research attempts to identify cognitive trait variables affecting cultivation, subprocesses or stages in the cultivation process, and the intervening impact of psychological factors such as memory accessibility, critical consumption of media, personal involvement, and personal experience. The subsequent part examines evidence of the cultivation process in various areas and various societies and cultures. Chapter 5 starts with the Mean World Syndrome. Modern media, such as video games, computer networks, computer games, Virtual Reality, Internet, and others—and, of course, television and movies—have become popular sites for experiencing, watching, and even activating aggression in various forms. Gerbner argued that we live now in a "charged environment," in a huge "cult of violence." This chapter looks at two questions: How mean is the media world, and what is the impact of violent media and violent contents on perceptions of the world as dangerous, mean, and violent.

In Chapter 6, another dimension of reconstructed reality is examined, that of sex and sexuality. One of the most studied and documented areas of reconstructed realities by the mass media is that of the portrayal of the sexes and its impact on popular stereotypes of sex roles. The role of the media in sex role socialization has become an area of considerable concern and the topic of many studies during the recent decades because of the women's movement's interest, the convincing findings on bias and cultivation within this domain, and the emerging recognition that the media play a crucial role in diffusing, preserving, and cultivating images of sex roles. This chapter reveals the sexist patterns in various media contents such as commercials, TV series, movies, magazines, advertisements, and children's media. How do these mediated images of the sexes affect our perceptions of the sexes, their roles, traits, similarities, and differences? This chapter also looks at the impact of the media on the image of thinness and their impact on eating disorders, especially among women. Finally, the chapter reports the findings on the cultivation of sexuality, perceptions of sexual relationships, and especially the impact of pornography.

Death and dying are relatively new areas for communication researchers. Chapter 7 reviews the studies on media presentations of death, dying, and suicide. This chapter also reports the impact of these mediated "facts" or images on people's perceptions of death and suicide. Of specific relevance are the findings on the distorted perceptions of who commits suicide and why, as cultivated by media contents. Chapter 8 is devoted to "the world according to MTV," the music video channel, highly popular among young viewers all over the world. Music videos are distinctive because they present fantasies and dreams rather than the typical contents of television programs. Music video's "dream worlds," "stories," and "loose narrative" often depict aggression, violence, conflict, sex, and sex roles. This chapter explores the messages of MTV's videos and commercials and their impact on young viewers as revealed by numerous studies.

How do we develop our impressions about certain groups, such as the aging? African Americans? AIDS patients? Gay people? Physicians? Arabs? One of the major images that mass media create for us involves stereotypical images of various groups of people. For many of these groups, it is only through TV and other media that we meet, learn about, and virtually "encounter" them. Chapter 9 looks at the part played by the media in the social reconstruction of several social groups. We examine here a sample of these portrayals, such as those of ethnic groups, race groups, professions, and other social categories.

In Chapter 10, we examine the images of the United States as portrayed in various countries and various media contents. We also look at the impact of these mediated images on various audiences all over the world. The choice of American images was guided by the dominance of the American media in the international flow of news and entertainment, the impact of U.S.-made media on world media, and the studies of the impact of American media on various societies. Chapter 11 focuses on another dramatic form of media's reconstruction of reality: the case of war, especially the mediated Gulf War of 1991. Finally, Chapter 12 takes us into the recent innovations in communication technologies, from the Internet and the information superhighway to Virtual Reality, and looks at the potential cultivation impact of these media: Are they virtual or real? The concluding chapter attempts to list all the factors and actors involved in the process of "communicating unreality" and to suggest a dynamic and transactional model of cultivation (DTC model) to combine all these factors and actors into one conceptual framework of analysis.

Acknowledgments

This book summarizes research that extended over 5 years and was hosted by five universities, supported by several foundations and grants, and assisted by many colleagues and friends. It reviews over 4,000 studies in this area including some of my own. Traversing various domains of mass-mediated realities, from war to sexuality, from death to gender, from international images to Virtual Reality technology or MTV's depiction of the world, *Communicating Unreality* provides a true journey through the reconstructed worlds of the mass media.

The research reported here could not have been done without the contributions of many individuals and institutions all over the world. Five universities hosted me and provided the required research facilities: the Annenberg School of Communication at the University of Pennsylvania, United States; the University of Mainz, Germany; Hofstra University, Long Island, United States; the National University of Singapore; and Haifa University, Israel. Several foundations contributed directly and indirectly to this project: the American Fulbright Foundation, the German Alexander von Humboldt Foundation, the Berman Center's research grant, the German National Research Foundation (DFG), and the Japanese Sasakawa Fellowship.

Many of my colleagues and friends are to be thanked for their support, advice, and contributions. I will name only a few: Mark Levy, Sheizaf Rafaeli, Tamar Katriel, Jonathan Cohen, Helga Weissbecker, Hans-Bernd Brosius, March Lim, Wu Wei, Baruch Nevo, Sondra Rubenstein, Nancy Kaplan, Clowi, Sandra Ball-Rokeach, Josephine Heth, and many others. I wish to express my appreciation and gratitude to three anonymous reviewers for their excellent suggestions and comments and to Sara Miller McCune, Margaret Seawell, and the rest of the editorial staff at Sage Publications for their resolute efforts. Finally, to my family, Nava, Oren, and Dana, who provided encouragement and support to a husband and parent who was at times more attentive to his research than to them.

PART I

The
Reconstruction
of Reality

CHAPTER ONE

Living in a Mediated World

Modern humanity, several communication scholars argue, is increasingly experiencing a mediated world rather than reality itself:

> One of the major features of our current transition into the Age of the Mass Communication, then, is that increasingly we are in contact with mediated representations of a complex physical and social world rather than only with the objective features of our narrow surroundings. (DeFleur & Ball-Rokeach, 1989, p. 259)

It was Walter Lippmann's classical work, *Public Opinion,* first published in 1922, that highlighted for the first time the possibility that factual features of the world often have little relation to the perception and beliefs that people entertain about the world. Lippmann argued that the press's depiction of events was often spurious: The images it created were misleading, distorted, and shaped false "pictures in our heads" of the "world outside." He claimed that people often act not on the basis of actual facts and events, but on the basis of what they think is the real situation as they perceive it from the press. For example, when the press falsely reported an armistice in November 1918, during World War I, people rejoiced over the event. Meanwhile, the war went on, and thousands continued to die on the European battlefields.

Although Lippmann never referred to his ideas in terms of a model or theory of reconstructed realities, his notion of the reliance of the public on the often distorted presentation of reality in the press should be acknowledged as such. He was certainly the first to note the role of the media ("the press" in his time) in the construction of meanings and perceptions of the "world outside." Lippmann made the important distinction between the real environment and the pseudo-environment sketched and delivered by the mass media. Moreover, Lippmann, in 1922, could not anticipate the emergence of the electronic media and the ever-growing role of the new media in shaping "the pictures in our heads." As radio, and then television, cable, and satellite technologies appeared, the world shrank to a global village, exposed to the flow of mass-produced news and entertainment, and the notion of a mediated world became more realistic.

We are a mass-mediated society. The mass media, especially television, play important, if often invisible and taken-for-granted roles in our daily lives. Television sets are usually placed in prominent positions in our homes, whether in the family room, the living room, the kitchen, the bedroom, or all of the above. Few can remember, or care to remember, what life was like before television. Each day, in the average American household, a television set is on for over 7 hours. Individual family members watch it for about 3 hours. Children and older people watch the most; adolescents watch the least, but even they view an average of 20 or more hours each week. Although most Americans report that they read a daily newspaper, television is often cited as their major source of news and information.

The electronic media have only strengthened the power of the media in the reconstruction of reality. For the same reasons that operated for the press during World War I, only more significantly, the electronic media and especially television continue to present and diffuse reconstructions of reality rather than accurate representations. And the impact, in terms of shaping the audience's perceptions, seems in the age of television to be more powerful than ever. As Gerbner and his associates (Gerbner, Gross, Morgan, & Signorielli, 1986), who studied television and cultivating constructed realities (discussed in detail in Part II), argue,

> Television is a centralized system of storytelling. It is part and parcel of our daily lives. Its drama, commercials, news, and other programs

bring a relatively coherent world of common images and messages into every home. Television cultivates from infancy the very predispositions and preferences that used to be acquired from other primary sources. Transcending historic barriers of literacy and mobility, television has become the primary common source of socialization and everyday information. (p. 18)

Although the terms *distortion, false presentation,* and *reconstructed realities* are frequently used and mentioned, one should note that the media, in general, do not set out deliberately to deceive anyone, to manipulate or to abuse their audiences. The ethical codes of journalism, the sacred principles of objectivity, accuracy, value detachment, and fairness, dominate most of the newsmaking process and the professional orientation of journalists and editors (see Gans, 1980, on "deciding what's news"). There are factors beyond the control of editors, reporters, and producers that cause this reconstruction of reality. The selection process in the media, due to the constraints of limited space and time is the first source of such partial and thus distorted presentation of reality: Not all events can survive the multistage selection process, and the remaining events are a poor sample of the full volume of occurrences. Moreover, the nature of news "stories" (note the storytelling nature of reporting news) is a reconstructed format of presenting events. The importance of the narrative presentation in the reconstruction of reality was noted by Schudson (1982):

> The power of media lies not only (and not even primarily) in its power to declare things to be true, but in the power to provide the form in which the declaration appears. News in a newspaper or on television has a relationship to the "real world," not only in content but in form; that is, in the way the world is incorporated into unquestionable and unnoticed conventions of narration, and then transfigured, no longer for discussion, but as a premise of any convention at all. (p. 98)

Journalism is mostly storytelling, thus providing a structured account of the environment, and like all stories, news stories structure events and experiences for us, filtering out many of the complexities of reality. An important element of the mass-mediated world is the integration of news and entertainment, facts and fiction, events and stories—into a symbolic environment in which reality and fiction are almost inseparable. Gerbner argued that the study of the flow of symbolic realities from the media should be regarded as a force for enculturation rather than as a selectively used medium of separate entertainment and information functions. Thus, the news becomes storytelling, and soap operas become news: They present to us realities from other cultures, other social strata, and—despite their fictional nature—are seen and interpreted as realities:

> The dominant stylistic convention of Western narrative art—novels, plays, films, TV dramas—is that of representational realism. However contrived television plots are, viewers assume that they take place against a backdrop of the real world. Nothing impeaches the basic "reality" of the world of television drama. It is highly informative. That is, it offers to the unsuspecting viewer a continuous stream of "facts" and impressions about the way of the world, about the constancies and vagaries of human nature, and about the consequences of actions. The premise of realism is a Trojan horse which carries within it a highly selective, synthetic, and purposeful image of the facts of life. (Gerbner & Gross, 1976, p. 178)

This Trojan horse, the so-called "infotainment" narrative of the modern media, affects us all. How can we make the distinction, asked Gerbner and his colleagues, between fictional representation and factual "real world" information? How many of us have ever been in an operating room, in a prison cell, in a criminal courtroom, or in a hijacked plane? How much of what we know about such places and activities has been learned from fictional mass-mediated worlds?

One of the most impressive cases of blurring fiction and reality that caused a behavioral as well as an emotional and cognitive impact was the case of the "invasion from Mars." On October 30, 1938, Orson Welles and the *Mercury Theater of the Air* presented a radio play called "War of the Worlds," based on the science-fiction novel written by H. G. Wells. Although the program was announced and presented as a radio play, its convincing realistic style caused a real panic. Many listeners thought that a real invasion of mean, destructive aliens from Mars was actually taking place. They believed that spaceships from Mars were landing in New Jersey and were killing the residents; the police and the military forces were being sent to block them. As the program progressed, more and more people became excited, distressed, and terrified.

The radio program scared people because they thought it was real, not fictitious (Cantril, Gaudet, & Hertzog, 1940). Accepting the radio play as a real event demanded action, and people responded as if to a real crisis situation and not to a scary science fiction story. Sometimes the impact is not on the behavioral level but more on the cognitive level, when attitudes and perceptions are altered or formed. Nevertheless, these effects may be significant, as the classic study by Kurt and Gladys Lang (1953) illustrates, this time with television as the medium. They studied the General MacArthur Parade in Chicago in 1952. The general returned from Korea after distinguished service during World War II and the Korean War. While thousands watched the parade in the streets of Chicago, many more stayed at home to view it on television. Thus, the Langs could compare the two "realities": the parade as it took place in the streets and as it appeared on the television screen. The comparison of the two revealed interesting differences: The parade on television appeared much more active and lively. The viewers at home got the impression of huge, enthusiastic crowds. The general was shown and perceived as constantly surrounded by excited, admiring people. However, the people in the street saw a rather boring and quiet parade. For most of them, it was a short glimpse of the general passing in his car. There were no huge crowds, no cheering people, no excitement, and a very different message in terms of the general's acceptance by the people. As the Langs concluded, television presented a "unique perspective," a constructed reality, selecting scenes and camera angles that conveyed a very different reality from the real occurrences.

Living in a mass-mediated world is the result of several processes: our reliance on media sources to know and interpret the "world out there," the distorting effect of the selection process in the media and the practice of writing news as storytelling, and the mixture of information and fiction where real and fictional worlds become a homogeneous, synthetic reality. We should also note the growing importance of the technology of communication and mainly the role played by the most dominant medium—television.

Television as "Environment"

Shortly after the end of World War II, television was a new medium that spread rapidly through North America and Western Europe. Within a decade, television reached almost 90% of the homes in the United

States. In most of the world, somewhat later and at a slower pace, television reached huge portions of the population, attracting growing slices of human leisure time. Television appealed to a larger audience than any other medium: it was powerfully attractive to all ages (including children), all levels of education, in all cultures and societies, and regardless of religion, politics, gender, or race. Television is a powerful tool of mass communication because of its wide appeal, its variety of contents (ranging from news to music and game shows), its appeal to our eyes and ears (we watch television, listen to it, read it), and its relevance to so many aspects of human life (politics, consumerism, violence, education, marketing, crime, and many more). When asked about their prime source of information or entertainment, the majority of respondents name television.

Television has become the world's most common and constant learning environment. It both mirrors and leads society. Television is first and foremost, however, a storyteller—it tells most of the stories to most of the people most of the time. As such, television is the wholesale distributor of images and forms the mainstream of our popular culture. Our children are born into homes in which, for the first time in human history, a centralized commercial institution rather than parents, the church, or the school tells most of the stories. The world of television shows and tells us about life: people, places, striving, power, and fate. It presents both the good and the bad, the happy and the sad, the powerful and the weak, and it lets us know who or what is a success or a failure.

As with the functions of culture in general, the substance of the consciousness cultivated by television is not so much composed of specific attitudes and opinions as it is by broad, underlying, global assumptions about the "facts" of life. Television is only one of the many things that serve to explain the world; yet, television is special because its socially constructed version of reality bombards all classes, groups, and ages with the same perspectives at the same time. The views of the world embedded in television drama do not differ appreciably from images presented in other media, and its rules of the social hierarchy are not easily distinguishable from those imparted by other powerful agents of socialization. What makes television unique, however, is its ability to standardize, streamline, amplify, and share common cultural norms with virtually all members of society.

Although television has a great deal in common with other media, it is different in some important ways. For one thing, people spend far more time with television than with other media; more time is spent watching television than doing anything else besides working and sleeping. Most people under 35 have been watching television since before they could read or probably even speak. Unlike print media, television does not require literacy; unlike theatrical movies, television runs almost continuously and can be watched without leaving one's home; unlike radio, television can show as well as tell. Each of these characteristics is significant; their combined force is unprecedented and overwhelming.

Compared with other media, television provides a restricted set of contents for a virtually unrestricted variety of interests, cultures, publics, and social groups. Its commercial nature creates the necessity of producing programs that will be watched and enjoyed by huge masses in a relatively nonselective fashion. Television is the most powerful system of cultural diffusion, influencing the initial and the final years of life as well as the years between. Children today are exposed to television long before they start to read. And if viewing time is summed up, an average viewer spends years in front of the screen. Never before have all classes, all age groups, all cultures been exposed to the same sources of information and influence and shared so much of the same culture. Gerbner (1990) argued, for example, that television today fulfills most of the functions of religion in former times: You watch television as you might attend a church service, except that most people watch television more religiously. Television, the flagship of industrial mass culture, now rivals ancient religions as a purveyor of organic patterns of symbols—news and other entertainment—that animate national and even global communities' senses of reality and value.

More than 1 billion TV sets now are spread throughout the world, a 50% increase within 5 years. The number is expected to continue growing by 5% annually—and by more than double that in Asia, where half of the world's population lives. Worldwide spending on television programming is now about $65 billion, and the tab is growing by 10% per year. TV programs are a major U.S. export, worth about $2.3 billion annually. Transnational networks cover the world (CNN, for example, is currently seen in 137 countries), and the global village never seemed more realistic. Television "shrunk" the world, abolishing most of the cultural, political, and geographical boundaries, borders, and distances. With satellites beaming down literally hundreds of TV channels over the continents and oceans, countries lose control over the information crossing their borders—an unstoppable flow of ideas, images, messages, and culture that creates a new world order in terms of synthetic international culture.

Television became the modern melting pot, bringing the previously disenfranchised into a new cultural mainstream in which all viewers, all over the world, live and learn, absorbing the same mediated realities. Television is how most people now experience history, even their very own history. During the Gulf War, Scud missiles were launched by the Iraqis against Israel. One of their preferred targets was my hometown, Haifa. I remember how all of us, sealed in shelters, watched CNN broadcasting from Atlanta the pictures from the next street. We relied on CNN, from the United States, to show us what was happening to us. Only after the war and for some people not even then, did we learn how distorted, manipulated, and censored the pictures, the numbers, and the facts transmitted to us were. We communicate with the world, with ourselves, with our past, present, and future, via television for an average of 5 to 8 hours a day. We live in television's environment.

Modes of Reconstructed Realities

C. Wright Mills (1967) presented the notion of "second-hand worlds," or realities experienced indirectly by people, using the mass media as mediators:

> The first rule for understanding the human condition is that men live in second-hand worlds. They are aware of much more than they have personally experienced; and their own experience is always indirect. . . . Their images of the world, and of themselves, are given to them by crowds of witnesses they have never met and never shall meet. . . . Between consciousness and existence stand meanings and designs and communications which other men have passed on. . . . For most of what he calls solid fact, sound interpretation, suitable presentations, every man is increasingly dependent upon the observation posts, the interpretation centers, the presentation depots. (pp. 405-406)

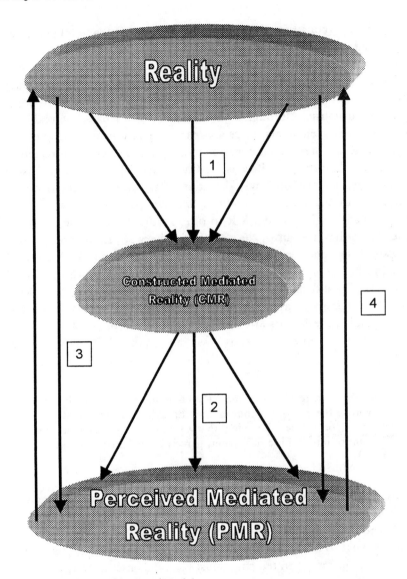

Figure 1.1   The Double Cone Model

The basic way to present the flow of mediated realities, the second-hand worlds, is in a double cone model, named after its two cones (see Figure 1.1).[1] According to this model, we have to distinguish between

(a) reality, (b) constructed mediated reality (or CMR), and (c) perceived mediated reality (or PMR). This model highlights a two-step process. In the first, certain aspects of real-life events and experiences are used by a communicator to form CMRs (Step 1 in the diagram). These may be in the form of news stories, fictional drama, newspaper reports, pictures, or music. Although many of the CMRs are based on reality or certain realistic elements, there are many differences between the two: The CMR is more dramatic, more colorful, more intense, more active, and faster than real life. Because of CMR's special qualities, because it is real life "blown up," we, the consumers/audiences, are not only attracted to the mediated realities, but we also expect them to be larger-than-life. We want CMR to offer us the unusual, the dramatic, the things that are out of the ordinary. Otherwise, there would be no reason to suspend real life for the sake of mediated reality.

In the second stage, the CMR is transmitted to the audience (Step 2). The audience, through selective processes of exposure, perception, and retention, adopts certain aspects of the CMR as reality (we will examine the factors affecting the level of acceptance later). What the audience accepts and perceives as reality is the PMR. As Whetmore (1991) argues,

> With the average TV set on more than 6 hours every day, with radios playing in the car, in the shower, and through the headphones as we walk, jog, or bicycle, it's obvious that we are exchanging an increasing amount of our real life for various perceived mediated realities. (pp. 12-13)

This stage is a highly selective process. We choose the channels of communication we are exposed to (selective exposure), we choose how to "read" and interpret the messages (selective perception), and we choose what to retain and remember (selective retention). These selection mechanisms, operated consciously and unconsciously, may further reconstruct the mediated reality that was already reconstructed by the communicator.

The model also suggests other directions of flow: One should note that a certain amount of reality's events, facts, and occurrences flows directly, without the mediating function of mass media, and contributes to the emergence of the PMR by joining those received from the media

(Step 3). Again, the amount of reliance on mass media sources or on personal experiences varies according to the subject's individual traits, the dependency on the media, and the circumstances. We will examine these factors more closely in the following chapters. Finally, the model also points to the flow from PMR to real life (Step 4): We often take information gleaned from mediated reality and apply it to our real lives. This book contains many examples, from images of a violent world and fear to "climate of opinion," from perceived sex roles to images of the "other." All are mediated presentations of reality that may affect our behavior in reality. The process is actually more complex than it may first appear. The model in Figure 1.1 conceals additional stages and subprocesses in the flow of constructed realities and thus oversimplifies the nature of this phenomenon. In the following chapters, we will examine the development of the theoretical and empirical tradition of studying this process and the complex set of social and psychological factors affecting the process.

NOTE

1. This model is a modified version of an earlier one suggested by Whetmore (1991).

CHAPTER TWO

The Debate Over Media Effects

According to cultivation theory, massive exposure to the mass media's highly distorted presentations of reality can result in distorted perceptions of reality among the audiences. The notion of cultivation as a "strong" media effect should be considered within the developing scientific framework of mass media impact. Thus, before focusing on the cultivation approach, let us briefly review the short but dramatic evolution of research in the area of media effects. First, we consider what *media effects* means, briefly trace the evolution in scholars' perspectives on media effects, and examine selected processes and theories by which media effects are thought to occur.

What Are Media Effects?

The most common general perspective in studying the media is a search for the effects of exposure to mass communication. Why study media effects? The mass media are considered an important social agent, transmitting attitudes, perceptions, images, and beliefs. There is increasing evidence that the media serve as important sources of information for a wide range of topics and populations. Television, for example, is often cited as the main source of information for most people. Parents and educators point to the (often negative) role of the media in the socialization of children and adolescents. It is not just the general public that is concerned with media effects; a significant portion of communication scholarship is devoted to examinations of media impact. In fact, the term *media effects* not only refers to the consequences or impacts of media use on individuals, society, and culture; media effects also is a rather well-defined area of scholarly inquiry that examines the impact of media. Most communication researchers, sociologists, psychologists, political scientists, and other scholars who have studied media effects tended to adhere to certain conventions or "rules" about what are considered the basic requirements for establishing the causal relationship of true media effect:

1. The presumed *cause* (e.g., a person watches a lot of violence on television or in films) and the presumed *effect* (e.g., a person becomes more aggressive or more frightened) must covary or change together in some verifiable way.

2. The presumed cause (e.g., viewing violence) must *precede in time* the presumed effect (e.g., engaging in aggression or being in panic).

3. *Rival causes* and explanations for these other causes (e.g., living in a volatile environment) must be *controlled for* and/or *eliminated.*

These stringent requirements for convincingly demonstrating media effects have led to a wealth of social scientific investigations as well as abundant critiques and critical analyses of these studies. Another problem relates to the source of the effect. Media effects may be the impact of a particular media *message content,* such as the impact on viewers' sexual arousal from watching sexually explicit films or the effects of "Joe Camel" ads on young people's predispositions to begin smoking. On other occasions, scholars are more concerned with the consequences of using a medium *as a totality,* relatively independent of the nature or content of its messages, thus referring to medium effects. This "the-medium-is-the-message" theme includes studies that focus on comparing the impact of televised and print news stories. Still other media effects research is concerned with the impact of particular *media message conventions,* including so-called "formal features" of a medium, which occur because of the way media messages typically are encoded. For example, it was suggested that video games are "addictive" to youngsters because they are so fast-paced and use so many "orienting devices" that they may control children's attention. Another increasingly popular category of effects research is media *context effects,* which focuses on the specific context in which potential effects occur. This category includes assessments of the impact of specific social settings and situations in which media are used, such as the impact of watching television alone or with others. Closely related to this category of effects research is the "uses and effects" research. This is a blending of the uses and gratifications approach with media effects research. Using this perspective, scholars seek to determine how the needs and motivations that people bring to their uses of media intervene in any effects that media may have. For example, if viewers are motivated to escape from their daily problems using soap operas, are they more likely to become addicted to this genre?

To further complicate the picture, scholars examine media effects at many different levels and in many different ways. Media impact is assessed at individual, family, reference group, community, societal, and cultural levels. Within each of these categories, different approaches to the study of media effects can be taken. For example, at the individual level, scholars might be concerned with media effects on the individual's behavior, attitudes, beliefs, or emotions. Other scholars might examine media effects on group behavior (riots, panic) or group values.

Some researchers are more interested in the short-term or transitory effects of media; others strive to determine whether media have more durable or long-term effects. Sometimes, the positive, beneficial, or prosocial effects of media are examined. More often, the focus is on the negative, detrimental, or antisocial consequences of using media. Methodology is another dimension in this area: Scholars approach the assessment of media effects through various methods. Some use observation whereas others conduct surveys, content analyses, or experiments. Still others examine archival records and accounts of media to conduct historical examinations of media effects. Increasingly, scholars use various techniques for combining and synthesizing the findings of various published investigations of media effects, using meta-analysis and other forms of macroanalysis to try to better understand the individual, social, and cultural effects of media use.

Given all of these different approaches to the study of media effects and the many different perspectives on media effects research, it may not be surprising to find so many media effects with such a diverse spectrum of findings and methods. It may also explain why this field is so divided by theoretical and empirical cleavages, conflicts, and debates. However, communication scholars in this research area generally divide themselves into two camps. One group is identified with the "strong effects" argument whereas the other group argues for "limited effects." As we will see, during the short history of media effects studies, these views have changed their explanatory power, their dominance, and even their own arguments.

The "Powerful Media" Paradigm

This paradigm, once labeled "the crudest form of a theoretical effects model," is the theory of uniform, powerful, direct media effects. This simple and yet popular notion assumes that individuals in a mass society perceive messages from media in the same fashion and react to them strongly and very similarly. Such ideas have inspired many potent metaphors to describe media effects—magic bullet, hypodermic needle, plug-in drug, and the like. Such perspectives of powerful media effects were shared by early scholars of communication. In fact, prior to the 1930s, many, if not most mass communication theorists assumed that mass media messages were immensely powerful and capable of directly influencing the values, opinions, and emotions of audience members. In assuming this, they embraced the concept of *mass society* that emerged from the study of the fundamental changes that had taken place in industrialized societies over the previous two centuries. The most crucial changes were those organizational changes accompanying the shift in the 19th and early 20th centuries from a rural, agriculture-based society to an urban-industrial society, including the erosion of open communication within tightly knit communities. The resulting psychological alienation and the decline of traditional social groups resulted, according to this paradigm, in an independent and culturally isolated mass of people. Early communication theorists assumed that, if individuals were no longer supported by traditional social units but shared the same psychological and emotional makeup, then media messages would presumably have a powerful, predictable, and uniform effect on all members of the audience.

The so-called bullet theories, hypodermic needle theories, stimulus-response theories, or theories of uniform influences seemed to receive some support from some studies. There is some dispute as to whether the bullet theory ever existed or whether it was simply a straw man invented by the critics of the notion of powerful media. Studies conducted shortly after World War I suggested that propaganda and advertising campaigns in newspapers were highly effective in shaping the attitudes, beliefs, and consumer behavior of their audiences. Messages had only to be loaded, directed to the target, and fired; if they hit their target audience, then the expected response would be forthcoming; thus, the notion of bullet theories of media effects. Audiences were assumed to act on impulse, emotion, instinct, and basic human nature rather than using reason and self-control.

As empirical social science techniques developed, researchers adopted and adapted them to study media effects. The Payne Fund studies of the 1920s and 1930s, for example, examined the impact of motion pictures on children, a group that traditionally has received heavy research attention. This specific audience has been thought to be especially susceptible to media influence, due to the incomplete social and moral development of children, their relatively extensive and presumably nonselective use of certain media, and their limited cognitive maturity. The Payne Fund studies, undertaken primarily to address public concern over adverse media effects, appeared to support those who feared the potency of media effects on children, and they influenced public opinion, which pressured for tightening self-regulation within the developing motion picture industry. These early studies appeared to support the notion that mass media messages exercise powerful influences over passive, trusting, and vulnerable consumers.

Television is perhaps the favorite target of powerful effects critics today, although video games, computer games, and the Internet are not far behind. Television has been accused of single-handedly inciting riots, promoting crime and violence, encouraging illicit sex, promoting alcohol and drug abuse, reducing the populace to mindless "couch potatoes," creating a nation of obese and passive illiterates, and breaking up the nuclear family, among other disastrous consequences. However, the finding that not all people are affected in the same way by the same media content or media exposure revealed the first weakness of the powerful media paradigm. Accumulating evidence on the failed attempts of campaigns to change attitudes and images and the revealed existence of mediating factors and intervening variables in the process led to the unavoidable decline of this paradigm.

The "Limited Effects" Paradigm

The emerging realization that media do not affect all people in the same manner all the time prompted some researchers to focus on divergent reactions of individuals to the same media messages. It was soon discovered that audience members were not weak, helpless, passive receivers of information. Moreover, various intervening variables affected audience members' uses of and reactions to media messages in rather dramatic ways. Researchers began to stress the individual differences in audience needs, attitudes, values, motivations, and moods, as well as the psychologically oriented personality variables of audience members. It was found that each of these factors, as well as environmental conditions, greatly influenced individuals' perceptions of the world and contributed to their diverse responses to the mass-mediated messages. Although media messages were still believed to influence individuals, the effects were not perceived to be as powerful, indiscriminate, and predictable as once thought.

The questions addressed by media researchers began to be not only What are the effects of mass-mediated messages? but How and why are particular media selected? and What factors influence the selection of one medium or message over another? Much of the early theory building at this time came from the then rapidly growing field of social psychology. Experiments in behaviorism, motivation, persuasion, and conditioning led researchers to examine the processes of habit formation and learning. Moreover, studies in human perception revealed that an individual's values, needs, beliefs, and attitudes are instrumental in determining how stimuli are selected from an increasingly rich media environment and how meaning is derived from those stimuli within an individual's frame of reference.

From these findings, the concepts of *selective attention* and *selective exposure, selective perception,* and *selective retention* were formulated to explain how individuals manage and manipulate the multitude of media messages available to them. Melvin DeFleur (1970) concluded that selective attention and selective perception are intervening psychological mechanisms that modify the stimulus-response model of mass communication. Individual audience members were found to selectively attend to messages, "particularly if they were related to his interests, consistent with his beliefs, and supportive of his values" (p. 122). Similarly, it was found that individuals tended to avoid messages that were contrary to their interests, attitudes, beliefs, and values. For example, if you are a heavy smoker, it is unlikely that you will watch a program on the links between smoking and cancer. Research revealed that message selection was not random; in fact, much media selection was quite purposeful and deliberate.

Selectivity was found to continue after the individual had selected media messages to listen to, read, or watch. Selective perception is the tendency for people to adapt media messages to fit their own preferences. *Perception* has been defined by Berelson and Steiner (1964) as a "complex process by which people select, organize, and interpret sensory stimulation into a meaningful and coherent picture of the world" (p. 88). Perception can be influenced by a myriad of psychological factors, including predispositions based on past experience, cultural expectations, motivations, moods, and attitudes. These factors can cause individuals to selectively perceive, process, and interpret media messages or, from the perception of the other party in the process, to misperceive and misinterpret messages, which reduces the potential for changing attitudes, values, opinions, or images once these are established.

The process of selective retention or recall reveals that people tend to remember messages they consciously perceive and accept rather than those they consciously reject. Factors that influence these selective processes include whether the messages are consistent with pre-existing attitudes and experiences, the perceived importance of the message for later use, the intensity of the message, and the medium used to transmit the message. As with selective perception, selective retention also involves the distortion of the message. The audience member may adapt the media message and retain it in a form that best suits his or her individual needs.

Concurrent with these accumulating studies of selectivity, coming largely from psychology, a group of sociologists began to look at the various characteristics shared by people within social groups. Called the *social categories perspective,* the sociologists' view assumed that people in various positions of the social structure shared similar demographic characteristics and, therefore, would have similar reactions to media messages. Variables such as lifestyles, values, age, gender, income, education, religious affiliation, and ethnic background seemed to have a powerful influence on the type of communication content selected and also seemed to have a discernible influence on the effects the media had.

A 1944 voting study conducted by Lazarsfeld, Berelson, and Gaudet during the presidential electoral campaign was the first to add a new dimension to the limited effects paradigm: the notion of personal influence. The researchers found that media messages alone seldom changed people's candidate preferences. They noted that those individuals who actually changed their minds during the campaign typically did so largely because of interpersonal communication. That is, other people influenced their voting more than media messages did. The research team labeled those individuals who influenced other people as *opinion leaders,* and they found that those people were different from other voters in only a few ways. Primarily, opinion leaders were especially interested in the political campaign, read a lot about the campaign, listened to many stories about the campaign on radio, and engaged in a great deal of political discussion and debate. These opinion leaders relied heavily on media for political content, in contrast to those voters who relied more on opinion leaders to make up their minds. Based on these findings, Lazarsfeld et al. formulated what was to become the classic "two-step flow" model.[1]

A second example of limited effects as explained by mediating variables is the case of television violence and its impact on children. A large, government-sponsored project (Surgeon General, 1971a) focused on televised violence and its influence on children and adolescents. In content analyses, experiments, and surveys, all indicators pointed to the conclusion that under specific kinds of circumstances, repeated exposure to violence on television did raise the probability among certain groups of children that they would be more aggressive. Yet, the findings were not compelling, and debates over the research report generated more heat than light. In a review of some 2,500 research studies of the effects of television (Surgeon General, 1971b), the link between exposure to televised portrayals of violence and aggressive behavior among children was somewhat complex: Causality was found to operate only among some children and under certain environmental contexts.

A Return to the Concept of "Powerful Media"?

We can summarize the early stages of media effects research with the following conclusions: When research began, the magic bullet theory was the leading conceptualization of the power of the media. Before empirical studies began, it was believed that the mass media produced direct, immediate, and powerful influences on all individuals in their audiences. The earliest research findings seemed to confirm the prevailing belief that the media had great power. However, it soon became apparent that this theory did not fit reality, and new formulations were needed. Selective influence theories replaced the magic bullet perspective. As research accumulated, and as methodology grew increasingly sophisticated, it became apparent that the media had very selective (nonuniform) influences on people. The factors causing people to expose themselves selectively to media or to perceive and retain the messages selectively, were found to be individual differences in preexisting attitudes, individual preferences, psychological traits, memberships in various kinds of social categories, and finally, patterns of social relationships (with family, friends, work associates, and so on).

The influence of mass communications was not only selective, but quite limited. The explanation of the effects of the mass media in an overall sense was that they were not powerful at all. They did influence some people, increasing somewhat the probability of change among certain subpopulations, and they could add to people's knowledge, modify their opinions, and even guide their purchases. However, they did not convert people to new political ideologies, cause them to vote for someone they did not like, drive them to sexual deviance, cause them to commit crimes or take drugs, or otherwise greatly influence their lives.

Thus, the basic theories of mass communication that emerged in the 1980s led to the general conclusion that the mass media are selective and quite limited in their influences on audiences that are exposed to their messages. In other words, although the media can change people in some ways, their influences are not particularly powerful. This general conclusion about the power of mass communication has itself come into question during the last decades. In a research paper published in 1973, German communication researcher Elisabeth Noelle-Neumann reviewed the state of mass communication effects research and called for a "return to the concept of a powerful media." Noelle-Neumann, insisting that "the decisive factors of mass media are not brought to bear in the traditional laboratory experiment designs" (p. 105) was joined in this attack on the minimal effects concept by other researchers.

One assault was on the selective perception theory, which limits the possibility of media effects. Noelle-Neumann (1973) said that "real life" is different from laboratory-controlled studies; the media are so ubiquitous that it is difficult for a person to escape a message; repetitive messages have reinforced impact; and news stories are so much the same that there are few options for selective perception. Noelle-Neumann's long-term studies demonstrated that the effects of mass media increase in proportion to the degree to which selective perception is minimized. Noelle-Neumann's argument was solidified by her theory of the Spiral of Silence. It states that one's perception of the distribution of public opinion motivates one's willingness to express political opinions. When people look to the media to determine the majority position on an issue, those who think they are in the majority are more willing to speak out, whereas those who perceive themselves to be in the minority have an extra incentive to stay silent. Groups of individuals, who perhaps may constitute a majority, lose confidence and withdraw from the public debate, thus speeding the demise of their position through the self-fulfilling prophecy of the Spiral of Silence. Despite the numerous studies conducted by Noelle-Neumann and her consistent findings, the theory of the Spiral of Silence was criticized both on the theoretical level and the methodological level.[2]

In another revisiting of the powerful media concept, mass communication researcher John P. Robinson (1974) found that the media can affect voting behavior after all. Data from studies of the presidential elections of 1968 and 1972 showed that "a newspaper's perceived support of one candidate rather than another was associated with about a 6 percent edge in the vote for the endorsed candidate over his opponent" (p. 592). The study of the 1972 election revealed that independent voters who had been exposed to a newspaper endorsing Democratic candidate George McGovern were twice as likely to vote for McGovern as independent voters exposed to a newspaper supporting President Richard Nixon for reelection. Robinson pointed out that the numbers of voters affected were small and the effects of newspaper endorsements peripheral. But in a closely contested election, a change in attitude and behavior by a small group of voters could be decisive.

More and more studies, in various areas of media effects, revealed indications of powerful media. Becker and Dunwoody, in a 1982 study involving a local election, linked media use to knowledge and knowledge, in turn, to voter behavior. Lemert's 1981 book, *Does Mass Communication Affect Public Opinion After All?* answered the query strongly in the affirmative. The power of the media to affect public opinion and produce an historic turn of events was dramatically evident during revolutions and rapid political changes, as in the Philippines in 1986, the collapse of East Germany and Communist Russia, the revolution in Rumania, and other situations.

As the search for better understanding of the power of media has continued, it now seems likely that the research done before the 1980s overlooked some crucial factors and that under certain kinds of circumstances the media may have a far more powerful influence than media researchers had previously believed. This caused a true "return to the concept of powerful media." The key to understanding this seemingly dramatic shift in the power attributed to the media lies in recognizing the difference between short-term influences and long-term effects and between the impact on individuals and effects on society and culture. More and more, media scholars have come to believe that the influences of mass communication are long-term, indirect, and accumulative. From the critical perspective of studying media and society came the notions of "ideological effects," political socialization, social control, and hegemony. If this is indeed the case, the influence of the media may be profound rather than trivial. Such subtle but powerful influences cannot be expected to show up in research strategies modeled after those of physical science, where a limited number of factors are measured and controlled. Obviously, new scientific procedures had to be devised to study long-term, large-scale, accumulative, and subtle processes.

Thus, the new wave of studies set forth a number of theories concerning long-term and indirect influences of the media—the theories of accumulation, adoption, modeling, meaning, and stereotypes. These candidate explanations of media influences are now at the forefront of investigations into the process and effects of mass communications, providing guidelines for continuing research. These interpretations of media effects go beyond what can currently be confirmed by empirical research evidence. That is, they are influences and effects that are not demonstrated in short-term experiments or one-time surveys. To bring these influences under the scrutiny of researchers requires new theories and new methods. Fortunately, as we will see in the following pages, some progress has already been made.

The important notion of *defense mechanisms* that help us to protect our existing attitudes, beliefs, and values and to maintain our cognitive consonance, thus minimizing the potential influence of external sources like mass media, may be accurate but only for existing attitudes and perceptions. But what about those many instances of events, "news," or processes that are totally new to us, when we depend on the media for information as well as for interpretation? In these cases, there are no pre-existing attitudes or images; thus, the defense mechanisms are not triggered. At this point, it is appropriate to propose what DeFleur and Ball-Rokeach (1982, 1989) have called an integrated *dependency theory* of mass communication. Such a theory depends on a recognition of various psychological and social defense mechanisms that prevent the media from having arbitrary control over their audiences. In traditional societies, most information needs are derived from firsthand, direct contacts with "reality" or from listening to other people who have experienced that reality (e.g., tribal elders or experienced men). Once that traditional structure breaks down and life becomes more complex, individuals and institutions assume a wide variety of divisions of labor— serving different functions to connect them to one another. A breakdown in traditional, face-to-face oral communication culture brings about societies that have ever greater needs for second- or third-hand information, and ever greater reliance on external sources. Mass media obviously play a key role in establishing and maintaining the function of monitoring reality. Simply by virtue of being part of a social system, today's citizens must put a great deal of reliance on the media. The media put our environment in perspective by giving its many aspects various meanings and explanations. They help establish our agendas by giving us things to think and talk about; they help us become socialized into our communities and political systems and to participate in change when necessary; and they help us cope with or escape from life's realities in a wide variety of ways. In short, the greater our need to belong, to understand, and to cope, the greater our reliance on the mass media. From this, it follows that the media must have some pervasive influences on our thoughts, beliefs, values, and even our behavior.

Another strong argument for the powerful media concept is that of the impact of continuous flow of media messages.

This flow was suggested as an accumulation of minimal effects that cause a powerful long-term effect. That is, even though the impact of any one message on any specific person may be minimal (as the research reveals), even minor changes in the public gradually occur over time. They accumulate as increasing numbers of individuals slowly modify their beliefs, interpretations, and orientations toward an issue that is repeatedly presented by the media in a way that consistently emphasizes a particular point of view. Thus, *accumulation theory* explains how significant changes take place in public orientation and action on a long-term basis. The second form of change is that which occurs within a society as people gradually adopt (individual by individual) some new form of technology, new ways of looking at reality, or a particular new way of believing and behaving. This kind of change can be explained in terms of a theory focusing on the adoption of innovation, which has already been well-confirmed. According to *adoption theory,* the media serve as one of the causal factors of social change. The mass media play a key role in bringing innovations to the attention of potential adopters. The adopters, in turn, make decisions to take actions, often on the basis of information supplied by the media. The theory of the accumulation of minimal effects offers one way to understand long-term media influences. Accumulation theory explains that significant changes can occur over a long period of time if the media focus repeatedly on a particular issue and are relatively consistent in presenting a uniform interpretation. They can have an especially strong influence under these circumstances when their audiences know little or nothing about the issue from other sources. Very obvious and impressive evidence for powerful media effects in this manner can be found in changing patterns of public response to certain events in recent American history (DeFleur & Dennis, 1991).

Many media effects researchers were preoccupied with the issue of televised portrayals of violence and their influence on children. This research preoccupation came about because parents, and government agencies who have paid the research bills, have been concerned about the socializing influence of television. That is, they have been concerned with the lessons the media present to young audiences and the degree to which youngsters learn such instructions concerning the rules of behavior that prevail in society. The fear is that television seems to legitimize the use violence as a means of settling disputes between people. Although this set of relationships—among portrayed violence, young audiences, and their actual behavior—illustrates the idea of socialization, it is only one form of media content and one kind of behavior that comes within the broad concept of socialization. Socialization is a long-term process that every human being undergoes and certainly includes much more than just learning to be aggressive as a result of exposure to violence on TV. Socialization refers to internalizing all of the lessons concerning ways of behaving that are approved and expected by society. And it continues as individuals mature through every stage in their life cycle.

Two rather different approaches to the process of socialization by the media have emerged. One focuses narrowly on individual audience members who feel that certain behavior portrayed is attractive and worth copying. Thus, *modeling theory* predicts that many activities observed in media portrayals will guide people to adopt them as part of their own behavior. The second look at socialization is much broader. *Social expectations theory* focuses on media-provided lessons about what constitutes acceptable behavior in various group settings.

According to the modeling theory, under certain circumstances, individuals who view particular actions that are performed by another person may adopt that behavior. Thus, *observational learning* from models who perform an activity is one means by which people acquire new ways of behaving (Bandura, 1977). Modeling theory, when applied to mass media, argues that the mass media, and especially television and movies, present many models that can be imitated. Individuals do pick up new ideas, action patterns, and modes of psychological orientation by attending to mass communication. When response patterns are acted out on television, or in the movies, for example, they are said to be "modeled" by the actors portraying the behavior. In other words, the more general idea of social learning theory becomes *modeling theory* when applied to acquisition of new behavior forms from exposure to portrayals of action in mass communication content. Although, presumably, behavior can be modeled in print, the theory seems far more relevant to accounting for influences on individuals from film and television. Virtually all of the research done thus far within this theoretical perspective has focused on television.

The modeling function of the media was found in several areas. The first method used was content analysis; this approach was used to reveal the modes of behavior that are available for people to imitate in their own personal activities. Findings from such analyses have often been dismissed in the past as relatively unimportant if it could not be shown convincingly that the content under study had some immediate and direct influence on a particular audience. As our review of changing perspectives on media theory has shown, such immediate and direct influences cannot easily be demonstrated because it is highly unlikely that they exist. The long-range, accumulative, and indirect influences that are provided by modeled behavior are more significant.

However, as Lowery and DeFleur (1983) argue,

> For the most part, research within the framework of modeling theory *has* not *addressed* long-range, accumulative influences. Many studies have established the fact that modeling effects *do* occur, but much research is still needed even at a basic level. Much remains to be uncovered regarding the conditions under which a subject will find a form of modeled behavior attractive, will identify with the actor, or find some other motivation for adopting the behavior and then make the behavior a permanent part of his or her habit patterns. (p. 377)

The second approach of social learning is the social expectations theory, which emphasizes learning group requirements. With modeling theory, the focus is on the acquisition of specific forms of behavior that are used by individuals in responding to stimuli they encounter in their mass-mediated world. In studying how people learn the rules and requirements for acting out parts within groups, the focus is not on isolated specific acts that are acquired from models but on developing an overall understanding of the customs and routines of group behavior. People in societies without media learn the requirements of different groups by a slow process. Others in the society teach them, or they acquire the needed knowledge by a process of trial and error, which can sometimes be a painful experience. In a media society, however, an enormous variety of groups and social activities are portrayed in mass communications. There is, in short, an almost endless parade of groups, with their norms, roles, ranks, and controls portrayed in the media. The media, then, provide broad but often distorted presentations of such social expectations. Through media contents, we can understand the requirements of social life, what is expected of a member of specific groups or occupations. This kind of influence is called the social expectations theory of media effects. We may go one more step and ask whether the media serve as a source of understanding our world and "social environment," not only that of social expectations but the meaning of our personal and shared interpretations of the physical and social world. This will lead us to the approach that looks at media as a source of our meaning, or the *meaning theory*.

Meaning Theory: Shaping Personal and Shared Interpretations

The meaning theory of the effects of mass communications sees the meanings people hold as strongly influenced by their exposure to mass communications. One of the most promising directions for media effects research lies in attempting to assess the role of mass communication in establishing, modifying, and reinforcing the meanings people share about the nature of the world around them. Central to shared meanings are the common symbols of language. Such meanings for words are used collectively and individually whenever people try to interpret and respond to any aspect of social or physical reality. Our personal structures of meaning are shaped by many forces. Through our participation in a variety of communication processes, we shape, reshape, and stabilize our meanings so that we can interact with others in predictable ways. These processes take place in our families, among peers, and in the community and society at large. In modern society, the mass media are a very important part of these communication processes. Not only do people attend to content directly from mass communications, but they discuss such information in conversations and pass on news and interpretations in a process of diffusion. Meanings are subjective experiences "in our heads," to use Walter Lippmann's words. We really do not know if they are actually the true features of what exists in "the world outside." Understanding the idea of meaning in this way reveals that the language we create and use together separates us in many ways from the objective world. That is, for every word in our culture, we have constructed a pattern of subjective meanings that are undoubtedly different from the detailed objective characteristics of that fact or situation. Therefore, we do not communicate by using realities; we communicate by referring to our own subjective meanings aroused by words. Once we learn a word in our language, we soon become accustomed to following the subjective experiences that it is supposed to arouse in each of us. Then, we use the word not only to communicate with each other but also to perceive and think about the reality for which it is a substitute.

In a similar way, our exposure to various communication processes enables us to share conventions of meaning about almost anything that can be described in language or shown in media portrayals. The important argument of the meaning theory of media effects is that the constant flow of subjective interpretations we receive from the media and personal communication constitutes the world to which we adjust. We cannot relate accurately to the objective world of reality itself because our access to that world is both selective and limited. We create our cultural and private worlds of meaning through communicated presentations of the realities "out there." By presenting endless portrayals of reality in its content, mass communications provide experiences from which we collectively shape our meanings. Meaning theory argues that people learn or modify at least some of the meanings they associate with experiences described by words through exposure to portrayals encountered in the media. Then, in their interpersonal communications, the meanings they derive from the media are further shaped, reshaped, and eventually stabilized into conventions that they share with others to become part of the general language and culture. The media also play a key role in stabilizing these meanings. Thus, the mass media are a source both of changes in language, as they modify meanings for individuals, and of stabilization, as they reinforce conventional usages. These may be subtle influences of media content, but they are of profound importance.

The analysis of the media as a cultural agent is particularly interested in their role as a provoker and circulator of meanings. The work of Stuart Hall (1981), John Fiske (1978, 1987), David Morley (1992), and others focused on the production of such mediated meanings, especially by looking at the encoding and decoding of meanings. In this approach, the message is treated neither as a unilateral sign, without ideological flux, nor as a disparate sign that can be read any way according to the needs or the uses of the decoder. The media messages are treated as complex signs in which a preferred reading has been inscribed, but which retain the potential for decoding in a manner different from the encoded meaning. Morley argues that before messages can have "effects" on the audience, they must be decoded: " 'Effects' is thus a shorthand, and inadequate, way of marking the point where audiences differentially read and make sense of messages which have been transmitted, and act on those meanings within the context of their situation and experience" (Morley, 1992, p. 86).

Meaning theory suggests four basic stages in the process of learning meanings from the media:

1. Meaning is linked to a label (a language symbol, such as a word, or some pattern of symbols) by a written, audio, or screen presentation describing an object, event, or situation.
2. A member of the audience perceives the portrayal and undergoes some change in his or her personal interpretation of the meaning of the label. The individual's subjective meanings may then shape behavior toward the object, event, or situation.
3. More often, the individual communicates with others using the new or revised meaning. In this interpersonal communication, the revised meaning is further shaped and reshaped until the interacting parties hold parallel (shared) interpretations, which gradually become cultural conventions of meaning.
4. As a result, individual behavior toward objects, situations, or events is guided by the meanings people hold, either individually or collectively, toward them.

According to meaning theory, there are various ways in which the media shape the meanings we associate with terms, situations, and realities. These include *establishment, extension, substitution,* and *stabilization.* Establishment is a process by which new words and new meanings become part of our language system through our exposure to media messages and portrayals. For example, the terms *gay, AIDS,* and *deviance* carry the meaning associated with their presentation and interpretation in the media. Extension or expansion of meanings is also an outcome of media portrayals. In this way, people learn to associate additional meanings with already familiar symbols. Finally, certain media contents can stabilize meanings when members of the audience already share a relatively similar set of meanings for symbols in the portrayal. By repeatedly showing the accepted meanings for these symbols, the media reinforce the conventions regarding their interpretation. For example, the public's attitudes and views about terrorism are reinforced by media portrayal and even terminology when reporting terrorist events (Weimann & Winn, 1994).

Three independent research directions emerged recently in the area of meanings provided by the media. One is the study of the *agenda-setting* functions of the news media; another is the investigation of the *theory of climate of opinion*; and the third is the *cultivation effects* of television on people's beliefs. At first glance, these independently developed approaches to the study of media effects may seem to have little in common. On closer analysis, however, they are in many respects focusing on similar underlying issues. All three are concerned in some way with the role of the media in shaping people's interpretations of the world around them. They differ primarily in terms of the type of meaning and the sphere of interpretation of reality on which they focus.

Agenda Setting

The basic idea of agenda setting is usually credited to several scholars. Kurt Lang and Gladys Engel Lang (1959) made an early statement of the agenda-setting idea: "The mass media force attention to certain issues. They build up public images of political figures. They are constantly presenting objects suggesting what individuals in the mass should think about, know about, have feelings about" (p. 202).

Another early reference to this idea is a brief passage in a book by political scientist Bernard Cohen. In 1963, he wrote, "The press may not be successful much of the time in telling people what to think, but it is stunningly successful in telling its readers what to think *about*" (p. 22). It has been well-known for a long time that the press surveys the environment, and the news media selectively present ideas to the public.

Presumably, the news media perform this surveillance function in a pattern that encourages the public to attach the most importance to what the media give the most prominent attention. Noted communication researchers McCombs and Shaw (1976) wrote, "Audiences not only learn about public issues and other matters from the media, they also learn how much *importance* to attach to an issue or topic from the emphasis the media place upon it" (p. 18).

This is the agenda-setting hypothesis. It concerns the news media rather than mass communication in general, and its dependent variable is the level of importance audiences attach to topics and issues given various coverage by the press. The degree of importance is, of course, a significant dimension of the meaning that people attach to the reports they encounter in the media.

McCombs and Shaw (1976) conducted a study on how political campaigns influence the salience of attitudes toward the political issues. The findings supported an agenda-setting effect. For major items, the correlation between emphasis in the media on an issue and voter perception of that issue as important was .967, a very high correlation that may stem from the very crude categorization of issues. As the authors point out, these data suggest a very strong relationship between the emphasis placed on different campaign issues by the media and the judgments of voters as to the salience and importance of campaign topics. Another issue closely related to the agenda-setting function of the press is the degree to which the meanings attached to issues by the public (e.g., perceived importance) play a part in formulating public policy. In other words, if the media emphasizes a given topic to a point where the public comes to believe that it is truly important, do political leaders then take action to "do something" about the issue? There is reason to suspect that policy makers' agenda might be affected by the media agenda and by the public, but at the same time policy makers, acting also as news makers, may be involved in creating the events and issues that appear on media agendas and consequently on public agendas. Rogers and Dearing (1988) concluded their review of the agenda-setting literature with the following generalizations:

1. The mass media influence the public agenda. This proposition has been generally supported by evidence from most public agenda-setting investigations, which cover a very wide range of agenda items, types of publics, and points in time.

2. An understanding of media agenda setting is a prerequisite to comprehending how the mass media agenda influences the public agenda.

3. The public agenda, once set by, or reflected by, the media agenda, influences the policy agenda of elite decision makers, and, in some cases, policy implementation.

4. The media agenda seems to have direct, sometimes strong, influence on the policy agenda of elite decision makers and, in some cases, policy implementation.

A related notion is that of *priming*: Priming is the process by which the media attend to some issues and not others and thereby alter the standards by which people evaluate candidates for election. Iyengar and his associates (Iyengar, 1991; Iyengar & Kinder, 1987; Iyengar, Peters, & Kinder, 1982) discovered a special way that television newscasts might be having an impact on presidential elections. By setting the agenda for an election campaign, the media also determine the criteria by which presidential candidates will be evaluated. The researchers found some evidence of priming in their experiments. Subjects in the experiments rated President Carter on his performance in the three specific problem areas—defense, pollution, and inflation. They also gave general ratings of Carter's overall performance, competence, and integrity. As predicted by the concept of priming, the correlation between the overall rating and the rating in a specific problem area was greater for respondents who saw coverage emphasizing that problem area than it was for respondents who saw coverage neglecting that problem area. In other words, respondents were evaluating President Carter in terms of topics they had seen emphasized in the news recently. This is a rather subtle but powerful way that agenda setting could be influencing voters' decision making.

"Climate of Opinion" and Spiral of Silence

A theory that gives the mass media more power than many other theories is the Spiral of Silence, developed by the German public opinion researcher Elisabeth Noelle-Neumann (1973, 1984, 1989). According to Noelle-Neumann, the mass media do have powerful effects on public opinion, and these effects have been underestimated or undetected in the past because of the limitations of research. She contends that three characteristics of mass communication—its cumulation, ubiquity, and consonance—combine to produce powerful effects on public opinion. Consonance refers to the unified picture of an event or issue that can develop and is often shared by different newspapers, magazines, television networks, and other media. This is the mass-mediated "climate of opinion." In fact, it is the media's (often distorted) presentation of what others are thinking, what is the dominant view among "the others." Consonance overcomes selective exposure, because people cannot select any other message, and it gives the impression that most people look at the issue in the way that the mass media are presenting it.

The impact of this climate of opinion is the initiation of the process called the Spiral of Silence. On controversial issues, people form impressions about the distribution of public opinion. They try to determine whether they are in the majority: whether public opinion tends to agree with them. If they feel they are in the minority, they tend to remain silent on the issue. If they think public opinion is changing away from them, they tend to remain silent on the issue. The more they remain silent, the more other people feel that their particular point of view is not represented, and the more they continue to remain silent. The mass media play an important part because they are the source that people use to find out about the distribution of public opinion. The mass media can affect the Spiral of Silence in three ways: (a) They shape impressions about which opinions are dominant, (b) they shape impressions about which opinions are on the increase, and (c) they shape impressions about which opinions one can utter in public without feeling isolated.

Elihu Katz (1983) summarized the notion of climate of opinion and Spiral of Silence in the following arguments: (a) Individuals have opinions; (b) Fearing isolation, individuals do not express their opinions if they perceive themselves as unsupported by others; (c) A "quasi-statistical sense" is employed by individuals to scan the environment for signs of support; (d) Mass media constitute the major source of information about the distribution of opinion and thus for the climate of support/nonsupport; (e) There are other reference groups but their relative importance is not clear; (f) The media tend to speak in one voice, almost monopolistically; (g) The media tend to distort the distribution of opinion in society, biased as they are by the views of journalists; (h) Perceiving themselves unsupported, groups of individuals—who may, at times, even constitute a majority—lose confidence and withdraw from public debate, thus speeding the demise of their position through the self-fulfilling Spiral of Silence. They may not change their own minds, but they stop attempting to recruit others and abandon the fight; thus the "powerful effect" assigned to mass communication is a subtle one. The media are not perceived as agents of direct influence, but rather as reporters on the distribution of (acceptable) opinion. The media are used by individuals as indicators to determine who may speak and who should remain silent.

Central to this argument of media effect is Floyd Allport's concept of *pluralistic ignorance.*[3] When people believe that they are the only ones who think something, and do not talk about their opinion for fear of violating a moral taboo or an authoritarian ruler, or of just being unpopular, it sometimes happens that a wave of publicity can sweep through the community, informing people that everybody else (or many others) think as they do. In such cases, what appears to be a basic change in attitude is, in fact, the result of changed perception of the distribution of opinion. Silence, according to Noelle-Neumann (1973, 1984, 1989), is a reaction to fear of isolation and shame for those who think differently than what they perceive others to be thinking. This relates to the findings of Asch (1958) that some people actually begin to see things as they think the others do.

The implication of these arguments, claims Katz (1983), is a re-emphasis on the powerful media conceptualization: "Noelle-Neumann wants us to consider the dark side of mass communication," argues Katz.

> Even in the democracies, media—like interpersonal communication—can impose acquiescence and silence, in defiance of the free flow of information. People will become disconnected from each other, warns Noelle-Neumann, if the media practice misrepresentation and monopolization. People, searching for support, will "scan" their environments in vain if the distribution of opinions is misrepresented and if the media arbitrarily shut out the plurality of voices. (p. 96)

Thus, Noelle-Neumann joins others who argue that the theories of mass society of 50 years ago are now becoming truly applicable to the modern, democratic society. They believe, first of all, that television is different from its predecessors. Viewing television is a more "total" experience, appealing, as it does, to eyes and ears, providing information, entertainment, and companionship—in short, a symbolic environment in place of the real world outside. Noelle-Neumann argues that by portraying the (false) climate of opinion, TV causes people to perceive a reality different from the one that surrounds them. Similarly, Gerbner and his colleagues argue that reality as perceived by heavy television viewers is a reflection of what they have seen and heard on television and not in the real world. Thus, a vicious circle is at work in which people fear the world portrayed by television because of its violence (Gerbner) or its misrepresentation of the climate of opinion (Noelle-Neumann), causing people to feel lonely, retreat into their small private "environments" to watch more television, and thus be further influenced by it. Under such circumstances, selectivity and interpersonal communication are neutralized as mediating factors, and the media of mass communication may indeed be described as "powerful."

In conclusion, we can find common assumptions among various perspectives calling for a return to the concept of powerful media despite their very different ideological and theoretical origins. They are anchored in the belief that the media can "construct reality" and impose their construction on defenseless minds. Central to all of them is the notion that the media have come to substitute for social relationships and reference groups. One of the most fruitful attempts to document the power of the media, and especially of television, in an accumulating process, on the audiences' perceived reality is that of the cultivation approach. The following chapter is devoted to this approach, its sources, arguments, methodology, findings, criticisms, and diffusion into other research areas.

NOTES

1. For a review of all studies on the opinion leaders, the two-step flow model, and the modification of these concepts, see Weimann (1995b).

2. The most severe criticism of Noelle-Neumann's work and her personal background during the Nazi regime originated from the work of Christopher Simpson (1996) and especially the debate following the publication of his paper.

3. Discussion of the concept of "pluralistic ignorance" can be found in Newcomb (1950) and in Krech, Crutchfild, and Ballachey (1972).

CHAPTER THREE

Cultivation and Mainstreaming

The cultivation research tradition started with a very specific goal. It was initially an attempt to provide "Cultural Indicators," a tool to identify, measure, and monitor various aspects of social life in American society.[1] The concept of a cultural indicator was developed to complement economic and social indicators and to provide a barometer of important cultural issues. In the United States, the focus has been on television, because TV is the country's most pervasive cultural institution and most visible disseminator of cultural symbols. Other media, however, can be studied as indicators of cultural patterns and trends. The Cultural Indicators project was launched as an independently funded enterprise with a very specific purpose: to ascertain the degree of violence on television (Gerbner, 1969). The research began during the late 1960s, a time of national turmoil after the assassinations of John F. Kennedy, Martin Luther King, and Robert F. Kennedy when the National Commission on the Causes and Prevention of Violence was set up to examine violence in society, including violence on television.

Nationwide unrest continued, as did concerns about television's impact on Americans. In 1969, even before the report of the National Commission on the Causes and Prevention of Violence was released, Congress appropriated $1 million and set up the Surgeon General's Scientific Advisory Committee on Television and Social Behavior to continue this area of investigation. All together, 23 projects, including

Cultural Indicators, were funded at this time. The Cultural Indicators research focused primarily on the content of prime-time and weekend-daytime network dramatic programming (Gerbner, 1972). The cultivation analysis phase of the Cultural Indicators research paradigm was fully implemented with the first national probability survey of adults during the early 1970s in research funded by the National Institute of Mental Health (Gerbner & Gross, 1976). The research continued in the 1970s and 1980s with funding by the National Institute of Mental Health (NIMH), the American Medical Association, the Office of Telecommunications Policy, the Administration on Aging, the National Science Foundation, the Ad Hoc Committee on Religious Television Research, and other agencies.

Although these early efforts focused primarily on the nature and functions of television violence, the Cultural Indicators project was broadly based from the outset. Major differences between television's reality and objective reality have been found in various areas, including the amount and type of violence and crime, depictions of women, and the presence and place of elderly people in society. Encouraged by the early findings, the Cultural Indicators research team has investigated the extent to which television viewing contributes to audience conceptions and actions in such realms as sex roles (e.g., Gerbner & Signorielli, 1979; Morgan, 1982; Preston, 1990; Signorielli, 1989), age-role stereotypes (e.g., Gerbner, Gross, Signorielli, & Morgan, 1980), health (e.g., Gerbner, Morgan, & Signorielli, 1982), science and scientists (e.g., Gerbner, Gross, Morgan, & Signorielli, 1981b), the family (e.g., Gerbner, Gross, Morgan, & Signorielli, 1980b), educational achievement and aspirations (e.g., Morgan & Gross, 1982), politics (e.g., Gerbner, Gross, Morgan, & Signorielli, 1982, 1984; Morgan, 1989), religion (e.g., Gerbner, Gross, Hoover, et al., 1984), and many other issues.

One of the major constructs of cultivation theory is *mainstreaming,* the homogenization of people's divergent perceptions of social reality into a convergent mainstream. This apparently happens through a process of construction, whereby viewers learn "facts" about the real world from observing the world of television. Memory traces from watching television are stored relatively automatically. We then use these stored images to formulate beliefs about the real world.[2] When this constructed world and the real world have a high degree of consistency, *resonance* occurs, and the effect is even stronger.

The Methodology of Cultivation Analysis

The methods of cultivation analysis are different from those tradition-ally used in mass communication research. Research and debate on the impact of mass communication has often focused on individual mes-sages, programs, episodes, series, or genres and their ability to produce immediate change in audience attitudes and behaviors. Cultiva-tion analysis is concerned with the more general and pervasive conse-quences of cumulative exposure to cultural media. Its underlying theo-retical framework could be applied to any dominant form of communication. Most cultivation analyses, however, have focused on television because of the medium's uniquely repetitive and pervasive message characteristics and its dominance among other media in most of the world.

Cultivation analysis generally begins with identifying and assessing the most recurrent and stable patterns in television content, emphasizing the consistent images, portrayals, and values that cut across most program genres. In the next step, cultivation analysis tries to ascertain if those who spend more time watching television are more likely to perceive the real world in ways that reflect the most common and repetitive messages and lessons of the television world, compared with people who watch less television but are otherwise comparable in important demographic characteristics.

The goal of cultivation analysis is to determine whether differences in the attitudes, beliefs, and actions of light and heavy viewers reflect differences in their viewing patterns and habits, independent of (or in interaction with) the social, cultural, and personal factors that differen-tiate light and heavy viewers. Thus, cultivation analysis attempts to document and analyze the independent contributions of television viewing to viewers' conceptions of social reality. The first stage in cultivation analysis is a careful study of television content to identify predominant themes and messages. It begins with content (message system) analysis: identifying and assessing the most recurrent and stable patterns of television content (the consistent images, portrayals, and values that cut across most types of programs). Findings from systematic analyses of television's content are then used to formulate questions about people's conceptions of social reality. Some of the questions are semiprojective, some use a forced-error format, and others simply measure beliefs, opinions, attitudes, or behaviors.

Since 1967, Gerbner and his colleagues have analyzed sample weeks of prime-time and daytime television programming. Each year since 1967, researchers have content-analyzed a week-long sample of U.S. network television drama to delineate selected features and trends in the overall world that television presents to its viewers. In the 1990s, this analysis has been extended to include the Fox television network, "reality" programs, and various cable channels. Through the years, message system analysis has focused on the most pervasive content patterns that are common to many different types of programs but characteristic of the system as a whole, because these hold the most significant potential lessons that television cultivates. Not surprisingly, television portrays a rather idiosyncratic world that is unlike reality in many ways. To mention a few examples, television's world usually has a preponderance of males. In fact, in an average season, about two thirds to three quarters of all leading characters are men. Moreover, in portraying occupations, television overemphasizes the professions and overrepresents the proportion of workers engaged in law enforcement and the detection of crime. Last, the TV world is a violent one: About 70% to 80% of all programs usually contain at least one instance of violence.

The second stage examines what viewers absorb from heavy exposure to the world of television compared with light exposure. Respondents are presented with questions concerning social reality and are asked to check one of two possible answers. One of these answers (the "TV answer") is more in line with the way things are portrayed on television; the other (the "real-world answer") more closely resembles situations in actual life. Television viewing is usually assessed by asking how much time the respondent watches television on an average day. Because amount of viewing is seen in relative terms, the determination of what constitutes light, medium, and heavy viewing is made on a sample-by-sample basis, using as close to a three-way split of hours of self-reported daily television viewing as possible. What is important is that there are basic differences in viewing levels, not the actual or specific amount of viewing. Heavy TV viewers are expected to choose the television answer more than are light TV viewers. Researchers then compute a "cultivation differential," which is the margin of heavy viewers over light viewers giving the television answers within and across groups, indicating conceptions about social reality that viewing tends to cultivate.

For example, in the case of violence and cultivation, the early (and later criticized) Cultivation Index included four items. The respondents were asked to read each item and to circle the response for each that best reflected their own feelings:

1. During any given week, what are your chances of being involved in some kind of violence? About 1 in 10? About 1 in 100?
2. What percentage of all males who have jobs work in law enforcement and crime detection? 1%? 5%?
3. What percentage of all crimes are violent crimes like murders, rape, robbery, and aggravated assault? 15%? 25%?
4. Does most fatal violence occur between strangers or between relatives or acquaintances?

The answers "One in 10," "5%," "25%," and "between strangers" are the television answers for the respective questions.

Gerbner and his associates did not address the reliability or validity of the Cultivation Index (see later in the section on the criticism of these studies). Gerbner and his associates reported mixed evidence about whether heavy viewers, as compared with light viewers, were more afraid to walk alone at night (gammas ranged from .03 to .18) or take more precautions against crime (gammas ranged from .03 to .18); several gammas were near .00 after statistical controls for age, gender, or education. Questioning a primary cultivation assumption about uniform messages, Hawkins and Pingree (1981a) noted that content type matters in cultivation relationships. They reported a significant .16 partial correlation (controlling for overall TV viewing and social class) between the Cultivation Index and crime-adventure viewing. Similarly, Rubin, Perse, and Taylor (1988) noted program-type relationships with their measures of social attitudes. For example, whereas total TV viewing positively predicted perceptions of safety, action-adventure program viewing was a negative predictor.

Gerbner and his colleagues compared the portrayals of men versus women and people in different occupations such as law enforcers, and, primarily, the depiction of televised violence in their message analyses

(Gerbner et al., 1977; Gerbner, Gross, Jackson-Beeck, Jeffries-Fox, & Signorielli, 1978). After controlling for some demographic and individual characteristics, they noted relationships for their Cultivation Index with estimates of incidence of violence and law enforcers. Because heavy TV viewers are more likely than light viewers to give the television answer than the real-world answer, heavy viewers overestimated the proportion of people employed as law enforcers and their chances of being a victim of crime. Others have found similar, statistically significant relationships. Hawkins and Pingree (1981a) reported a .25 partial correlation (controlling for social class) between the Cultivation Index (which they labeled "violence in society") and total TV viewing. Pingree (1983) noted a .18 correlation between the Cultivation Index (which she labeled "demographics of violence") and total TV viewing. Cultivation studies have differed in their definition of heavy and light viewing. For example, Gerbner and his associates regarded light viewing as a daily viewing of 2 hours or less, medium viewing was 2 to 6 hours, and heavy viewing was 6 hours or more each day. Later, Gerbner, Gross, Morgan, and Signorielli (1980a) defined light viewing as under 2 hours, medium viewing as 2 to 4 hours, and heavy viewing as more than 4 hours.

Mainstreaming

Cultivation is both dependent on and a manifestation of the extent to which television's imagery dominates viewers' sources of information. Television viewing usually relates in different but consistent ways to different groups' life situations and worldviews. Every society, every culture, consists of many diverse currents of which one or some are more dominant. This dominant current or mainstream is not simply the sum total of all the crosscurrents and subcurrents; rather, it is the most general and stable mainstream, representing the broadest and most common dimensions of shared meanings and beliefs. The mass media, as a central social factor, can serve as the primary carrier and manifestation of the mainstream in modern society. Morgan and Signorielli (1990) argue,

> Transcending historic barriers of literacy and mobility, television has become a primary, common source of everyday culture of an otherwise

heterogeneous population. Television provides, perhaps for the first time since preindustrial religion, a strong cultural link between the elites and all other publics. It provides a shared daily ritual of highly compelling and informative content for millions of otherwise diverse people in all regions, ethnic groups, social classes, and walks of life. Television provides a relatively restricted set of choices for a virtually unrestricted variety of interests and publics; its programs eliminate boundaries of age, class, and region and are designed by commercial necessity to be watched by nearly everyone. (p. 22)

Mainstreaming means that heavy viewing may absorb or override differences in perspectives, values, and habits that stem from other social factors and individual differences. Thus, differences associated with the varied cultural, social, and political characteristics of various groups and individuals are diminished by the unifying influence of heavy viewing. Mainstreaming represents the theoretical elaboration and empirical verification of the assertion that television cultivates common views and perceptions. It represents a process of homogenization, an absorption of divergent views, and a convergence of disparate viewers. Former and traditional distinctions become blurred as more and more people from successive generations and groups become encultured by television's reconstructed world.

The theory of cultivation was designed primarily for television and has focused on television's pervasive and recurrent patterns representing reconstructed realities in various areas. This emphasis on its being a long-term process led to the notion of "growing up with and living with television": the cultivation of enduring, stable, resistant, and widely shared assumptions, images, and conceptions reflecting the institutional characteristics and interests of the medium itself and the larger society. Through the process of mainstreaming, modern media may have become the true "melting pot" of many societies around the globe.

Cultivation and Mainstreaming Versus Media Effects

Cultivation does not imply any sort of simple, linear stimulus-response model of the relationships between media content and audiences. Rather, it implies long-term, cumulative consequences of exposure to an essentially repetitive and stable system of messages, not immediate short-term responses or individual interpretations of content. It is concerned with continuity, stabilization, and gradual shifts rather than outright change. A slight but pervasive shift in the cultivation of common perspectives may not change much in individual outlooks and behavior but may later change the meaning of those perspectives and actions profoundly. As Morgan and Shanahan concluded (1997),

> Gerbner's original conception of cultivation was a break from conventional academic discourse about the social and cultural implications of mass communication. His goal was to develop an approach to mass communication distinct from the then-dominant paradigm of persuasion and propaganda research and to escape the scientism and positivism of the "effects" tradition. (p. 4)

Thus, the use of the term *cultivation* for television's contribution to conceptions of social reality is not simply another form of effect. Most of all, it does not imply a one-way, monolithic process. Cultivation also should not be confused with "mere" reinforcement (as if reaffirmation and stability in the face of intense pressures for change were a trivial feat); nor should it suggest that media exposure is simply symptomatic of other dispositions and outlook systems. Finally, it should not be assumed that no change is involved. The "independent contribution" of the media means, quite specifically, that the generation (in some) and maintenance (in others) of some sets of outlooks or beliefs can be traced to steady, cumulative exposure to the world of the mass media.

The cultivation process is not thought of as a unidirectional flow of influence from the media to their audiences, but rather as part of a continual, dynamic, ongoing process of interaction among messages and contexts. It is designed to understand gradual, long-term shifts and transformations in the way generations are socialized (not short-term, dramatic changes in individuals' beliefs or behaviors).

This required a reworking of the traditional methodological tactics that had been used to assess effects. Early mass communication research focused on prediction and control, with a clear-cut criterion for an effect: some change in attitude or behavior following exposure to some message. But from the cultivation perspective, rather than seeing communication research as a way to achieve a specific practical aim (e.g., selling soap, winning votes, improving public health), it is seen as an "interaction through messages," a production of symbolic environment. Thus, the cultivation theory is, most of all, about the cultural process of storytelling. Much of what we know and think we know comes not from personal experience but from the stories we hear. In earlier times, the stories of a culture were generally told face-to-face by members of a community, parents, teachers, or the church. Today, storytelling is in the hands of global commercial interests: The great cultural stories of mythology, religion, legends, education, art, science, laws, fairy tales, and politics are increasingly packaged and disseminated by commercial television, movies, books, magazines, and newspapers. Thus, "cultivation is what a culture does," because "culture is the basic medium in which humans live and learn" (Gerbner, 1990, p. 251). Cultivation analysis is not merely a measurement of media effect: it is a cultural analysis of our most pervasive and widely shared stories, the mass storyteller (mass media), and their impact on common beliefs, values, and ideologies.

The Debate Over Cultivation

Despite its great influence on media effects research, cultivation theory is not without its critics. It is difficult to discuss cultivation theory without acknowledging the somewhat heated controversy that has developed around this tradition. Several critics have shown that careful controls of certain other sociodemographic and personality variables tend to reduce or eliminate cultivation effects (Carveth & Alexander, 1985; Doob & Macdonald, 1979; Hawkins & Pingree, 1981a, 1981b; Hirsch, 1980; Hughes, 1980; Perse, 1986). Second, cultivation studies have been criticized on conceptual and methodological grounds, including response biases and problems with the measuring instruments (Hirsch, 1980, 1981a, 1981b; Hughes, 1980; Perse, 1986; Potter, 1986; Wober, 1978). There have also been criticisms of some of the assumptions underlying cultivation theory. It is not possible to review all the arguments and counterarguments here: There are several detailed reviews of the lingering debate,[3] but most of it revolved around the humanistic criticism, failed replications, issues of spuriousness and controls, and the linearity of the cultivation effect (Morgan & Shana-han, 1997). The numerous and serious challenges to the cultivation paradigm could be grouped into the following categories.

The humanistic criticism: Newcomb (1978), one of the earliest critics of cultivation, pointed out the supposed differences between a quantitative and qualitative approach. Newcomb argued that violence has had many symbolic meanings and that all viewers do not interpret acts of violence in the same way. He defended the value of in-depth analysis of individual programs against the Cultural Indicators focus on aggregate patterns. He questioned whether viewers would "read" the messages that Gerbner and his colleagues claimed they should from exposure to television violence. In response to Newcomb, cultivation scholars justified the focus on the broad similarities that cut across program types. Cultivation theory, they claimed, does not assert that every act of violence observed on television means the same thing to every viewer. The relationships observed between amount of viewing and viewers' perceptions are precisely the test of whether the patterns and meanings inferred from message data are indeed absorbed by viewers. The relative statistical weakness of cultivation relationships is, of course, itself a proof of the operation of individual readings.

More recently, Potter (1994) has reiterated Newcomb's argument by asking how cultivation researchers can "be confident that their designated television world answer has taken into account all the factors" that influence viewers' inferences from television content. The answer, given by Gerbner and later by his followers, was that individual programs and variations in interpretation are interesting and valuable things to study, but cultivation research tries to illuminate broad pat-terns across large groups of people. The key distinction, they argue, is not humanism versus social science, or even qualitative versus quanti-tative; more simply, it is macro versus micro.

Failed replication: Around the same time, research conducted by Wober (1978) at the Independent Broadcasting Authority (IBA) in the United Kingdom was reported as failing to replicate Gerbner's findings. Wober analyzed the results of a public opinion poll asking questions, among other things, about the "prevalence of violence," and "inter-personal distrust," concepts similar to the Mean World Index. Wober did not find any relationship between watching television and feelings of security or a lack of it. Gerbner, however, argued that this difference stemmed from cultural and institutional differences between the United States and Great Britain (Gerbner, Gross, Morgan, & Signorielli, 1979; Neville, 1980; Wober, 1979). Questions have been raised about the validity of Wober's dependent measures and his survey question: the question presented to respondents was on "attitudes to broadcasting." Gerbner and his colleagues have always been extremely careful not to introduce "television" in any way before asking respondents about their conceptions of social reality. Any explicit prior mention of television may subtly invoke some of the medium's images in respondents' minds when they answer the social reality questions or may sensitize them to the purposes of the study.

Spuriousness relationship? In a study with residents of Toronto, Canada, Doob and Macdonald (1979) attempted to replicate earlier American findings indicating that television causes people to overestimate the amount of danger that exists in their own neighborhoods, while controlling for a previously uncontrolled factor, the actual incidence of crime in the respondent's neighborhood. They found that when neighborhood is used as a control rather than income, the correlation between television viewing and fear of crime disappears for all groups but the most poor, living in the most dangerous neighborhoods in the city. This finding does run contrary to Gerbner's argument that heavy viewing should make all income groups more similar, but it offers some support for the idea of resonance: Gerbner, Gross, Morgan, and Signorielli (1980a) proposed that television's messages about violence may be most congruent, and thus "resonate," with the everyday reality of those who live in high-crime areas. They asserted that this "double dose" of messages may amplify cultivation. Doob and Macdonald acknowledged that their results do not unequivocally reject Gerbner's theory, but they questioned the use of controls for income rather than neighborhood. In addition to finding some support among one social class for Gerbner's theory, Doob and Macdonald also found that when the questions asked are divided into those that are personal in nature ("are you afraid of being mugged?") versus those that are about society ("how many muggings were there in your neighborhood last year?")—there is evidence for a cultivation effect with the social questions, but not so much with personal ones: "Thus, television may well act as a source of information with regard to questions of fact, whereas it does not change people's views of how afraid they should be" (Doob & Macdonald, 1979, p. 179).

Same data—different results? The publication of the cultivation studies' findings in the early 1980s brought a new, and sometimes almost aggressive wave of criticism, described by Morgan and Signorielli (1990) as "fierce, prolonged battles" (p. 21). The main argument of the main critic, Paul Hirsch (1980, 1981a, 1981b), was that a reanalysis of the same database with a better control of other variables yields no cultivation effects. Using the National Opinion Research Center's (NORC) General Social Surveys, Hirsch came up with quite different results. The conventional cultivation analyses had been implementing controls by examining associations between amount of viewing and attitudes within subgroups, *one at a time.*

That is, the comparisons were done separately within groups of males, older people, those with less education, and so on. Reanalyzing the same database, Hirsch found that multiple controls (i.e., controlling for age, sex, education, etc., all at once), tended to reduce or completely eliminate those relationships. The main counterargument presented by Gerbner, Gross, Morgan, et al. (1980a) was that the absence of an overall relationship under multiple controls does not mean that there are not nonspurious and theoretically meaningful associations within specific subgroups. The idea of mainstreaming, first noted in research relating to conceptions about sex roles, has been found since then in more and more substantive areas, to be reviewed in the following chapters. Recently, there has been some tendency to reinterpret cultivation theory in line with a uses and gratifications approach, stressing the active mental activity of the viewer while watching TV (e.g., Weaver & Wakshlag, 1986; Levy & Windahl, 1985; Rubin & Perse, 1987a, 1987b).

The nonlinearity of cultivation: Both Hughes (1980) and Hirsch (1980) reported that the relationships they examined were nonlinear. Hirsch added to the usual light/medium/heavy viewing categories two additional categories—nonviewers (those reporting "zero hours" on "an average day") and extreme viewers (those watching more than 8 hours a day). He found that the nonviewers were often more alienated and fearful than were the light viewers, whereas the extreme viewers were less so than the heavy viewers. This appears to contradict dramatically the cultivation prediction of a generally monotonic pattern across all viewing levels. Yet, both of the "extreme" groups are small (about 4% of the sample); Hawkins and Pingree (1982) noted that they "are unusual enough that they probably differ from other groups on possibly relevant third variables" (p. 235). Moreover, Gerbner, Gross, Signorielli, et al. (1980) conducted tests for linearity on the same variables Hirsch used, across Hirsch's own viewing categories; 17 of the 22 tests showed significant linear trends, and only one showed significant nonlinearity. Thus, Morgan and Shanahan (1997) argue,

> Hirsch's analysis does not clearly show that cultivation relationships are indeed nonlinear. If the extreme groups are eliminated, a practice that some statisticians recommend, should be done routinely, . . . then the associations become even stronger for the remaining 90% of the NORC respondents. (p. 18)

Potter (1991b) also claimed to show that cultivation relationships are nonlinear, based on data from 308 adolescents. He divided the viewing distribution in various ways, such as into an even three-way split (the method preferred by Gerbner), into quintals, into stanines (nine equal-sized groups), and so on. He looked at the means of the dependent variables at each viewing level and ran correlations within each viewing group. He then regressed the dependent indices on demographics and various transformations of the viewing measure. He found that the magnitude of association varied within the different subgroups and claimed that this showed a nonlinear association. This, of course, raises the issue of too small subsamples: The quintiles and stanines represent at most about 34 cases. Such small samples are certain to produce unstable coefficients.

Nevertheless, this criticism raises important issues about how television viewing should be handled as a variable. Overall exposure measures can be expected only to indicate relatively more or less exposure to television. Variations in question wording, response options, and the ages of people in the sample all produce different distributions and mean that the numbers of actual hours reported are not relevant. That is why

Gerbner and his associates have consistently divided the sample into three groups of roughly equal sizes regardless of the actual cutoff points. One should note that correlations should not be used with television viewing; even though it is measured as a ratio-level variable, it is usually not distributed normally. As Potter (1991b) argued, the viewing measure "would probably be better treated as a categorical variable from a statistical point of view because the distributions do not meet the assumptions of normalcy" (p. 574).

Thus, applying advanced and sophisticated precision to the viewing measures is likely to result in unreliable results and findings. Viewing is not a variable that can be regarded as a highly accurate measure: Volgy and Schwartz (1980) note that many of their medium viewers (determined by the number of hours of viewing reported) also indicated watching a lot of specific programs; they suggest that this group may include both real medium and many real heavy viewers. Cultural Indicators' analyses of a 1979 national sample showed that 15% of those claiming to be nonviewers also listed "watching television" as one of their favorite leisure activities. Another example is evident in the 1993 General Social Survey, in which "nonviewers" were found to be watching dramas or sitcoms at least several times a month. A third of the nonviewers said they watch programs on the Public Broadcasting System at least a few times a month. More than half said they watch the news that often, and 13% said they watch the news every day! All this makes the suggested linearity tests unsupportable, as they imply a level of precision that the measures cannot justify. Rough approximations of general patterns are all that cultivation analysis assumes or can achieve.

Some Genres Have Some Effects on Some Viewers

Viewers do not simply watch TV, they watch specific shows. They tend to prefer certain types of shows over others, and their choice of shows, or "TV diets," often consist of a mix of shows from a limited number of genres. Weimann, Brosius, and Wober (1992) studied these TV diets and found four types. These were in fact four types of viewers that differed both in the amount of overall TV they viewed and in the degree of devotion to specific program types or genres. About half the viewers were found to be especially devoted to a specific genre. The study concluded that to understand viewing behaviors, and consequently the effects of TV viewing, we must consider the content that is viewed as well as the amount of overall viewing.

Kaminsky and Mahan (1988) suggest that TV genres differ in conventions regarding the type of protagonist, the location of the action, the people and objects that are portrayed, the ways in which the stories unfold, and the technical production conventions. More important, genres also differ in their focus on social reality. Police dramas, news, and current event shows focus on social order, foreground public rather than domestic life, and stress formal social roles. In contrast, soap operas, sit-coms, and family dramas highlight the personal and intimate, and accentuate friendship and family relationships. News, police, and action genres stress actions and events and use characters to maintain coherence of the plot and to present the context and motives for action. Soaps, on the other hand, use events as a way to present characters and explore their relationships (see Rubin & Perse, 1987a). Because of genre conventions, the images of the world as seen on television are not similar across genres. It is not so much that different genres present conflicting images of the world, just that genres focus on different aspects of reality. Viewers devoted to programs of one genre are, therefore, exposed to different views of the world and therefore to different effects than viewers devoted to another genre. The world as presented in light-hearted comedies is quite different than the scary world of police dramas and horror films. The world on the news does not resemble the images of MTV.

If media content shapes our attitudes and cultivates our images of the world, it seems plausible that different media would shape different attitudes. If TV can create a scary world, why should it not be able to create a more trusting and friendly world? If dramas and police shows are associated with attitudes about personal safety and crime, it seems logical that soaps should be associated with attitudes about interpersonal relationships. The importance of studying media cultivation effects by genres has been demonstrated in several studies. Genre differences were found in a study of the effects of TV viewing on interpersonal trust and civic participation (Shah, 1997). Whereas an index of total TV viewing was associated with less interpersonal trust, friendship sitcoms and science fiction were associated with a higher level of interpersonal trust. Another study that found differential genre effects was conducted by Rubin et al. (1988), who found that viewers of daytime serials had less faith in others and that viewers of action/ adventure felt that they had less control in life and were less safe. Interestingly, they found no positive effects of any media genres. Viewers of sit-coms held no more positive beliefs about life and human nature than nonviewers. Similarly, viewing of news was uncorrelated with personal beliefs. Thus, this study found few effects of viewing on attitudes, and all the effects of heavy viewing were in the direction of less positive beliefs about others, life control, political efficacy, and safety. Each belief, however, was affected by devotion to a different genre. Strouse and Buerkel-Rothfuss (1987) found sex- and topic-specific genre effects. Permissive sexual attitudes among female college students were associated with viewing of MTV and among male students with watching soaps. No effects on sexual attitudes were found for sitcoms, action-adventure, or overall TV viewing.

Finally, Cohen and Weimann (1998) conducted a study in Israel, among a sample 4,848 Israeli teenagers. The survey included questions about the amount of TV they viewed, their genre preferences, "scary world" beliefs about Israel, and their degree of interpersonal trust. The results suggest that TV's cultivation of beliefs depends on viewer characteristics and genre preferences. Genres are related to cultivation: Some genres are clearly "yielding" significant cultivation differences. These are, in descending order, comedy programs and soaps (each yielding differences on five of the seven scales), MTV, movies, horror and suspense, sports and news (differences on three scales), and politics and game shows (differences on two scales). The belief most frequently related to the amount of viewing was seen in the violence scale (interestingly, this was also the first scale ever used by cultivation scholars back in the early 1970s). The violence scale is followed by the police scale, again a measure of the Mean World Syndrome, and then by the probability of being victimized scale, an additional Mean World measure. In fact, the Mean World measures differentiated clearly between heavy and light viewers, whereas the mistrust and alienation measures related to the amount of viewing only in certain genres. These findings demonstrate the importance of analyzing each genre separately. One of the more surprising findings of this study was the reverse cultivation effects. Devotees of certain genres believe the world to be a somewhat nicer place than light viewers of these genres. These reverse findings were selective, however. First, they applied more to beliefs about interpersonal trust than to fear of crime. Also, they applied only to girls and only to older teenagers. Together, these findings fit our more specific understanding of the cultivation process. Because girls tend to watch shows that deal with interpersonal relations more than boys, and because these are the shows that present the world as somewhat less scary and mean, they are more likely to believe that the world is nicer. Because the shows they watch deal with interpersonal issues, these are the beliefs most likely to be cultivated. The age difference reflects the argument that cultivation is a long-term, cumulative effect. Thus, we found that heavy viewing cultivated attitudes and beliefs in both directions, but only at heavy doses of viewing of specific genres.

Where Is Cultivation Theory Today?

It has been over 20 years since the first cultivation findings were published. Since then, many studies have explored, enhanced, critiqued, dismissed, or defended the conceptual assumptions and methodological procedures of cultivation analysis. Although cultivation analysis was once closely identified with the issue of violence, over the years, researchers have looked at a broad range of topics, including sex roles, aging, political orientations, environmental attitudes, science, health, religion, minorities, and occupations. Replications have been carried out in Argentina, Australia, Brazil, Canada, China, England, Hungary, Israel, the Netherlands, Russia, South Korea, Sweden, Taiwan, and other countries.

So where did the cultivation tradition lead us and where is it today? A very comprehensive and detailed answer was recently given by Morgan and Shanahan (1997), who conducted a meta-analysis of all the cultivation studies. Meta-analysis is a statistical integration of the results of independent studies that has an advantage over the traditional narrative review: In meta-analysis, each observed result is assumed to be a random sampling from a distribution whose mean represents the "true" effect. The analysis thus gives a better estimate of that true effect, adjusted for sample size, than does any individual study. But meta-analysis does more than that: The cumulated data are examined to see if the set of relationships is homogeneous and to measure how much of the variation in results observed across studies simply reflects sampling error. Morgan and Shanahan used this method to examine the accomplishments of cultivation research in its first 20 years.

To do it, they began with the regularly updated, comprehensive bibliography of cultivation studies that have been published since 1976. From the list of more than 300 publications, they built a database of studies that (a) tested a relationship between amount of exposure to television (however measured) and a dependent variable that could be thought of as providing a "television answer" and (b) specifically adduced or criticized cultivation theory as an explanation of the results. Some studies that met these criteria could not be included for other reasons. Almost all cultivation studies were survey-based. There are experimental tests of cultivation relationships or experimental manipulations of cognitive variables, but these deal with short-term phenomena and hence do not really estimate cultivation processes. Thus, they included only survey-type cultivation studies, which are by far the most common, and ignored the small handful of relevant experiments. Because there were numerous dependent variables in the cultivation literature, the meta-analysis focused only on cultivation findings in three areas: (a) violence (including fear and the Mean World Syndrome), (b) sex roles, and (c) political beliefs and orientations. Cultivation studies of images of aging, minorities, religion, occupations, science, health, the family, and other topics were not included.

The first analysis selected all findings that were (a) overall findings (that dealt with an entire set of data); (b) about one of the three dependent areas of violence, sex roles, or political orientations; and (c) measured as Pearson's r (or as gammas transformed to r values). This yielded 52 independent samples that could contribute to the overall meta-analysis. All overall coefficients from each sample were weighted and averaged to produce a single r for that sample. These averaged coefficients were then weighted by the average sample size. The analysis shows that the average overall effect size for cultivation studies is rather weak, $r = .091$. This confirms what most observers have assumed about cultivation: Its effect size tends to be small.

The meta-analysis reveals that when we consider several other factors, there are stronger or weaker coefficients. Studies conducted by those associated with Gerbner (i.e., "core" studies), studies that use larger samples, and studies that make sure not to sensitize respondents to the purposes of the research—all tend to produce somewhat smaller estimates of cultivation. It is interesting that the findings produced by researchers and methods most connected to Gerbner have been, in a meta-analytic sense, more conservative than those of the critics and others, who have sometimes used smaller and less representative samples.

Some would argue that such a small average effect means that the cultivation relationship, although perhaps true, is too trivial to be meaningful. However, Morgan and Shanahan (1997) argue that one should not expect to find statistically large effects from television viewing. Very few people in this society do not accumulate substantial exposure to television over the years, comparable messages are disseminated by other media, and light and heavy viewers live in the same general culture. The forces that shape our beliefs are many and varied; television is just one. Gerbner and his associates have repeatedly argued over the years that television is by no means the most powerful influence on people, but it is the most common. The cultivation scholars have also argued that the *size* of an effect is less important than its *direction* and the nature of its steady contribution. As Morgan and Shanahan concluded their meta-analysis,

> In slow but steady ways, cultivation means that long-term, regular exposure to television's dramatic portrayals contributes to and helps reproduce our ideologies of individualism and consumerism; perceptions of the roles of women, children, and the family; notions of progress, technology, equality, and opportunity; and images of different groups of people. These in turn reflect and define the cultural climate from which actions and policies draw meaning; they subtly keep some values and perspectives alive while marginalizing or neglecting others. Bit by bit, the long-term accumulation of small changes and the maintenance of "common sense" can have far-reaching implications for many disparate realms of social policy. (p. 37)

As we will demonstrate in our concluding section (Part III), the reason for the weak support for many cultivation studies is their failure to consider, include, and control for the multitude of variables or actors involved in the complex process of encoding and decoding media messages. We will propose a model that presents these multi-actor processes and the numerous combinations of these variables. This will provide a better understanding of the futility of so many cultivation studies.

NOTES

1. This brief review of the history of cultivation research is based on Morgan and Signorielli (1990).

2. On this process, see Hawkins and Pingree (1990), Hawkins, Pingree, and Adler (1987), Potter (1989, 1991a, 1991b), and Shapiro (1991).

3. For reviews of conceptual and methodological issues, see Doob and Macdonald (1979); Gerbner, Gross, Morgan, and Signorielli (1981a), and Rubin et al. (1988).

CHAPTER FOUR

The Psychology of Cultivation

The cultivation hypothesis—that the media's presentation of social reality influences the social reality beliefs of their audiences—has been studied from various angles and perspectives. Most studies attempted to measure the simple existence or robustness of the cultivation effect. Very few studies explore and attempt to understand the psychological processes that may underlie cultivation effects. How is it that watching television or Internet websites contributes to certain social reality beliefs and not others? What are the psychological processes that lead individuals to construct their own social reality in ways that mirror both the facts and the ostensible meaning of television's social reality? Hawkins and Pingree (1990), who conducted several cultivation studies and reviewed many others (e.g., Hawkins & Pingree, 1980, 1981b, 1982, 1990; Hawkins, Pingree, & Adler, 1987), have concluded,

> Even though years of research have provided considerable evidence of a small but consistent relationship between television viewing and beliefs about the social world that are similar to or plausibly implied by the images in television programs, the research community still does not understand how this relationship occurs. And since most evidence of cultivation is based on cross-sectional survey research (although supported by an occasional experiment or panel survey), as long as these effects occur within a "black box," the whole enterprise remains vulnerable to questions of spuriousness. (p. 35)

Demonstrating a plausible psychological process for cultivation results has proved surprisingly difficult. Sociologically oriented cultivation research typically sums up the psychology involved as "learning": Viewers learn the actions and characteristics of television, and heavy viewers, who see so many television examples, come to accept television images as representative of the real world. But how and what is learned? How is that learning stored in memory? What kind of processing translates learning into generalizations about social reality? Hawkins and Pingree were the first to suggest five different subprocesses that might be involved in the process of cultivation: (a) information processing, (b) critical attention to television, (c) direct experience or other sources providing confirmation or disconfirmation of media messages, (d) social structural influences, and (e) cultivation related to specific content and selective viewing instead of habitual viewing in general. Although comparatively little research has been conducted within each of these areas, there appears to be growing interest in studying these psychological mechanisms. Let us review some of the emerging findings and ideas about the psychology of cultivation.

Cultivation as a Two-Step Process?

One central distinction between subprocesses was based on the two different sets of measures used to study cultivation. The first, labeled first-order measures, were the demographic characteristics of television or the real world, whereas second-order beliefs were the value-system measures. Thus, first-order measures required the respondents to make quantitative estimates of the occurrences of certain things (crime, murder, police violence, etc.). For first-order measures, real-world figures (from formal and official statistical sources such as U.S. Statistical Abstracts) and television-world figures (from content analysis of television programs) were compared so that researchers could access the respondents' answers to see which reality they resembled. Second-order measures, however, are generalized beliefs that are supposedly derived or inferred by viewers from first-order information. These second-order measures required the respondents to express their general beliefs about the world (how mean or violent it is, whether women are as competent as men, can people be trusted, etc.).

The logical and basic hypothesis suggested that second-order beliefs might be derived by inference from an individual's first-order beliefs. This idea led to a two-component model of cultivation based on the subprocesses of learning and construction. Learning is the relationship between amount of television viewing and first-order measures. The more people view, the more information they learn from television. Construction is the process of using that incidental information to form beliefs about social reality. So, a test of construction is an examination of the degree to which first-order measures are related to second-order measures. Hawkins et al. (1987) conducted an empirical test of this model on three samples of adolescents ranging from the 6th through the 11th grades. Using the topics of working women, perceptions of violence, police procedures, sex roles, and family makeup, they found a general cultivation relationship on about one third of their first-order measures and on about one third of their second-order measures. They used first-order measures as test variables to see if these were intervening in the overall relationship between amount of television viewing and second-order beliefs and found them not to be intervening variables. This was interpreted as a lack of relationship between first- and second-order measures. In fact, of 19 correlations, 6 were significant, but no correlation exceeded .20. The researchers concluded that there was no support for their subprocess model, and in a later article, Hawkins and Pingree (1990) argued that it may be time to look for an entirely different set of processes to account for relationships between television viewing and second-order beliefs or to see the two types as constructed independently of each other. Hawkins and Pingree (1990) argued that

> in fact, it is possible that research on processes has been hampered by the implicit assumption that similar processes apply to both. The different cognitive demands of the two, recent work in cognitive psychology, and the available evidence on processes in social reality effects all point toward very different ways of constructing social reality in first- and second-order beliefs. (p. 43)

In contrast, Potter (1989) argued that it is too early to abandon the subprocess model, especially the notion that viewers may construct their second-order beliefs from first-order estimates. Although Hawkins et al. (1987) failed to find a relationship between first- and second-order measures, their search for relationships was limited to a general bivariate test. Potter suggested other alternatives by examining contingent and asymmetric forms of relationships. Potter's studies (1991a, 1991c) attempted to test the possibility of asymmetric relationships: A finding of a weak or nonrelationship does not necessarily mean that there is no relationship, only that there is no symmetric relationship. There is still a question about whether the two types of measures might be related in an asymmetric way. For example, second-order scores may provide a good basis for predicting first-order scores only at the high end of the score distribution, which is the focus of cultivation interest. His studies led Potter to three conclusions: First, this investigation confirmed the findings of Hawkins et al. that first- and second-order measures are not related in a bivariate, samplewide, symmetric manner. The intercorrelations between these measures on the same topic were very modest and indicate an ability for one of these measures to predict a maximum of less than 5% of the variance of the other. Second, there are some types of respondents who differ from the general pattern of no relationship. Younger respondents and those with higher IQs seem to exhibit more evidence of a relationship. Contingent patterns were also found in a differential manner across topics, and these patterns are related to relevant situational variables. Third, there is evidence of asymmetric relationships. The fact that an asymmetric pattern was strong on the topics of affluence and divorce/affairs but nonexistent on the topic of working women indicates that the relationship is not a general one but is sensitive to some topics and not so to others.

When asymmetric relationships were found, they were almost always in the direction where second-order measures were dependent, that is, where first-order estimates formed a basis for second-order beliefs. What does this relationship between first- and second-order measure tell us? Potter suggested that there is a construction process operating. Television viewers learn about the real world from observing patterns in the television world and then use these facts in some way to formulate their beliefs about the real world. This construction process has been hypothesized as a subprocess within cultivation and is found to depend on characteristics of viewers and the topics (to be discussed later).

In conclusion, there seems to be more complexity in the cultivation process than early researchers of this phenomenon assumed. The overall cultivation effect appears to be a complex process embracing several components, each of which displays different patterns. Researchers must distinguish between various stages of the cultivation process, determine what types of topics, subgroups of respondents, and orders measures interact, and only then find the true nature and magnitude of this process.

Individual Cognitive Traits

There have been several research attempts to identify cognitive trait variables affecting cultivation. That is, if cultivation occurs in the presence of some enduring cognitive trait or habit, then that trait may be an important condition for the process. For example, Hawkins and his colleagues found that subgroups based on school achievement scores or current events knowledge differed in the size of various cultivation relationships, especially for second-order social reality belief measures. To interpret those results, they argued that school achievement and knowledge of current events were surrogates tapping some portion of either cognitive activity, cognitive effort, or both. Several other studies attempted to measure a cognitive process directly as a trait variable. For example, Potter (1986) assessed adolescents' and adults' beliefs about the reality of television on several dimensions (their perceived reality). Correlations between amount of viewing and social reality beliefs occurred for those who believed television to be an accurate representation of actual life and not for those skeptical of television. Potter's argument is that people who believe entertainment television to be realistic accept its messages as more applicable to their social reality judgments. Weaver and Wakshlag (1986) concluded that people actively interpret televised information and relate that information to their own personal experiences when using television as a basis for social reality beliefs. Many other researchers observed that perceptions of television realism were substantial contributors to cultivation (e.g., Perse, 1986; Potter, 1986; Slater & Elliott, 1982). Others, such as Tamborini,

Zillmann, and Bryant (1984), argued that cultivation is the result of a cognitive priming process. According to this argument, television exposure provides salient information about facts, images, events, and values. Frequent viewing makes television information easy to access and retrieve and, because people make judgments based on the most available sources, judgments about social reality are often based on television images. Tamborini and his colleagues conducted a study based on indirect experimental evidence, which supported this priming function.

Another potential intervening variable was IQ: Is low IQ an inhibitor of cultivation effects? The evidence here is sparse. Gerbner, Gross, Signorielli, and Morgan (1979) reported separate cultivation differentials at high, medium, and low relative levels of achievement for their New York sample of schoolchildren. In estimating the proportion of people involved in violence, the cultivation differential is significant for low and medium achievement but not for high achievement. Achievement, even as a surrogate for IQ, subsumes too much and thus is rather distant from processing abilities that would give us an idea of what goes on as television influences social reality. Ideally, one should determine individual performance on various processing abilities and then use these individual differences in conditional analyses for the same sample of individuals.

Comparisons across age groups would provide another method of comparison whenever developmental changes in processing abilities run parallel to changes in cultivation. For example, stronger television influences on young children could be based on cognitive-developmental theories suggesting that concrete-operational reasoning may be more inflexible and dogmatic than formal-operational reasoning. Two samples from the Cultural Indicators group provide comparisons across age ranges. Cultivation in their youngest group (fourth to sixth grade) was reported to be as strong as among the seventh to ninth graders at the same school. Moreover, a variety of studies suggested that young children (before ages 8-10) have difficulty comprehending and making use of the order of isolated events in a plot, lose track of order and relationships between events separated in a plot, have difficulty making inferences about the causes and meanings of televised actions, and have difficulty understanding, let alone applying, dramatic characters' motives and the consequences of their actions. Very young children may simply not understand enough of what they watch to be cultivated by it.

The assumption behind these attempts is that the cognitive characteristics are traitlike: Cognitive orientations are stable over time so that those who say they perceive television to be real will also see it as real when watching or when constructing social reality beliefs. Still, perceived reality, although relatively close, is not itself the process it implicates as constructing social reality. As with grade point average or achievement test scores, perceived reality is argued to be a surrogate for skeptical or accepting evaluations of television content, or more or less active rational processing of television. It is the hypothesized evaluation or activity that determines the degree to which television influence occurs. One such process that may be a cognitive trait influencing cultivation is the accessibility of information in memory, or construct accessibility.

Memory Accessibility and Cultivation

One of the central psychological subprocesses involved in cultivation is the storage of information in the memory and then the access and retrieval of this information from the memory. Contemporary theory in the area of social cognition and personal memory clearly points out that one of the primary determinants of the probability of a particular bit of information being retrieved is the accessibility of that information in memory. Thus, Shrum and O'Guinn (1993) suggested studying memory access, or construct accessibility, as a key factor affecting the influence of television viewing on perceptions of social reality. Shrum and O'Guinn direct our attention to the fact that one of the most consistent findings in social cognition research has been that people tend to use surprisingly little information in constructing a judgment or inference. Rather than making an exhaustive search of memory for information bearing on a particular object or proposition, people instead attempt to retrieve sufficient information to form a judgment, which clearly does not include all possible information. More specifically, studies show that subjects tend to search memory and use the information that is most accessible to form these judgments (Wyer & Srull, 1989).

Memory accessibility can generally be viewed as the ease with which information is retrieved, and information that is more easily retrieved is considered more accessible. Several studies have shown that this accessibility increased the probability that the accessible construct would be used as a basis for judgment. Shrum and O'Guinn (1993) applied the notion of construct accessibility to the process of cultivation. They argued that information related to a particular social reality topic is more accessible for those who watch comparatively more television. Television provides its viewers with frequent representations of information pertaining to typical social reality topics. Thus, by definition, heavy viewers would be more likely to possess these television-related cognitions relative to light viewers, and thus, for heavy viewers, these cognitions would be more accessible. Specifically applying the above reasoning to a typical social reality question—when people are asked to estimate the frequency of violent crime perpetrated by strangers or the number of workers who are police—they may perceive the task to be quite difficult. Rather than performing an exhaustive search of memory and weighing and balancing each piece of information, people may simply use the information that comes to mind most easily. If, indeed, relevant information is more accessible for heavy compared to light viewers, then heavy viewers should give higher estimates.

The crucial question of this theoretical reasoning is whether the assumption that relevant information is indeed more accessible for heavy viewers relative to light viewers is a valid one. Cultivation measures are specifically constructed with the idea that the object or behavior in question occurs frequently on television. Thus, this information should be stored more frequently and more recently by heavy viewers. It is also reasonable to assume that the television information is often more vivid. Indeed, that is the essence of television programming: removal of the more mundane, everyday aspects of life in favor of vivid portrayals of spectacular events. All of these factors have been shown to heighten the accessibility of information in memory. Shrum and O'Guinn's (1993) study attempted to test the hypothesis that relevant information is more accessible for heavy viewers than light viewers and that this enhanced accessibility contributes to higher frequency and probability of estimates for social reality measures. The researchers tested their hypothesis with a sample of 130 female students in an American university, using an exercise on a microcomputer to test construct accessibility and then a survey to study television viewing and perceptions of social reality (the prevalence of crime, alcoholism, drug addiction, prostitution).

The results supported the central thesis that the accessibility of information in memory contributes to the cultivation effect. In virtually every case, a cultivation effect was noted within a specifically predicted viewing category. Moreover, when controlling for speed of memory accessibility in the correlation between television viewing and estimates of social reality, the relationship diminished or disappeared entirely. This suggests that enhanced memory accessibility of relevant information for heavier viewers can at least partially account for the cultivation effect. "These results," argued the researchers, "are consistent with the hypothesis that the cultivation effect is related to the accessibility of information in memory" (Shrum & O'Guinn, 1993, p. 460). Relevant images of reality, "cultivated" from television viewing, are more accessible in memory for heavier viewers.

In a later study, Shrum (1996) retested the notion of construct accessibility as mediating the cultivation effect. Accessibility was operationalized as the time needed to generate frequency estimates of the real-world prevalence of crime, marital discord, and particular occupations. The independent variable was amount of soap opera viewing, and the study used only very heavy (5 or more hours per week) and very light (0 hours per week) viewers. Heavy viewers gave significantly higher frequency estimates (cultivation effect) and responded significantly faster (accessibility effect) than did light viewers, replicating the findings of Shrum and O'Guinn (1993). Soap opera viewing also had an indirect effect on the frequency estimates of crime and occupational prevalence through its effect on response latency, supporting the notion of accessibility as a mediating variable. These results support the model by again showing that heavy television viewing creates an accessibility bias and that this bias has an effect on real-world frequency estimates. If an individual's estimates of such things as the incidence of crime or occupational prevalence is indeed at least partially the result of the accessibility of relevant exemplars in memory, this process has very important implications for the study of media effects. Accessibility is affected by a number of factors that may be related to media consumption, including frequency of presentation, recency of presentation, vividness, and distinctiveness. Thus, from an accessibility perspective, it is not necessary that instances of violence be portrayed often for these instances to be easily accessible from memory. A very vivid portrayal of violence, which television certainly can and does provide, may be sufficient. In addition, simply having seen a television portrayal of violence recently may affect perceptions of violence (although the effect of recency would be temporary). Thus, a light viewer who recently happened to view television just prior to making a cultivation judgment, or a light viewer who viewed a particularly vivid portrayal, may be affected. Schrum (1996) argues that this may account for the relatively weak television effects that are often found in cultivation studies. In particular, it calls for a greater emphasis on "critical portrayals" rather than "total number of portrayals."

Shapiro (1987) pursued the implications for social reality beliefs of memory models. The individual's construction of social reality based on television might be combining two steps: (a) learning incidental content from viewing and (b) constructing beliefs from that store of memories. Shapiro reasoned that if cultivation occurs by abstraction from a memory store, it should be possible to assess the relevant stored memories and their individual sources directly and find them more closely associated with social reality beliefs than is any measure of television viewing. To test this hypothesis, Shapiro asked college students to provide "memory dumps": listing all examples they could think of in a category, such as "victims of crime" or "law enforcement personnel." After a fixed period for the memory dump ended, respondents went back and marked one of eight communication sources (a mix of direct, interpersonal, and mediated) for each exemplar. He found that the number of relevant exemplars recalled from various sources was a much better predictor of beliefs than were media-use variables, although media use was generally correlated with the number of exemplars produced. These results provide support for a model in which social reality beliefs are constructed from multiple memory traces of individual events. Although Shapiro's research may tell us something about the origins of social reality beliefs, it is not clear that this process is the one responsible for relationships between viewing and beliefs. Given the predictive strength of the memory dump procedure, further work attempting to link the dump back to media use is clearly needed.

Critical Consumption and Cultivation

Another psychological process that may affect cultivation is critical weighing of television messages. Hawkins and Pingree (1980, 1981a, 1982) argued that what may be important here is not the beliefs about television but what they may indicate about the "activity" with which people watch television. It may be that inactive viewing is necessary for social reality effects or that active viewing inhibits the influence. In one study, social reality effects were compared for soap opera fans (who had paid to attend a soap opera convention and luncheon with several stars) and a random sample of women from the same city. The evidence suggested that the fans watched much more actively and discussed the programs with friends. Amount of soap opera viewing and soap opera-biased social reality was related for the random sample of women but not for the fans, suggesting that active processing and involvement may inhibit cultivation. The researchers suggested the term *critical consumption,* by which they meant evaluation of information during reception, greater retention of the bits and pieces of information provided by television, awareness of exceptions to patterns, more active search (not simply exposure) for confirming or disconfirming information, a more rational weighing of evidence in constructing social reality, and so on.

Shapiro (1991) attempted to explain cultivation effects in terms of a weighing and balancing mechanism. Shapiro suggested that, when individuals attempt to construct a social reality estimate, they first retrieve relevant information to form the judgment and then weigh and balance the information with respect to its veracity. According to Shapiro, the reliability of the source may be an important factor, affecting the veracity of the retrieved information, and information retrieved from unreliable sources such as television may be discounted. Shapiro's results showed that people could generate the perceptions or estimates pertaining to a typical social reality topic (e.g., crime, occupations) and also showed that they could determine where they had acquired this information (the source). Although Shapiro claimed support for the weighing and balancing model, the study was considered problematic on a conceptual level as an explanation for a cultivation effect. In fact, it may be the reluctance or inability of viewers to weigh and balance information that is responsible for the cultivation effect. A later work of Shapiro and Lang (1991) suggested this very possibility.

Source Confusion and Cultivation

Another important psychological factor in the process of accepting the unreal as real is the credibility attributed to the source. As noted above, Shapiro (1991) hypothesized that when people make a social reality judgment, they call up lots of event memories and then weigh and balance the memories based on the source. Event memories from low credibility sources should have less influence on social reality judgments. What if individuals make mistakes about the source of their information? Mares (1996) argued that individuals who tend to misremember events as coming from reliable sources will be more likely to label remembered examples as accurate and hence will be quicker to retrieve a seemingly trustworthy example relevant to the social reality judgment. Mares exposed individuals to news and fictional television programming and then asked them to recall whether specific events had been part of the news or part of the fictional programming. This provided measures of fiction-to-news confusions (mislabeling fiction as news) and news-to-fiction confusions (mislabeling news as fiction). Participants also made social reality judgments and answered questions about their television viewing habits. Two hypotheses were tested: (a) source confusions in which fictional television content is remembered as news will be positively correlated with measures of social reality beliefs and (b) source confusions in which news content is remembered as fiction will be negatively correlated with measures of social reality beliefs. Thus, the type of source confusion habitually made by the viewers is considered a key factor. Fiction-to-news confusions should intensify the effects of viewing, such that heavy viewers who make fiction-to-news confusions will be the quickest to find a seemingly useful example and will make the highest social reality estimates. On the other hand, news-to-fiction confusions will minimize the effects of viewing, such that even if heavy viewers can quickly think of an example, they will be likely to reject it as untrustworthy. Two samples, adolescents and elderly people, were subjected to an experimental procedure. They were shown a televised news story and trailer (fiction). Source confusions were identified by a list of 24 specific events: 8 of these events came from the target news story, 8 were from the movie trailer, and 8 had not been in either.[1] Subjects chose whether the event had been in the news, the trailer, both the news and the trailer, neither the news nor the trailer, or "don't know." Scores were created for fiction-to-news confusions and for news-to-fiction confusions. Social reality measures, testing cultivation, were the Perceptions of Violence Scale (subjects were asked about the prevalence and nature of violence and were given two possible responses for each question. One response reflected real-world statistics; the other was the "television world" answer) and the Mean World Scale (the scale contains items about how helpful or trustworthy most people are, as well as items about personal vulnerability).

The hypotheses were strongly supported. Those subjects who remembered more events depicted in the movie trailer as having been part of the news had higher scores on all cultivation measures. Even after income and daily viewing were entered on the first step, fiction-to-news confusions explained between 22% and 33% of the variance in social reality measures. In contrast, remembering events shown in the news as having been part of the fictional trailer was significantly associated with lower violence estimates and mean world scores. The results supported the argument that source confusions play a role in the effects of television viewing on social reality beliefs. That is, when individuals misremember whether items depicted on television really occurred, their beliefs about the real world may be affected, either in the direction of television's biased version of reality or away from that version. The direction of effects of television viewing appears to depend, in part, on the type of source confusions made by viewers. Fiction-to-news confusions appeared to strengthen the cultivation effect. That is, these confusions (particularly in combination with heavy television viewing) were associated with beliefs that the world is dangerous and full of mean people.

Involvement and Cultivation

The notion of involvement stemmed from a study on another factor. Pingree (1983) studied individual differences in the ability to draw inferences from implicit television content. Specifically, Pingree hypothesized that those who are best at drawing such inferences would show a greater cultivation effect. The results, however, indicated just the opposite: Those who were worst at drawing inferences from the program content were most affected. This led Pingree to suggest that cultivation effects are most prominent for low involvement viewers, as her results also showed that those exhibiting less ability to draw inferences also indicated that they tended to be more passive viewers.

In mass communication research, involvement is seen as intellectual and emotional participation during message reception. Petty and Cacioppo (1984), for example, found that issue involvement is reflected in more intense cognitive activity. When people encounter messages about topics important to them, they pay attention to and evaluate the content. The researchers concluded that involved individuals process information more deeply. Besides the critical consumption discussed earlier, which prevents many social reality effects, it is equally appropriate to suggest that uninvolved or passive reception can enhance some media effects. Advertising researchers propose that, instead of a sequence from attentive learning to evaluation and attitude formation and finally behavior, our understanding of much of television viewing, and especially viewing commercials, will be increased if we consider an uninvolved, uninterested viewer assimilating only the simplest facts, names, and then only into short-term memory.

Perse (1990), who applied the notion of involvement to cultivation analysis, suggested that involvement has two dimensions: orientation and intensity. Orientation marks the direction of the cognitive-emotional processing. People may become involved with any aspect of the message: issue information, personalities, plot, music, or audience. Intensity marks the depth of the processing. As people become more involved, they process the information more deeply, moving from paying attention to the information, categorizing it as familiar or unfamiliar, relating the information to prior knowledge, and reacting emotionally to it. Her study tested the following hypotheses regarding cultivation and dimension of involvement. Specifically, she hypothesized that individual perceptions of less personal safety will be predicted by (a) higher levels of local news exposure and non-news television exposure, (b) more salient diversionary local television news viewing motives, (c) higher levels of local news perceived realism, (d) higher levels of attention to local television crime news, (e) higher levels of recognition of local television crime news, (f) higher levels of elaboration on local television crime news, and (g) more emotional reactions to local television news.

Perse (1990) found that attention to the news is a significant positive contributor to the cultivation of perceptions of personal safety. The orientation of involvement was an important aspect to perceptions of personal safety. Higher levels of perceived personal risk were predicted by entertainment news viewing motives, attention to crime news stories, and lower levels of more utilitarian viewing motives. Consistent with cultivation studies, perceptions of personal safety were linked to an entertainment orientation to local news. Perse (1990) argued, "the consideration of the influence of involvement has added to knowledge about the individual-level cultivation process that is consistent with earlier speculations" (p. 63). Moreover, the negative contribution of recognition to perception of personal safety may reflect the greater impact of mass media: When the individual does not have direct personal experience, television becomes a source for social reality beliefs.

Finally, the findings support the view that cultivation is an incidental learning process. Incidental learning occurs unintentionally without motivation to learn. The findings show that perceptions of personal safety are learned at lower levels of involvement, thus through unintentional learning. However, Perse (1990) argued that because perceptions of personal safety were associated with lower levels of involvement, cultivation due to television exposure may not be long-lasting. Previous research has shown that lower levels of cognitive activity result in less enduring effects because less intense information processing does not link the information very strongly to prior knowledge (Petty, Cacioppo, & Kasmer, 1987).

In conclusion, the tests of the role of involvement in the cultivation process support the view that involvement is an important variable in media effects. Both the intensity and orientation dimensions of involvement increased understanding of individual-level cultivation. The inclusion of involvement in cultivation analysis was found to add to the understanding of the process.

Personal Experience

Even if television messages affect the construction of social reality, it is not done in a vacuum. Viewers have their own experience, other mass media, friends, family, and their beliefs as filters for television's images. As Hawkins and Pingree (1982) argued, these factors may form conditions for television influence in at least three ways. First, for any given television content or message, some degree of confirmation from real-world experience, other sources, or even pre-existing beliefs about social reality may be necessary to validate the television message (Gerbner labeled this process resonance). Second, messages from other sources that are heavily used or relied on could provide sufficient disconfirmation that the amount of exposure to television becomes less relevant or even irrelevant. Third, Gerbner suggested (see Chapter 3) that, for some social reality beliefs, television's portrayals both form and match the mainstream of beliefs. Many population subgroups share these beliefs, and the amount of television viewed adds little; but for divergent population subgroups, the extent of viewing becomes important, with the beliefs of heavy viewers in the divergent group converging on the population mainstream.

Many dimensions of an individual's experience might be relevant. For example, the daily experiences of lower class lifestyle could provide confirmation of television messages about interpersonal mistrust and possibly about the prevalence of violence and fear of crime. Confirmation of television's messages about violence could come from exposure to news media or personal experience or personal knowledge of victimization. Hawkins and Pingree (1982) cited several studies that found this mainstreaming pattern (for example, in the NORC 1975 sample, there is a significant cultivation differential for interpersonal mistrust at middle- and upper-income levels, but not for those with low income). Confirmation (or resonance) results were also reported by Gerbner's team (see Chapter 3), as well as other researchers. Thus Doob and Macdonald (1979) found that television viewing and fear were significantly related only in the high-crime city area; this may suggest that living in such an area provides confirmation that television's messages are relevant and believable.

Additional support for the importance of personal experience may come from the comparisons of adolescent and adult samples. In general, the relationships are much weaker in the adult samples. Hawkins and Pingree (1982) argued that children younger than about 10 may lack some processing abilities necessary to construct social reality from television:

> What we may have here instead is an application of what has become almost a communication research truism—that effects of communication are strongest when competing sources of information and preexisting knowledge are lowest. For adolescents, these social reality beliefs are still in the process of formation and thus more amenable to influence. (p. 241)

There is, of course, a close association between the notion of personal experience and the process of critical consumption or the weighing and balancing of information from different sources. Moreover, there is an interesting connection with the notion of two-step cultivation. First, the individual must acquire from television various bits of information about actions and characterization and associations between these bits of information; this may be best explained as the learning stage. Second, the individual may use these bits of information to construct more general and integrated conceptions of the world, and it is probably here, in the construction stage, that the processes such as weighing television against other sources of information occur. At this stage, personal experience may be used for the evaluation of the information and the reconstruction of meanings.

Conclusions

The need to relate the cultivation paradigm to psychological processes is clear. However, this integration of the disciplines, despite its potential, is far from easy. As Hawkins and Pingree (1990) noted,

One problem in applying cognitively oriented psychology to problems of psychological processes in effects on social reality beliefs is that there is a mismatch between the narrow, particularistic research paradigms of cognitive psychology and the long-term, television-content-as-a-whole nature of the potential stimulus here. That problem has not been resolved . . . There will have to be many creative solutions, each devised to match an individual problem of time-order, duration, and the particular constructs and processes involved. (p. 47)

And yet, the few studies in this area did demonstrate the need to treat first- and second-order beliefs separately, propose specific theory-based processes for each, and study their role in the cultivation process. We also learned about the importance of individual traits that may promote or block the media's cultivation impact, and we know that memory accessibility, critical media consumption, or personal involvement may be important subprocesses in the cultivation process. More psychological process research on the cultivation hypothesis will be necessary to establish the nature and effectiveness of various individual traits and psychological mechanisms. The recent advances in theory and operationalization in cognitive social psychology, the improvement of methods and analysis, and the pioneering process studies cited here all combine to provide a promising research agenda.

NOTE

1. The news stories were part of an ABC nightly news program aired in 1987, selected because they did not appear dated and were unconnected to news events occuring at the time of the study. The three distraction items included stories about techniques to help autistic children, an arms dealer being captured, and political struggles in South Africa. The target story was about ongoing border disputes betwen Libya and Chad (three different versions). The movie trailer was created from an obscure movie about a U.S. marine embroiled in the political struggle in the Middle East.

PART II

Mediated
Realities

CHAPTER FIVE

The Mean and Scary World

*It was another L.A. murder, but when the victim turned out
to be the son of a beloved television father [Bill Cosby], it was
as if America had suffered a death in the family. . . . It was
almost natural to confuse real and imagined.*

—*Time,* January 27, 1997, p. 23

The body sprawled next to the Mercedes convertible might have been just another victim of random robbery or murder in Los Angeles. But when recognition took place, America shuddered: The body on the roadside was Ennis William Cosby, the only son of Bill Cosby. But for many television viewers all over the world, it was not Ennis who was murdered, it was Theo Huxtable, the son of Dr. Huxtable, a member of the Huxtable family on Bill Cosby's popular TV sitcom. In Israel, for example, the headline in the leading Israeli daily, *Yediot Achronot,* was "Theo Huxtable is dead." The images of Ennis Cosby killed in Los Angeles melded myth and reality: Cosby's television family was combined with his real family, and the figures overlapped. Virtual figures melded with real people, and a real murder was related to the fictional figures. The situation comedy turned into a situation tragedy:

The virtual American family has suffered a real death. . . . Had a human being been slain, or a sitcom character? How was Dr. Huxtable—Bill Cosby, rather—going to handle this one? How would he break such news to Phylicia Rashad, his TV wife, and how could the tragedy be resolved in under 30 minutes? (*Time*, January 27, 1997, p. 27)

For more than a decade, the Huxtables were America's first family, and Bill Cosby was everyone's dad. The Huxtables were warm, friendly, comfortable, and a very American family. They were confronted with many problems shared by many other American (and other) families. So when Cosby's son was killed, it was regarded as another moving episode in the Huxtables' life, not the Cosbys'. Moreover, the murder and the victim were depicted and treated according to the Huxtables' fictional setting and relationship. The real story, that of Ennis Cosby and his father, was mostly invisible to the public while the virtual son and father became the "real" story. But there is an additional dimension to the event: the way it was evoking deeper emotions, existing fears, and perceptions of reality. Everyone is afraid of being victimized; every parent dreads an unfortunate disaster happening to his or her child. This fear was described by Cosby himself: "the feeling of your child going out to play, going to the store, going to visit Grandma or Uncle, and not coming back home" (*Time*, January 27, 1997, p. 24). These fears reflect a deeper sense of threat, of the "mean world out there." Are these perceptions and fears products of "media realities"? The present chapter attempts to reveal the impact of media contents on perceptions of reality as a dangerous, mean, and violent one.

The Attractiveness of Violence

Men have always been fascinated by violence and aggressive actions. Paintings on cave walls, created many thousands of years ago, include scenes of hunting and killing, as do pictographs in the tombs of ancient Egyptian pharaohs. Legends, myths, and tales were always rich with scenes of war, hatred, aggression, murder, and revenge. Even the Bible describes many forms of human aggression and violence. Aggression has always been one of the principal themes of literature and art. Preoccupation with aggression is not restricted to adult contents. Children's fairy tales and stories have their violent, frightening giants, hungry wolves, cruel stepmothers, evil witches, and scary criminals. The description of violence is frequent in every mode of communication, from oral to print, from small media to mass media. Although oral storytelling is the oldest form, visual means of communication developed quickly. Plays and dance forms combined oral and visual "pretend" aggression. Printing permitted the communication of fantasy aggression to mass audiences, and illustrated books presented violence both verbally and pictorially. Radio provided a new way of communicating aggressive themes. Radio was followed by the movies, which combined oral and visual in vivid presentations of violence to mass audiences. Genres like the Westerns, war movies, and horror and gangster films have been the most successful since the early days of cinema. Then came television. Like the movies, television has exploited most known forms of aggression and violence but in a greater quantity than was known before. Objections to the heavy load of such violence on television brought the issue to public awareness and debate. More modern media of communication (see Chapter 12), such as video games, computer networks, computer games, virtual reality, the Internet, and others, have become popular sites for experiencing, watching, and even activating aggression in various forms. Gerbner (1992) argued that we live now in a "charged environment," in a huge "cult of violence": Mass-mediated violence bears little relationship in volume or in type—and especially in consequence—to violence in real life. Yet, much of it looks realistic, and we tend to project it onto the real world.

Relating Media Violence to Real Violence

An unpublished UNESCO study in February 1998 found that the *Terminator*, the killer robot played by Arnold Schwarzenegger, was the most popular character among the world's children. The study, conducted by Professor Groebel of the Dutch University of Utrecht, sampled 5,000 children from various countries on all continents. For 88% of the children studied, the killer robot was the prime hero. The researcher concluded his report with the statement that the impact of media violence on children was largely explained by the fact that aggressive behavior on the screen was at worst rewarded, at best unpunished, in most cases.

The United States, the world's strongest nation, is also one of the world's most violent societies. As a nation, the United States ranks first among all developed countries in the world in homicides per capita. The pervasiveness of violence is staggering, particularly violence involving children and adolescents. For example, consider the following statistics cited by the American Psychiatric Association (1994):

- Every 5 minutes, a child is arrested for a violent crime.
- Gun-related violence takes the life of an American child every 3 hours.
- Every day, over 100,000 children carry guns to schools.
- In a recent survey of fifth graders in New Orleans, more than 50% reported they had been victims of violence, and 70% had seen weapons being used.
- Adolescents account for 24% of all violent crimes leading to arrest. The rate has increased over time for the age group 12 to 19 and has decreased for age groups 35 and older.
- Among individuals ages 15 to 24 years old, homicide is the second leading cause of death, and for African American youth, it is the leading cause.
- A child growing up in Chicago is 15 times more likely to be murdered than a child growing up in Northern Ireland.

What accounts for these alarming figures? There is universal agreement that many factors contribute to violent behavior: Institutions such as the American Psychological Association, American Medical Association, National Academy of Science, and Centers for Disease Control and Prevention have all recently examined the perplexing problem of the causes of violence. Although they recognize the complexity in determining the causes of violent behavior, all of these groups have concluded that the mass media bear some responsibility for contributing to real world violence. A number of theories have attempted to describe the relationships between violent media contents and subsequent behavior of those exposed to them. Two types of theories and models emerged: the behavioral effects theories and the cognitive effects theories. The behavioral effects of media violence are thought to act via a number of mechanisms, principal among them: the catharsis hypothesis, social learning theory, priming theory, the social developmental model, and arousal theory. The cognitive effects of mass-mediated violence relate to individuals' beliefs and opinions about the world around them, their fears, attitudes, and perceptions. The most dominant models in the cognitive domain are the disinhibition theory, the desensitization theory, and the social construction of reality theory.

From the perspective highlighted by the present book, violence in the media may be regarded as construction of social reality. The media, and in particular television, communicate facts, norms, and values about our social world. For many people, television is the main source of information about critical aspects of their social environment. Learning about violence in the news and in fictional programming may lead to the belief that the world is generally a scary and dangerous place. In numerous areas, including violence, researchers have found that people store media information and use it to formulate their perceptions and beliefs about the world. No wonder many communications scholars consider this influence on people's conceptions of social reality to be one of the most important mass media effects (Tan, 1986). The cultivation analysis is one of a number of theories concerned with the media's role in the social reconstruction of reality. Cultivation theory presumes that extensive, cumulative television exposure shapes viewers' perceptions of social reality. The assumption is that individuals develop beliefs about the "real world" from observing the world of television. According to the basic cultivation hypothesis, those who spend more time watching television are more likely to perceive the real world in ways that reflect the most common and repetitive messages and lessons of the television world. The cultivation approach is perhaps best known for its research on violence and fear, postulating that the lessons of television violence, and especially the patterns of victimization, are fear, intimidation, and a sense of vulnerability. Work in this area generally explores the hypothesis that those who watch more television will express greater interpersonal mistrust, perceive the world as a "mean" place, and endorse statements that reflect alienation, gloom, and fear (Signorielli, 1990). Gerbner and colleagues have presented elaborate evidence that heavy viewers of television believe the world they live in is more violent and unsafe than do light viewers. For example, heavy viewers evidence greater fear of walking alone at night, make greater estimations of the prevalence of violence, and express greater overall fear of crime. For cultivation theory, television viewing is a life-long process. Whether television shapes or merely maintains beliefs about the world is not as important as its role in a dynamic process that leads to enduring and stable assumptions about the world, particularly violence.

How Mean Is the Media World?

Numerous content analyses have been conducted since the early 1950s. The earliest studies coded programs "off-the air" and found a considerable amount of violence in samples of New York City television programming (Head, 1954). In the 1950s, violence appeared in two thirds to three quarters of all television plays at a rate of between 6 and 10 incidents per hour in prime time and at rates three or four times as large in children's programming (mostly cartoons). Clark and Blankenberg (1972) found violence in one third of a sample of movies released between 1930 and 1969, and in half of all movies shown on television. They also found that violence was prevalent in network television news, making up 16% of all news items. These stories were longer than nonviolent stories and unrelated to crime statistics. Dominick (1990) found that two thirds of all prime-time television programs contained some violence and that 60% of the violence could be categorized as assault, armed robbery, or murder. Unlike the situation in real life, violence by strangers was more frequent than violence by those who were known to the victim. An analysis of television series with law enforcement or other violent themes broadcast between 1950 and 1976 found that violence was systematically presented within a framework that suggests people have an unquestioned moral and/or legal right to use violence, including deadly force, to protect the status quo (Taylor & Dozier, 1983).

The first extensive series of content analyses of television violence was the work of the Cultural Indicators Project, which began in 1967-1968 with a study for the National Commission on the Causes and Prevention of Violence. This series has continued for almost 25 years under the sponsorship of the Surgeon General's Scientific Advisory Committee on Television and Social Behavior, the National Institute of

Mental Health, the White House Office of Telecommunications Policy, the American Medical Association, and other agencies. The research consisted of two steps: (a) content analysis of a week-long sample of prime-time and weekend-daytime programs on American television networks and (b) cultivation analysis, determining conceptions of social reality that television viewing cultivates among various viewers. The Cultural Indicators Project has published annual reports on violence in television programming, usually called Violence Profiles; the most recent of these reports was released in January 1990. These studies did not attempt to reflect what any particular individual viewer might see on any one evening of viewing but what large numbers of viewers absorb over long periods of time, thus to provide systematic, cumulative, and objective observations of television's world and violence in particular. Violence was defined in a simple easy-to-measure way: any overt episodes of physical violence; hurting or killing or the threat of hurting and/or killing in any context. Idle threats, verbal abuse, or gestures without credible violent consequences were not coded as violence. Violence was included in both realistic/serious and fantasy/humorous contexts.

These studies have consistently found that the world of prime time and children's weekend-daytime network dramatic programming is a world of action, power, and danger (see, e.g., Gerbner, 1969, 1972; Gerbner & Gross, 1976; Gerbner, Gross, Morgan, & Signorielli, 1986; Gerbner et al., 1977, 1978, 1979, 1980a, 1986; Signorielli, 1990). Crime is at least 10 times as frequent as in the real world; an average of 5 acts of violence per hour in prime time and 22 acts of violence per hour in children's weekend-daytime programs victimize half of the major characters in prime time and 8 out of 10 of the major characters in children's programs. The analyses reveal a remarkable stability in violent (as in most other) representations. During more than 20 years, 9 out of 10 children's weekend-daytime programs have contained violence at the overall rate of 6 violent actions per program (often a 10-minute cartoon) and 22 violent actions per hour of programming. Individual programs and characters change, but the overall structure of dramatic representations endures over time. These studies have consistently revealed that symbolic violence serves to resolve conflict and illustrate power by demonstrating who can get away with what against whom: It tells us who wins and who loses; who is likely to be on the top and who on the bottom. Hardly anyone dies a natural death on television.

In prime-time network programs, for every 10 male characters who commit violence, there are 11 who fall victim to it. But for every 10 female perpetrators of violence, there are 16 victims. Minority and foreign women pay the highest price: For every 10 perpetrators, they suffer 22 and 21 victims, respectively. Among the 10 groups most likely to be victimized, only one, elderly men, is not female; the only group, however, that is more likely to commit violence than be victimized is formerly married women—for every 10 of these women who are victimized, 11 commit violence. "Bad" men and "bad" women are equally likely to commit violence as be victimized. On the whole, groups of male characters are about equally likely to be victimized as to commit violence. The heavy presence of violence was very clear and very stable. Even more alarming were the findings on children's television, as shown in Table 5.1 for the weekend-daytime programs, which are mainly children's programs.

Prime-time television is certainly packed with violent contents but even more so are children's programs: 93.7% of children's programs (weekend-daytime) have violence in them (compared with 79.9% of all programs and 71.0% for prime-time television), and children might see 17.7 violent acts per hour whereas the equivalent rate for prime time is "only" 5.1 acts per hour. Almost all characters on children's television (80.3%) were involved in violence, a higher rate than among adult programs (55.7%). These figures have continued to rise during the 1980s and the 1990s. The proliferation of toy-based programs increased the amount of violence even more. Many of the new toys have war, fighting, and violence as their central theme, thus turning the programs into "program-length commercials" with violent contents targeting children. Between 1984 and 1987, following the U.S. deregulation of television in 1984, the networks increased war and fighting cartoons from 1.5 hours per week to 48 hours per week. Between 1985 and 1989, children's programming reached the rate of 25 violent acts per hour (far above the 8 to 9 acts per hour in prime-time television), committed by 7 out of 10 characters in 9 out of 10 children's programs (Gerbner & Signorielli, 1990).

The most recent monitoring of television violence is the National Television Violence study, published in 1997. This study was a 3-year

TABLE 5.1 Violence on Television: Trends in Violence Profiles

Measure	All Programs	Prime-Time	Weekend-Daytime
Percentage of programs with violence	79.9	71.0	93.7
Violent acts per program	5.2	4.8	5.9
Violent acts per hour	7.5	5.1	17.7
Percetage of characters involved in violence	64.0	55.7	80.3

NOTE: Table is based on measures presented in various tables in Gerbner, Gross, Signorielli, & Morgan (1979).

effort to assess violence on American television. The project, which began in June 1994, included the participation of media scholars at four university sites and an oversight council of representatives from national policy organizations. It was funded by the National Cable Television Association. This project had two primary goals: (a) to identify the contextual features associated with violent depictions that most significantly increase the risk of a harmful effect on the audience and (b) to analyze the television environment in depth to report on the nature and extent of violent depictions, focusing in particular on the relative presence of the most problematic portrayals. The sample consisted of programs on 23 of the most frequently viewed broadcast and cable television channels, over a 20-week period. The study monitored programs between the hours of 6 a.m. and 11 p.m., a total of 17 hours a day across 7 days of the week. In total, the project examined about 2,500 hours of television, which included 2,693 programs, representing one of the largest and most representative samples of television ever studied using scientific content-analysis procedures. The working definition of violence had three main components: (a) behavior acts, (b) credible threats, and (c) harmful consequences of unseen violence.

The analysis revealed that 57% of the sampled programs were classified as violent (having at least one act of violence). A total of more than 18,000 violent interactions were observed in the sampled programs. Two thirds of the violent incidents (66%) on television involve behavioral acts of aggression. In other words, a majority of violent interactions involve a perpetrator committing an actual physical act of violence. In the majority of violent scenes (58%), aggression is neither rewarded nor punished when it occurs. A much smaller proportion of scenes show violence being explicitly punished (19%) or rewarded (15%), and even fewer depict violence as both rewarded and punished (8%). Taken together, the findings indicate that almost three quarters of the violent scenes on television (73%) portray no punishment for violence within the immediate context in which it occurs. This robust pattern holds across all genres, including children's series. The pattern also holds across different channels and times of day. The findings also reveal another distorted element in the presentation of violence: its unharmful nature. Across all violent interactions, 44% depict *no* physical injury to the target. In an additional 3% of the violent interactions, the target is not even shown on screen (camera moves away or the scene changes abruptly). Thus, almost half of violent incidents (47%) on television contain no observable indications of harm to the victim. Let us briefly review some of this study's main findings (see also Table 5.2):

- 57% of coded programs contain some violence. Cable television is more likely to contain violence.
- About one third of violent programs contain nine or more violent interactions.
- Movies and drama series are more likely to contain violence.
- About two thirds of the violence involves behavioral acts of aggression.
- Very few involve harmful consequences of unseen violence.
- Perpetrators of violence are overwhelmingly adult White men.
- Most violence is committed for one of three reasons: personal gain, anger, or protection.
- Nearly half of the violence on television is portrayed as justified.
- The majority of violent interactions involve repeated behavioral acts of aggression (16% of violent interactions include 10 or more acts of aggression against a victim).
- A small portion of TV violence is based on actual events in the real world, but most events seem fairly realistic in that they could happen in real life.
- The vast majority of violence is not punished at the time that it occurs.
- Good characters who engage in violence are rarely punished at all.
- Characters who engage in violence almost never show remorse.
- Roughly half of the violent interactions on TV contain no observable harm or pain to the victim.

TABLE 5.2 Violence on Television: The 1997 Findings

Percentage of Programs With Violence	57
Violent programs	
Percentage with nine or more violent interactions	33
Percentage with advisory or content code	15
Percentage with an antiviolence theme	4
Percentage that show long-term negative consequences	16
Percentage with violence in realistic settings	51
Violent scenes	
Percentage with unpunished violence	73
Percentage with blood and gore	15
Percentage with humor	39
Violent interactions	
Percentage that show no pain	58
Percentage that depict harm unrealistically	35
Percentage with use of a gun	25
Percentage with repeated behavioral violence	57
Percentage that appear justified	44
Characters involved in violence	
Percentage of perpetrators who are attractive	37
Percentage of targets who are attractive	43

NOTE: Table based on various findings presented in *The National Television Violence Study*, 1997, Thousand Oaks, CA: Sage.

- Children's series contain the highest percentage of unrealistic depictions of harm.
- Very few programs depict the long-term negative repercussions of violence.

The made-in-America media violence is exported around the world. In fact, some of the best-selling American products are violent movies, TV series, and programs. Consequently, television contents all over the world are extremely violent. A study in Canada analyzed all the fiction programs on major Canadian networks (Gosselin, DeGuise, & Paquette, 1997). These were public networks (Société Radio-Canada and the Canadian Broadcasting Corporation), private (TVA, Television Quatre Saisons, CTV, and Global Television), and educational networks (Radio-Quebec in Quebec and TVO in Ontario). Only prime-time programs were analyzed. The violence index was measured using a series of variables.[1] These indexes indicated 23.4% less violence on Canadian television than on American television. In both countries, children's programs were more violent than adult programs: They contained four times more violent scenes per hour, and 76.9% of these programs contained violence, compared to only 58.9% for adult programs. About the same differences were observed in the United States. Among the networks, CTV (161.9) and TQS (159.1) had the highest violence ratings. As was expected, educational television (RQ and TVO) showed the least amount of violence (25.1 and 40.0). It is interesting to note that SRC scored higher than TVA mainly because of children's programming, which mostly consisted of violent cartoons. Private networks had more violent programming than public television, yet this score remained lower than that of the American networks. The English- and French-language networks showed almost the same amount of violence. Analysis of programs broadcast by noneducational networks according to production location revealed that programs originating in the United States were the most violent.

Programs broadcast in Canada were significantly less violent than those broadcast in the United States. This difference would have been significantly higher if Canadians did not import so many programs from their American neighbor. American programming not only contained more violence, but the study revealed that 65 of the 96 violent programs broadcast in Canada (67.7%), as well as 579 of the 733 violent scenes (79%), were produced in the United States. Although Canadians were not forced to choose these programs, the fact remains that the violent nature of their programming is influenced by American culture. In analyzing format, it was found that apart from the cartoons, films showed the most violence, followed by weekly series, and, far behind, by soap operas. In fact, the same order was obtained when rating programs according to cost, suggesting that the higher the production costs, the more violent a program was likely to be. This, perhaps, explains the violent nature of American productions, which benefit from more generous budgets than Canadian productions.

Finally, movies, for the cinema as well as on television, are important carriers of violence. Escalation of the cinematic body count appears to be one indication of the growing rates of victimization. *Robocop's* first rampage for law and order in 1987 killed 32 people. The 1990 *Robocop 2*, targeting a 12-year-old "drug lord," among others, slaughtered 81. The movie *Death Wish* claimed "only" 9 victims in 1974. In the 1988 version, the "hero" disposed of 52 men. *Rambo: First Blood,* released in 1985, rambled through Southeast Asia leaving 62 corpses. In 1988, *Rambo III* visited Afghanistan, killing 106. *Godfather I* produced 12 corpses, *Godfather II* produced 18 victims, and *Godfather III* killed no less than 53. The courageous yet deadly cop in the original *Die Hard* movie in 1988 left 18 dead. Two years later, *Die Hard 2* achieved a phenomenal body count of 264! *Terminator 2* dominated the list of box-office blockbusters from 14 major movie markets around the world. The National Coalition on Television Violence named Schwarzenegger, the movie's leading actor and promoter, "the most violent actor" of 1987 and found that 10 of Schwarzenegger's 12 movies averaged 109 violent acts per hour. Higher rates of deadly heroes appear in children's movies. For example, the *Teenage Mutant Ninja Turtles* (released in 1991) had 133 acts of aggressive behavior per hour, but the follow-up version, *Turtles II,* was even more aggressive and violent.

The movies' obsession with violence is illustrated by their titles: The October 14, 1991, international edition of *Variety* featured 123 pages of ads for new movies, with pictures of shooting, killing, or corpses on every other page and verbal appeal to violence, on the average, on every page. The most frequently used words were *kill, murder, death,* and *dead* (33 times), followed by *terror, fatal, lethal,* and *dangerous* (12 times). Then came *rage, frenzy, revenge, gun-crazy, kickboxer, maniac, warrior, invader, hawk, battle, war, shoot, fight, slaughter,* and *blood.*

Violence is thus an important element in various media contents, affecting both story lines and characterizations. This led Gerbner (1992), among others, to suggest that mass-mediated violence, or "retail violence," is cultivating a "mass cult of violence": It is more like a charged environment affecting many aspects of social relations, control, and power. The facts of violence are both celebrated and concealed in the cult of violence that surrounds us.

How Real Is the "Mean World" of the Media?

One of the most significant claims of the cultivation paradigm is that media presentation reconstructs reality, creating a "meaner" than real world. Let us examine one of the clear and simple comparisons of real violence with the world of television violence, as performed by Gerbner and his associates (1977) for one of the earlier Violence Profiles (see Table 5.3).

Whereas 64.4% of the characters on television are involved in violence, in reality, the proportion of violent crimes per capita is less than a third of 1%. Thus, the proportion of violent characters on television is 201 times larger than in reality. The number of people involved in law enforcement and detection of crime is 15 times larger on television than in reality, and although most crimes (90%) in reality are not violent, on television, the majority of crimes (77%) involve the use of violence. Finally, whereas most actual murders occur among people who know each other (family, relatives, and coworkers), in television reality, murder occurs mainly among strangers. In a later study, Gerbner (1977) found that the percentage of characters involved in violence on television had risen to 74.9% (from 64.4%) and that 9 out of every 10 programs sampled contained some violence. The saturation of programs with violence, indicated by the rate of violent episodes, rose to 6.2 episodes per program and 9.2 per hour.

How realistic is the portrayal of violence in the media? First, let us examine the notion of *realism*. What are the elements in the portrayals of aggression that make it real to viewers? Potter and his colleagues (1995) suggested that there are two useful ways to answer this question. First, there is the issue of *replicated reality,* which is assessed by comparing television portrayals with actual patterns in real life. By counting the number of acts of violence and comparing this sum to the real world figure, a determination can be made if the television world underportrays, overportrays, or accurately portrays the amount of real world violence. Thus, if television is to replicate reality, the proportions of violence on television should be an accurate reflection of violence in real life. Second, *contextual reality* focuses on how violence is portrayed rather than on how often. The contextual reality is an inference built from the variables of intention, motivation, reward, consequences, humor, and realism of the portrayal. Thus, replicated reality and contextual reality are two alternative ways of conceptualizing the match between television content and the real world.

Potter and his associates (1995) used these two concepts of realism to study the match between media reality and real reality. The database for their study contained 3,844 acts of aggression found in a composite

TABLE 5.3 Violence in "Real Reality" Versus "Television Reality"

	Real World	Television World
Percentage of violent crimes per person	0.32	64.4
Percentage of all males who work in law enforcement and crime detection	1	15
Percentage of crimes that are violent	10	77
Percentage of fatal violence among strangers	16	58

week of over 100 hours of entertainment programming. The results presented evidence for replicated reality in the patterns and seriousness of the aggression, as well as gender patterns of perpetrators and victims. However, portrayals of race and age were not found to be close to real world patterns of aggression. As for contextual reality, the researchers found that "when we use a morality play template as a guide, we must conclude that the portrayal of aggression is not realistic" (p. 514). This was clearly revealed by the contextual elements of reward and consequences: Fewer than one in six aggressive acts were shown with major consequences, and only one in six such acts were shown as being punished. From a social learning point of view, lack of punishment has the same effect as a reward—it signals to the viewer that the act is acceptable. Therefore, in the aggregate, television is signaling to viewers that almost all aggression is acceptable.

In a content analysis of the so-called "reality-based" police shows (e.g., *America's Most Wanted, Cops, Top Cops, FBI, The Untold Story*, and *American Detective*), Oliver (1994) attempted to explore portrayals of crime, race, and aggression. This content analysis of police programs yielded several important findings. First, these programs not only strongly overrepresent violent crime but also overrepresent the percentage of crimes that are solved by law enforcement personnel. Second, in terms of racial representation, these programs tend to underrepresent blacks and overrepresent whites as police officers in comparison to government statistics (U.S. Department of Labor, 1992). These programs are also much more likely to portray whites as police officers (or heroes) and nonwhites as criminal suspects (or villains). Finally, in terms of aggression, police officers are generally more likely than criminal suspects to be portrayed as using aggressive behaviors, and criminal suspects are generally more likely than police officers to be portrayed as suffering from aggressive behaviors. In addition, Black and Hispanic criminal suspects are significantly more likely than white criminal suspects to suffer from unarmed physical aggression from police officers.

Thus, the argument of media's cultivating function should not be based solely on the amount of violence in media contents but also on its forms of representation. Media violence differs in form, amount, and consequences from violence in real life. Media violence is a structured, fabricated, and very unrealistic form of violence. Yet, much of it looks realistic, so realistic that we tend to accept it as "real reality" and project it onto our perceptions of the real world. The regular portrayal of mayhem and crime in the media, and especially in movies, television, video, and computer games, misrepresents the actual forms and nature of victimization of real-life violence. So heavy is the "violence diet" on commercial television and movies that one cannot avoid the question of cumulative impact. If we are so exposed to so many violence-laden contents, what will be the impact of the cumulative, long-term exposure to these messages? After all, in 1992, the American Psychological Association concluded,

> By the time the average child graduates from elementary school, she or he will have witnessed at least 8,000 murders and more than 100,000 other assorted acts of violence. Depending on the amount of television viewed, our youngsters could see more than 200,000 violent acts before they hit the schools and streets as teenagers. (Huston et al., 1992, p. 54)

In 1994, a survey by the Center for Media and Public Affairs, which examined all programs on all channels (including cable) for one day only (April 7, 1994) in Washington, D.C., tallied 2,605 acts of violence that day only, the majority of them appearing in the early morning when children were most likely to be watching. Another study, published in 1992 in the *Journal of the American Medical Association,* found that the typical American child, spending 27 hours a week watching television, witnesses 40,000 murders and over 200,000 other violent acts by the age of 18. These studies and numerous other analyses of media depiction of violence are cited by Potter et al. (1995).

Effects of Media Violence on Aggressive Behavior

Over the years, the topic of the effects of television violence has received growing attention: There are over 4,000 studies documented in this area only. Most of the research conducted in this area grew out of society's concern about the level of violence in society and whether or not television might be a contributing factor. In the United States, television violence specifically has been identified as a potential health hazard: In 1976, and again in 1982, the American Medical Association took several actions, including issuing a policy statement that (a) said TV violence was a risk factor threatening the health and welfare of American children, (b) committed them to finding ways to make television better, and (c) encouraged people to oppose TV violence and boycott companies that sponsored violent programs. Similar campaigns were undertaken by the National Parent-Teacher Association, the American Psychological Association, and the National Coalition on Television Violence.

A considerable amount of research as well as debate on the effects of television violence has been conducted over recent decades (see, e.g., Andison, 1977; Dorr & Kovaric, 1980; Hearold, 1986; Heath, Bresolin, & Rinaldi, 1989). A number of laboratory experiments provided evidence of a causal relationship between viewing violence on television and aggression (e.g., Atkin, 1983; Bryant, Carveth, & Brown, 1981; Drabman & Thomas, 1974, 1976). Nonexperimental field studies and, to some extent, field experiments also provide support for this conclusion (see, e.g., Belson, 1967; Huesmann, Lagerspetz, & Eron, 1984; Joy, Kimball, & Zabrack, 1986; Singer & Singer, 1981; Steuer, Applefield, & Smith, 1971). Thus, for example, Centerwall (1989a, 1989b) examined exposure to television as a risk factor for violence, using the tools of epidemiology. He found that homicide rates doubled in Canada and the United States after the introduction of television; in South Africa, where television was not available, white homicide rates remained the same. Specifically, in the United States, white homicide deaths went from 3.0 homicides per 100,000 in 1945 to 5.8 homicides per 100,000 in 1974, an increase of 93%. Similarly, in Canada, homicides went from 1.3 homicides per 100,000 in 1945 to 2.5 homicides per 100,000 in 1974, an increase of 92%. In South Africa, where television was banned until 1974, white homicide deaths went from 2.7

homicides per 100,000 in 1943-1948 to 2.5 homicides per 100,000 in 1974, a decrease of 7%. In 1983, after television had been available for almost 10 years in South Africa, the white homicide rate had reached 3.9 homicide deaths per 100,000, an increase of 56% over the rates in 1974 (the last year without television).

Many studies in this area focused on children and adolescents, both because of children's heavy exposure to media violence and their naive, gullible, and submissive acceptance of media contents. Among the earliest studies of television and aggression were those conducted by Stanford psychologist Albert Bandura. Bandura, Ross, and Ross (1963a, 1963b) exposed children in a controlled laboratory setting to aggressive content on television and observed their increasing aggression toward "Bobo dolls" placed in their vicinity. The tendency to imitate the aggression was enforced when it was portrayed as being rewarded and not punished. Similar results were found by other studies conducted within a laboratory (e.g., Lovaas, 1961; Mussen & Rutherford, 1961). In field experiments, it was observed that children exposed to aggressive cartoons were subsequently more aggressive to their playmates than those who had watched nonaggressive cartoons (e.g., Ellis & Sekyra, 1972). Although these experiments were often criticized for their artificial setting, which bears little resemblance to natural social conditions, correlational studies have identified a potential relationship between viewing violence and aggression in the home or at school.

Longitudinal studies have largely supported the hypothesis that violence viewing and aggression are causally related, and the relation persists over time (e.g., Huesmann, Eron, Berkowitz, & Chaffee, 1987; Huesmann et al., 1984; Singer & Singer, 1981, 1988). The most extended longitudinal study began with the work of Leonard Eron in 1963 and eventually led to a 22-year follow-up study (Eron, 1982, 1986; Eron & Huesmann, 1987). Eron studied third-graders in Columbia County in semirural New York. He found that the more violent television these 8-year-olds watched at home, the more aggressive they were in school. Eron returned to Columbia County in 1971, when the children from his sample were 19. He found that the boys who had watched a lot of violent television when they were 8 were more likely to get in trouble with the law when older. Eron returned to Columbia County a third time in 1982, when his subjects were 30. He discovered that those who had watched the most television violence at age 8 inflicted more violent punishments on their children, were convicted of more serious crimes, and were reported as more aggressive by their spouses than those who had watched less violent television. Eron concluded that viewing television violence leads to aggression that can persist over time and become a characteristic way of solving interpersonal and personal problems.

Although Eron's study did not make a special effort to control for other potentially violence-inducing variables, other longitudinal studies have done so. For example, in 1971, Lefkowitz and his colleagues published "Television Violence and Child Aggression: A Follow-Up Study," which confirmed that the more violence an 8-year-old boy watched, the more aggressive his behavior would be at age 18. Lefkowitz controlled for other possible variables, directly implicating media violence as an instigator of violent behavior.[2]

Since 1968, when President Lyndon Johnson convened the National Commission on the Causes and Prevention of Violence, commissions, hearings, and a Surgeon General's report have all found that television is a "major contributory factor" in violent behavior in society. One of the recent bursts of activity around the issue of television violence, culminating in the V-chip legislation, can be traced to a night in the mid-1980s when U.S. Senator Paul Simon of Illinois, lying in his motel bed, flipped on the television and saw, in graphic detail, a man being sliced in half with a chain saw—a victim of Colombian drug dealers in the movie *Scarface*. Appalled that there was nothing to prevent a child from witnessing such horror, Simon urged the passage of a law reducing gore on television. The result, the 1990 Television Violence Act, was a compromise between the broadcasting industry and those who, like Simon, wanted somehow to reduce the violence on shows that children might be watching. Ordinarily, antitrust laws prohibit broadcast networks from collaborating, but Simon's proposal gave the networks a 3-year exemption from the laws so that they could jointly work out a policy to curb violence. Although Simon hailed the networks' (except Fox) announcement in December 1992 of a set of guidelines governing television violence, this basically toothless bit of legislation had little effect until it was about to expire, at which point network executives promised that they would place parental advisories at the beginning of violent programs ("Due to violent content, parental discretion is advised"). When the act expired, in December 1993, television was as violent as ever.

Meanwhile, in Canada, the invention of a Vancouver engineer had come to the attention of Keith Spicer, then the chairman of the Canadian Radio-Television and Telecommunications Commission (Canada's FCC equivalent). This invention was the V-chip. Using this device, which receives encoded information about each show as part of the broadcast transmission, parents can program their television to block out shows that have been coded as violent or sexually explicit. The Canadian government adapted a law mandating the use of the V-chip in all new television sets sold in Canada. In the United States, after the Television Violence Act expired, Representative Edward J. Markey of Massachusetts introduced legislation requiring manufacturers to install the V-chip in all U.S. television sets. President Bill Clinton extolled the V-chip in his State of the Union Address and then signed its use into law as part of the 1996 Telecommunications Act. According to Clinton's plan, all new television sets (Americans buy 24 million of them a year) must have the chip. Meanwhile, the broadcasting industry has established a rating system to be employed in conjunction with the chip.

Thus, the convergence of cumulative research, both experimental and nonexperimental, makes a strong and "solid case" for the correlation of viewing violence and aggressive behavior. As Signorielli (1993b) concluded,

> Most of the scientific evidence thus reveals a relationship between television and aggressive behavior. Although few would say that there is absolute proof that watching television causes aggressive behavior, the overall cumulative weight of all the studies gives credence to the position that they are related. (p. 11)

And yet, television violence is only one of the social forces that may lead to aggressive, antisocial, or criminal behavior; and it usually works in conjunction with other factors. As noted by Dorr and Kovaric (1980), television violence may influence "some of the people some of the time" (p. 183). In fact, there are several known variables or factors that may increase or decrease the behavioral effect of viewing violence in the media. As we will note, many of these mediating variables are attributes of the cognitive setting of the viewers.

Although most children and adolescents watch many hours of television violence, most of them will not become violent or aggressive. In fact, most of them will be able to "digest" a huge amount of violent contents and programs without any behavioral change. There are only a few who will be vulnerable and thus affected. This indicates the existence and functioning of several important mediating variables that heighten or attenuate the effect. First, several characteristics of the content play a crucial role. People are more likely to imitate or be disinhibited by the aggressive behavior of an attractive, respected, prestigious hero or model than one who does not have such qualities. Thus, violence committed by the "good guys," that is, the characters we admire and like to identify with, may have a stronger influence than violence of the "bad guys." This, of course, has important ramifications for assessing effects of action-adventure and police shows. It also matters whether or not the violence is reinforced or rewarded. If acting violently appears to pay off for the violent character (in money, power, relationship, etc.), it is thus reinforced in the context of the story. Some evidence suggests that reinforced violence is more likely to be modeled than nonreinforced or punished violence (as revealed in Bandura's experiments with the Bobo doll). In most television programs and movies, the rewarded violence is that of the good guys. This is a second reason that good-guy violence may have more powerful effects than bad-guy violence.

Another important mediating factor is whether the violence is presented as real or fictional: that is, the degree of perceived reality. There is some evidence of stronger effects of violence that is perceived as real than that which is perceived as unreal (Van der Voort, 1986). For example, the most violent genre of TV shows is the children's cartoon, yet, it is the most stylized and unrealistic violence of all. Some studies (like those of Feshbach; see Feshbach, 1976; Feshbach & Singer, 1971) have shown cartoon violence to have less negative effects than more realistic violence. These mediating variables are all related to the viewer's cognitive understanding of television. A very young child might think that a violent death in a movie or in a television program actually shows someone dying, rather than an actor pretending to die. Children who believe such staged violence to be real are often more disturbed by it than those who understand the convention of acting and fiction. Hence, the most difficult forms of TV violence for children to deal with are news and documentaries, because violence there is real rather than staged.

Another set of mediating factors highlights the individual's tendencies. Many studies found a strong effect only in people who are somewhat prone to violence to begin with (Heller & Polsky, 1975; Parke, Berkowitz, Leyens, West, & Sebastian, 1977). Another personal trait factor is the level of arousal. A person who is already aroused for whatever reason is more likely to engage in violence in response to seeing a violent media model than an unaroused person. The arousal may come from the movie itself, as violent movies and television series tend to be emotionally arousing and exciting, or it may come from some prior and unrelated source. This was tested in experiments where some subjects were made angry before exposing them to a violent media model (Berkowitz, 1965; Hartmann, 1969; Tannenbaum, 1971, 1980; Zillmann, 1979). Although these personal traits have not been found consistently, studies suggesting such conclusions have often been used to argue that the lack of a general effect indicates no substantial effects of media violence.

Cognitive Effects: Cultivation of the Mean World Syndrome

Although most studies of television and aggression have focused on behaviors, the cultivation approach focused its attention on the cognitive and more subtle impact of violent contents. George Gerbner and his colleagues (1980, 1982a, 1982b, 1986) have argued that the more exposure people have to television, the more their perception of social realities will match what is presented on TV. Although these researchers are best known for their research on TV violence, the notion of cultivation is much broader. Gerbner and his partners argued that cultivation is part of a continual, dynamic process of interaction among messages and contexts. They distinguish cultivation from direct effects and reinforcement by attributing a more active role to the viewer, who is interacting with the medium, not being passively manipulated by it.

Cultivation theory is best known, however, for its research on cultivation of attitudes related to violence.

According to the cultivation hypothesis, growing up in a violence-laden cultural environment cultivates fear, insecurity, mistrust, and anxiety in most people. The cultivation approach attempted to show that heavy viewers believe the world to be a more dangerous and crime-ridden place than do light viewers. This, of course, could be due either to TV teaching that this is what the world is like or to the fact that more fearful people are drawn to watching more TV. If it is the former, as argued by Gerbner and his followers, mass media can induce a general mind-set about the position of violence in the world, completely aside from any effects it might have in teaching violent behavior. Finally, cultivation theory speaks of TV teaching the role of victim. From watching lots of crime and adventure shows, viewers learn what it is like to be the victim of violence, and this role becomes very real to them, even if it is completely outside their own experience.

As we saw in Chapter 3, Gerbner began his Cultural Indicators research project in the mid-1960s in an attempt to describe the "world" of television, and particularly the amount of violence on television. The two stages of the Cultural Indicators Project were message system analysis and cultivation analysis. As we saw, the message analysis involved a content analysis done by coders, who made detailed observations about the characters and the action on television drama. The second aspect, cultivation analysis, is to determine what influence these messages have on viewers. The first step, the content analysis, revealed the heavy load of violent actions and actors television carries. It also revealed that many aspects of "real" reality are distorted and misrepresented on television programs. But do the viewers accept this media reality as a real one? Table 5.4 presents selected findings regarding the Mean World Syndrome as revealed in various studies. This was done within and across groups, but at this stage let us look at the overall trend.

The findings of many cultivation analysis studies provided evidence for a small but significant influence of television's content on attitudes and beliefs about the real world. In every measure used to study perceptions of reality (selected measures are presented in Table 5.4), the heavy viewers more frequently gave the pessimistic, mean world answer. When these comparisons were computed controlling for age, education, gender, income, experience as victim, social class, and other variables,

TABLE 5.4 Summary of Cultivation Analyses

	Percentage overestimating:				*Percentage saying that:*			
	their chances of involvement in violence		number of people employed in law enforcement		their neighborhoods are only somewhat safe or not safe at all		"you can't be too careful" (when asked about trusting others)	
Viewership:	Light	Heavy	Light	Heavy	Light	Heavy	Light	Heavy
Percentage:	39	52	59	59	55	66	48	65

	Percentage saying that:					
	crime is rising		fear of crime is a very serious problem		women are more likely to be victims of crime	
Viewership:	Light	Heavy	Light	Heavy	Light	Heavy
Percentage:	94	98	20	29	72	82

NOTE: The coefficients in this table were gathered from various tables included in the Violence Profiles (No. 8, 9, and 11) of Gerbner and his colleagues.

the pattern did not change. Heavy viewers believed that the real world incidence of violence is higher than light viewers from the same group, subpopulation, or class. Apparently, the "facts" of the television reality tend to slip into the perceptions of individuals who are heavy consumers of it. Gerbner referred to this effect as *mainstreaming* and described it in terms of a "homogeneity" (or sameness) of outlook. One convincing example of a homogeneous outlook is the misperception of the prevalence of true violence in the society:

> The results of our . . . surveys showed . . . that violence-laden television not only cultivates aggressive tendencies in a minority but, perhaps more importantly, also generates a pervasive and exaggerated sense of danger and mistrust. Heavy viewers revealed a significantly higher sense of personal risk and suspicion than did light viewers in the same demographic groups who were exposed to the same real risks of life. (Gerbner & Gross, 1980, p. 158)

For example, Gerbner and his colleagues asked American subjects such questions as: During any week, what are your chances of being involved in some kind of violence? What percentage of all men who have jobs work in law enforcement and crime detection? What percentage of all crimes are violent crimes? Does most fatal violence occur between strangers or between relatives and acquaintances? Note that all these questions relate to the measures used to compare television reality with real reality, thus enabling testing the hypothesis that heavy viewers will adopt the television reality. Indeed, when correlated with television viewing, the zero-order correlation (with no control variables removed statistically) between amount of viewing and the choice of television reality's answers was positive and significant. When the influence of several variables (sex, grade, newspaper reading, father's education, socioeconomic status, and IQ) was controlled, the correlation was reduced but was still significant.

Support for these claims about reconstruction of reality, cultivation, and mainstreaming was found in numerous studies conducted all over the world. Pingree and Hawkins (1981) applied the cultivation idea in Australia, studying the social attitudes and television viewing of school children in Perth (the largest city in western Australia). Questionnaires were given to a sample of 1,280 elementary school children (2nd through 11th grade) assessing their opinions and knowledge about life in Australia. At a later stage, these same children filled out a 4-day television viewing diary. The questions were designed to get at television bias on the part of the children (heavy viewers giving more of the television answer) and at beliefs about the prevalence of violence in Australia. The two sets of beliefs were then correlated to determine how much television viewing contributes to attitudes and values.

In general, Pingree and Hawkins (1981) found evidence for a cultivation effect: They reported a significant correlation between the total amount of television viewed and a television bias, leading heavy viewers to see Australia as a mean and violent place. Moreover, when these correlations were broken down by type of content watched, these authors found that the most consistent and strongest correlate of television-biased answers to questions about social reality was one specific type of U.S. program: crime adventure. The children who most thought that Australia was a mean and dangerous place were those who most watched U.S. crime adventure programs shown on Australian television. Thus, their findings have led Hawkins and Pingree (1981b) to question two of the central assumptions made by Gerbner and his colleagues: First, they suggest that breakdowns by content type are more useful than the less meaningful measures of total viewing. And second, they suggest that viewing is not nonselective, as Gerbner and his group have long suggested. Instead, Hawkins and Pingree (1981a) find evidence that people do view by content type—that is, they view selectively—and if this is taken into consideration, as they did in their Australian study, stronger correlations would emerge from cultivation analysis research.

A more recent study that replicated the cultivation hypothesis and applied it to four samples (adults and adolescents) in Australia and the United States found supportive findings (Hawkins, Pingree, & Adler, 1987). The researchers correlated four beliefs about real-world violence with amount of television viewing. In the American adult sample, they found significant and even quite strong correlations between viewing and three out of the four beliefs about real-world violence (.39 with estimating chances of violence, .22 with estimating percentages of men in law enforcement, and .33 with estimating violence committed by relatives and by strangers). All these coefficients remained significant even when partialed to control for age and education. In the samples of schoolchildren in Australia and the United States, cultivation correlations were found for perceptions of violence, police procedures, and even sex roles, leading the researchers to conclude, "Heavy viewers of television often hold beliefs about the world that are more television-like or television-implied than the beliefs of light viewers" (Hawkins et al., 1987, p. 572).

In a recent study conducted in Canada, a survey was used to study 360 first-year students at Quebec City's Université Laval. Television viewing itself, as hypothesized, was found to have an effect on cognition: Each hour of television viewing adds .05 to the score on the cognition scale (seeing the world as dangerous). Viewing was not found to have any direct effect on fear. Cognition, on the other hand, had a positive influence on the level of fear: people who believe the world is dangerous appear to fear it the most. Thus, the researchers concluded,

> Our analyses show that television viewing affects the beliefs people have about the level of danger in society, even when controlled for the effects of age and gender and even in a population made of people who are prone to know the media and how they work much more than the general population. (Gosselin et al., 1997, p. 155)

An experimental test of the cultivation hypothesis provided additional support. In this experiment, undergraduates were assigned to watch 30 hours of programming in addition to the television that they normally watched. Half of the subjects were shown program material featuring a "clear restoration of justice," whereas the other half saw programs in which the "outcomes were not just." The strongest effect observed was for those students who were heavy viewers of materials in which injustice was habitually depicted: These students showed significant increases in anxiety under these viewing conditions, with the greatest increment in anxiety occurring among those students who were already highly anxious. The authors view this experiment as support for the cultivation hypothesis: "These findings indicate that heavy exposure to the world of televised action drama does cultivate conceptions of an overly dangerous social reality for some viewers, especially when the adventure drama does not feature the triumph of retributive justice" (Bryant et al., 1981, p. 118).

The notion of cultivating a Mean World Syndrome was further expanded by studies that looked at the cultivation of "sad, gloomy world" perceptions. Signorielli's (1990) study on "Television's Mean and Dangerous World" looked at the relationship between television viewing and views reflecting a mean world in the sense of interpersonal mistrust, alienation, and gloom. She used the data from the 1980, 1982, 1983, 1985, and 1986 NORC General Social Surveys, which examined the relationships between television viewing and two indices: the Mean World Index and the Index of Alienation and Gloom (Anomie Index). Both scales are additive in nature, summing respondents' agreement with statements reflecting interpersonal mistrust (a mean world) and statements reflecting alienation and gloom (anomie).[3]

The first analysis looked at the relationship between television viewing and these indices by calculating partial correlation coefficients, controlling for sex, age, education, race, income, subjective social class, and political orientation. Television viewing was found to be significantly associated with the tendency to agree with the items in the Mean World Index ($r = .14$, $p < .001$). Although simultaneous controls for sex, age, income, race, subjective social class, and political views reduced its strength, the relationship remained statistically significant (seventh order partial correlation was .06, $p < .001$).

Although a small overall correlation was found between television viewing and mean-world views, stronger correlations were reported in several subpopulations. As found in previous analyses, the relationship was strongest for respondents who have had higher education: They are least likely to express interpersonal mistrust (the correlation between education and the Mean World Index is −.25, $p < .001$). This study also revealed the mainstreaming implications of viewing. For example, combining data from the 1980, 1983, and 1986 General Social Surveys, heavy and light viewers who have not been to college are equally likely to agree with the items in the Mean World Index: 53% of both the heavy and light viewers agree with two or three of these items. Among those who have had some exposure to college, however, television viewing makes a considerable difference: 28% of the light viewers compared to 43% of the heavy viewers in this subgroup have a high score on this index. There is thus a 25 percentage-point difference between these two subgroups of light viewers but only a 10-point spread between these two subgroups of heavy viewers.

Similar patterns, although weaker, were found for the Alienation and Gloom Index. The overall correlation (.111) was rather weak but significant and withstood simultaneous controls for sex, age, education, income, race, social class, and political orientation. In every subgroup, according to these above variables, heavy viewers endorsed more statements of gloom and alienation than did light viewers in this subgroup. Again, there were a number of examples of mainstreaming. For example, light-viewing men were somewhat less likely to express feelings of gloom than light-viewing women, whereas about the same percentage of men and women who were heavy viewers had a high score on this index. Similarly, among the subjective social class subgroups, heavy viewers were more homogeneous in their likelihood to have high scores on this index, and the percentages of light viewers in these subgroups who endorsed these statements were more dissimilar. Among low-, medium-, and high-income groups, the light viewers were more dissimilar whereas the heavy viewers were more similar in their likelihood to endorse these statements. Signorielli (1990) also found that the patterns exhibited for the education and social class subgroups were quite similar to those found for the Mean World Index. In short, the heavy viewers in these demographic subgroups seemed to be more homogeneous and more likely to express gloom and alienation than their light-viewing counterparts.

These findings were summarized by Signorielli (1990): "Those who watch more television tend to express a heightened sense of living in a

mean world of danger and mistrust and alienation and gloom" (p. 102).
This conclusion supports the findings of Morgan (1984), who also
found that heavy viewers tend to feel more lonely, bored, and depressed.
Moreover, the cultivation of such anxieties is most pronounced in
groups whose light viewers (for example, those who have been to
college) are the least likely to be mistrustful and apprehensive. This, of
course, has serious social implications for society, quality of life, and
social order:

> This unequal sense of danger, vulnerability, and general malaise culti-
> vated by what is called "entertainment" invites not only aggression but
> also exploitation and repression. Fearful people are more dependent,
> more easily manipulated and controlled, more susceptible to decep-
> tively simple, strong, tough measures and hard-line postures—both
> political and religious. They may accept and even welcome repression
> if it promises to relieve their insecurities and other anxieties. That is
> the deeper problem of violence-laden television. (Signorielli, 1990,
> p. 102)

Cultivating Fear

Studies of cultivation have revealed that violence on television plays an
important role in communicating fear of victimization. Symbolic victimization on television and real-world fear (especially among certain
groups) are highly related. Studies have consistently revealed that in
most subgroups, those who watch more television tend to express a
heightened sense of living in a mean world of danger and mistrust, as
well as alienation and gloom (e.g., Morgan, 1983; Signorielli, 1990).
Fear of victimization (FOV) was the dependent variable in numerous
studies. Sparks and Ogles (1990) suggested a distinction between the
probability of being victimized (first measure) and the fear of being
victimized (second measure). They argued that the traditional measures,
depending on the respondents' estimates of probabilities (chances of
being victimized, chances of being involved in violence) differ from fear
of being attacked, murdered, or beaten up. Thus, they applied the two
types of measures and related them to amount of television viewing.
First, they found that the two victimization measures were not corre-

lated, thus supporting the contention that there is a conceptual distinction between measurement of fear of crime and measurement of probability of criminal victimization. Second, when related to television viewing, stronger correlations were found between fear of being victimized and viewing than between the probability measures and viewing. Thus, the coefficient of viewing and fear of being murdered was .28, it was .21 with the fear of being threatened by a knife, it was .18 with the fear of being beaten up by a stranger, and it was .24 with the combined index of fear (all coefficients were statistically significant, and all were fourth-order partial correlations, controlling for sex, age, previous victimization, and city of residence). These relationships were stronger than those found in this study and in previous ones when the traditional measures of victimization probabilities were used.

A recent review of mass media and fear of crime research by Heath and Gilbert (1996) concluded that the relationship is contingent on "characteristics of the message, of the audience, and of the dependent measure" (p. 384). Relevant message characteristics include the proportion of a newspaper devoted to crime, whether the crime is local versus distant, whether the crime is random or is the subject of sensational crime reports, and whether there is "just" closure of a crime on television drama. Concerning dependent measures, Heath and Gilbert reported stronger links between media and fear when the issue is a societal concern as opposed to a personal fear or apprehension about "the world out there" versus the immediate neighborhood, and for urban as opposed to rural settings.

Audience characteristics were the focus of several studies. Heath and Gilbert (1996) concluded that "belief in the reality of television drama and viewer apprehension about crime victimization affect the relationship with fear of crime" (p. 384). One potentially salient factor in the reception of media crime messages is whether audience members have direct victim experience or share characteristics making them more likely crime victims. Weaver and Wakshlag's (1986) study of crime-related television watching and crime-related anxiety demonstrated precisely this point. Similarly, Liska and Baccaglini (1990) hypothesized that newspaper crime stories will have their strongest fear effects for those least likely to be victimized, such as whites, the elderly, and females. Their content analysis of newspapers and use of fear measures (perceived safety) for 26 cities showed fear was related only to local homicide stories in the first part of the paper. Although this finding held for diverse demographic groups, the media influence was weakest for those statuses (nonwhites, young, men) most likely to experience victimization.

Another possibility raised by Gerbner and his associates could be described as *audience affinity*. This approach posits that we may be especially receptive to seeing how characters like ourselves fare in the world of television. Because Gerbner's analyses of programs in the 1970s showed women, older women, and blacks (men and women) to be most victimized in television drama, one may hypothesize that heavy television viewing should cultivate the greatest fear among these groups. Skogan and Maxfield (1981) suggested that vulnerability to attack, as opposed to victim risk per se, could make some audiences "more sensitive to messages." Thus, they hypothesized that women and the elderly would be more responsive to personal or media messages about crime. Their 1977 telephone survey ($N = 1,389$) of San Francisco, Chicago, and Philadelphia residents failed to find any support for this notion because the relationship between fear and ability to recall a recent crime story (television or newspaper) was constant among more vulnerable and less vulnerable groups. Heath and Petraitis (1987) conducted telephone interviews with 372 respondents in 26 medium-size U.S. cities. They found that total TV viewing increased respondents' fear of distant, urban settings but only among men. Viewing crime drama increased the perceived likelihood of victimization in New York City and in one's own neighborhood, but again, only for men. They suggested that the absence of a media relationship for women could be due to their consistently high fear levels and a kind of "ceiling effect" that mitigates additional influences.

This evidence may identify five audience circumstances that can influence the media-FOV relationship. These are (including examples of the kinds of people who are expected to experience those circumstances):

Substitution: Lacks victim experience or has reduced victim likelihood (women, elderly, whites, nonvictims)

Resonance: Has victim experience or higher victim likelihood (urban, high-crime neighborhood residents, males, young, blacks)

Vulnerability: Less able to defend against attack (women, elderly)

Affinity: Shares characteristics of more likely media victims (women, older women, black women, victims)

Ceiling effect: Has such high fear that media can have little influence (women, blacks)

A recent study attempted to examine and compare the above suggested models (Chirocos, Eschholz, & Gertz, 1997). A survey of 2,092 adults in Tallahassee, Florida, was used, with scales measuring fear of crime and news exposure (six different measures). The analysis revealed that all television news effects were limited to women. There were no audience traits associated with men, black or white, for which television news had a significant relationship to fear of victimization. Moreover, almost all effects were limited to white women.

The data clearly indicated that the relationship between television news and fear of crime is exclusive to women and almost entirely exclusive to white women. At first glance, the pattern of these findings appears to rule out the relevance of ceiling effects. Women in the sample had levels of fear of victimization that were 25% higher than men and still, all the revealed effects involved women. The issue of vulnerability, the presumption that women and the elderly are more defenseless against attack, is sometimes used to explain their higher fear levels despite lower risk and experience of crime. It has also prompted the hypothesis that the most vulnerable will be most responsive to media messages. This pattern was not supported by the data: White middle-aged women should be no more vulnerable than black middle-aged women or older women of either race. In fact, in terms of the ability to resist victimization, it is not certain that a 35-year-old white woman would be more vulnerable than, for example, a 70-year-old man of either race. In the sample, there were no effects for older females, who presumably would feel the most vulnerable. Moreover, the concentration of significant effects among white middle-aged women is not entirely consistent with a resonance interpretation. In general, white middle-aged women have consistently low victim risk and for most, media messages would not resonate with their experience. In this sample, crime news was significantly related to fear among white women with recent victim experience, and for those with low income or living in disproportionately black neighborhoods, a pattern consistent with resonance. This interpretation would have greater relevance if men and blacks with those same characteristics also had significant effects, but they do not.

Because white women without recent victim experience and living in high-income circumstances also demonstrated significant effects, it seems likely that for them, something other than resonance is at work. A possibility to explain relationships between news and fear of victimization among these white women (high-income or no victim experience) is that media messages substitute for real experience in the genesis of fear. The researchers also conducted a content analysis of the TV news on crime. The distribution of the news items was consistent with the notion of affinity. The audience most likely to see itself victimized in the news, white women, is the only audience for which significant effects were found. "This suggests," concluded the researchers (Chirocos et al., 1997), "that regardless of actual victim experience, seeing people like themselves victimized frequently in televised news may have contributed to the fear of crime among white women" (p. 354). The affinity appeared to be the most supported explanation.

Finally, Zillmann and Wakshlag (1985) raised the issue of direction: "What about the reverse causal chain? Instead of heavy exposure causing fear, fear might cause heavy exposure. And to make matters even more complicated, causation could be bidirectional" (p. 141). The research addressing the association between fear of crime and crime-drama watching has established that apprehensions can foster increased selective exposure. The drama variable that emerged as most significant in this connection is that of justice-injustice. Drama that features the restoration of justice after the commission of criminal transgressions appears to hold great appeal to people who are apprehensive about crime. As justice restoration commonly relies on violent action, the appeal of the justice theme entails the acceptance and appreciation of some degree of violence: the violence needed to achieve the punitive objectives involved in the restoration of justice. The research also provides some evidence that crime-apprehensive people experience greater excitement from crime drama than others do and that emotional responses to drama, including enjoyment of favorable resolutions, are accordingly more intense. And yet, Zillmann and Wakshlag (1985) noted,

It should be recognized, however, that all of this does not preclude cultivation effects such as perceptions of crime in society that fail to correspond with reality, esteem for those instrumental in restoring justice and safety for citizens, and an acceptance of violence in the service of justice and security. (p. 154)

Strong or Weak Impact?

What can we conclude from the data, findings, debates, arguments, and evidence on the cultivation of Mean World Syndrome? There are three alternative answers: The first, violence on television does not matter, and people are not affected by what they see on television. Second, violence on television will affect some people some of the time. Third, violence will always have a very negative impact on anyone who comes in contact with it. Given the evidence gathered by hundreds of studies, both the first and third of these interpretations are too extreme. The first position—television violence does not matter—has only a few supporters, a number of whom are involved with the television industry. For example, NBC researchers reported no evidence of a relationship between television violence and aggressive behavior in their 3-year longitudinal study of 2,400 elementary school children and 800 teenage boys conducted between 1970 and 1973 (Milavsky, Kessler, Stipp, & Rubens, 1982). However, when the same data were analyzed by more appropriate statistical procedures, the researchers found a real effect of TV violence on aggression (Turner, Hesse, & Petterson-Lewis, 1986). At the other extreme, the powerful impact notion was not based on solid research. Even the experiments that revealed a strong impact on learning aggression and imitating it were criticized for their use of invalid measures of aggression (e.g., the Bobo doll); their pressure to yield to experimenter demand (subjects try to do what they think the experimenter wants them to do); and their use of experimental materials that were much more violent (and taken out of context) than programs seen in movies or on television. Hence, the third position, that television violence will always have an extremely negative impact on people, is also too extreme. Although the research overwhelmingly reveals that there is a relationship between viewing and aggression, media violence may be only one cause of aggression. Very often, its effects are mediated by other factors (e.g., family background, personality traits), thus limiting the real impact to very few vulnerable individuals.

Most studies in this area show only very moderate or even small effects. In many studies, the absolute size of the effect accounts for less than 10% of the variability in aggression measures. Small effects, however, should not be dismissed out of hand; small effects may have profound consequences. When the dependent variable is aggression or fear of it, gloom and alienation, mistrust and suspicion—small effects may have very serious consequences. The most sensible interpretation, and that supported by a majority of the studies, indicates that television violence does have some type of impact—it may have a large effect on small numbers of children and adults, as well as a small effect on large numbers of people. For example, Gadow and Sprafkin (1989), who conducted a thorough meta-analysis of the studies in this domain, concluded that although there is little support for the hypothesis that viewing violence on television leads to aggressive behavior, viewing television in general may itself lead to antisocial behavior and that for certain children, viewing aggressive programming may be particularly toxic.

Although most of the public and scientific attention, and consequently the public and academic debate, have focused on behavioral hazards (the few who will imitate the violence), concern should also focus on the many who may become more fearful, insecure, and dependent on authority, who may demand protection and even welcome repression in the name of security.

Who Will Be Influenced?

One of the most agreed on and consistent findings in the studies of media violence and its impact is that the most affected audiences are children and adolescents. Although some of the early studies of media effects examined the effects of scary images on children, this area of investigation has not received much attention until recently. Children and adolescents are always the heaviest viewers in general and of violent material in particular. For most children in Western societies, exposure to television begins shortly after birth. Parents report using television to pacify infants, and by 6 months of age, many babies are engaged in "watching" television (see, e.g., Hollenbeck & Slaby, 1979; Huston et al., 1992). According to Nielsen surveys, the average American preschool child, ages 2 to 5, watches about 28 hours a week, whereas school-age children, ages 6 to 11, average about 24 hours a week.

Most modern children grow up in homes where the television is on an average of 7 hours a day, and many children grow up in "constant television households," where the television, continually on, provides an ever-present background to family life (Medrich, 1979). Moreover, recent technological changes have added new modes of exposure: video recorders, computers, video discs, and movies downloaded from the Internet provide additional media sources for children and adolescents. However, television continues to be children's primary medium. Even in multimedia households, television viewing accounts for 74.3% of children's media usage. At high school graduation, American and many European children will have spent more time watching television than any other form of activity except sleeping. When looking at absolute amount of time, television viewing surpasses the time modern children spend with their parents or teachers (Dorr & Kunkel, 1990).

In addition to a general amount of viewing, some children are heavy viewers. Although home viewing is an equal opportunity experience, poor and minority children with limited access to diverse educational opportunities and other leisure activities rely on television as a prime source of entertainment, education, information, and social contact (Comstock & Cobbey, 1982; Greenberg, 1986; Himmelweit & Swift, 1976; Huston, Watkins, & Kunkel, 1989). Many low-income single parents who live alone with their children and cannot afford leisure activities are the heaviest adult viewers, and their children are living in homes where television is always on (see Kubey & Csikszentmihalyi, 1990). The combination of a huge amount of television viewing with the heavy load of violence in most programs—and especially in children's programs—makes them digest enormous quantities of real and fictional violence.

To their heavy diet of mass-mediated violence, we have to add their naive and submissive trust in media realities. In their study of children's perceptions of television reality, Nikken and Peeters (1988) found out that young children (ages 4-9) could make little distinction between the real and unreal on television. Children's developing cognitive abilities and limited world experiences leave them particularly vulnerable to media messages, fictional or real (Dorr, 1986; Eron & Huesmann, 1987; Singer & Singer, 1988). Television is one of the most powerful social agents in the modern child's world, if not the most important. And when learning from their environment, children will find television handy, easy to access, rich in messages and suggestions, and appealing as an environment. As Lazar (1994) concluded,

> Although television violence may not be the most important cultural source for learning societal prescriptions, it is one source. Although television may not be the only material that child viewers have to create meanings with, it is a consistently available resource. . . . Although children can fill in the picture to a certain extent, the frame they are offered provides an ordering and delimiting structure. Children who are embedded in the world of television may be most vulnerable to its stories. (p. 9)

And indeed children are attracted to violent contents and are affected by them: Cantor and Reilly (1982) found that 80% of the 6th- and 10th-grade students in their samples said that they liked scary media (e.g., films such as *Jaws*) *a lot* or *somewhat* and that three quarters of these adolescents watched these films *sometimes* or *often*. Cantor and Sparks's (1984) survey of parents of children in preschool, first grade, or fourth grade found that parents were more likely to mention that their younger children (those at a pre-operational developmental stage) were frightened by media content categorized as fantasy (events that could not happen in the real world and superhuman characters such as the Incredible Hulk, Batman) than parents of the older children (concrete operational stage). On the other hand, the parents mentioned that fictional content (did not actually occur but could occur, e.g., *Jaws*) was more frightening to the older children than to the younger children. Continuing this line of research, Cantor and Hoffner (1990) found that children ages 5 to 8 were more fearful after a scary segment of a movie where they believed that the same threat existed locally.

When children see a scary movie or television program, parents usually attempt to reduce fear by reminding children that the program and/or the character "is not real." In an experimental setting using scary scenes from *The Wizard of Oz,* Cantor and Wilson (1984) found that these kinds of strategies did not reduce the fear of young children (3 to

5 year olds) but did help older children (9 to 11 year olds). Moreover, even though all the children said that the witch in this movie was not real, the younger children probably did not know what this really meant. Children have always been exposed to storytelling. But in the past, the storytellers were parents or other acceptable extrafamilial storytellers. Modern mass media and especially television have replaced the traditional storytellers: Beginning with the widespread availability of printed materials for the literate, enlarged by the availability of movies and radio, and culminating with the omnipresence of television, the opportunities for children to directly consume mass-produced stories have rivaled traditional methods of instruction about the world. When the stories told to children and adolescents are so violent, when this violence is so attractive for the younger consumers, and when the viewers of the mediated violence are so submissive and naive, the results, in terms of impact on the child's perceptions of the world, might be powerful. Data were collected among samples of adolescents in public schools from New York and New Jersey.

In each of the four areas—personal mistrust, fear of victimization, perceived activity of police, and estimation of crime and violence—heavy viewers among the adolescents always gave the mean, pessimistic, and gloomy answer more frequently. Heavy viewers see the world as more violent and scary and express more fear than do light viewers in a variety of ways, ranging from overestimating the number of criminals and victims to assumptions about the violence used by the police. These comparisons revealed consistent differences even when other factors were controlled, thus leading the researchers to conclude that adolescent heavy viewers perceive social reality differently from light viewers. There is considerable variation between groups in the scope and magnitude of these differences, and yet, the pattern remains stable. The finding about alienation and mistrust should be more alarming when one considers the potential vicious cycle: Children who are alienated and/or scared may find refuge in heavier television viewing, which in turn would cultivate more alienation and fear. In fact, the findings of a study on television viewing among children revealed that children expressing less interpersonal trust tend to spend more time watching television. The direction of causality is not clear, but the pattern of alienation-viewing correlation is established (Ridley-Johnson, Chance, & Cooper, 1984).

The impact of television's violent world on children is mediated by three main factors: First, the degree to which the children perceive what they see as real. Numerous studies have found that the perceived reality of media violence is associated with increased aggression or fear of aggression. The second factor is the social environment: Children who live in constant television homes, children in violent neighborhoods, or children who live with aggressive relatives are more heavily influenced by violent media contents and also are more exposed to such contents. Finally, a third factor relates to personality traits and characteristics. Emotionally disturbed children, children with behavioral disorders or social isolation problems, are heavier viewers and also are more affected by the messages. Thus, for these groups, the Double Dosage Syndrome may be very harmful: It may lead some to imitate the violence and aggression they saw on television, and it could lead many more to perceive the world as a violent, scary place where mistrust, anxiety, power, and alienation prevail. We may conclude that although behavioral effects in terms of promoting aggression are found only for some people some of the time, the latent cultivation of fear and alienation, although moderate in magnitude, is found for many people most of the time.

New Technologies: A Meaner World?

Although this chapter, like many studies within this domain, focuses on television, one should not overlook the role of other media. Thus, for example, a study on homicide reporting in Chicago dailies revealed clear patterns of reconstruction of reality (Johnstone, Hawkins, & Michener, 1994). Whereas only a third of all the homicides committed in Chicago were reported by the Chicago press, certain murders receive more attention than others. The press was more likely to report homicides if the offender was a man and the victim a woman, if there were more than one victim, and if the victim was not African American or Hispanic. As in the case of television, the presentation of crime in the press did not reflect the crime rates in reality.

Even television itself changed: The Cultural Indicators group conducted the cultivation studies in a different television environment than the one we live in now. Then, for example, 90% of all American television viewing centered on network prime-time programming. But the introduction of and subsequent widespread adoption of cable television, videocassette recorders (VCRs), and remote control devices (RCDs) has dramatically changed our media environment. Between 1980 and 1990, U.S. cable subscription increased from 22% to 61.2%, VCR ownership increased from 1% to 73%, and RCD ownership increased from 18% to 77%. Today, people are no longer television viewers; they are video users with more programming options and greater opportunity for viewing selectivity (Gross, 1992; Shagrin, 1990; Sheridan, 1991).

These trends may affect the potential for a cultivation process, but in which direction? There are two perspectives on the impact of new technologies on cultivation effects. On one hand, Gerbner (1990), Morgan, Alexander, Shanahan, and Harris (1990), and Morgan and Shanahan (1991) argue that the new television environment will have little impact on cultivation effects. New television technologies should be viewed as changes in delivery systems rather than as real changes in content. These technologies do not necessarily replace television exposure, but they do add to it. Thus, these new technologies may even increase cultivation effects because they increase the availability of network-type programming at times when they were not typically available before. Moreover, cable channels and video rentals that contain violent themes may add to the amount of violent content that can be viewed.

However, a different approach to the new technologies may suggest weaker cultivation effects. Cable, VCRs, and RCDs allow people to be more selective by facilitating their exposure to different programming. Access to this greater range of available programming and increased opportunity for audience selectivity may limit the cultivation of fear and mistrust. Cable television, for example, might increase fear and interpersonal mistrust because it is related to increased television viewing (Garay, 1988; Weimann, 1995a, 1996). Basic cable subscribers watch more television than nonsubscribers; pay cable subscribers watch the most television. On the other hand, cable television increases the capacity for audience selectivity because it increases the programming options available to viewers. Cable makes some very specialized channels available. The content carried by these channels (news, weather, shopping, documentaries, public affairs, etc.) differs from traditional prime-time television content and is produced by new program suppliers. Because television's ability to cultivate fear and mistrust is based on the content and themes of dramatic prime-time programming, television's cultivation effects may be reduced because cable makes a wider range of nondramatic programming available during prime-time hours.

A study of the new technologies and cultivation set out to test these conflicting ideas (Perse, Ferguson, & McLeod, 1994). Using two American samples, the researchers measured the use of cable, VCRs, and RCDs and tried to relate it to perceptions of social reality (four items measuring mistrust/anomie and two items measuring fear of crime). Fear of crime ($r = .24$, $p < .01$) and mistrust ($r = .41$, $p < .001$) were both positively related to amount of television viewing. The relationships remained significant even after controlling for various demographic variables and the use of new television technologies. However, although interpersonal mistrust was positively correlated with greater exposure to cable's broadcast-type channels, both fear of crime and mistrust were negatively correlated with increased exposure to more specialized and diverse cable channels. None of the hypotheses regarding VCRs or RCDs was supported, and the relationships were mostly weak and insignificant. The results, however, have some implications for cultivation research. The changing television environment may have an impact on television's ability to pull television viewers to social reality beliefs consistent with themes in television's prime-time dramatic programming. As Bryant (1986) pointed out, new television technologies offer increased program diversity and audience selectivity. These newer technologies do not reinforce effects identified by earlier research, they modify them.

These studies' findings suggest that cable television has the strongest impact on television's mainstreaming impact: Cable subscription was linked to stronger feelings of interpersonal mistrust. But channel repertoire, or the channels that viewers typically watch, was also a strong predictor of both fear of crime and interpersonal mistrust. Watching channels that present programming most like that traditionally carried by the television networks was a positive significant predictor of interpersonal mistrust. When viewers are exposed to "more of the same" programming, relationships between television exposure and fear and mistrust are consistent with previous research and are even stronger. But cable television does not carry only broadcast-type channels. Cable offers new sorts of channels that present specialized and alternative programming. So, watching channels that carry programming that differs from the networks' prime-time dramatic offerings was related negatively to cultivated perceptions. However, heavy viewers were less likely to own a VCR and more likely to watch time-shifted programs and have higher broadcast channel repertoires. For heavy viewers, cable television was used for more of the same, and accordingly, the cultivating impact was stronger.

When we consider more recent technologies, such as virtual reality, computer videos, and computer networks (the Internet and others), the cultivation effects may be very different from those pointed out by studying only television's contents and impact. In Chapter 12, we will look at the technology of virtual reality and its consequences, but at this point, we may highlight the fact that many of the new-age technologies, and especially computer games, video-on-line, virtual reality games, and such—are highly violent and involve more vivid (and even three-dimensional) presentations of killings, executions, fights, wars, and so on. Future research should explore the cognitive impact of these new mediated and virtual realities. The results of the existing studies of new communication technologies point out that it is useful to consider their content and repertoires. If indeed they present a meaner world, their devoted consumers may become more alienated, fearful, suspicious, and isolated.

NOTES

1. This scale is composed of five elements: the percentage of programs containing violence (P), the number of violent acts per program (AP), the number of violent acts per hour (AH), the percentage of leading characters involved in acts of violence (V), and the percentage of leading characters involved in killings (K). These five elements are then combined into one index, based on the formula: $VI = P + 2AP + 2AH + V + K$.

2. Additional support for the causal relationship is reported by later studies: see, for example, Lefkowitz, Eron, Walder, and Huesmann (1977).

3. The Alienation and Gloom Index was based on the following questions:

1. In spite of what some people say, the lot (situation/condition) of the average man is getting worse, not better. (Agree/Disagree)

2. It's hardly fair to bring a child into the world with the way things look for the future. (Agree/Disagree)

3. Most public officials (people in public office) are not interested in the problems of the average man. (Agree/ Disagree)

Those who agreed with two or more of these statements were categorized in the *high* alienation and gloom group. The Mean World Index was based on the following questions:

1. Would you say that most of the time people try to be helpful, or that they are mostly just looking out for themselves?

2. Do you think that most people would try to take advantage of you if they got a chance, or would they try to be fair?

3. Generally speaking, would you say that most people can be trusted or that you can't be too careful in dealing with people?

Those who gave the pessimistic reply to two or more of these questions were included in the high-scoring group.

CHAPTER SIX

Sex and Sexuality

One of the most studied and documented areas of reconstructed realities by the mass media is that of the portrayal of the sexes and its impact on popular stereotypes of sex roles. Sex roles are an integral and important part of human life, values, and behavior. We learn the roles we exhibit from numerous sources—families, friends, teachers, books, movies, and, of course, television. The role of the media in sex role socialization has become an area of considerable concern and the topic of many studies during recent decades because of the women's movement, the convincing findings on bias and cultivation within this domain, and the emerging recognition that the media play a crucial role in diffusing, preserving, and cultivating images of sex roles. Recently, the notion of sex role stereotyping has broadened from the classical notion of differences based on gender to include an examination of the media reconstruction of femininity and masculinity. In media studies, the topic of masculinity is in the early stages of emerging as a research area in its own right. As noted by Durkin (1985), such research has "concentrated on the female role, and the male sex role tends to be illustrated by default, and is often assumed to be the converse of whatever characteristics are identified as associated with the female stereotype" (p. 110).

However, there is a research tradition that focuses on sex roles and the media. This area deals both with the investigation of the images of men and women that are presented in the media and with the effects such portrayals have on an individual's notion of his or her own gender. The growing empirical research on pornography presents another exploration of masculinity. In this chapter, we will look at the different images of men and women in various media, the impact of these gender-based images on the public's perceptions of sex roles, and the cultivation of sexual stereotypes by the media.

Sexism on Television

Perhaps the most basic gender bias, a clear asymmetry, is that there are far fewer women than men on television, whereas in reality, there is no question of their equal proportions. On American television, for example, there are three times as many men as women in prime-time dramas and four times as many in Saturday morning children's shows (see, e.g., Fejes, 1992; Greenberg, 1980; Levinson, 1975; Signorielli, 1989). Even on *Sesame Street,* most of the classic characters are male. Among the Smurfs, there is only one female, and she is blonde, helpless, and dependent on the males around her. This bias may be due to the far greater numbers of men that are editors, writers, and producers or to a common, although never established belief that women find the opposite sex more interesting to watch than men do. Men are also more likely to be found in action/drama programming and less likely to be found in situation comedies and soap operas (e.g., Greenberg, Richards, & Henderson, 1980; Greenberg, Simmons, Hogan, & Atkin, 1980; Gunter, 1986). Thus, viewers tend to see men in programming contexts that emphasize action and drama rather than humor, emotions, or interpersonal relationships. In terms of occupation, men are more likely to be shown as employed in higher status jobs and are less likely to be shown in a home environment (Barcus, 1983; Downs, 1981). Other aspects of the portrayal of men in television reveal that men are less likely to be shown as being married, are generally shown as being older, and are less likely to be shown involved in a romantic relationship (Fejes, 1992). Men are portrayed as being more dominant than women, as more likely to engage in acts of violence and to give directions and orders, and as possessors of both power and status through their greater control of rewards and punishment.

More women watch daytime television than men. The two popular genres of daytime programming are soap operas and talk shows, and both target female audiences. In daytime soap operas, viewed primarily by women, characters also are presented in traditional and stereotypical ways (Cantor & Pingree, 1983). Compared to men, women in these series are frequently depicted as weak and helpless, displaying avoidance behaviors. Men more than women are depicted as directive and good problem solvers. These shows may particularly appeal to women because of the complex and ongoing nature of the stories and the characters involved, and thus they seem to satisfy their viewers' needs for a sense of involvement, connection, and community, despite the fact that such a community is not real (Modleski, 1982). During daytime talk shows, sensationalism and exploitation are very common. As Rapping (1995) notes, such shows as *Oprah Winfrey* take some of the contributions of feminism—consciousness raising, personal sympathetic questioning—and use them to exploit the feelings of both the guests and the studio audience. The topics very often concern women in stereotypical roles involving romance, children, sex, emotions, betrayal, and such.

Sex-based bias on prime-time TV has been amply documented since the early 1970s. Men consistently outnumber women three to one as leading characters of shows. In exciting adventure shows, men outnumber women more than four to one. Men are more likely than women to be depicted as wage earners, and men appear in a greater variety of jobs than women. Since 1979, increasing numbers of female characters on TV have had jobs, but their representation has been less than realistic. Although professional women on TV can serve as positive role models for young girls, the lack of realism may cause viewers to underestimate the extent of gender inequities in the labor force. Not only are more women on TV now shown as employed (75% in the United States) than is the case in real life (56% in the United States), but most of these TV women have professional careers (e.g., as lawyers or managers), whereas women typically work in low-paying, low-status jobs. Furthermore, most shows with female professionals still focus on family issues rather than on work. Despite such changes in depictions of women, they still are more often identified by their relationships with men (as girlfriend, wife, mother) than men are identified by their relationships to women. In fact, both women and men on TV tend to interact with men much more frequently than they interact with women (Lott, 1989).

Even more alarming are the consistent findings of numerous studies, all over the world, on the stereotypical and traditional media presentations of male and female sex roles. For example, women on television were found to be presented as passive, emotional, dependent, and less valued than men. The overall image is traditional, in that women are presented as weak and dependent on men, seeking a man if unmarried or being nurturing mothers and wives (e.g., Busby, 1985; Levinson, 1975; Long & Simon, 1974). Although a sizable portion of this research started in the 1970s, most of these patterns are found today. Although more than half of the female characters in prime-time television are shown working outside the home, their occupations tend to be limited and stereotyped (nurses, secretaries, etc.). In addition, women on television have a hard time mixing work outside the home with marriage. Among major characters, half of the single and formerly married women but only one third of the married women work outside the home. Among the men, by comparison, no matter what their marital status, three quarters are shown in an occupation (Signorielli, 1989).

Many studies reveal that female characters on TV are more concerned than male characters with sex and marriage. Women are more often portrayed as youthful beauties whose duty it is to stay young and attractive and to please their men. Once a woman is no longer young and attractive, she becomes an object of ridicule. Support for this criticism comes especially from all of the subtle messages that a woman must not allow herself to age, a message transmitted especially, although not exclusively, by television commercials and television series. Female characters are more likely than males to show helpless and incompetent behaviors. For example, even in a show where a woman is a major character, she often must be rescued from a difficult situation by a male. Examining the visual portrayal of men on television, Copeland (1989) found in commercial television programming a tendency to portray men in close-up face shots, whereas women were portrayed in full body shots. The researcher suggested that this example of "face-ism" may be a manifestation of deeply rooted cultural myths of men, pictorially represented by their faces, as intellect, and women, pictorially represented by their bodies, as heart or emotion.

A more recent concern, focusing on the unrealistic "superwoman," is directed specifically at a relatively new media portrayal that has arisen in an attempt to represent modern women more accurately and fairly.

Most TV series women are employed full-time and yet, these super-women manage to be young and attractive and raise beautiful children while having a brilliant career. Characters like Clair Huxtable (*The Cosby Show*) seem to handle the demands of career, wife, and parent with amazingly little stress and difficulty. Real women in two-career families may find great difficulties when balancing all their responsibilities, whereas Clair Huxtable and her sitcom counterparts ("super-moms") make it look all too easy. As Harris (1994) noted, the super-woman myth is also reinforced by some prime-time commercials and advertising. For example, one perfume ad says that a woman can "bring home the bacon, fry it up in a pan, but never let him forget he's a man." In other words, a woman can (or at least should) work outside the home all day, come home and cook dinner for her husband, and still have enough energy left to be charming, active, and sexy for him.

Sexism in Commercials and Advertising

Commercials on prime-time television as well as children's weekend-daytime programs are rife with female images that do not reflect reality. Ferrante, Haynes, and Kingsley (1988), replicating Dominick and Rauch's (1972) seminal research, as well as Lovdal's (1989) replication of O'Donnell and O'Donnell's (1978) study, found that men and women are not treated equally in television commercials. Women in television commercials are seen in narrowly defined roles, such as housewives or low-level employees: Typically, women are placed in the kitchen or bathroom to sell products used exclusively by women. O'Donnell and O'Donnell (1978) discovered that women were product representatives for 86% of the domestic products advertised. More specifically, researchers of television commercials in the 1970s found that women were seven times more likely to appear in ads for personal hygiene products, cosmetics, and domestic items; and they were significantly less likely to appear in ads for cars, trucks, and gas (Busby, 1975; Courtney & Whipple, 1974).

Although commercials depicted women in more narrowly defined social roles, women were not portrayed as autonomous, independent human beings. Men in advertisements and commercials were shown as nondomestic product representatives: They were represented as independent, employed, and speaking with the voice of authority. Sex-stereotyped elements are not confined merely to gender portrayals, they also pervade the formal features of commercials. Welch, Huston-Stein, Wright, and Plehal (1979) found that commercials aimed at boys have a different format than commercials aimed at girls. Commercials aimed at boys have rapid action, frequent cuts, loud music, sound effects, and frequent scene changes. In contrast, commercials aimed at girls contain many fades and dissolves, background music, and female narration.

Another dimension of latent stereotypes is in the voice-over: The majority of commercials featured an overriding male voice-over (when a voice is heard but no person is visible). Male voice-overs were used more frequently in the early 1970s (87%-89% of the voice-overs, according to several studies). Later, a high percentage was found (the O'Donnell and O'Donnell, 1978, study determined that 93% of the commercials used male voice-overs whereas 83% was reported by Ferrante, Haynes, and Kingsley, 1988). Commercials using male voice-overs reinforce the idea that men are more credible, convincing, and knowledgeable.

Children are most likely to view commercials on prime-time, adult-oriented programming as well as afternoon and Saturday morning programming made specifically for child audiences. During their viewing, children ages 2 through 11 years are exposed to about 20,000 television advertisements (between 150 and 200 hours) each year. Despite the potential influence of television advertising on children, few content analyses of children's advertising have been published, in comparison with the research on commercials for adults. Generally, although the majority of ads aimed at children contain both boys and girls, boys are the dominant characters (Macklin & Kolbe, 1983). Ads aimed at boys include far more activity than those aimed at girls and contain more aggressive behavior. A study of the traits associated with boy and girl characters portrayed in children's advertising indicated that boys were typically shown to be active, aggressive, and rational (Peirce, 1989). Male voice-overs predominate in male-oriented and neutral ads, and male-oriented ads are far louder than either female-oriented or neutral ads.

In her study of gender differences in children's commercials, Smith (1994) examined the differences between television advertisements featuring only one sex of actors. The advertisements that were studied aired during a week of afterschool and Saturday morning children's programming. The findings indicated that children's advertisements featuring characters of only one sex portrayed traditional stereotypes for male/female roles. As would be expected from adult advertising, advertisers positioned many products that would generally not be considered to be used by predominantly one sex toward the male viewing audience. The commercials showed stark stereotyped differences for boys and girls. Ads using only boys portrayed them in away-from-home and fantasy settings. Girls' commercials, on the other hand, pictured them at home over 70% of the time. Thus, girls stayed at home; boys roamed the world. Boys used a wider variety of products and performed more varying activities than girls did.

Research on the portrayal of gender in advertising in other countries tends to duplicate the findings of American research. In Italy, Furnham and Voli (1989) conducted a study on the portrayal of men and women in television commercials using advertisements broadcast on Italian television. Three hundred and thirty-three daytime and evening commercials were content-analyzed by classifying the attributes of their central figures into 11 categories: gender, mode, credibility, role, location, reward, product price, argument, background, humor, and comment. Gender stereotyping in Italy was constant across time of day and more apparent than in America, but as frequent as in England. The results of this study show that men and women in Italian television advertisements were portrayed in several significantly different ways in accordance with traditional gender stereotypes. In the Italian study, the tendency for men to predominate (64.3%) was comparable to the English study (66%) and greater than in the American study (57%).

In a study conducted in Israel, all 3,223 commercials aired on Israel TV (Channel 2, the only commercial station) during its 3 years of operation (1993-1995) were content-analyzed (Weimann, 1999). The study revealed gender-based stereotyping in Israeli commercials, similar to the stereotyping found in the early 1970s in American studies. Men outnumbered women in every measure of appearance (visual, vocal): The ratios, male to female, were 2.19 (to whom the commercial is directed), 1.59 (who speaks in the commercial), 4.25 (the voice-over), and 3.14 (who is last seen in the commercial). The dominance of men is related to the price of the product being advertised: The more expensive the product, the more frequently male figures and voices are used. Women are almost completely absent from commercials for the top-priced products. Even the location of the commercial is highly stereotypical: Male figures appear mostly outdoors, in workplaces, and in nature whereas female figures appear mostly in the home. Finally, the way the products were "sold" (type of appeals) was strongly related to gender: In commercials aimed at a female customer, the appeals were mainly emotional, and the promised rewards concerned mainly physical appearance. The appeals directed at men were mostly rational, and the promised rewards were mostly practical (income, efficiency, saving, etc.) or social (enhanced status).

Studies of British television reported that men were typically portrayed as having expertise and authority, as being objective and knowledgeable about reasons for buying particular products, as occupying roles that are autonomous, and as being concerned with the practical consequences of product purchases (Harris & Stobart, 1986; Livingstone & Green, 1986; Manstead & McCulloch, 1981). A study of British radio advertising found similar results, and a study of Italian television found that it is very similar to British television in the portrayal of men (Furnham & Schofield, 1986; Furnham & Voli, 1989). A comparative study of sex-role portrayals in television advertising in Australia, Mexico, and the United States revealed that although the commercials of all three countries contained traditional stereotypes, Australian commercials were less stereotyped in a number of different elements, such as occupation, setting, marital status, whether a man or woman acted as a spokesperson, their credibility in the role, and whether they were recipients or providers of aid (Gilly, 1988). Mexican commercials, on the other hand, were the most stereotyped on all the factors studied.

Print advertising, in magazines and newspapers, reveals the same patterns. Goffman (1976/1979) found numerous examples of genderism, illustrating the position of men and women in our society: function ranking (male taller, in front, and in authoritative position), ritualization of subordination (e.g., a woman at a man's feet), snuggling, mock assault games, and an overabundance of images of women on beds and floors. Other research has confirmed Goffman's findings. Masse and Rosenblum (1988), using Goffman's approach, analyzed 564 ads from three male-oriented and three female-oriented magazines. In male-oriented magazines, men tended to be portrayed in a dominant stance; were less likely to be shown smiling; were less likely to be touching one another, themselves, or an object; and gazed full-faced at the viewer or an object, but not at others. In female-oriented magazines, the portrayal was similar, except that men were more likely to touch and gaze at others. Men are also pictured seated above, and leaning over the woman; men also are more likely than women to be depicted with their faces prominent, as opposed to their bodies. Such face-ism, which has been documented in periodicals both in the United States and in 11 other cultures, over six centuries, and in TV interview shows, is argued to "affect the viewers' perception of the person; for example, a person is perceived more favorably and is rated as more intelligent when the face is prominent than when it is not" (Basow, 1992, p. 166).

Skelly and Lundstrom (1981) used a scale designed to measure the level of sexual stereotyping in an analysis of 660 magazine ads from three decades to determine whether there was any change in the portrayal of men in print advertising over the three decades. They found a small and gradual movement toward a nonsexist portrayal of men over the 20-year period. Lysonski's (1985) study of sex roles in British magazine advertising showed similar results: Looking at a sample of ads from British magazines in 1976 and 1983, he concluded that although the sex stereotyping had decreased slightly, men still were more likely to be depicted in themes of sex appeal, as career-oriented, and in activities and life outside the home. Several studies used the Consciousness Scale for Sexism (see Pingree, Hawkins, Butler, & Paisley, 1976). In the late 1980s, Lazier-Smith (1988) used this scale for a content analysis of print advertisements. The scale was applied to ads portraying women in four magazines: *Ms., Playboy, Time,* and *Newsweek,* coding 10 ads in each monthly issue for 1 year. This scale attempts to measure sexism by analyzing ad visuals on five levels:

Level 1: Put her down (the sex object, dumb blonde, decorative object)

Level 2: Keep her in her place (women shown mostly in traditional womanly roles or struggling with roles "beyond them")

Level 3: Give her two places (women can have an occupation as long as they are still primarily wives/mothers; the career may be something "extra")

Level 4: Acknowledge that she is fully equal (women in multiple roles without reminders that housework and mothering are nonnegotiable woman's work)
Level 5: Nonstereotypic (true individuals, not judged by sex)

In the 1973-1974 study, 75% of all ads were at the two lowest (most sexist) levels: 48% at Level 2 and 27% at Level 1 (sex object). Table 6.1 presents the results of the same analysis performed in 1986. As the rates in Table 6.1 reveal, the ads at the lowest level of sexism became more frequent (from 27% to 37%) whereas for the two lowest categories combined, there was no real change (75% of the ads in 1973 and 72% in 1986).

The selective targeting of print advertising is also biased. For example, although women account for 39% of new car purchases and participate in buying another 42% of all new cars and trucks, automobile companies spend less than 3% of their advertising money in women's magazines (Basow, 1992). A study of computer ads in magazines showed that men appeared in such advertisements almost twice as often as women; were overrepresented as managers, experts, and technicians; and were portrayed as more active and accepting of new computer technology (Ware & Stuck, 1985). In a first study, Silverstein, Perdue, Peterson, and Kelly (1986) examined over 1,200 ads and articles in both women's and men's magazines, as well as photographs of models in selected women's magazines. The results, in terms of product types in ads and in articles and gender, are presented in Table 6.2.

The findings in Table 6.2 supported the authors' hypothesis that women receive more messages about slimness and staying in shape than do men. In a second study, the same researchers attempted to obtain a measure of the changes in standards of bodily attractiveness for women since the turn of the century (Silverstein et al., 1986). Photographs of women in bathing suits or underwear in *Ladies Home Journal* and *Vogue* were used to collect data on the ratios of bust to waist. The results show that mean bust-to-waist ratios exhibited a steady decline over the years. This reveals a trend that continued into the present of a steady stream of "thin-is-in" messages to young and middle-aged women of today. Advertisements in magazines aimed at one sex tend to use models predominantly of that sex (Masse & Rosenblum, 1988). Women in print ads tend to be extremely young and extremely thin, setting a standard

TABLE 6.1 Comparison of Female Portrayals in 1973 and 1986 (in percentages)

	Year	
Consciousness Scale for Sexism	*1973*	*1986*
Put her down	27	37
Keep her in her place	48	35
Give her two places	4	3
Acknowledge equality	19	15
Nonstereotypic	2	10
Total:	100	100

NOTE: Table is based on findings presented by Lazier-Smith (1988).

TABLE 6.2 Ads and Articles in 48 Women's Versus 48 Men's Magazines

	Type of Ad or Article				
	Diet Foods	*Body Ads and Articles*	*Total Food Ads*	*Food Articles*	*Alcoholic Beverages*
Women's magazines	63	96	1,179	228	19
Men's magazines	1	12	15	10	624
Ratio (women/men):	63	8	78.6	22.8	0.03

NOTE: Table is based on findings reported by Silverstein, Perdue, Peterson, and Kelly (1986).

of attractiveness that few women can attain. Equality between the images of men and women in ads has increased slightly over the last decades and yet the most prominent female features in ads are still sexuality and "decoration."

Sexism in Children's Programs

Children's television programs were found to be even more sexist than adult programs. For example, children's TV has been found to depict more than twice as many male as female roles. The behaviors of the female and male characters are strikingly different, as are the conse-

quences of these behaviors (Sternglanz & Serbin, 1974). Male characters are more likely than female characters to be aggressive, constructive, direct, and helpful and to be rewarded for their actions. Women
are more likely to be shown as deferent and as being punished for
displaying a high level of activity. Women also use indirect manipulative
strategies to get their way (for example, acting helpless or seductive).
In general, female behavior has no environmental consequence. This
pattern parallels the practices of socializing agents: Men get more
attention and reinforcement; women are usually ignored and are expected to be passive and sedate.

Even in educational programs such as *Sesame Street,* gender stereotypes appear. The Muppets, the major characters on *Sesame Street,* have
mostly male names or voices or both, whereas Miss Piggy represents the
blond, desperately-trying-to-be-sexy, manipulative female, trying to
charm the males around her. These puppets not only are television
characters but also are prominent in books, toys, and other commercial
articles. Their influence on children is strong. In one study, children ages
4 to 6 would not play with non-sex-typed toys that had been labeled by
two Muppets as appropriate only for the other sex (Cobb, Stevens-Long,
& Goldstein, 1982). This behavior change occurred after only 5 minutes
of TV exposure.

In the United States since the early 1990s, all Saturday morning
programs have featured dominant male characters with females playing
peripheral roles, if any. This was, according to a *New York Times* report
(Carter, 1991), a deliberate marketing decision by television executives
based on the finding that girls will watch shows with male or female
lead characters, but boys will only watch shows with male leads. Because
commercial TV is driven by advertisers, and because boys are 53% of
the Saturday morning television audience, programmers aimed to attract and please boys. Because boys prefer animated, high-action programs (often involving violence), such programs predominate on children's TV.

Sexism in Movies

According to several studies, two frequent female images appear in
movies: virgin or saint and whore (see review by Basow, 1992). These

images were clearly exemplified in the 1950s and 1960s by the brainless sexy woman (e.g., Marilyn Monroe) and the feminine homebody (e.g., Doris Day). In 1990, we had Madonna playing the roles of both the whore and the virgin. It was only during the second World War, when increased numbers of women were in the labor force, that different images of women emerged (as working, fighting, ambitious, successful, independent). This ended when the war ended: The woman of the 1950s, 1960s, and 1970s, although sexually active and more independent than her predecessors, usually was depicted in a negative way or was punished for her sexuality (Mellen, 1977).

The women's movement had some effect on film images of women in the late 1970s, with credible and strong female characters in such films as *Alice Doesn't Live Here Anymore* and *An Unmarried Woman*. But the 1980s brought a considerable backlash, with such retrogressive film images as the brainless young woman *(The Woman in Red)* and the prostitute *(Pretty Woman)*. Motherhood and family came back, even (or especially) for working women *(Terms of Endearment, Baby Boom)*. The backlash against strong women led to a surprising absence of women in films; the roles for women have been smaller and their action more submissive. The intense reaction to the 1991 film *Thelma and Louise*, which depicted two strong women friends who used guns to protect themselves against male violence, clearly revealed how problematic and even unacceptable strong women can be.

Images of men and of masculinity also have held strongly to the gender stereotype. Whereas the realms of passivity, domesticity, and sexual allure have been reserved for women, those of aggression, as in Westerns, war, and gangster movies, moral superiority, and intelligence, as in detective and mystery movies, have been reserved for men. Then came a strange twist, with men taking over what were once considered female issues—for example, single parenting *(Kramer vs. Kramer)* and problems of divorce *(Starting Over)*. But then came the return to the traditional definitions of maleness—adventure *(Indiana Jones* movies), sports *(Field of Dreams)*, and violence *(48 Hours)*.

An alarming trend is related to the rise in home video viewing, which has led to increased concern about R- and X-rated films. Although the effects of pornography will be discussed later in this chapter, it is worth noting that most such films are aimed at a male audience and depict male dominance and/or exploitation of women (Cowan Lee, Levy, & Snyder, 1988). Maybe even more alarming is the combination of sex with violence against women. As we will see later in this chapter, films that do this negatively shape men's attitudes toward women and toward sexual violence (Linz, Donnerstein, & Penrod, 1984, 1988).

Sexism in Print Media

Gender stereotypes are as present in print media—books, magazines and newspapers—as they are in visual and audio media. For example, children's books markedly portray boys and girls in stereotypic roles, and male characters tend to predominate. In books aimed at an adult audience, a wider variety of roles and behaviors are portrayed. However, the 1980s mark a turning point in the acceptance of female writers and their works, resulting in more inclusivity and gender equality. Yet, a popular female literature, the romantic novel, written and read primarily by women, still presents stereotypical sex roles. In these stories, the heroine is usually helpless or dependent on a man to bring meaning to her life (Modleski, 1982). Popular books and fiction aimed at men, on the other hand, tend to present the male going off on some adventure, unencumbered by family ties. Themes of aggression predominate, and if women are presented, they are usually cast in a stereotyped sexual role (Weitz, 1977). Griffin's (1981) work as well as Dworkin's (1981) analysis revealed that much male fiction is pornographic, with interconnected themes of sexuality, dominance, and violence against women.

Gender-based stereotypes are found in magazines as well. A study by Thomas (1986) of gender and social class coding in photographs in heterosexual erotic magazines (*Playboy, Penthouse, Mandate, Playgirl,* and so on) found that in magazines aimed at upwardly mobile heterosexual men, women were portrayed in a highly sexualized and idealized manner. Their physical attributes and beauty were uncommon, and there was a great deal of photographic manipulation (airbrushing, lighting, and so on) of the figures. On the other hand, magazines aimed at heterosexual women showed men with average physical attributes, and the degree of photographic manipulation was nowhere near as great. In contrast, the images of men found in homosexual erotica were comparable to the images of women found in erotica aimed at the upwardly mobile heterosexual male, in that men had uncommon physical attributes and were of above-average attractiveness. Thus, it seems that erotica aimed at men, either heterosexual or homosexual, relies on an idealized image of sexuality and sexual attractiveness. Finally, magazines aimed at men focus on themes of sexuality *(Playboy, Hustler)*, sports, cars, racing, action, and adventure. Magazines aimed at women emphasize women's appearance, fashion, house care, children, and shopping (Peirce, 1990).

Newspapers also frequently contain a sexist bias in the treatment of women and men: A study by Luebke (1989) of gender and newspaper pictures revealed that photos of men outnumbered women in all sections of the newspaper except lifestyle pages. In a gatekeeper study of newspaper sports photos, Wanta and Leggett (1989) examined sports photographs of the 1987 Wimbledon Tennis Tournament sent over the Associated Press (AP) wire and compared those with the photos that were then actually used by eight newspapers. They found that newspaper sports editors tended to select photos of women that showed them in emotional and helpless states and rejected similar photos of men. The newspaper comic strips also perpetuate gender stereotypes. Men, especially white men, are represented far more than their proportion in the population (Brabant & Mooney, 1986). Furthermore, men are given preferential treatment not only in number of appearances but also in number of careers depicted. Although many male and female characters are described in equally favorable or unfavorable terms, sex-typed characteristics often are emphasized for women. Although a few comic strips portray employed mothers, these women are depicted as superwomen (Mooney & Brabant, 1987). Furthermore, the home life of employed mothers is portrayed as less happy than that of traditional mothers. Thus, in the world of comic strips, as elsewhere in the media, traditional gender roles are frequently presented and endorsed.

In sum, in all forms of media, gender stereotypes are conveyed often in the most exaggerated way. What is most striking from the above review of media and gender is the consistency of the gender stereotypes conveyed. Television commercials, print advertisements, children's programs, and music videos tend to be particularly stereotypic. Given the pervasiveness of the gender stereotypes in most media contents and presentations, let us now look at the consequences of mediated sexism.

Cultivation Effects of Media Sexism

Although it is relatively easy to find persistent gender role portrayals in various media, the question of their effect is a far more difficult research problem and a less investigated one. However, it appears that gender stereotypes in the media may affect us in powerful ways. As we have seen, media consumers see a world in which men dominate. Men are more visible than women and are depicted as more important, rational, competent, authoritative, and aggressive. How does it affect our perceptions of the sexes, their roles, traits, similarities, and differences? Are we influenced by the media's distorted presentations of men and women?

There are good reasons to consider media effects on sex role perceptions: People learn about sex roles from numerous sources—families, friends, teachers, books, movies, and television. The role of the media in sex role socialization has become an area of considerable concern and the topic of a good deal of research. Most research about the effects of television in sex role socialization focuses on children and examines perceptions of sex-typed behaviors or personality traits and tendencies to identify with specific characters. Miller and Reeves (1976), for example, found that children selected television characters as people they wanted to be like when they grew up. Reeves and Miller (1978) also found a strong tendency for children, especially boys, to identify with same-sex television characters. The identification of boys with television characters was positively related to perceptions of masculine attitudes (physical strength and activity level); girls' identification was positively related to perceptions of physical attractiveness. Reeves and Miller also found that girls were more likely to identify with male characters than boys were likely to identify with female characters. Indeed, TV is a powerful source of influence on children, who, as a group, are not as skilled as adults in distinguishing fantasy from reality (Eysenck & Nias, 1978). The amount of time children spend watching TV is directly and positively related to their degree of acceptance of traditional sex roles as early as kindergarten age (see, e.g., Frueh & McGhee, 1975; Liebert & Sprafkin, 1988; Zuckerman, Singer, & Singer, 1980). Furthermore, whereas the perception of male stereotypes declines with increasing age among light viewers of TV, among heavy viewers no such decline occurs.

Numerous studies supported the notion of gender stereotypes cultivated by the media: In a study of 3- to 6-year-old children, Beuf (1974) found that children who watched more television were more likely to stereotype occupational roles. Gross and Jeffries-Fox (1978), in a panel study of 250 8th-, 9th-, and 10th-grade children, found that television viewing was related to giving sexist responses to questions about the nature of men and women and how they are treated by society. Atkin and Miller (1975), in an experimental setting, found that children who viewed commercials in which women were cast in typically male occupations were more likely to say that this occupation was appropriate for women. Morgan (1982, 1987), in a 2-year panel study of 6th to 8th graders found that television cultivates notions such as "women are happiest at home raising children" and "men are born with more ambition than women." Overall, children who watched more television tended to be more sexist.

The simple same-time correlations between television viewing and the sexism index were positive and significant each year for both boys and girls. When Morgan (1982) tested the correlations with second- and third-year level of sexism, significant correlations were found. When controls were implemented for grade, socioeconomic status, IQ, and whether the respondent's mother works, only IQ seemed to lower the simple associations. The other controls by themselves had little impact. These results parallel those found in other studies. Thus, TV may "mainstream" children, creating in all viewers a homogeneous commonality of outlooks. Curiously, early sexism on the part of boys was a strong predictor of TV watching a year later, suggesting that those with strong stereotypes may enjoy the reinforcement of those attitudes that occur on TV.

In his second study of 287 adolescents, using measures taken at two points in time, Morgan (1987) investigated the effects of viewing on adolescents' sex role attitudes and behavior over time. The results regarding attitudes were consistent with previous research in that they showed that adolescents who spend more time watching television are more likely to express attitudes that reflect traditional sex role stereotypes. However, Morgan went beyond previous research by also considering the impact on behavior. He added behavior both as a dependent variable and as a factor that may mediate between amount of viewing and attitudes. The analysis found no relationships at all between amount of viewing and sex role behavior, but there were complex interactions between viewing and behavior over time. Behavior, argued Morgan, mediates the relationship between viewing and impact on attitudes: For boys, the relationship between viewing and attitudes is enhanced among those who are less likely to perform in traditionally male-stereotyped ways, whereas for women, high sex-role behavior seems to constitute a condition under which television's influence is heightened. For boys, the overall result is one of convergence; conversely, television has no impact on girls' attitudes unless their behavior tends toward traditional sex roles. Finally, despite the not very strong correlations, there is some indication of a reciprocal, dynamic relationship between television viewing and the degree of congruence between attitudes and behavior. Heavy viewing seems to increase consistency between attitudes and behavior (supporting the argument that exposure to television's messages helps maintain stable patterns of behaviors and beliefs), and congruence also contributes to greater amounts of viewing. Thus, Morgan's second study suggests that television viewing, sex role attitudes, and sex role behavior among adolescents should be seen as loosely related but nonetheless intertwined aspects of an ongoing system. As Morgan (1987) concluded,

> In sum, adolescents' exposure to television's stable lessons about sex-roles helps cultivate adherence to more stereotyped ways of thinking about sex-roles. Actual behavior mediates that process, but television also works to increase consistency between attitudes and behaviors. . . . Whatever general changes are occurring in adolescents' ideas about sex-roles, television, the mainstream of the culture, is lagging behind as it continues to contribute to intersections between traditional attitudes and behavior that fit its socially functional myths. (p. 280)

Signorielli and Lears (1992) continued Morgan's research. In their study, they examined the relationship between television viewing and sex role attitudes and behaviors among children. They used a sample of fourth- and fifth-grade children to examine if television viewing is related to children's attitudes and behaviors in relation to household chores that are typically viewed as "something boys do" or "something girls do." The sample was equally divided into fourth- and fifth-graders as well as into boys and girls. There were statistically significant relationships between television viewing and scores on an index of attitudes toward sex-stereotyped chores that maintained statistical significance under conditions of multiple controls. The correlation and regression analyses revealed that television viewing was positively related to children's attitudes toward sex-stereotyped chores. Those children who watched more television were likely to say that only girls should do those chores traditionally associated with women and that only boys should do those chores traditionally associated with men. These relationships maintained statistical significance when controlling for demographic characteristics as well as the children's specific behaviors in regard to these chores. Although viewing was not related to which chores the children actually performed, there were statistically significant relationships between attitudes, behaviors, and viewing. For both boys and girls, there were moderate to strong statistically significant relationships, which increased with television viewing, between attitudes about who should do certain chores and about whether or not the children said they did chores typically associated with the other sex.

Pingree (1978) was interested in the effects of commercials on sex role perceptions of children. To test the hypothesis that television content can teach sex-typed attitudes, this study presented third- and eighth-graders with television commercials showing either traditional or nontraditional women. Crossing this manipulation, the children's perceptions of the reality of the commercials were altered with instructions that the characters in the commercials were all real people (reality set), that they were all acting (acting set), or that the commercials were just like ones seen at home (no instructions). Results showed that the children's perceptions of reality were successfully manipulated and that younger children thought all content was more real. The two sets of commercials were found to have a significant differential impact on the children's attitudes about women only for groups that had been instructed about reality. For these groups, there was an interaction with sex of subject so that eighth-grade boys had more traditional attitudes about women after viewing the nontraditional women, whereas all other groups showed the reverse pattern of means. Finally, rather than the predicted interaction, perceived reality had a main effect such that children who believed the characters to be acting were less traditional in their attitudes about women.

An interesting research design was used by Kimball (1986) in three Canadian communities (nicknamed NOTEL, UNITEL, and MUL-

TITEL). In NOTEL, she compared the situation before and after the time NOTEL received television. She found that in NOTEL, children's perceptions relating to sex roles were less strongly sex-typed before the introduction of television. Two years after the introduction of television, however, the perceptions of these children were more sex-typed and did not differ from the perceptions relating to sex roles of the children in UNITEL and MULTITEL.

There are few studies examining this impact on adult populations. Volgy and Schwartz (1980), in a study conducted in the southwestern United States, found a positive relationship between viewing entertainment programs and acceptance of traditional sex roles. Pingree, Starrett, and Hawkins (1979), using a small sample of women in Madison, Wisconsin, found a positive relationship between viewing daytime serial dramas and supporting traditional family values and family structures. Ross, Anderson, and Wisocki (1982), using a sample of 78 college students and a group of 19 older adults, found that the amount of sex role stereotyping in self-descriptions was positively correlated with amount of viewing of stereotyped television programs. A cultivation study was conducted by Signorielli (1989), using a secondary analysis of data from the 1975, 1977, 1978, 1983, 1985, and 1986 NORC General Social Surveys. The hypotheses were tested by examining the relationship between television viewing and responses to an index of sexism made up of four questions in these surveys. The index was additive in nature, summing respondents' agreement with sexist statements about women's role in society and included the following items:

- Do you agree or disagree with this statement: Women should take care of running their homes and leave running the country up to men.
- Do you approve or disapprove of a married woman earning money in business or industry if she has a husband capable of supporting her?
- If your party nominated a woman for President, would you vote for her if she were qualified for the job—yes or no?
- Tell me if you agree or disagree with this statement: Most men are better suited emotionally for politics than are most women.

The analysis found significant evidence for the cultivation of sexist perceptions: Heavy viewers overall and in most subgroups tend to give the stereotypical answer more often. Although the differences vary across groups, the direction is almost always consistent. One should note that despite the decline over the years in the popularity of gender stereotypes, cultivation effects are not disappearing (Cultivation Differential values remain the same). Finally, Morgan and Rothschild (1983) investigated "new" television (namely, cable TV) and its impact on cultivation of gender-based stereotypes. Their findings replicate the findings of the previous studies and also show that the cultivation impact is intensified by new television offerings, such as cable television. As they concluded their study, the results offer a rather pessimistic glimpse of the future:

> The economic structure of the cable industry, the cost of programming, and the track record so far all suggest that cable will follow the course of other media institutions. . . . Thus, the new electronic environment will not ensure diversity, but, like its predecessors, will monopolize the message systems by further standardization and homogenization of this culture's most common social myths. (p. 48)

Finally, a recent study attempted to test whether media images of men influence the gender role attitudes that men express soon after exposure to the images (Bodenhausen, 1997). A sample of American men viewed magazine advertisements containing images of men that varied in terms of how traditionally masculine or androgynous they were and whether the models were the same age or much older than the viewers. Men who had initially been less traditional espoused more traditional attitudes than any other group after exposure to traditionally masculine models, although they continued to endorse relatively nontraditional views after exposure to androgynous models. These findings suggest that nontraditional men's gender role attitudes may be rather unstable and susceptible to momentary influences such as those found in advertising.

The Cultivation of Thinness

A model chosen for her skeletal appearance was at the center of a new advertising campaign, launched for the 1997/1998 season by Accurist, a London-based luxury watches company. Accurist had commissioned a

$3 million press and poster campaign featuring a skinny model whose ribs are clearly visible under her vest. In fact, she is so thin that she wears the watch around her upper arm rather her wrist. Ironically, the slogan in the ads was "Put some weight on," suggesting that the weight added is that of the watch. This ad caused several experts, organizations, and groups to react. Among them were eating-disorders experts, who pointed to the exploitation of extreme thinness. The spokesman for the Eating Disorders Association was quoted in the *Singapore Sunday Times* for September 11, 1997, saying that he never saw anything like this and that "the organization is very concerned and will be taking it up with the company" (p. 3). The company said the advertisement simply sought to make a point about the weight of its watches, but the advertising agency issued a different statement to the *Singapore Times,* arguing that "while being provocatively contentious, the idea does not seek to condone the vogue for anorexic models but takes a fashion icon and uses it to emphasize the point of difference . . . , the weight." The advertising agency also argued that "we are absolutely not saying that it is right to be thin or anorexic. The model was chosen because she looks thin, not because she looks unwell." This debate illustrates the potential harmful messages related to the extremely thin models used in advertising.

The rapidly growing problem of eating disorders among young Western women has prompted some media critics to suggest that unattainable physical ideals portrayed in the media are contributing to an eating disorder epidemic. The two most alarming disorders are anorexia nervosa and bulimia nervosa, threatening the physical and mental health of growing numbers of women. Anorexia nervosa is a potentially life-threatening disorder characterized by the refusal to eat enough to maintain body weight over a minimal norm for age and height, as well as an intense fear of gaining weight, body image disturbances, and amenorrhea (temporary cessation of menstruation). Bulimia nervosa is a related disorder characterized by a pattern of binging (eating large quantities of food in a short time) followed by attempts to compensate for the excessive caloric intake by vomiting, using laxatives, severe restrictive dieting, or overexercising. These problems are clearly related to gender: The American Psychiatric Association (1994) estimated that among eating-disordered individuals, women outnumber men 10 to 1.

Most of the theories of the origin of eating disorders point to the prominent role played by the social environment, so it is no coincidence that media messages and especially advertising were suggested as important promoters of this phenomenon. Lazier and Gagnard-Kendrick (1993) argue that in the media, they find two themes related to women's appearance: "First, thin is in (translation: fat is out) and secondly, thinness is associated with good health and attractiveness" (p. 210). It is evident that fashion models' bodies, for example, are still consistently thin. Garfinkel and Garner (1982) argued, "The media have capitalized upon and promoted this image (of thinness) and through popular programming have portrayed the successful and beautiful protagonists as thin. Thinness has thus become associated with self-control and success" (p. 145). Content analyses revealed this growing trend of thinness messages targeting women: Gagnard (1986) reported a significant increase in thin models in popular magazine advertisements from 1950 to 1984, reaching a high of 46% in the 1980s. Another study reported a significant decrease in the body measurements and weights of *Playboy* centerfolds and Miss America Pageant contestants (Garner, Garfinkel, Schwartz, & Thompson, 1980). The same study also reported a concurrent and substantial increase in the number of diet articles in popular women's magazines, from a yearly mean of 17.1 for the 1960s to a yearly mean of 29.6 for the 1970s. An update of this study, conducted by Wiseman, Gray, Mosimann, and Ahrens (1990) reported that this slimming trend continued from 1979 to 1988. They found that 69% of the *Playboy* centerfolds and 60% of the pageant contestants studied were at a weight considered symptomatic of anorexia nervosa (American Psychiatric Association, 1994). At the same time, the number of dieting and exercise articles in popular women's magazines increased year by year during the period of study, as the normal weight range of American women and the reported prevalence of eating disorders in the United States both continued to rise.

Several content analyses have revealed television's increasing preoccupation with beauty, thinness, and food (see, e.g., Garner et al., 1980; Silverstein et al., 1986; Toro, Cervera, & Perez, 1988; Wiseman et al., 1990). Klassen, Wauer, and Cassel (1990), who studied food advertisements aimed at women, found an increasing trend for food advertisers to incorporate weight-loss claims in magazine ads for their products. In addition, Andersen and DiDomenico (1992) found that a sample of popular women's magazines contained about 10 times as many dieting advertisements and articles as a similar sample of men's magazines. Andersen and DiDomenico suggested that there is a "dose-response" relationship between media content that emphasizes the ideal slim figure and the incidence of eating disorders in the dominant female target audience, such that greater exposure to such media content is associated with greater levels of disordered eating.

Are the mediated messages of thinness affecting eating disorders? Some empirical evidence has been produced to show that exposure to media images of thinness leads directly to disordered eating. An experiment by Myers and Biocca (1992) involving a mood test and a body image detection device found that as little as 30 minutes of television programming and commercials affected self-perceived body size estimates and mood of young women. Results supported the notion that an "elastic body image" exists for young women, in which their actual body size is in conflict with media messages about ideal body image. In another study involving a sample of female college undergraduates, the researchers tested a structural equation model involving media exposure as an exogenous variable; gender role endorsement, ideal body stereotype internalization, and body dissatisfaction as mediating variables; and eating disorder symptomatology as the final criterion variable (Stice, Schupak-Neuberg, Shaw, & Stein, 1994). The path coefficient for the direct link from media exposure to eating disorder symptomatology was significant. In addition, media exposure was found to be indirectly related to eating disorder symptomatology through gender-role endorsement, ideal body stereotype internalization, and body dissatisfaction. In a related study, Stice and Shaw (1994) found significant links between exposure to thin female magazine models and bulimic symptomatology in a sample of female college undergraduates.

A more recent attempt to relate media messages and eating disorders was conducted by Harrison and Cantor (1997). They based their hypothesis on the Social Learning Theory, arguing that the mass media operate as transmitters of cultural ideals including that of a slim female physique. The study used a sample of 232 female and 190 male undergraduate students at a large midwestern university. Both female and male respondents were asked to indicate the number of hours they watched television on an average weekday, an average Saturday, and an average Sunday, as well as the frequency with which they viewed six popular television shows: *Beverly Hills 90210, Melrose Place, Seinfeld, Northern Exposure, Designing Women*, and *Roseanne*. These shows were popular among the population of interest and represented the widest possible range of body types featured in popular prime-time television entertainment. Female main characters with very thin bodies *(Beverly Hills 90210 and Melrose Place)*, average bodies *(Seinfeld and Northern Exposure)*, and heavy bodies *(Designing Women and Roseanne)*. Respondents also indicated how many issues of popular magazines they read each month in each of five categories: health and fitness, beauty and fashion, entertainment and gossip, news and current events, and men's entertainment magazines (men only). The extent of disordered eating was measured by the Eating Attitudes Test (EAT). Representative items from this scale include "Am preoccupied with a desire to be thinner" and "Exercise strenuously to burn off calories," with six possible frequency-based responses. The Eating Disorders Inventory (EDI) was used also, based on five subscales (dissatisfaction, drive for thinness, perfectionism, ineffectiveness, and bulimia). Representative samples include: "I think my hips are too big" (body dissatisfaction), "I exaggerate or magnify the importance of weight" (drive for thinness), "I feel that I must do things perfectly or not do them at all" (perfectionism), "I feel generally in control of things in my life" (ineffectiveness), and "I have gone on eating binges where I felt that I could not stop" (bulimia). For the male respondents in the sample, a 14-item scale was constructed to measure their endorsement of personal thinness and dieting for women. Finally, a six-item scale was used to measure female respondents' endorsement of thinness for women.

Because the study involved multiple predictor and criterion variables, a multivariate multiple-regression analysis was first performed on all variables. Disordered eating, body dissatisfaction, drive for thinness, perfectionism, ineffectiveness, anorexia, and bulimia were entered as dependent variables. Overall television viewing, overall magazine reading, and other media variables were entered as predictor variables. All the statistical tests showed that the set of media consumption variables significantly predicted the following criterion variables: overall disordered eating ($R^2 = .12$, $F = 3.79$, $p < .001$), anorexia ($R^2 = .13$, $F = 4.18$, $p < .001$), bulimia ($R^2 = .07$, $F = 2.07$, $p < .05$), body dissatisfaction ($R^2 = .07$, $F = 1.92$, $p < .05$), and drive for thinness ($R^2 = .07$,

$F = 1.92, p < .05$). The findings supported the hypothesis that certain media, and especially thinness-promoting media, significantly predicted women's eating disorder symptomatology and men's attitudes in favor of personal thinness and dieting. These findings were more consistent for overall magazine reading than for overall television viewing. However, both types of these media, fitness and fashion magazines and "thin" TV shows, were generally consistent predictors of the dependent variables for both men and women. Multiple regression analyses revealed that both anorexic and bulimic behaviors were significantly predicted by overall magazine reading, even after interest in dieting and fitness as magazine topics had been partialled out of the regression equations. The effect magnitudes found in this study were relatively small (as expected, given that eating disorders are believed to result from multiple sources including familial, psychological, biological, and sociocultural factors, only one of which was examined in this study). Nevertheless, the effects found in this study are impressive because they demonstrate the contribution of television and magazines to disordered eating.

In another study, Harrison (1997) examined the link between women's attraction to female media personalities and eating disorders. The analysis revealed that attraction to thin media personalities was related to eating disorder symptomatology and its related psychological and behavioral states.

Finally, Heinberg and Thompson (1995) conducted a laboratory experiment on the impact of television commercials on body images regarding thinness and attractiveness. One hundred and thirty-nine women viewed television commercials that contained either appearance-related commercials (demonstrating societally endorsed images of thinness and attractiveness) or non-appearance-related advertisements. Pre-post measures of depression, anger, anxiety, and body dissatisfaction were examined. Participants were blocked by a median split on dispositional levels of body image disturbance and sociocultural attitudes regarding appearance. Individuals high on these measures became significantly more depressed following exposure to the appearance videotape and significantly less depressed following a viewing of the non-appearance advertisements. In addition, individuals high on the level of sociocultural awareness became more angry, and participants high on body image disturbance became more dissatisfied with their appearance following exposure to commercials illustrating thinness/attractiveness. Participants who scored below the median on dispositional levels of disturbance either improved or showed no change on dependent measures in both video conditions. These findings suggest that media-presented images of thinness and attractiveness may negatively affect mood and body satisfaction, especially for certain individuals.

Mediated Realities of Sex and Sexuality

Sex, sexual behavior, and sexuality are important elements in most media contents. Signorielli (1993c) argues,

> The media, because of their nonthreatening, story-telling style, have become an important source of sexual information for children and adolescents. The media, however, have their own agenda, the most important of which is to attract and maintain an audience. Consequently, media images are created not to inform but to attract; sexuality thus is one of the ways in which the media attract and hold their audience. (p. 51)

Sexuality is presented on television, in the movies, in magazines, in commercials, and in magazine advertisements.

Sexual content on television has risen steadily in most of the world. Signorielli (1987) found that, since the late seventies, the amount of sex on prime-time dramatic programs has remained at consistently high levels, occurring in 9 out of 10 programs. Although most programs do have some sexual references, most of the sex on television is incidental to the story line (sex was incidental to the plot in 60% of these programs, and sex was a major or significant plot feature in 35% of the programs). Not surprisingly, most sex that was a significant or major plot focus was found in general dramatic programs; nevertheless, almost a third of all situation comedies and almost a third of the action-adventure programs had sexual references that were a significant or major aspect of the story. Lowry and Towles (1989a) examined references to sex (explicit behaviors including erotic touching and heterosexual intercourse, aggressive sexual contact, prostitution, homosexuality, unnatural sexual behaviors,

contraception, sexually transmitted diseases, AIDS, and verbal sugges-
tiveness) in a week of prime-time network dramatic programming. This
study found an increase in the rates of sexual behaviors over those
reported in studies examining samples of programming broadcast in the
mid to late 1970s. Sapolsky and Tabarlet (1991) compared a week of
prime-time network programming in 1989 to a similar sample from
1979. They found that the amount of sex on prime time had increased:
Sexual language or behavior occurred once every 5 minutes of programming in 1979, compared with once every 4 minutes in 1989. Most of
the sexual portrayals, as in the previously discussed studies, took place
in situation comedies and consisted of innuendos, double entendres, or
jokes about doing "it." More programs containing implied or explicit
references to heterosexual intercourse were found in 1989. Again, little
attention was paid to the possible consequences of sexual behavior or
to prostitution, rape, and homosexuality.

Sex on prime time is related to genre. The evening serial dramas
were considerably more sexually explicit than other types of dramatic
programming. Sitcoms treat sex with humor; such programs are rife
with sexual taboos, innuendo, and ironic humor. The nighttime soap
operas, on the other hand, treat sex in an ultraserious fashion, and sex
is often linked with power. Characters are often involved with numerous
romantic partners, leaving a convoluted and interconnected sexual past.
Action-adventure and detective shows have their own sexuality, often
focusing on sex as related to criminal investigations and the sexual
underworld. As Signorielli (1993c) concludes,

> Overall the image of sex in prime-time programming is troublesome
> and has been getting more risqué. Most importantly, the networks
> continue to present sex in a titillating manner but fail to acknowledge
> the serious ramifications of sexual behavior. AIDS, sexually transmit-
> ted diseases, and teen pregnancy are very real threats for today's
> society. Polls over the past 20 to 30 years show that there has been an
> increase in the approval of premarital sex (including cohabitation),
> birth control, and sex education, yet little change (with perhaps some
> conservative movement) in attitudes toward homosexuality, pornog-
> raphy, and extramarital sex. . . . Prime-time television, however, has
> not helped our young people by providing the information in terms
> of imagery and characterizations (role models) they need to develop
> the attitudes that will help them to protect themselves against un-
> wanted pregnancy and/or sexually transmitted diseases. (p. 56)

The serial dramas have traditionally relied on sex and sexual liaisons as an important feature of their continuing stories. Sex on the soaps is often impersonal, exploitative, and emotionless. Numerous studies reveal that sexual relationships are most likely to occur between partners who are not likely to be married to each other and that sexual acts and references occur quite frequently (see, e.g., Greenberg, Abelman, & Neuendorf, 1981; Greenberg, Richards, & Henderson, 1980; Lowry, Love, & Kirby, 1981; Lowry & Towles, 1989b). Comparing samples over the years revealed that the level of sexual behavior grew steadily. Most important, the world of the soap opera, like that of prime-time programming, does not adequately deal with the negative aspects of sexual behavior: unwanted pregnancy, sexually transmitted diseases, and AIDS. Sex continues to be the norm for unmarried partners, with little thought given to the consequences.

Movies are another carrier of sexual contents and a potential source of information affecting the sexual socialization of teenagers. Moreover, with many households now having VCRs, this source of sexual images is even more likely to be available to youngsters. The sexual element is one of the most frequent features of today's movies, and it is getting more and more difficult to find movies without sexual content. Greenberg and his partners (1986, 1987) found in a survey of adolescents in three Michigan cities that more than half of the 15- and 16-year-old respondents had seen either in a movie theater or on video half of the most popular R-rated movies distributed between 1982 and 1984. The content analysis of these movies revealed that sexual acts and references occurred at a rate seven times higher than prime-time commercial programming. Characters in the movies were more likely to respond positively to sex, and there were more visual depictions of sexual acts.

As Signorielli's review reveals, in the popular press, sexual matters have undergone considerable change in recent decades. Newspapers' treatment of sex has become more frank and frequent, yet, coverage tends to focus on sensational or sensitive sexual issues (e.g., homosexuality, rape, child molesting, infidelity, and impotence). The consequence of this type of coverage is that sexual deviance, rather than sexual normalcy, becomes the focus of attention. Studies of women's mass-circulation magazines reveal a change from a focus on romantic to sexual issues (e.g., Baily, 1969; Herold & Foster, 1975). Another revealing change was the shift from articles examining sexual morality to those talking about sexual quality and espousing more liberal views about sex (e.g., premarital and extramarital sex).

Among the most sex-laden media channels are the music videos. We have devoted an entire chapter to this domain (see Chapter 8). Sex, sexuality, and sexually explicit images are included in the majority of music videos. Sherman and Dominick's (1986) analysis of a sample of music videos broadcast over a 7-week period in 1984 found that sexual intimacy, much of it adolescent and titillating, appeared in three quarters of the videos, a rate of almost five acts per video. Sex in the videos was seldom overt and usually involved casual flirtations and nonintimate touching. The sexual motive in these videos is also found in the music and the lyrics: Three quarters of the popular songs of the 1960s had lyrics dealing with sex and love. Brown and Campbell (1986) found that half of the sample of videos were songs about sex, love, courtship, sexual relationships, or breaking up. Similarly, love and sex appeared in half of the videos in six randomly taped hours of MTV programming telecast (Greeson & Williams, 1986).

Overall, sexual messages and images are frequent and important features of all media contents. Later, we will examine sexuality in pornography, but at this stage, we may conclude that even the conventional media are heavily laden with sex and sexuality. What do these messages and images create? Do they cultivate expectations and perceptions regarding sex?

The Cultivation of Sexual Perceptions and Expectations

Today's youth are growing up in an electronic environment that barrages them with a constant flow of sexual symbols, images, and messages. Concerned parents, educators, and researchers have questioned the potential effects of such mediated sexual contents. We may hypothesize that the enormous and often distorted presentations of sex and sexuality in the mass media may breed popular images of sex among the audiences, cultivating unrealistic expectations about sex. Just what do we learn from the media about sexuality? Although research in this area is sparse, there are a few studies that begin to shed some light on this issue. Thus, for example, the media play an important role in imparting information about sex, particularly for teenagers. In fact, most studies have found that youth are woefully misinformed about sex and depend heavily on the media for such information and guidance. Studies of youth's perceived sources of sexual information found that peer groups and the mass media always rated first sources. Furthermore, some recent studies suggest that media usage has increased in importance as a source of sexual information. As one report concluded,

> American teenagers seem to have inherited the worst of all possible worlds regarding their exposure to messages about sex: Movies, music, radio and TV tell them that sex is romantic, exciting, titillating; premarital sex and cohabitation are visible ways of life among adults they see and hear about. . . . Yet, at the same time, young people get the message good girls should say no. Almost nothing that they see or hear about sex informs them about contraception or the importance of avoiding pregnancy. For example, they are more likely to hear about abortions than about contraception on the daily TV soap opera. Such messages lead to an ambivalence about sex that stifles communication and exposes young people to increased risk of pregnancy, out-of-wedlock births and abortions. (Jones, 1985, p. 61)

Fabes and Strouse (1984, 1987) found that college students tend to select media figures as models of both responsible and irresponsible sexual behavior. In particular, those students who select media figures as models of responsible sexual behavior were more likely to have permissive attitudes about sex and more likely to be sexually active. Brown and Newcomer (1991) report that teens believe that television is more supportive or encouraging than best friends about having sex. Moreover, television, movies, and video clips, with their presentations of handsome, "sexy" men and women, provide important messages about beauty and attractiveness, which, in turn, are related to messages about sex appeal. Such images may affect perceptions of the importance of physical appearance. For example, Tan (1979) conducted a laboratory experiment to test the effects of exposure to beauty commercials. The results revealed that high school girls exposed to beauty commercials saw beauty as significantly more important "to be popular with men" than those girls who saw neutral commercials. Those girls exposed to beauty commercials also rated beauty as personally more important than those who saw neutral commercials. Other studies have examined the relationship between mediated "beauty" and perceptions of beauty. Kendrick and Gutierres (1980), using a sample of college men, found that subjects who saw an episode of *Charlie's Angels* (an action-adventure program about three beautiful women) rated pictures of women who were possible dates less positively than the men who had not seen this program. Weaver, Masland, and Zillmann (1984) found that male college students described their own girlfriends as less sexually appealing after seeing nude women centerfolds from *Penthouse* and *Playboy*.

Media presentations of sex were found to affect individuals' satisfaction from actual sexual relationships: Baran's (1976a, 1976b) study of high school and undergraduate students revealed a relationship between perceptions of portrayals of sex on television and initial sexual satisfaction. Students who perceived that television characters enjoyed sex and were more proficient reported less satisfaction with their own coital experiences. Moreover, among the sample of college students, Baran found that those who perceived that media portrayals of sex were real and that characters experienced sexual satisfaction reported that they were not satisfied with their current state of virginity. Several studies have examined the relationship between television viewing and initiation of sexual intercourse (e.g., Brown & Newcomer, 1991; Furstenberg, Moore, & Peterson, 1985). They all reported a positive relationship between watching "sexy" television programs and having had sexual intercourse. A number of experiment-based studies have also revealed relationships between viewing of sexually explicit materials and the acceptance of less stringent views about sex. Greeson and Williams (1986) found that after seeing less than an hour of videos on MTV, adolescents in the 7th and 12th grades were more likely to approve of premarital sex than their peers who had not been exposed to the music videos. In addition, in studies of male and female college students, Zillmann and Bryant (1988b) found that exposure to nonviolent sexually explicit films was related to the acceptance of promiscuity and sexual infidelity.

Another study examined the relationship between popular media consumption and sexual attitudes and behavior (Strouse & Buerkel-Rothfuss, 1987). The subjects of this study were 457 American college students. The results indicated that women consume more sexually suggestive media (soap operas and pop music) than men. General media consumption was not a powerful predictor of permissiveness. Regression analyses revealed that MTV was the only medium where consumption was strongly associated with permissiveness for women. The issue of genre viewing (and not of general consumption) was also revealed by another study: Brown and Newcomer (1991) found that adolescents who chose heavier diets of sexy television shows were more likely to have had sexual intercourse than those who viewed a smaller proportion of sexual content on television. This relationship held regardless of perceived peer encouragement to engage in sex and across race and gender groups.

Another studied area was that of perceptions about sexually related matters. Using a sample of college students, Buerkel-Rothfuss and Mayes (1981) found a positive relationship between viewing daytime serial dramas and perceiving greater numbers of men and women who have had affairs, been divorced, and had illegitimate children. There was also a positive relationship between viewing and overestimating the number of women who had abortions. The correlations between viewing and overestimation of these occurrences remained statistically significant when controlling for age, sex, grade point average, class, and self-concept. Similarly, Carveth and Alexander (1985) found that college-age respondents who watched soap operas to be entertained overestimated the prevalence of abortions and affairs (personal problems) in society. As discussed earlier, video music and MTV video clips are rife with sexual messages. Several studies found significant relationships between viewing of music videos and attitudes relating to sex roles and music appeal. One such study found that a brief (17-minute) exposure to heavy-metal rock music compared to an easy-listening condition increased the amount of sex-role stereotyping of male college students (St. Lawrence & Joyner, 1991).

Pornography: Images of Sex and Sexuality

During recent decades, sexually explicit materials (i.e., pornography and erotic material) in the entertainment marketplace has been radically transformed and substantially expanded. The production and distribution of such materials have been characterized, for instance, as rapidly evolving from "a seedy and illicit cottage industry to a stable and well-refined, mass production business employing the latest know-how" and yielding annual worldwide revenues of more than $5 billion (Hebditch & Anning, 1988, p. 32). Much of this income has been derived from the retail videotape marketplace where, almost since the domestication of videotape technology, sexually explicit software has produced lucrative sales and rentals (Weaver, 1991, 1992). Brosius, Weaver, and Staab (1993) produced data on wholesale sales of pornographic material, reaching $400 million, or about 15% of the total prerecorded video cassette sales in the United States, 25% of the total income from videotape sales and rentals in Germany, and an analogous pattern in the United Kingdom, Italy, and other countries. In short, contemporary sexually explicit materials appear to enjoy considerable popularity.

The growing popularity of pornography led to a growing interest in its presentations of sexual relationships and sexuality, as well as the impact on its audiences. It has long been "asserted that a distinguishing characteristic of sexually explicit materials is the degrading and demeaning portrayal of the role and status of the human female" (from the report of the U.S. Commission on Obscenity and Pornography, 1970, p. 239). Many analysts have argued that the social and sexual "reality" conveyed by contemporary pornography consistently and persistently portrays women as sexually and socially subservient to and dominated by men. From their vantage point, these analysts maintain that such materials disparage and demean women by portraying them as "obsessed with sex, and willing to engage in any sexual act with any available partner" (Diamond, 1985, p. 51); that sexually explicit materials require "that women be subordinate to men and mere instruments for the fulfillment of male fantasies . . . that our pleasure consists of pleasing men, and not ourselves" (Longino, 1980, pp. 45-46); and that they consistently depict women as "anonymous, panting play things, adult toys, dehumanized objects to be used, abused, broken and discarded" (Brownmiller, 1975, p. 394).

What are the social roles and contexts projected in modern pornography? Why do characters engage in sexual activities and under what circumstances? To what extent are female and male characters inequitably portrayed? Are there, for example, substantial differences in the nature of their discourse and the posture they assume during sex? Have there been significant shifts in the themes of modern pornography over time?

Several studies examined pornography and sexually explicit images in the media, including films, paperbacks, magazines, and X-rated videocassettes. Smith (1976) examined 4,588 sexual episodes in 428 "adults-only" paperbacks. He found a consistent pattern of male dominance in these sexual episodes. Rape appeared frequently; one in five sexual episodes was a rape (most often of a woman by a man). In addition, the books perpetuated the rape myth (women actually enjoy being raped even though they may initially resist forcible sexual intercourse). Malamuth and Spinner (1980) found that sexual violence increased in *Playboy* and *Penthouse,* while Dietz and Evans (1982) found that images of domination and bondage increased on adult magazine covers between 1970 and 1981. Winick (1985) found that hard-core magazines sold in adults-only bookstores typically presented mutually consenting relationships. Representations of force were very stylized, with men dominating women in more than 7 out of 10 instances of bondage-discipline. The accumulating empirical data show that contemporary pornographic productions typically involve a narrow range of highly stylized content conventions that strongly emphasize a chauvinistically male or macho orientation toward sexual behavior. Most notable among these conventions is a seemingly complete preoccupation with sexual activity to the exclusion of all other facets of human social behavior. Depictions of other basic aspects of human sexuality—such as communication between sexual partners; expressions of affection or emotion (except fear and lust); depictions of foreplay, afterplay, or friendly cuddling; and concern about sanitation or the consequences of sexual activities—are minimized (Cowan, Lee, Levy, & Snyder, 1988; Prince, 1990; Rimmer, 1986). Furthermore, women are normatively portrayed as eagerly soliciting participation in, and responding with hysterical euphoria to, any of a variety of sexual encounters. Coercion and/or violence are depicted as means of initiating sexual activities, and in such circumstances women, as a rule, are portrayed as experiencing sexual arousal and, ultimately, enjoyment because of the assault. Even less frequent are productions that portray sexual behavior within the context of a loving, affectionate relationship.

Palys (1986) examined the amount of aggression, sex, and sex combined with aggression in a sample of XXX-rated and adult-rated videocassettes in Vancouver, Canada. This analysis revealed more male domination in the adult videos than those rated XXX. The adult videos also had more time devoted to and more graphic depictions of aggression than the XXX videos. Moreover, women were more likely to be victims or targets of sexual violence in the adult-rated videos than in the XXX-rated videos. Brosius et al. (1993) studied the "social and sexual realities" in pornographic videos, looking at a sample drawn from a period of 10 years to allow for changes over time. Their analysis revealed that contemporary pornography typically portrays a "reality" in which men and women assume inequitable social and sexual roles. In the pornographic reality, for example, women were shown as more sexually active with a greater variety of partners than were men. A strong age bias (i.e., only young women) was apparent for female but not for male characters. Essentially all sexual scenes involved at least one woman with almost a quarter of the scenes portraying female characters only. Women were far more expressive than men during sexual interactions, with most dialogues consisting of oral and nonverbal expressions of delight and pleasure. In scenes involving heterosexual couples, women typically initiated sexual interactions through penile fondling or fellatio. Furthermore, fellatio was usually performed with the female in a subordinate posture (i.e., kneeling before rather than over her partner). The experience of orgasm was clearly the domain of the male and typically involved extravaginal ejaculation onto the body, face, or mouth of the female. In other words, although always the focus of attention, women were, as a group, portrayed as promiscuous sexual creatures who were subordinate and subservient to men.

The pornographic reality also frequently depicted sexual behavior, in general, and female sexuality, in particular, as very unreal: For example, more than half of all sexual scenes portrayed intercourse between total strangers or casual acquaintances. Sex between committed partners (e.g., a married couple) was infrequently presented. Even more alarming are the findings concerning changes over time: The study revealed significant increases in the frequency of portrayals of sex between casual acquaintances, women persuading men to engage in sexual activities, and sex among strangers, with decreases in cases of sex among committed partners. As the researchers concluded, their findings show that a chauvinistic, macho orientation toward sex is the most prevalent component of the reality presented in pornographic fare. Modern pornography does not, as a rule, simply present adults engaged in affectionate, egalitarian sexual behavior in which mutual satisfaction is paramount. Instead, the findings illustrate that pornography spotlights the sexual desires and prowess of men, and, to this end, it consistently and persistently portrays women as sexually willing and available.

Virtual Sex: Pornography "Sites"

A new medium for pornography is the Internet (see also Chapter 12). The electronic information superhighway can be used for accessing pornography. The absence of control, censorship, limits, or grading made this new medium an ideal site for pornography. Indeed, several analyses reveal that the most frequently visited websites are those with pornographic and erotic material. The Internet contains thousands of pornography sites, mainly hard pornography, without any limit on accessing the material shown. A study of news groups on the Internet revealed that "pornography is readily available in a large quantity to any determined user" (Mehta & Plaza, 1997, p. 62). A simple search by one of the Internet's search engines reveals the number of such sites, identified mainly by titles, such as cunts, tits, clit, sex, fuck, breasts, teens, ass, anal, cum, blowjob, gangbang, fetish, lesbian, sluts, pussy, whore, hardcore, cock, dick, suck, XXX, and others. For example, the Alta Vista search engine provided a list of hundreds of thousands (!) of pornography sites: There were, according to the search results

- 112,070 websites that included *pussy* in their title
- 63,550 sites with *cunt*
- 42,480 sites with *clit*
- 73,270 sites with *tits*
- 58,290 sites with *breasts*
- 29,990 sites with *nipples*
- 197,190 sites with *cum*
- 120,840 sites with *anal*
- 41,410 sites with *blowjob*
- 102,570 sites with *fuck*
- 137,240 sites with *porn*
- 348,980 sites with *xxx*

- 9,130 sites with *bestiality*
- 42,480 sites with *sluts*
- 26,160 sites with *whores*

A short "voyage" through a random sample of these numerous sites reveals very intriguing patterns: Most of these sites are male-oriented (few are homosexual-lesbian sites), and the references to women (usually called sluts, babes, cunts, clits, whores, and teens) are degrading, humiliating, and dehumanizing. The pictures, the video clips, the movies offered and shown, are promoted with such descriptions as: "fist fucking," "cunt stretching," "teens getting fucked by animals," "ass busting," "teen nipple torture," "teen gang bang," "they take it in their tight little holes," "cum-sucking teens," "horny pregnant teens," "wild animal sex," "12 guys fucking one teen," "young cuties eating huge cocks," "open her teen ass wide," "kinky teens take anything," and more. Women are shown as enjoying rape, torture, and beating, exposing their most intimate parts to the camera, posing in positions desired by men, enjoying sex with animals, instruments, and parties of men, and often being sodomized. Very frequently, the female models are described as teens, schoolgirls, or cheerleaders, a clear reference to their youth. The pedophilic elements are presented both in text ("virgins," "tight vaginas," "barely legal sex," "first fuck," "open her up") and in the pictures (young girls partly dressed in school uniforms, naked girls, shaved pubic hair, etc.). There is no doubt that the women on these sites are always ready, eager to satisfy the men, willing to do anything, enjoying everything, and lacking any moral standards or limits (thus referred to as "cum-thirsty sluts," "hungry teens," "submissive Asian girls," "they wait for you").

Although various attempts have been made to block access to these sites, there is actually no efficient method. Ironically, I am writing this chapter while in Singapore, where all pornography (magazines, movies, videos) is strictly forbidden by law. The Singaporean authorities try to prevent Internet users from accessing the porno sites: The law requires each Internet access provider in Singapore to block access, and they try to do so by installing in their servers a "black list" of keywords (sex, porno, fuck, etc.) that denies access to sites using these terms. And yet, any user can bypass these measures and access thousands of sites.

Protective measures include the following statement, copied from one of the porno sites:

You must be 18 years of age (21 in some areas) or older to visit this online adult site. This site contains adult material not suitable for minors. Viewing this site if you are under age is prohibited by federal, state, and local laws and is subject to prosecution by the applicable authorities. By clicking below you agree to being familiar with the laws of your community, being 18 (21 in some areas) or older and that the viewing of adult material is legal in your area. Furthermore you agree that you do not find this type of material offensive and you release and discharge all involved in the production and maintenance of this site from any and all liabilities.

Needless to say, any user can "accept" these terms by clicking on the *agree,* regardless of his or her age.

The Effects of Pornography

Questions about the potentially harmful effects of pornography have been asked for a long time (for a review, see Buss & Malamuth, 1996; Donnerstein, Linz, & Penrod, 1987; Linz & Malamuth, 1993; McNair, 1996). In 1970, the U.S. Commission on Obscenity and Pornography concluded that the available evidence was not sufficient to support the contention that exposure to explicit sexual materials causes increased physical or sexual aggression toward women or delinquent or criminal behavior. In the mid-1980s, the question of the potential effects of pornography again emerged and was examined by two simultaneously appointed commissions: the U.S. Attorney General's Commission on Pornography (appointed by Attorney General Meese) and the Workshop on Pornography and Public Health (organized by Surgeon General C. Everett Koop). Each of these commissions, however, came up with very different interpretations of the same body of literature. The surgeon general's workshop acknowledged a relationship between pornography and sexual aggression; the attorney general's commission, on the other hand, concluded that there was a causal relationship between exposure to sexually violent pornography and sexually violent behavior.

One should note the political dimension of the research in this area. Social scientists select and address issues for a variety of rather personal reasons. In this area, as in many other research fields, the resulting body of knowledge is not necessarily "clean" from ideology, values, interests, and personal views and thus cannot be considered an optimal basis for policy decisions (on this aspect of pornography research, see Zillmann, 1989). Linsley (1989), for example, presents the two camps: On the law and order side are

> the self-righteous, the indignant, and the outraged who sincerely believe that today's flood of pornography assuredly will portend the downfall of western civilization . . . [whereas] the opposite camp, made up of free expressionists who are paradoxically intolerant of intolerance, contends that the identification and preservation of safe societal norms is assured best by unrestrained discussion and debate. (p. 343)

Most of the studies to date have concentrated primarily on the relationship between pornography and aggression/sexual aggression, focusing on pornography as an agent of change in laboratory studies using a basic stimulus-response model of human behavior. Such research, noted Hall-Preston (1990), ignores feminist contentions that although isolated incidents of sexual aggression directed against women may be triggered by exposure to pornography, such incidents are dramatic symptoms in a culture that structurally and ideologically creates and re-creates the context in which such events occur. Preston argued that from a feminist perspective, laboratory research focusing on the relationship between pornography and male sexual aggression is ethically questionable, epistemologically unsound, and theoretically misguided; it ignores the subtle yet potentially far more powerful ways in which pornography may function to maintain the sex-based inequalities of a patriarchal culture. As Zillmann and Bryant (1984) noted,

> Sexual reality tends to fall short of such magic. Men, inspired by pornography, may well feel cheated and accuse perfectly sensitive women of frigidity. Lacking corrective information, women might actually come to doubt their own sexual sensitivities. Regarding untried activities, pornography again projects euphoria where it might not exist—at least, not for many. That pornography thus entices

actions, and that the resultant experimentation leads to less than satisfactory results, can hardly be doubted. (p. 12)

Indeed, several scholars argued that the impact of pornography extends far beyond the simple and isolated behavioral and attitudinal changes evoked in laboratory studies.[1] One of the suggested directions was that of cultivation analysis: "Merged with feminist analyses of pornography and the social construction of gender and sexuality, the cultivation model provides a concise and attractive framework for researching the impact of pornography" (Hall-Preston, 1990, p. 108). The cultivation framework provides an alternative way of thinking about the effects of pornography, looking at social construction and the symbolic reality of pornography and their cumulative impact. Thus, cultivation analysis of pornography is based on the premise that pornography is an agent of enculturation, one of many social institutions contributing to our perceptions of social reality. Because the content of pornography is primarily concerned with the representation of women, sexuality, and sexual behavior, it is assumed that it is in those interrelated areas that pornography contributes most heavily in shaping the boundaries of social reality. It is likewise assumed that pornography re-creates a specifically patriarchal pattern of images of women and sexuality. Individuals who are more heavily exposed to pornography may be expected to share a perception of social reality that reflects the patriarchal lessons of pornography more intensely than others who are similar in demographic terms but have had less exposure to pornography. These were the basic assumptions of a cultivation analysis of pornography, conducted by Hall-Preston: High exposure to pornography is associated with strong sex-role and sex-trait stereotyping; it is also associated with strong stereotyping about male and female sexuality; and, ultimately, exposure to pornography is associated with an increased acceptance of myths about rape.

Hall-Preston's study used several samples of undergraduate students and a questionnaire containing a series of items designed to be combined into additive indices: (a) sex-role stereotypes, (b) sex traits, (c) sexuality stereotypes, and (d) rape myths. The first measure, sex-role stereotyping, asked if respondents would have more confidence in a man or a woman holding each of eight specific positions. The simple correlations clearly reveal a strong positive relationship between exposure to pornography and scores on the sex-role stereotyping index for men; the relationship holds across all demographic subgroups, as well as under simultaneous controls. Simultaneously controlling for age, income, grade point average, self-designated political orientation, and religious convictions as well as current involvement in and satisfaction with current sexual relations yields a correlation of .24 ($p < .001$). Among women, however, there is no apparent relation between exposure to pornography and sex-role stereotyping. This is perhaps not surprising, given women's overall low score on the sex-role stereotyping index and their lower degree of exposure to pornography. It may be that the greater sex typing among men predisposes them to the implicit messages of pornography.

Finally, the last measure examined the stereotyping of sexuality. This was measured by agreement with the statement, "In general, men have stronger sex drives than women" and the respondent's sense of whether men and women (or both, or neither) "are more likely to say 'no' to sex when they don't really mean it," "are more concerned with their partner's satisfaction than their own," and more. As the analysis reveals, men who are exposed to pornography express more agreement with sexuality stereotypes (strong and significant correlations that are not affected by any control variable). No such relationship is found for women. For the last measure, acceptance of the rape myth, Hall-Preston found no correlation, either for men or women.

These findings indicate a relationship, but not a causality, between exposure to pornography and sex-based stereotypes for men only (one should note that pornography is a male-oriented production, and almost all of its consumers are men). Several studies went beyond this association and attempted to find causality. Examples are studies that examined the relationship between exposure to pornography, especially violent pornography, and attitudes about rape and women. In a number of controlled laboratory studies, Zillmann and Bryant (1982, 1984, 1988a, 1988b, 1989) have examined exposure to pornography in relation to a number of different issues. In one study, college students, both men and women, who had been exposed to massive doses of pornography perceived that particular sexual practices, including unusual sexual practices, occurred more frequently (and grossly overestimated the frequency of such patterns) than those students who had viewed less pornography. Using a paradigm of showing subjects weekly films and testing them 1 to 3 weeks later, Zillmann and Bryant (1982, 1984, 1988a, 1988b, 1989) found that subjects seeing the films overestimated the popularity of sexual practices such as fellatio, cunnilingus, anal intercourse, sadomasochism, and bestiality, relative to perceptions of a control group seeing non-sexually explicit films. The students in this condition also overestimated the number of people who were sexually active and considered pornography less offensive. These studies also revealed that exposure to pornography was related to the trivialization of rape: Those students who had been exposed to the most pornography were more likely to recommend minimal sentences for those found guilty of committing rape. The women, however, treated rape as a more serious offense and indicated more strict sentencing for someone convicted of rape.

Other studies have shown pornography's effects on attitudes and values about sex: After seeing slides and movies of beautiful female nudes engaged in sexual activity, male subjects rated their own partners as being less physically attractive, although they reported undiminished sexual satisfaction (Weaver et al., 1984). In another study, men reported loving their own mates less after seeing sexually explicit videos of highly attractive models (Kendrick & Gutierres, 1980). All of these studies show significant attitude changes after a very limited exposure to sexual media. Zillmann and Bryant found that subjects seeing the explicit films, relative to a control group, reported less satisfaction with the affection, physical appearance, sexual curiosity, and sexual performance of their real-life partners. They also saw sex without emotional involvement as being relatively more important than the control group did. They showed greater acceptance of premarital and extramarital sex and lower evaluations of marriage and monogamy. They also showed less desire to have children and greater acceptance of male dominance and female submission. Results generally did not differ for men versus women or students versus nonstudents.

Studies testing the effects of short-term exposure to sexual materials usually expose subjects to the stimulus materials for less than 1 hour. In one of the earliest of these studies, the researchers exposed male and female subjects to neutral materials or to issues of *Penthouse* and *Playboy* that contained nonaggressive and aggressive (sadomasochism and rape) portrayals (Malamuth, Reisin, & Spinner, 1979). Two weeks later, subjects in both sexual conditions were less likely than the subjects in the neutral condition to perceive that pornography was a cause of rape. In a similar experimental design, the researchers compared groups exposed to nonviolent sexually explicit material, sexual violence, and neutral presentations (Intons-Peterson & Reskos-Ewoldsen, 1989). Those subjects in the sexual violence group (slasher films) were more likely to accept rape myths than subjects in the other two conditions. The frequent combination of violence and sex in pornography was found to be rather toxic for the viewers: Linz (1989) found that subjects in both the violent nonpornographic film condition and the violent pornographic film condition had higher scores on the Rape Myth Acceptance Scale. Subjects in these conditions also indicated they would be willing to use force to have sex with a woman or that they would commit a rape if they were assured they would not be caught or punished. Similar results were found in another study: In this case, the subjects were more likely to say that women enjoy rape and/or forced sex when they were exposed to a stimulus in which a nonconsenting woman became sexually aroused than when they saw a film in which a consenting woman was sexually aroused (Malamuth & Check, 1985).

We may conclude that pornography, and especially violent pornography, may have a strong impact on its consumers. Although the evidence on direct behavioral impact is less consistent, there is convincing evidence of strong cognitive effects. Men exposed to such material were very likely to accept and use sexist images, justify violence against women, accept the rape myth, criticize their partner, be less satisfied with their own sexual relationships, and perceive that particular sexual practices, including unusual sexual practices, occurred more frequently. Pornography, especially for heavy users, cultivates distorted and rather mean perceptions of sex, sexuality, and women's place in a sexual relationship. With the growing availability of pornography on the Internet and its easy accessibility for youth—the effects might be even more alarming.

NOTE

1. On the debate about the generalizability of laboratory experiments in this area to real-world behavior, see Donnerstein et al. (1987, pp. 1-22).

CHAPTER SEVEN

Death and Suicide

*Our own death is indeed unimaginable, and whenever we
make the attempt to imagine it, we can perceive that we
really survive as spectators.*

—Sigmund Freud (1915/1963, p. 122)

Dying and death are important aspects of human life, human culture,
and religion. We are all concerned with our own mortality, with our
loved ones passing away, with forms of dying, and with what may
happen after death. Death comes to everyone, and all human societies
have developed social arrangements for managing its impact on the
living. Early in the 1960s, social scientists became increasingly interested in studying the process of death and dying in contemporary
society. The study of attitudes toward death has made that topic one of
the most productive sources of theoretical and applied insight into
human behavior. The basic problem that humans have in dealing with
death is fear. Several studies on attitudes toward death have pointed out
that death has been and remains a fearful event for most human beings
and that fear of death is universal throughout the human species. Many
studies in psychology and psychiatry have documented the fact that this
strong fear motivates many people to seek secure environments and to
avoid activities and situations that could result in premature death.

Sigmund Freud, for example, believed that fear of death was a primary motivation for social cohesion, as people sought security and strength from group membership. Several types of fears have been identified in connection with death, but the primary fear is fear of the unknown, the dread of not knowing what happens when you die and after you are dead.

Some sociologists explored the notion of "death is a forbidden social issue," or in Mellor's (1993) phrase, death is publicly absent but privately present. A similar claim was made by the historian Philippe Aries (1974, 1981). He argued that death is "forbidden" in modern society because of the high value placed by Western culture on happiness, life, love, and joy. Later, Aries spoke of death more as "invisible" or "hidden," particularly from public view. However, Aries did not consider the mass media, as noted in the criticism published by Walter, Littlewood, and Pickering (1995), who studied death in British news stories. As they concluded, death is not that invisible if one considers its frequent appearances in both news media and entertainment media. Thus, death is a key element in many media genres and narratives, challenging the public absence of death thesis. Moreover, Gorer's (1965) much-cited notion of the "pornography of death" adds additional importance to media's presentations of death. Gorer argued that when something as central to human life as sex or death becomes taboo, it is not likely to disappear but to re-appear in a pornographic way. This, he argued, is what happened to death in modern societies: "While natural death became more and more smothered in prudery, violent death has played an ever-growing part in the fantasies offered to mass audiences—detective stories, thrillers, Westerns, war stories, spy stories, science fiction, and eventually horror comics" (p. 173).

The mass media is but one source of images about death and dying, but as we will explore in this chapter, they present reconstructed and selective images of death. Although violence abounds on television (see Chapter 5), death and dying, particularly death from natural causes, do not. Death caused by suicide or murder prevails. On American TV, on prime-time network dramatic programming, about 1 in 10 major characters is involved in killing or being killed. Death from natural causes almost never occurs in television's world (Signorielli, 1993a). In soap operas, where death is very frequent, people rarely died of a disease that might plague a member of the audience. Rather, death typically comes as a result of improbable accidents (Soares, 1978). Despite the statistical reality that most humans die from natural causes, most deaths on soap operas are due to accidents or violence; far fewer characters die as a result of disease (Cassata, Skill, & Boadu, 1983). In the press, despite its more true-to-reality nature, similar distortion in presenting causes of death were found. In a content analysis of two regional newspapers, Combs and Slovic (1979) found that disease was very underreported, whereas catastrophic events (fires, tornadoes, drownings, homicides, and all accidents) were overreported. The researchers suggested that accidents and homicides are overreported because such events represent types of societal vulnerability as well as newsworthiness. Diseases, on the other hand, are not given extensive newspaper coverage except in the cases when they threaten to become epidemics (e.g., Legionnaires' disease, AIDS) and consequently may result in societal vulnerability.

There are a number of approaches researchers use to explore death's depiction in mass media. Kearl (1989) suggested four: First, they can speculate on the cultural context stimulating the presentation of death and dying. Media contents are a product of their times and perhaps are more sensitive than most to shifts in cultural concerns or the unfolding of social events. Second, researchers can analyze the patterns of death themes developed within various media, specifically content-analyzing longitudinal patterns of who dies, how they die, where, and when, as well as the centrality of death to the entire presentation. Third, the death orientations can be studied, examining how the producer's (author/ performer/artist/actor) biographical experiences, age, preoccupations, and immortality urges motivated the direction of his or her artistic expression. And finally, researchers can gauge how an audience is affected by the death messages presented.

The first direction relates cultural and political environments to media presentations of death. Thus, for example, fears of ecological destruction following the first detonation of hydrogen bombs, leading to the 1950s genre of science fiction movies that featured mutated creatures preying on the remnants of the human race. The moral upheavals in the United States following the Vietnam War, Watergate, and the changing lifestyles and values of Western societies contributed to the public fascination with evil, producing a receptive climate for such demonic movies as *The Exorcist* and *The Omen*. Kearl (1989) argues that the increasing cultural violence and homicide rates during the late 1970s and early 1980s stimulated a genre of revenge movies, such as the *Dirty Harry* and Charles Bronson series, just as the militarism of World War II produced an abundance of war valor movies. Various media contents reflect, reinforce, and shape the death fears that exist within a culture at any given time.

Another approach examines media presentations of death, in an attempt to categorize their themes. Thus, one can analyze a song, a novel, a television show, or a movie, using various scales: death as incidental or central theme, death as tragedy or comedy, the degree of death's realism versus abstractness, and whether death serves a didactic or cathartic function for the audience. Let us examine some of the media's portrayals of death and dying, their motives and background.

Death in Cinema

Gorer (1965) suggested the term *pornographic death,* referring to the public's appetite for violence and perverse forms of death. The motif is pornographic as it involves modern culture's prudery toward and denial of natural death. As sex becomes pornographic when divorced from its natural human emotion, which is affection, so death becomes pornographic when abstracted from its natural human emotion, which is grief. Perhaps nowhere is this more evident than in the cinematic medium, wherein, over time, such deaths have become increasingly vivid. According to Kearl (1989), there are a number of ways to approach the evolution of pornographic death in cinema:

> In part, it is a function of the medium itself, which focuses on observable action and not on the subjective perspectives of individuals, one of the hallmarks of literature. The medium, depicted as larger than life and ready for public viewing, must be attention-getting to hold the interest of large numbers of people, and it is death, not grief, that commands attention. (p. 387)

To continue holding interest, producers must constantly outdo themselves, whether by producing increasingly absorbing plots (seasoned with shock or surprise), showing increasing amounts of action sequences with increasingly spectacular special effects, or featuring more death scenes.

One of the cinematic death genres was the Western, which used death to differentiate the good from the bad. During the 1930s and 1940s, the heroes—Roy Rogers, Gene Autry, and Red Ryder—avenged the deaths of innocents with more death. There was not much blood in these black-and-white episodes and always time for the outlaw to acknowledge his guilt before expiring. By the late 1960s and early 1970s, however, in the context of the Vietnam War, the bloody protest movements, and the assassinations of John and Robert Kennedy and Martin Luther King, the death-pornographic productions were then the "spaghetti Westerns." Here, the cowboy, now the symbol of true individualism, took it upon himself to execute evil, this time very graphically and with a lot of bloody scenes. The Vietnam War triggered new cinematic explorations of war and death *(The Deer Hunter, Apocalypse Now)*, as did urban violence. Finally, an additional death motif of cinema during the 1970s involved attacks on humanity by natural forces. Why during this era should people be attacked by rats, frogs, bees, sharks, meteors, earthquakes, and tidal waves? Kearl argues that people had grown tired of man-made death and had become desensitized to its terror. Furthermore, as people became fully urbanized, nature became an unknown, its forces of destruction no longer respected when compared to our own potential for evil. In a sense, then, the motif represented a rediscovery of the natural order, bolstered by the culture's growing environmental awareness and new appreciation of ecological interdependencies.

During the 1970s, the "New Wave" of cinema emerged, with its distinctive stylistic and cultural features. In her analysis of death in these New Wave films, *Narrative Mortality,* Russel (1995) relates the presentation of death to social, political, and cultural conditions. Looking at death presentations in numerous films during 25 years of New Wave film making, Russel examines the relationships between mortality and narrative. Not only does she point to the reconstruction of death and dying in these films but also to the factors leading to these formats and presentations. One of her conclusions is that

> the prevalence of violent death in the mass media is thus immediately attributable to the demands of the medium: speed and spectacle,

but also to the melodramatic desire to "see the unseeable" . . . Narrative mortality is the allegory of crisis of historical vision . . . , the loss of social consensus . . . The Analyses of these films should demonstrate the parameters of narrative mortality as a discourse of apocalypse in the Vietnam and Watergate periods of American history. (pp. 175-176)

During the 1980s, cinema returned death to human control in an era marked by international terrorism and increasing militarization. By the mid-1980s, it was military violence that gained immense popularity, epitomized by *Rambo* and its sequels and imitators. In the original, not counting the groups of individuals who were slaughtered in more than 70 explosions, there were 44 specific killings—one every 2.1 minutes. The Russians responded in 1986 with their own *Rambo* in *Odinochnoye Plavaniye*, or *Solo Voyage*, wherein it was Americans who were killed when trying to carry out a scheme to start a third world war. Thus, war and killing in fighting became romanticized, and the message was that it takes violence to resolve complex problems.

With the advent of videocassettes, the ability to view uncensored death in the privacy of one's home further dramatizes Gorer's (1965) notion of pornographic death. As opposed to the obscene, which produces social embarrassment and is enjoyed socially, pornography produces fantasy and is enjoyed privately. In 1985, *Faces of Death* appeared in American video rental outlets. Here, actual death was displayed, with images of suicides, executions, and autopsies. The popularity of this film among teenagers, while teenagers' suicide rate was increasing, prompted public debate and editorial reflection. One movie reviewer said he couldn't tell what was acting and what was real, illustrating the notion of reconstructed reality.

Death on Television

In the world of television, no one ever dies a natural death. Assembly-line drama, television series, and movies generally deny the inevitable reality of death and prefer the more dramatic forms of dying. Violent death befalls 5% of all prime-time dramatic characters every week, with about twice as many killers (many of whom also get killed) stalking the world of prime time. By the age of 16, according to several reports discussed in Chapter 5, the typical American has witnessed some 18,000 homicides on television. One 15-year-old youth, accused of murdering an 83-year-old woman in her Miami Beach home, held the defense that he had become intoxicated with violence from watching violent television. Although the jury was not convinced, the case marked an interesting precedent and further legitimized the belief that we are all possibly subconsciously susceptible to media violence. Television's killings come in various guises, mostly during conflicts between "goods" and "bads," cowboys and Indians, cops and robbers, earthlings and aliens, or the living and the dead. These homicides are packaged either individually, such as when the good guy outdraws and kills the outlaw, or collectively, as when an entire populated planet is destroyed by hostile invaders. Gerbner (1980) claims that TV death "is just another invented characterization, a negative resource, a sign of fatal flaw or ineptitude, a punishment for sins or mark of tragedy" when death lessons are unwittingly "calculated to cultivate a sense of insecurity, anxiety, fear of the 'mean world' out there, and dependence on some strong protector" (p. 66).

So who is most likely to kill, and who is most likely to die? Gerbner's (1980) sample of television programs presents the results in terms of killers/victims on American TV. He found that women and minorities are most likely to be presented as victims. Also evident in the data, the good characters are more likely to be victors than the bad, whites more likely than nonwhites, the young more likely than the old, and the upper class more likely than the lower class. These ratios do not represent the actual reality but may shape people's conceptions (and fears) about killings and being killed, or the perception of "good killings." Thus, for example, the good characters of television are at the top of the killing order: For every 10 good characters killed, there are 38 good characters who are killers! Moreover, those killed have a tendency to reappear on other shows, an important lesson in death denial for the young viewer.

In addition to the action programs, many other TV programs present death as a frequent feature. But most televised death stories are to be found on the evening news. Death is news, and it attracts viewers just as it sells newspapers. The day the space shuttle *Challenger* exploded, the regular network evening newscasts scored a combined rating of 40 in 12 major markets, compared to a 30 rating the preceding week. War death became another frequent news feature: the synchronization of the Vietnam War with the development and dispersal of color television and satellite relays produced a new death experience: live war deaths during the supper hour. Since the mid-1970s, television viewers have witnessed a local newscaster committing suicide during the evening news; Los Angeles police killing members of the Symbionese Liberation Army during a 1975 shootout (carried live and commercial-free on California television stations); and numerous victims of disasters, plane and train crashes, terrorism, sabotage, wars, and executions. In Israel, television cameras carried live the terrible pictures of victims of bus bombings (in Jerusalem and Tel Aviv), including close-up shots of body parts, dead victims, and the corpses of the terrorists.

Special attention was paid by researchers to the popular genre of daytime serials, the familiar soap opera. In an article in *Time* magazine, critic Renata Adler (1976) described her 6-year addiction to *Another World* and the meaning of death in this soap opera:

> When Lee Randolph died, a suicide who had lingered on for weeks, I watched her face being covered by a sheet and I was ridden by the event. But it was not at all like losing a character in fiction of any other kind. I saw the characters in the soaps more often than my friends. . . . It had a continuity stronger even than the news. (p. 46)

Life and death on soap operas are presented in a unique reconstructed way. For example, Downing (1975) found, on the basis of her research, that the field of medicine accounts for 68% of all professionals shown in the serials. Comparing this to the census figure of 2.3% of the population practicing medicine or otherwise being engaged in related health occupations, she reached the obvious conclusion that health care in the serials was vastly overrepresented. A study by Cassata et al. (1983) set out to investigate the role that death, illness, accidents, and violence play in the current daytime television serial world and, where possible, to make comparisons with the real world. They guided a content analysis of 13 popular daytime TV serials, focusing on the occurrence and distribution of health-related conditions. Subjects for the study were the soap opera characters of 13 daytime serial dramas, which occupied 8,314 hours of broadcast time daily and whose summaries appeared in *Soap Opera Digest*. Overall, the study involved 341 characters, 170 of whom were men and 171 of whom were women.

A total of 191 occurrences of health-related conditions for the 341 persons portrayed in the 13 soap operas were recorded. Forty-three (22.5%) of these occurrences ended in the death of the soap opera character. The main reasons were presented as illnesses of a psychiatric nature (25 occurrences, 13.1% of the total). This was followed closely by 21 occurrences (10.9%) of cardiovascular disease and 17 occurrences of symptomatic disorders (9% of the total). Pregnancies accounted for nearly 10% (19 occurrences) of all the health-related disorders in the study. Because soap opera pregnancies generally are unplanned, truly accidental calamities having serious physical and emotional consequences, the majority of which befall either unmarried people or married people not married to each other. Looking at the number of deaths resulting from all the health-related conditions, the analysis revealed that by far the greatest number occurred in the category of accidents and violence; that is, 8.2 of every 10 dying soap opera characters died as a result of accidents or violence of some kind. On the other hand, diseases were rarely the reason for death (only 2.6 of every 100 characters in the soaps world died as a result of a disease).

As Table 7.1 reveals, cases of violent death are the most common: Most soap deaths are related to homicides and accidents. Diseases of all sorts, even when combined, are presented very rarely as causes for death. This distribution does not reflect the real world causes of death. Thus, whereas death, illnesses, accidents, violence, and suicide appear to take up a major part of the story line of the daytime television serials, the soaps' version distorts their nature and form in reality. It is striking that although women have typically been characterized as being superior to men in terms of their capacity to handle stress and keep the families together, and men have been cast in a less prominent role, the study found women to be more vulnerable than men, less mentally stable, more prone to attempt suicide or more successful at it, and more likely to die from cardiovascular disease.

Finally, one should note the importance of death in modern rock videos. We discuss this issue in Chapter 8, The World According to MTV.

TABLE 7.1 The 10 Leading Causes of Death in Soap Operas

Cause of Death	Ratio of Occurrence to Total Occurrences of Causes of Death	Incidence per 100 Persons
Homicides	5.2	2.9
Motor vehicle	4.7	2.6
Cardiovascular disease	2.6	1.5
Suicide	1.6	.88
Pregnancy-related	1.6	.88
Symptomologies	1.5	.58
Neurological disease	.5	.29
Pulmonary disease	.5	.29
Congenital disease	.5	.29
Infectious disease	.5	.29

NOTE: Table based on data from Cassata et al. (1983).

ER for Error: Miracles in Emergency Rooms

One of the most popular shows on television all over the world is *ER,* a Chicago-based drama that depicts the professional and personal lives of physicians, nurses, and medical students working in the emergency department of a public hospital. In its depiction of a busy trauma center, ER presents exciting cases of cardiopulmonary resuscitation (CPR), often performed on young victims of violence. *Chicago Hope,* another hospital series, details the perpetually hectic lives of surgeons, whereas *Rescue 911* focuses on amazing, often miraculous rescues based on true incidents throughout the country. One must consider the fact that most of the decisions on prospective use of CPR and other operations are made jointly by patients and physicians. But the patients' information may rely on many sources, including the physicians, friends, and family and . . . television series like *ER* or *Chicago Hope.* Thus, Schonwetter, Walker, Kramer, and Robinson (1993) found that 92% of patients over 62 years of age reported obtaining information about CPR from television, 82% from newspapers, and 72% from books. In another study, by Schonwetter, Teasdale, Taffet, Robinson, and Luchi (1991), 70% of patients over 74 years of age reported obtaining information about CPR from television. An alarming indication of the impact of relying on television is that patients overestimate their likelihood of survival after CPR, and this might lead them to choose this option in situations in which survival is extremely unlikely (Murphy et al., 1994).

This led Diem, Lantos, and Tulsky (1996) to look at the depiction of CPR in three popular television programs, comparing the media reality with "real world" statistics on CPR. The content analysis was of all the episodes of *ER* and *Chicago Hope* during the 1994-1995 season and 50 episodes of *Rescue 911* during 1995. The analysis found 60 occurrences of CPR, mostly caused by trauma, such as gunshot wounds, car accidents, and near drowning. Only a few were caused by cardiac causes. Most of the cases on TV involved children, teenagers, or young adults. Survival after CPR was very high in these series: 77% on average and 100% on *Rescue 911*. However, the survival rate in these programs was significantly higher than the real rate (40%). Comparisons between TV reality and real reality led the researchers to conclude that these three television programs give misleading information on various aspects of CPR and thus may lead the patients who rely on this "evidence" to make wrong decisions.

First, the distortion starts with the kind of people most commonly given CPR. On television, these are mostly children and very young adults whereas in reality, this problem is much more common in the elderly. Second, cardiac arrest on television was often due to acute injury such as accident or near drowning whereas in reality, 75% to 95% of the cases result from underlying cardiac disease. Third, CPR succeeds more frequently on television than in reality. Finally, on television, the outcome of CPR was portrayed as either full recovery or death. However, in reality, CPR can lead to prolonged suffering, severe neurological damage, and death. Such outcomes were not portrayed on these television series. As Diem and his colleagues (1996) argue, these findings may have an undesirable impact:

> In a subtle way, the misrepresentation of CPR on television shows undermines trust in data and fosters trust in miracles. . . . We acknowledge that this drama produces good television, as evidenced by the large viewing audiences. However, these exceptional cases may encourage the public to disregard the advice of physicians and hope that such a miracle will occur for them as well. Faith is central to our ability to maintain hope in difficult situations and often is important adjunct

to the therapy physicians offer. Belief in miracles, however, can lead to decisions that harm patients. The portrayal of miracles as relatively common events can undermine trust in doctors and data. (p. 1581)

One of the coproducers of *ER,* Dr. Neal Baer, responded to the criticism of Diem and his colleagues (1996). The critical question raised by their study was whether viewers, particularly elderly people, have an unrealistic view of CPR because of what they see on television. Baer (1996) argued that it is difficult to determine exactly how the depiction of CPR on television influences beliefs and attitudes:

> Diem et al. suggest that because of the high rates of survival after CPR on these television shows, patients and their families may have overly optimistic expectations of CPR. This criticism would have some merit if people indeed had unrealistic expectations of CPR after viewing these programs. (p. 1605)

Yet, Baer is certainly ignoring the studies on media and cultivation. These studies show not only that the public relies heavily on the media for impressions of CPR and other medical procedures, but that this leads them to overestimate success rates.

Suicide, the Media, and the "Contagion Effect"

Suicide is frequently reported in the media. The study of mass media and suicide has focused mainly on the impact of suicide stories on subsequent acts of suicide, called "contagion" or "imitation." The leading theme in these studies has been that publicized suicide stories seem to function as "natural advertisements" for suicide and thus constitute one of the factors that may lead a distressed individual to suicide (Phillips, Lesyna, & Paight, 1991; Stack, 1990). This phenomenon was referred to as "the Werther Effect," after Goethe's fictional hero, whose suicide was believed to have triggered many imitative acts. Work on the impact of suicide stories on real suicide has been extensive during the last decade but has yielded inconsistent, confusing, and even contradictory findings. Based on theoretical explanations such as social learning, contagion, imitation, and suggestion, several researchers have tried to explore the Werther effect. Phillips, for example, reported increases in both suicides and equivocal suicides (single-vehicle motor vehicle fatalities) after the airing of a daytime television series that included suicides or the publication of suicide stories (Phillips, 1979, 1980, 1982; Phillips & Carstensen, 1986, 1988; Phillips & Paight, 1987). However, others used Phillips's methodology and in reanalyses invalidated his findings. Gould and Shaffer (1986) found that there were more suicide attempts (and more actual suicides) by teenagers in the greater New York area in the 2 weeks after broadcasts of movies focusing on suicide than in the 2 weeks before the broadcast of these programs. When the studies were extended to other geographic areas, the data revealed differences by geographic location—suicides were found in some areas of the country, but not others. This study has been criticized, however, in that there was no evidence that those teens who committed suicide after the movies were broadcast had actually seen these movies. A replication of this study did not find support for the hypothesis that there would be an increase in teenage suicides in 2 weeks following the broadcast of these programs (Berman, 1988).

Other studies have revealed mixed support for behavioral contagion effects after media suicides. Range, Goggin, and Steed (1988) found some evidence of possible contagion effects when giving a sample of college students information about a potential suicide and asking them to estimate whether or not suicide would occur. A similar study, using a sample of adolescents who viewed one of three versions of a 4-minute vignette about a troubled teen, however, did not find any evidence of suicide contagion (Steed & Range, 1989). Similarly, researchers from NBC found no relationship between viewing suicides and attempted suicides on television (in soap operas or newscasts) and subsequent teenage suicides (Kessler, Downey, Stipp, & Milavsky, 1989; Kessler & Stipp, 1984).

The evidence from European studies has also been inconsistent. Holding (1975) examined the impact of television series that depicted a suicidal person: Evidence on the series' effect on subsequent suicides and deaths of undetermined causes was inconclusive. Another study on British soap opera suicides documented no increase in imitative suicides: Examining the aftermath of an attempted suicide on *EastEnders*, a popular BBC soap opera, found that the total number of hospital-treated attempted suicides in Great Britain did not increase in the week immediately after this broadcast (Platt, 1987). In contrast, a study of the effects of a six-part serial shown on West German television that dealt with a 19-year-old student who threw himself in front of a train found a significant increase in railway suicides by young males following the broadcast (Schmidtke & Hafner, 1988).

The lingering debate on the effects of mass-mediated suicides on imitative suicides has been fueled by these inconsistencies. However, Weimann and Fishman (1995) suggested a possible factor that may account for at least some of the confusion: the way suicide is presented in the media, or, in other words, the reconstruction of suicide in press reports. They claimed that these inconsistencies can be explained by the use of different methods and measures to study the effect, the application of these methods and measures to different populations and subpopulations, the various media contents suggested as triggers (ranging from fictional soap operas to press reports on celebrity suicides), and the varying presentations of suicides in the media.

There is some information about the prevalence of suicide stories in the press or on television. Farberow (1989) noted that there seems to have been a shift in the reporting of suicides. Twenty-five years ago, any mention of suicide in the media was a sensationalized report of the suicide of a celebrity. Suicide was usually seen as a manifestation of mental illness. News reports provided information about the suicide but typically perpetuated the taboos and myths associated with suicide. In the past few years, however, there has been a proliferation of news reports and magazine articles about suicide. These publications (particularly popular magazine articles) frequently focus on teen suicide and provide information on suicide prevention and how to recognize a potentially suicidal person. There have also been increases in the number of television and radio talk shows focusing on teen suicide. Finally, there has been an increase in the number of dramatic programs including suicide as a plot element; such programs have often portrayed teen suicide. For example, Signorielli (1993a) reported that during the prime-time hours in the 1984-1985 television season, half a dozen feature films on teen suicide were broadcast. These shows treated the topic in a sensitive manner, focusing on the factors leading to teen suicide and the impact such actions may have had on family and friends. Suicides also occur more frequently on soap operas. On 13 serial dramas, suicide was the fourth most frequent cause of death (Cassata et al., 1983). Suicide and attempted suicide ranked seventh in terms of health-related events in these programs. Overall, there were 10 attempted suicides and 3 actual suicides—about 1 for every 100 characters (in reality about 1 in 10,000 people commit suicide). Characters between 22 and 45 years old, particularly female characters, were most likely to attempt or commit suicide in the soaps. Suicides were found in 7 of the 13 series examined in this study.

Reconstructing Suicide

The renowned French sociologist, Emile Durkheim, was the first to study suicide as a sociological phenomenon, using the methods of social investigation. He was also the first to suggest that official statistics about suicide were socially constructed. Many years after Durkheim's *Le Suicide,* Weimann and Fishman (1995) chose to focus on the presentation of real suicides in the media. Their study attempted to relate the concept of reconstructed realities to the case of suicide. Specifically, are there any discrepancies between real and mediated suicides, and if so, which dimensions of this phenomenon are being distorted or reconstructed. Data for Weimann and Fishman's study were derived from a systematic content analysis of over 430 suicide cases published in the two leading daily newspapers in Israel (*Maariv* and *Yediot Achronot*) from 1955 to 1990. A sample of the dailies published every other month of every 5th year (January, March, May, July, September, November of 1955, 1960, and so on) resulted in 480 issues scanned for every report on suicide. The coders were trained to analyze every suicide story, using a preset manual of coding categories. The variables used by the coders were (a) form of coverage: space allocation, placement in the paper, date, and inclusion of picture and (b) content of coverage: inclusion of information on the person's age, gender, religion, name, residence, motive for suicide, and mode of suicide; sources used for obtaining information about the act and the victim; attribution of responsibility (to the person himself, to others, or to circumstances)[1]; and finally, the general attitude of the article toward the act or the person (positive, neutral, negative). The coders were trained prior to the investigation and were subjected to an intercoder reliability test. The coefficients of reliability (i.e., the average proportion of agreement between pairs of coders) ranged from .90 to .92 in form variables, and from .87 to .91 in the content variables.

The first analysis was based on comparing media reality with real reality (drawn from official statistics).[2] Thus, Table 7.2 presents the changes in the rates of suicide in reality and in the press, using 1955 as the base (base rate = 100).

The change rates in real Israeli suicides show a steady growth, although this growth actually reflects a decline when compared to the population growth. A comparison of suicide statistics in Israel with those of other countries reveals that the Israeli suicide rate showed a noticeable reduction in recent decades: It decreased from 13.8 (per 100,000) in 1952-1954 and 12.6 in 1962-1963, to 9.6 in 1982. However, reported suicides, as measured by the frequency of suicide stories in the press, did not reflect this tendency accurately. A comparison of the two change rate columns in Table 7.2 indicates the gap between the two realities: The frequency of suicide stories in the press is only partially explained by the frequency of actual suicide. The number of press reports on suicides declined during the 1960s, increased moderately during the 1970s, and increased dramatically during the 1980s and 1990 (an increase of over 400% compared to 1955), despite the relative consistency of suicide acts in reality. Moreover, the prominence of reporting changed significantly. Over the years, the space devoted to suicide stories increased steadily, as did the prominence of the stories in the newspapers. Whereas in the 1955 to 1970 period, no suicide story exceeded a half page in size, the frequency of over half-page articles increased from 2% of the articles in 1975 to 5.6% in 1980, 6.1% in 1985, and 7.2% in 1990. More and more suicide stories were placed prominently on the front page, reaching a peak of almost 20% of all of the articles published in 1990 (lower rates were found in earlier years with a steady increase in the 1980s and 1990). A comparison of the two papers did not reveal any significant differences in the measures of coverage. Thus, although suicide in Israel remained relatively stable in terms of relative frequency, the press coverage changed in terms of increased reporting, space, and prominence. The growing interest of the press in reporting suicide may be related to the tough competition between the two leading dailies (starting during the 1980s with *Yediot* taking the lead from *Maariv*), a competition that led to

TABLE 7.2 Changes in Suicide Frequencies in Reality and in the Press

	Population (Reality)		Press Reports	
Year	Frequency[a]	Change Rate	Frequency	Change Rate
1955	85	100	66	100
1960	132	155.3	46	69.6
1965	140	164.7	54	81.8
1970	146	171.7	70	106.1
1975	245	288.2	96	145.4
1980	231	271.7	118	178.8
1985	223	262.3	136	206.1
1990	331	389.4	278	421.1

a. The population frequencies are based on statistics published by the Israeli Central Bureau of Statistics.

sensationalizing the news and increasing the space devoted to violence and crime.

Another dimension of presenting suicide is the content of the stories. Various measures may be used to indicate the nature of suicide stories. Let us first look at gender and suicide reports; Table 7.3 presents the distribution of men and women in real suicide rates and their share in press stories about suicide.

The consistency of men's higher frequency in the suicide population is also revealed in the press reports. However, the press overreports male suicide: In the entire sample, male suicide accounted for 74.6% of the suicide stories, far beyond men's share in real suicide (ranging from 47% to 69%). The press preference for male suicide may be related to another dimension of suicide stories: the mode and motive of the suicide. Suicides committed by a person serving in the Israeli army were more likely to be reported by the press than civilian suicides: Almost all cases of military suicides were reported whereas only an average of 42% of the nonmilitary suicides were covered. As all military suicides were committed by men, this preference for military suicides affected the frequency of male stories.

The *modus operandi* of suicides may be another factor that influences the selective reporting. Statistical reports on Israeli suicides compiled by the Israeli Central Bureau of Statistics compared the methods of male and female suicide victims. The differences were significant and consistent: Males preferred more violent modes (29.9% of male suicides

TABLE 7.3 Suicide and Gender in Reality and in the Press

	Population (Reality)			Press Reports		
Year	Men	Women	Total	Men	Women	Total
1955	47.1	52.9	100%	66.6	33.3	100%
1960	53.2	46.8	100%	86.9	13.1	100%
1965	58.6	41.4	100%	66.6	33.3	100%
1970	60.1	39.9	100%	84.4	15.6	100%
1975	57.5	42.5	100%	55.2	45.8	100%
1980	62.8	37.2	100%	65.2	34.8	100%
1985	68.6	31.4	100%	76.7	23.3	100%
1990	69.3	30.7	100%	82.9	17.1	100%

were by hanging and 16.9% by shooting, compared with only 3.0% and 18.1% among the women's, respectively). Women's most frequent mode was self-poisoning (34.2%). The press reports clearly focused on the more violent modes of suicide: shooting (28.8% of the reports), hanging (20.2%), and jumping from high buildings (17.4%). The less violent modes were less attractive to the press, with self-poisoning making up only 8.4% of the stories, far below their actual frequency (34.2% among females, 20.9% among males).

Age was another dimension of distortion: The age distribution was identical in both data sets only for the age group 22 to 65, which included 69.2% of the suicide victims reported by the press and 68.1% of the victims reported by the official health statistics. In the other age groups, however, there was quite a marked discrepancy. The very young age groups (0-14 and 15-21) were highly overrepresented in the press reports (4.5%, and 18.3% respectively) compared with the official rates (0.4%, and 9.1% respectively). On the other hand, representation of the oldest age group (65 and older) was noticeably smaller in the press (8.0%) than in the official reports (22.4%). We also collapsed the entire study period into four quartiles to assess if this trend held over time, and indeed this was the case: The press consistently misrepresented the real frequency of suicides among the very young and the very old.

The press reports also misrepresented the motive for suicide (see below), and did so in a very gender-based stereotypical form. According to statistical sources, the leading motive for suicide in Israel has been personal depression (motivating 42.7% of the men and 53.3% of the women who committed suicide). The press stories underreported stories with such a motive (18.1% of the stories) and instead highlighted other motives according to the person's gender. The economic/financial motive was mainly attributed to men (10.6% of male stories compared with 0.9% of female stories). Romantic motives or problems with partner/spouse were attributed mainly to women (18.9% of stories) and less so to men (11.1%), but both frequencies overrepresented this motive (only 4.5% of real suicide cases, with no significant difference among men and women).

Finally, Weimann and Fishman (1995) examined the attitude expressed in the story in terms of inclusion of any positive or negative reference. Most of the reports (73.3%) did not contain any judgment, nor did they express an attitude toward the act or the person. Among those that did, 18.3% were positive and 8.4% were negative. Using attitude as the dependent variable in numerous analyses of variance, we tried to find the factors associated with the attitude of the story. We used all the characteristics of the act (e.g., mode, year, motive) and the person (e.g., age, sex, soldier or citizen) as independent variables in separate analyses. The analyses revealed that the most powerful predictors of attitude were attributed external responsibility ($F = 20.01$, $df = 1$, $p < .0001$),[3] military versus civilian suicide ($F = 2.81$, $df = 1$, $p < .007$), motive ($F = 2.05$, $df = 9$, $p < .03$), and space or size of story ($F = 8.74$, $df = 4$, $p < .0001$). A suicide attributed to external reasons, a suicide committed in the army, and more lengthy coverage of the event were all associated with a more positive attitude of the report.

Although most of the stories were neutral when the cause for the suicide was presented as external to the person who committed the act, a clear tendency toward positive attitude of the story was revealed, particularly when compared to cases where there was no external attribution. This significant association was even stronger in the case of military suicides: All of the suicides committed during military service and reported as externally motivated were treated positively by the press.

Why Kill Yourself? Mediated Motives

A second study of suicide reports in the press, based on the same sample, focused on the notion of motives to commit suicide (Fishman &

Weimann, 1997). First, does the press portray suicide motives accurately? Second, what are the variables affecting the media's assignment of motives to suicides? To answer these questions, a real-world criterion must be established from which one can measure the deviation by the mediated reality; the official suicide records maintained by Israel's Ministry of Health serve as the reference point. The other set of data, the press reports, totally independent of the official statistics, was derived from the suicide reports that served as the database for our content analysis. As Table 7.4 reveals, the three suicide motives most frequently cited in the press were found: economic hardships, romantic disappointment, and mental problems.

For almost all of the motives, significant differences were found between their media frequency and their real frequency. The three most frequent motives, namely economic problems, romance, and mental problems, were also found to have the largest discrepancies between official statistics and press reports. The first two were overplayed in press reports. The economic hardship motive accounted for 9.5% of all the motives reported in the press, whereas in the official statistics, it only constituted 1.6% of the motives. Similarly, the romantic disappointment motive accounted for 16.1% of the motives reported by the press and only for 1.2% of the official statistics. The motive of mental problems was more frequently identified as a reason for suicide by the official statistics than it was by the press reports: 58.9% and 27.6% respectively. These differences were quite consistent over the decades (1950s through 1990s). The second stage of the analysis involved a comparison across motives: What are the profiles of those who were most likely and least likely to be assigned the three suicide motives? Do these relationships resemble the official statistics? For that purpose, a logistic regression analysis was conducted using a different motive as the dependent variable for each analysis.

Based on the logistic regression conducted on the official health statistics and the press data, Fishman and Weimann (1997) reported noticeable differences between the media and reality in terms of the variables predicting the attribution of suicide motives. Some of the predictive variables were found to be significant in one data set and not significant in the other, and other variables were statistically significant in one data set but showed reverse trends in the other. For instance, the official statistics showed age to be a significant predictor of economic

TABLE 7.4 Distribution of Motives for Suicide: Press Versus Reality

Motive	Press Reports	Official Statistics	Difference
Economic hardship	9.5	1.6	+7.9***
Academic/school	2.3	0.2	+2.1*
Romantic/love	16.1	1.2	+14.9***
Relations with parents	2.8	0.6	+2.2*
Army problems	3.0	0.6	+2.4*
Illness	6.2	7.4	−1.2
Mental problems	27.6	58.9	−31.3***
Absorption problems	0.8	0.3	+0.5
Other	31.7	29.1	+2.6**

$*p < .05; **p < .01; ***p < .001$ (when testing the differences under the null hypothesis of no significant difference).

and romantic motives for suicide, whereas in the press data set, age had no significant predictive value for attribution of any of the three motives. The different motive assignment in the two data sets also illustrates that whereas in reality (official statistics), being a woman was a significantly better predictor (than being a man) for assigning an economic motive to suicide, in the press, suicide driven by economic hardship was solely associated with the men. Similarly, whereas being married, according to the press, accounted better for the attribution of the mental problem motive for suicide, the official statistics reflected the exact opposite, that is, that the unmarried were more likely to be driven to suicide by mental problems.

The results of this study demonstrated significant differences between reality according to official statistics, and the portrayal of that reality in the press.

Do these reconstructed realities of suicide affect the public's perceptions of suicide? In a survey of 568 undergraduate students (University of Haifa, Israel, 1996), we asked the respondents to describe their impressions of the distribution of suicide cases in Israel. The pattern that almost all of them portrayed matched perfectly the media reality. Most of them described the people who commit suicide as very young (87% said that they are mostly under the age of 21) and motivated mainly by love and romantic problems (54% presented it as the prime motive), economic problems (32%), and adjustment to military service (18%). They also overestimated the number of suicides in Israel. Suicides of the elderly and suicides caused by mental problems were totally ignored by the respondents, just as they were underreported by the media. These perceptions reflect the mediated reality and not the real one. Although no causality was established, when the students were asked about the sources of their estimates, they usually indicated the media (and mostly the press).

The presentation of suicide in the Israeli press was found to be a reconstructed reflection shaped by media selection, newsworthiness, access to information, and other factors. The changes over time add a dynamic dimension to this process with newsworthiness, competition, public interest, or values changing the nature of selection and the content of the report. However, the unique contribution of the study (aside from relating the cultivation analysis concept and method to the case of suicide stories) is in its relevance to the debate on the effect of suicide stories on imitative behavior. Much of the lingering debate on the persuasive appeal of suicide stories has disregarded the mediated presentation of suicide. Many inconsistencies and conflicting findings can be attributed to the use of various contents with significantly different presentations of suicide. This explanation has been previously suggested by scholars who were challenged by the confusion and inconsistency: "It is conceivable that this variation in results is due to the fact that certain types of stories are more influential than others" (Kessler et al., 1989, p. 551).

Studies of celebrity suicide also found that the imitation effect holds only for stories on certain celebrities (political figures and entertainers) and not for others (artists, villains, and the economic elite). Stack and Gundlach (1992) explored the relationship between country music and suicide and reported a significant impact of certain country music themes. They argued that country music encourages suicidal mood through its concerns with problems such as marital discord, alcohol abuse, and alienation from work. In conclusion, the study of imitative suicide and the role of the media in this process should recognize the need to include the study of the form and contents of suicide presentations in the media. Our findings, revealing the reconstruction of the suicide reality in press reports, point to the depiction of suicide as being selectively related to certain motives, certain subpopulations, and in varying levels of justification. These may be causing significant variance in the impact on ideation, suggestion, and imitation. Without the study and control of the presentation factor, debate on media effects on imitative suicides will linger on.

NOTES

1. This typology was conceptualized by De Charms (1968) and has been operationalized by several researchers, for example: Hodges, Brandt, and Kline (1981) and Weimann and Fishman (1988).

2. However, one should remember Durkheim's note on how official statistics about suicide are themselves socially constructed and thus may not serve as perfect objective measures of reality.

3. This variable consisted of two categories: Was there a reference to any external cause (such as problems with parents, lovers, spouses, friends, commanders, employers, etc.) or not.

CHAPTER EIGHT

The World According to MTV

MTV is an advertiser-supported cable television channel dedicated to the programming of record company-produced music video clips for a target audience ages 12 to 34. MTV premiered on cable television systems on August 21, 1981, at 12:01 a.m. EST with a video of the song, "Video Killed the Radio Star" by The Buggies. Although no early ratings were available, MTV's premiere was carried by 225 cable systems in 2.1 million homes, and by the end of August, MTV was available in 2.5 million homes. MTV was not offered on cable systems in New York or Los Angeles during its early years, contributing to a lack of national media attention to the new service. Its owner/operator is the Warner Amex Satellite Entertainment Company, a joint venture between Warner Communications and American Express. In 1985, MTV was sold to Viacom, a television syndication company.

MTV was launched by a 29-year-old founder, Robert Pittman, who was already running the Movie Channel for Warner Amex Satellite Entertainment Company. The creators of MTV believed that a fusion of "album-oriented rock" with an advertising-style televisual sequence of images that would move very quickly with fast cuts and no transitions would have maximum appeal for the target audience. Pittman persuaded the executives of the cable company (Warner-Amex), the recording industry, and, ultimately, the corporate advertisers that the format of "an around-the-clock, circular flow of interchangeably artistic and commercial appeals to the viewer's senses" would attract and hold the attention of the desired audience. Warner executives sought to establish a certain style and mood for MTV, distinguishing it from traditional television. Unlike commercial television's tightly structured shows, MTV would be "a channel with no programs, no beginning, no middle, no end," according to Bob Pittman. Banks (1996) argues that MTV developed a noncerebral approach to programming that "relies on mood and emotion rather than on the traditional television approach of story and plot" (p. 44). Accordingly, claims Banks, MTV tried to cultivate an irreverent, informal style that appeared to be unplanned and unscripted. The program service intentionally departed from the technical perfection of conventional broadcast television by having a messy, cluttered set and poor lighting and allowing the hosts to make mistakes on the air, all of which gave the channel a spontaneous, casual feel.

In its early years, MTV largely consisted of an endless succession of video clips, introduced by on-air announcers called "vee-jays" (or VJs), a video age update of the radio's disk jockeys or DJs. Video clips constituted about 80% of MTV's programming at its premiere. The remaining time was devoted largely to music news and promotional campaigns. This emphasis on music clips was a problem because MTV had a limited library of video clips—no more than 125 selections—at its premiere. Most major record labels cooperated with MTV, providing access to their music videos, but they did not have many videos to offer MTV because their production of video music was quite limited. However, many English groups had produced clips for exposure in the United Kingdom and European markets, where television was more established as a way to promote recording acts. MTV's early emphasis on these British artists and other musicians relatively unknown in the United States placed the channel in the forefront of introducing new music to the public and prompted much interest in MTV. Ironically, argues Banks (1996), despite MTV's heavy reliance on audience research, the decision to feature United Kingdom artists and new music was based more on the historical fluke of clip availability than on research analysis. MTV could not feature many U.S. rock stars and groups favored by survey respondents because many had no videos available.

Reports of increasing record sales at music stores soon after MTV's premiere demonstrated that claims by Warner executives about MTV's potential promotional power had not been mistaken. In October 1981,

Billboard magazine did a survey of record stores in certain cities with cable systems carrying MTV. They reported increased sales of records and tapes, which store managers directly attributed to MTV. Industry analysts claimed MTV was also largely responsible for a significant increase in sales in major music chain stores, ranging from 5% to 30% in November 1983. An A. C. Nielsen study of MTV viewers in October 1982 provided further evidence of MTV's promotional influence, reporting that 85% of the 2,000 respondents in the intended demographic group watched MTV, and those who did viewed it an average of 4.6 hours a week. MTV clearly influenced viewers' music purchases because 63% of the survey respondents said they purchased an artist's album after viewing a clip featuring the artist's music. Record company executives came to believe MTV could create consumer interest in their artists' music.

However, MTV still faced serious obstacles from cable companies in its early years. Cable operators, who provided MTV with its means of distribution, were reluctant to offer the program service on their systems. MTV executives commissioned a promotional campaign to convince cable companies to carry MTV. The success of the promotional campaign as well as increasing publicity about the channel convinced several cable stations to add MTV to their systems, rapidly expanding MTV's potential audience base. In January 1983, cable systems in New York City and Los Angeles began offering MTV. MTV grew dramatically in 1983, reaching 18 million homes by that December, more than double the previous year, making it available to 22% of all U.S. homes with television. MTV's rapidly growing subscriber figures attracted major advertisers: By June 1983, MTV sold advertising time to 140 companies representing more than 240 consumer products.

According to Pettegrew (1995), MTV's success in commercial television depended on achieving three interrelated goals. First, to establish the content of its programming, the new station needed to make connections with the rock music industry. This was accomplished rather easily. The recording business had experienced a serious slump in the late 1970s, so many record companies welcomed the added exposure of their performers through a music television station. By the time telecasting began in August 1981, Arista, MCA, Polygram, and other major companies had agreed to supply MTV with music videos at no cost. The investment paid off. Record sales increased dramatically and, in general, the added dimension of television stimulated greater attention to pop music. MTV not only advertised albums, but it also developed a new form of entertainment. MTV quickly rivaled FM radio as the leading medium for promoting new talent; mega-stars Michael Jackson and Madonna, among others, made their names on MTV. MTV's second challenge was convincing cable operators to distribute its programming to American viewers. The station began in only 1.5 million homes, as many local cable operators were reluctant to include a 24-hour music video channel in their package of cable stations. So MTV executives decided to skip over the operators and promote the station by contacting viewers through leaflets, television commercials, and other advertising. Within a year, the station increased its viewership 10-fold: 10.7 million homes had MTV by 1982, and that number grew to 18.9 million homes after another year.

The third and most important key to MTV's success was the sale of advertising time on the station. Even after record companies supplied music videos and cable operators agreed to distribute its programming, MTV's long-term success in commercial television depended on showing profits to its corporate backers. Thus, MTV needed to attract advertisers by "selling its audience." The audience became the subject of considerable attention and research. These studies suggested that the audience to be targeted by MTV was those most interested in pop music—the 13- to 35-year-olds. Accordingly, MTV focused on upcoming trends in rock music, television, Hollywood, and youth culture and fashion. This turned out to be a successful combination, at least from the advertisers' point of view: By 1985, 23 of the top 25 network advertisers had bought time on MTV. Pepsi Cola and Ford Motor Company were the first major accounts in 1981, followed by others like Proctor and Gamble, General Foods, Dr. Pepper, Wendy's, Swatch, U.S. Navy, Doritos, Honda, Miller Beer, Quaker Oats, Nabisco, and AMC. What advertisers liked most about MTV was the station's ability to deliver its target audience: MTV was considered the perfect medium for reaching teens and young adults. This meant large profits for MTV and Warner Communications. After earning just $7 million in advertising revenue in its first 18 months, MTV took in $25 million in 1983. That amount more than doubled to $54 million the next year, and by 1985, MTV made $96 million in advertising. But MTV is not just music for young people. As Pettegrew (1995) noted,

The station's format went further than anything else on television in breaking down the distinction between commercial and program. Advertisers looked at MTV and knew they were getting a viewing environment in which it made less and less sense to separate selling from entertainment and consumption from enjoyment. MTV's programming amounted to almost a complete context of selling. The music videos themselves were produced by the record companies as advertisements for performers' albums. (p. 490)

In the 1990s, MTV has expanded its operations globally, launching derivations of MTV in other countries and regions (MTV Europe, MTV Asia, MTV Australia, MTV Japan, MTV Latino). MTV is now a significant factor on the Asian, South American, and European media scene (Banks, 1997). Of the various versions produced around the world, MTV Europe is the most elaborate and successful venture. It mainly presents music clips of American and British artists, calling into question just how European the channel really is. MTV's reach throughout Europe is expanding steadily. In 1993, its subscriber base in Europe increased 38% from the previous year to 46 million homes. The channel has crafted a loyal audience of young people in 31 countries, including a significant expansion into Eastern Europe and Russia.

In Asia, the battle between two foreign-owned music television networks, Viacom's MTV and News Corporation's Channel V, is getting hot. MTV has surpassed Channel V in all the major markets except Thailand, where the two are neck and neck, and Hong Kong, where neither has much of a presence. In 1997, MTV's Asian revenues doubled, and its audience grew five-fold, whereas Channel V's business was flat. China remains the big market for both firms, but so far, both companies have been making slow progress there (according to *The Economist*, April 11, 1998, p. 51). MTV's most ambitious project to date in Latin America is MTV Latino, which premiered in 1993 with a reach of 3 million homes in 20 countries in this region. Most of the videos presented on this channel (70%) are by English-speaking artists. The primary threat to MTV's dominance of global music video programming are several competitors, such as Viva in Germany, MuchMusic in Canada, VH-1 in the United States, MCM in France, the Scandinavian channel Z-TV, and Italy's Videomusic.

According to Banks (1997), MTV attempts "to develop and exploit an international youth culture" by using music as a "global language":

> MTV wants to provide a program service that will attract the world's youth, ... a pliable worldwide audience that can be sold to transnational advertisers seeking to reach this demographic audience on a global basis. A program service successfully targeting youth throughout the world would be much sought after by advertisers seeking to expand their share of the world market. (p. 51)

MTV's blend of music, lyrics, and commercials carries, like other media genres and contents, some common presentations of reality as well as some unique images. In this chapter, we will examine some of these images, both in the videos and in the commercials.

The MTV "Stories"

Music videos are distinctive because they present fantasies and dreams rather than the common contents of television programs. Kinder (1984) has noted five parallels between dreams and music videos: unlimited access (MTV's continuous format and people's ability to both sleep and daydream), structural discontinuity (for instance, abrupt scene shifts), decentering (a loosely connected flow of action around a theme), structural reliance on memory retrieval (both videos and dreams trigger associations with pungent images), and the omnipresence of the spectator. Morse (1985) noted many of the same features, particularly the absence of reliance on "conventional" narrative. She focused on the magical quality of the word as lip-synched by the performer, who can appear anywhere in the video without being linked with the images or events, as if a dreamer who could create a world.

According to Aufderheide's (1986) analysis, many MTV videos begin with someone dreaming or daydreaming. She found that although many of the fantasies of music videos are open-ended, they do play on story lines, such as boy-meets-loses-wins-girl and child-is-monster-and-conquers-it. Some weave fairy tale themes into the dream, and the performers easily switch identities, magical transformations occur, and sets are expressionistically large or small. These parallels between dream structure and music video structure may have important implications for their viewers:

> Music videos offer a ready-made alternative to social life. With no beginnings or endings—no history—there may be nightmarish instability, even horror. . . . Dreams by contrast create gestalts, in which sensations build and dissolve. And so they nicely match the promise and threat of consumer-constructed identity, endlessly flexible. Like fashion, identity can change with a switch of scene, a change in the beat. (Aufderheide, 1986, p. 66)

Music video's dream worlds, stories, and loose narrative often depict aggression, violence, conflict, sex, and sex roles. According to Aufderheide (1986), male images include sailors, thugs, gang members, and gangsters. Female images include prostitutes, nightclub performers, goddesses, temptresses, and servants. Most often, these images are drawn not from myths, but from old movies, ads, and other pop culture features. They are the commodified forms of cultural stereotyping. Social critics, especially feminists, have denounced sadomasochistic elements and stereotypes of sexual relationships in most of the videos. For instance, women are often portrayed in videos as outsiders or agents of trouble, which reflects in part the macho traditions of rock. Similar accusations have been made about the portrayal of sexual relations. Although romance is the theme of most popular songs, music videos rarely present love affairs. Very often in these videos, the action is an endless transformation of identities with the grotesque being the norm. Combined with shifting sexual identities, the result is androgyny: Gender is no longer fixed; male and female are fractured into dynamic and underdefined images.

Aufderheide (1986) also noted the videos' settings: Many of the videos' stories take place in a spooky universe. The landscape is strange, ordinary sunlight is uncommon, dark colors—especially blue and silver—are typical, and natural settings are extreme—desert sands, deep tropical forests, oceans. It is often a very lonely world, a very strange and scary world. This world, however, is also one of cosmic threat and magical power. The self-transforming figures are often triggering powerful fantasy acts of destruction, violence, and salvation. Parents, school principals, teachers, police, and judges provide a cultural iconography of repression. Aufderheide also points to the way these videos "play on the overlapping sexual and political iconography of power in Naziesque sadomasochistic fetishes, with symbols connoting total power without moral or social context" (p. 67).

MTV has two formats of videos: In the first, *performance videos,* the artists simply perform as though they were in concert or studio settings. The second type, *concept videos,* consists of videos that interpret or embellish a song. These concept videos have been variously described as "video minimovies," "surrealistic visual riffs," "three-minute visual fantasies," "complex and surreal passion plays," "hyperhybrid of commercials, cartoons, concerts, and selected short subjects," and "narrative mini-melodramas." Concept videos have attracted much of the criticism directed at rock video. Two of the most common charges maintain that such videos are sexist and violent.

Sexism in MTV and Music Video

One of the most frequent visual elements in MTV's videos during the early 1980s was the sexualized female form, used decoratively to enhance the emotional appeal of the video for the (presumed young white male) viewer/listener. Because MTV was born into a world in which the feminist movement's perspectives were already active, from the founding moment, it encountered criticism of its representations of women. Content analyses of MTV imagery explored its potentially damaging effects on adolescents, and there was also a wave of public criticism of sexist and sexually violent imagery on MTV (from groups such as the Parents Music Resource Center and the Parents Choice Foundation.[1]

The most troubling issue appears to be that MTV and the rock videos are viewed predominantly by young children, teenagers, and adolescents (Brown, Campbell, & Fisher, 1986). Sherman and Dominick (1986) reported results of a Nielsen survey: The median age of MTV viewers was 23, and they watched for 1 hour each weekday and longer on the weekends. By 1987, 40% of U.S. households had access to MTV, and its programming reached 43% of the U.S. adolescent market. Sun and Lull (1986) reported that in a sample of 900 teenagers in the Southwest, those who had access to MTV watched it about 2 hours each day.

Several studies have analyzed the characters in music videos. For example, Brown and Campbell (1986), using a sample of music videos from MTV and BET (Black Entertainment Television), found that women and blacks were in the minority on MTV. White men were seen most often and usually were the center of attention, whereas women and blacks remained in the background. Similarly, Sherman and Dominick (1986) found that women and minorities were underrepresented in samples of music videos on MTV and on network television. Men were found to constitute 78.3% of MTV video performers, 71.2% of the characters shown in these videos, 84.3% of the aggressors in the videos, and 80.7% of their victims. Another study examined 40 MTV music videos across gender role-based content categories (Sommers-Flanagan, Sommers-Flanagan, & Davis, 1993). The analysis revealed that men appeared nearly twice as often as women; men engaged in significantly more aggressive and dominant behavior; women engaged in significantly more implicitly sexual and subservient behavior; and women were more frequently the object of explicit, implicit, and aggressive sexual advances. Overall, MTV video content primarily included implicit sexuality, objectification, dominance, and implicit aggression.

Vincent, Davis, and Boruszkowski (1987) conducted a content analysis of MTV's music videos. A random cluster sample was drawn from MTV weekday programming, in blocks representing daytime and late night hours. One hundred and ten music videos were analyzed, using a scale of sexism developed by Butler and Paisley, originally designed to test for sexism in print advertisements. The scale measures how women are portrayed in specific roles and relationships. Because of the range of story lines found in rock videos, such a scale, by necessity, must address both sexuality and occupational roles. These four levels were:

- *Condescending (Put Her Down):* The woman is portrayed as being less than a person, a two-dimensional image. Includes the dumb blonde, the sex object, and the whimpering victim.
- *Keep Her Place:* Some strengths, skills, and capacities of women are acknowledged, but tradition also dictates "womanly" roles. The tradition also dictates emphasis on subservience in romantic or secondary roles. There is still high emphasis on sexual attributes.
- *Contradictory:* Emphasizes a dual role where a woman plays a traditional, subservient role while also displaying a certain degree of inde-

pendence. Anything she does outside of domesticity and nurturance is viewed as "something extra."

- *Fully Equal:* Treated as a person (possibly a professional) with no mention of her private life. Does not remind us that domesticity and nurturance remain women's work. Women are viewed nonstereotypically.

Besides the measurement of sexism, additional scales were used to evaluate the degree of male-female physical contact, the type of seductive clothing (if any), the occurrence of violence, and the type of narrative situation shown. The analysis revealed that of those videos with women, 56.9% were rated "Put Her Down" on the sexism scale. The next highest level found was "Keep Her in Place" (17.1%), followed by the level "Fully Equal" (13.8%). Most videos (76.4%) used male performers exclusively, whereas 23.6% were all female or mixed. The results support the notion that sexism is fairly high in music videos:

> In the videos examined it was very common for women to be used exclusively as decorative objects. In these productions women are often portrayed as background decoration, clad in bathing suits, underclothing or highly seductive clothing. They are shown in sexually alluring dance, . . . even when the portrayal is less sexually inveigling, there is a tendency for women to fall into simple ornamental roles. (Vincent et al., 1987, p. 754)

Women are less likely than men to be portrayed in professional work. Overall, most concept videos, which dramatize the music, contain violence, graphic sexual content, and women as sex objects. Using the consciousness scale, Vincent and his colleagues found that 56.9% of the portrayals of women in concept music videos (videos that told a story) were condescending. Overall, the depiction of gender roles was traditional, and sexism was high. In a follow-up study using samples of concept videos taken 18 months apart, most of the videos had all male performers and portrayed women condescendingly (Vincent, 1989). There was, however, a significant rise in the number of videos that presented women as fully equal to men between the videos taped during the summer of 1985 and those taped during the winter of 1986-1987, from 15.5% to 38.5%. Conversely, there were also small but significant increases in the amount of sexy or alluring clothing (lingerie, bathing suits) and nudity in the later sample as compared to the earlier one. Similarly, Seidman (1992) found that women were more likely than men to wear sexually revealing clothing. Finally, both men and women were portrayed in sex-typed occupations.

A recent study of MTV's videos found that in the 1990s, they continued to underrepresent women, with men outnumbering women in lead roles by almost a 5-to-1 margin; women are presented in a much narrower range of lead roles (Goe, 1996). Goe also found that popular music videos portrayed women in a manner that emphasized physical appearance rather than musical ability. Another frequently used element is the combination of sexuality and religion, as revealed by several analyses of MTV videos (McKee & Purdun, 1996; Purdun & McKee, 1995).

Rap music videos, a newer form of music videos, are mainly populated by black men who present themselves as dominant and sexually successful. Women in these videos are presented almost exclusively as objects of male lust. Many male rappers have been criticized for their sexist and homophobic lyrics. However, there a are few female rappers who challenge the stereotypes by appearing to be dominant, aggressive, and in control. Yet, overall, sexism abounds in rock videos: The young viewers of rock videos are confronted with images of male dominance and female subordination, and the sexualization of both. Jones (1997) studied the prevalence of sex and violence in MTV according to music styles. These styles were rap, hip-hop, rhythm and blues (R&B) and soul, country and western, and rock. Rap videos were consistently higher in certain socially questionable behaviors, such as gun talk, drug talk, presence of alcohol, bleeping and profanity, and gambling. Hip-hops and R&B included the most sexual variables.

As research findings suggest, the meaning viewers take from music television cannot always be predicted or controlled. For example, white and black female and black male teenagers are more likely than white male teenagers to say they watch music videos to learn the latest fashions and dances. Girls appear to use MTV to gain information about dominant male culture, whereas blacks more often than whites say they watch because they want to be like the people in the videos. Female viewers of MTV show a strong relationship between amount of exposure and acceptance of sexual violence. That is, the more females watch MTV, the more likely they are to believe that men are violent toward women, that violence is part of love and sex, and that women cannot or should not defend themselves from male sexual aggression. Male viewers show less of a correlation, perhaps because males tend to accept sexual violence more than females, regardless of the amount of MTV viewing. For both sexes, however, amount of MTV viewing is positively correlated with the view that both sexes tease and manipulate each other. Although the correlations exist, we do not know whether watching MTV causes attitudes to change or whether people with certain attitudes are more likely to watch MTV.

Sexism in MTV's Commercials

Most of the studies on gender and MTV focus only on the content in music videos themselves and not on the ads in the programs. As MTV grew in popularity and its audience increased in size, companies who wanted to reach young people found that MTV was an important vehicle for their commercial messages. In 1991, 80% of MTV's audience was between the ages of 12 and 34. Moreover, one quarter of the audience was between the ages of 12 and 17, an adolescent audience much larger than that reported for other television networks (MTV Research, 1991). In addition, adolescent viewers were found to spend an average of over 2 hours a day watching MTV, including the commercials. A study of gender portrayals examined a sample of commercials aired on MTV (Signorielli, McLeod, & Healy, 1994). Two research questions were considered: The first asks how men and women are portrayed in MTV commercials and hypothesizes that both men and women will be portrayed in stereotypical ways. The second research question focuses on whether commercials for different types of products have a male or female gender orientation. A sample of 550 MTV commercials was recorded (in 1991). Eliminating repeat commercials, the final sample consisted of 119 individual commercials, each subjected to a systematic content analysis. The results revealed that commercials on MTV were gender-stereotyped. Even though a large percentage of commercials were geared toward both men and women, the data consistently showed that when one gender was the target of a commercial, the target was typically male. The visual gender makeup of the commercial and the gender of the user had more than twice as many only-male commercials as only-female commercials. It is particularly interesting to note that men were far more likely than women to handle or control the object being advertised. This may reveal a bias on the part of advertisers that men are more effectively associated with the strengths of a particular product than women.

The analyses of character attributes also revealed that commercials on MTV were filled with stereotypical information about gender roles. First, there were fewer female characters. Analyses show that popular songs in the 1950s and early 1960s tended toward the romantic, but now songs emphasize violence, death, and suicide. The frequent reference to death is reflected even in the names of the groups: the Grateful Dead, the Zombies, the Dead Kennedys, Sharon Tate's Baby, the Clash, D-Day, the Explosives, Megadeath, and Terminal Mind. In the early years of rock, the death of a loved one was often romanticized in song. In the 1960s, death in music was affected by the Vietnam war, with dead soldiers being returned in body bags by the thousands and with the assassinations of Robert Kennedy and Martin Luther King. Death was not only a frequent theme of the music of the time, but it also was to become the fate of many of its performers (Buddy Holly, Elvis Presley, Jim Morrison, Jimi Hendrix, Janis Joplin, Otis Redding, Keith Relf, Jim Croce, Ronnie Van Zant, Keith Moon, Brian Jones, Lowell George, Sid Vicious, Pig Pen, Cass Elliot, Minnie Ripperton, Duane Allman, John Lennon, Bill Haley, John Denver, Karen Carpenter, and many more). Not only was death a theme of rock-and-roll songs and the fate of some performers, but the audience became involved as well. Mass murderer Charles Manson supposedly believed that the Beatles were sending him messages through the lyrics of songs from their *White Album,* particularly "Helter Skelter." In Cincinnati, Ohio, the crush of a crowd at a Who concert left six trampled to death. In Pueblo, Mexico, during a 1983 performance of the Puerto Rican group Menudo, thousands of fans stampeded toward the only open exit after a concert, crushing three to death and injuring 80 others.

Violence on MTV

A frequent criticism of MTV's videos is its presentation of violence in various forms. A number of content analytic studies have examined violence in rock music videos. Albert (1978) found that intensity and violence were the most important factors in discriminating among rock songs; evaluations of beauty, levels of interest, and goodness played very minor roles. A study by the National Coalition on Television Violence (1984) investigated 160 hours of music videos, estimating that viewers are exposed to an average of 18 instances of violence per hour. Sherman and Dominick (1986) found 57% of concept videos to contain violent acts, with an average of 2.9 separate acts per video, whereas Baxter, De Riemer, Landini, Leslie, and Singletary (1985) found that 57% of their sample contained some violence or crime. After analyzing 139 music videos, Caplan (1985) concluded that rock videos "are dominated by violence" with "almost twice as many acts of violence in music videos" compared to commercial television (p. 146).

Kalis and Neuendorf (1989) conducted a study of MTV, focusing on the pervasiveness of aggressive cues in MTV's videos, and the relationships between gender and violence in these videos. Over a period of 7 days in 1985, 14 hours of MTV content in 2-hour units were randomly videotaped off cable. Three sets of content analysis and surveys were used to measure (a) the occurrence of and audience identification of aggressive cues; (b) the prominence and cue type, and the initiators and recipients of validated aggressive cues; and (c) the pacing, video type, and real-time length of music videos. An aggressive cue was defined as "the occurrence(s) of objects or events actually occurring or simulated representing physical harm or the threat thereof." Each of the 1,108 cues identified was assessed for "perceived aggressiveness" by a response survey of at least 50 respondents. The study found that only 40% of the videos were free of aggressive cues (cues validated by the surveys as aggressive). However, there were significant differences across video types: 75% of the concept videos contained at least one aggressive cue, whereas only 29% of the performance videos did. Table 8.1 presents selected findings on the pervasiveness of violence on MTV.

Although most videos (61%) contained at least some aggressive cues, the proportion of video shots devoted to aggressive content was small: Aggressive cues were found in 13% of all shots, with such content more prevalent in concept videos (16% of shots) than in performance videos (4.8%). Real time devoted to aggressive cues was correspondingly brief: 9% of the total music video time (12% for concept videos,

TABLE 8.1 Violent Cues in MTV Videos

	Total Sample	Concept Video	Performance Video
Videos containing validated aggressive cues	60.7%	75.0%	29.4%
Shots containing aggressive cues	12.7%	16.0%	4.8%
Total time devoted to aggressive cues	9.4%	12.2%	3.1%

3% for performance videos). Nevertheless, an analysis of camera shots indicated that focal prominence is given to aggressive cues when they appear. Applying the results of the survey to the 333 validated aggressive cues, a "total aggressiveness score" was calculated for each video (i.e., a simple sum of the mean perceived aggressiveness scores for all validated cues in a video). The average total aggressiveness score was 62.6. For concept videos, this average was 86.4, and for performance videos 16.6—a statistically significant difference. Concept videos were 8 of the top 10 most aggressive videos.

Gender was strongly related to violence: Men were the most frequent recipients of aggression (58% of all recipients) and the most frequent initiators of aggression. Women were infrequently identified as recipients of aggression (13% of recipients) and were slightly more likely to be identified as initiators of aggression (15% of initiators). However, female recipients of aggression were likely to receive aggression from men. The MTV female is certainly more violent than the "ordinary" or "average" TV woman. In the MTV world, some women are more likely to be initiators of violence than its recipients (this reversal was labeled as the "predatory woman" typical of MTV videos). The researchers concluded that although aggressive cues might be less frequent on MTV than common criticisms would lead one to believe, the aggressive cues are given prominence and shown in close-up to make it more attractive, effective, and memorable.

What Do MTV Viewers "Read" From the Videos?

The rapid growth of MTV, its unique features of content and pace, and its appeal to children and adolescents have triggered concern about its impact on viewers. Critics of MTV have argued that the high levels of violence in its music videos could produce harmful effects, especially among young viewers, or could promote violence against women. These arguments relied on the numerous content analyses of MTV and music videos, which found high levels of violence and antisocial behavior in music videos. However, content analysis can provide evidence on the messages, but it cannot tell us about the impact these messages have on audiences. Indeed, content analyses of MTV have not led to any published study demonstrating the effects of violent videos on viewers. The same applies to gender stereotyping: Although MTV was found to promote and maintain a gender ideology of male power and dominance of men over women, little is known about how viewers actually interpret these messages.

Walker (1987) explains the lack of research showing harmful effects of MTV's videos:

> It is important to remember that the violence in music videos does not exist in a media vacuum. Violence is a standard ingredient in several other types of media. . . . Given the violent nature of many types of television programs, motion pictures and books, should the additional violence in music videos be of much concern? (p. 762)

Walker argued that a particular type of media content, such as the violence in MTV, should not be studied in isolation but in the context of other media that provide similar kinds of content. Thus, we need to establish the relationship between MTV viewing and exposure to other sources of violent content to assess more precisely the impact of MTV's contribution to mediated violence. Walker conducted a study to test the relationships between viewing MTV and other violent media contents (in television, books, movies), using a survey and a sample of under-graduate students.

The correlations between MTV viewing and the viewing of other forms of mediated violence were statistically significant ($p < .05$) and negative. In a strong inverse pattern, MTV viewing was found to be negatively related to high violence television programs, motion pictures, and books. Of the 13 significant correlations reported by Walker (1987), 11 were consistent with the inverse pattern. This may indicate that MTV's heavy viewers have a very unique television diet. They are not exposed to other forms of mediated violence, and this may reduce the potential for overall impact of violence in the media on these specific viewers: "In any event," argues Walker, "This tendency toward an inverse pattern of relationships suggests that researchers examining MTV viewing are likely to find few effects related to mediated violence" (p. 762). Walker himself found evidence for such "weak" effects: He examined the relationship between amount of MTV viewing and perceived violence in society and found a weak and nonsignificant correlation.

Other communication scholars have only just begun to analyze the cultural content and impact of music television. Nevertheless, observers of youth culture suggest that the traditional portrayal of gender and sexual images have important consequences on adolescent consumers of popular culture. For example, Brake (1985) argues that female adolescents receive "distinct signals about the cult of femininity" (p. 166) from popular fiction and the mass media, and these cues have a central theme—romantic attachment and dependency on men. There is evidence that viewers make connections between MTV texts and their personal experiences. For example, in a study of gender ideology and MTV, Lewis (1990) argues that MTV's "female-address videos" have had an important impact on the female audience. She discusses the history of MTV as a popular culture product that reflects an ideological struggle over gender inequality; thus women bring psychological, sociological, and political interests to their interpretations of female video texts.

How do young people "read" the images of gender and sexuality as portrayed in the "texts" of MTV? This question guided several studies. In the first study, Kalof (1990) found a large gender difference in the interpretation of female images in about 42 different MTV videos. Six key categories emerged in the description of the female images: using sex as a weapon, sex object, passive/indecisive, love dependent, competitive/aggressive, and vulnerable/weak. Women were much more likely than men to describe the females on MTV as individuals who use their sexuality as a lure to get attention. In addition, although MTV major performers are primarily male, female images were "noticed" far more often than male images by both female and male respondents. Finally, there was no gender difference in the description of male images on MTV. Both female and male respondents interpreted the male images as controlled/decisive, in pursuit of women, love dependent, and competitive/aggressive.

In her second study, Kalof (1993) focused on the active role viewers assume in constructing their interpretations of the images of gender, power, and sexuality in one of Michael Jackson's music videos, "The Way You Make Me Feel." This study explores the meanings attributed to MTV imagery by analyzing young viewers' descriptions of gender and sexuality as portrayed in the video. Jackson's "The Way You Make Me Feel" was selected because of its popularity among adolescents and the considerable airtime devoted to it on MTV. Second, the video depicts strikingly traditional images of gender and sexuality. The video portrays Michael Jackson as a young man who becomes infatuated with a beautiful woman as she walks down a dark, urban street. Michael Jackson follows, indeed stalks, the woman, singing and dancing his adoration for her, becoming more insistent on his need and desire for her, and clearly not allowing the woman to escape his attention. The young woman says nothing, initially ignoring and rejecting him, but eventually warms to the "cat and mouse" game. In the end, she opens her arms to him after a somewhat frightening and threatening scene that suggests a gang rape by a group of tough street men, implying that beautiful women are in danger unless they have a man to protect them. The Jackson video was shown to 80 young women and men, ranging in age from 13 to 22 years and primarily from white middle- and working-class backgrounds. After watching the video, the subjects were asked to respond to a self-administered open-ended questionnaire about the images of women and men as portrayed in the video. The open-ended descriptions of imagery in the Michael Jackson video were content-analyzed.

The first analysis revealed two major male image categories: (a) powerful and in control (decisive, forceful, persistent, confident, bold, aggressive, dominant, demanding) and (b) vulnerable and weak (infatuated, inferior, looking for sex, needing to impress). Both female and male respondents had strikingly similar readings of the male image in the Jackson video. For example, 62% of the females and 65% of the males interpreted the male image as powerful and in control by describing him as the one who "pursues and should be able to get what he wants," "is self-centered and can have whatever he wants," and "goes after what he likes and shows the women how much he is in control."

Another 20% of the women and 20% of the men interpreted the male image as vulnerable and weak, primarily because of the character's infatuation with women and sex. Thus, the findings indicate that there is essentially no gender difference in the interpretation of the male image, with the same proportion of female and male respondents constructing the masculine image as either powerful and in control or as vulnerable and weak.

Large gender differences were found in the interpretation of the female image. The most striking difference is in the interpretation of the young woman in the video as vulnerable and weak. Whereas 26% of the female respondents described the woman as vulnerable (scared, frightened, trapped, helpless), only 6% of the males had the same interpretation of the female image. Of course, one explanation of this finding is that females are more likely to recognize the predicament of the pursued and somewhat frightened young woman. On the other hand, male respondents were much more likely to construct the female image as a tease, or playing hard-to-get, with 35% of the males noting this as a major image, compared to 18% of the female respondents (some of the males' interpretations were "women are supposed to play hard to get and make the male suffer," or "woman is running away from the man even though she is having fun doing it").

Another important gender difference is found in the reading of the female image as powerful versus indecisive and submissive. About one third of the female respondents described the woman as powerful, in control, and independent. Most of these image descriptions dealt with the woman's physical attractiveness and sensuality. Overall, whereas the male respondents tended to construct the female image as teasing and hard-to-get (35%) or submissive and indecisive (24%), women tended to describe her as either powerful and in control (29%) or vulnerable and weak (26%).

This research shows that there are multiple interpretations of MTV texts, and the reading of a text is an interactive, interpretive process of viewers who make sense of the text according to their gender identity and their experiences as gendered individuals. The same music video, or cultural event, was read differently by young women and men, and there were also diverse readings within gender. Women were more likely than men to observe the female as vulnerable and in a threatening situation. This finding, argues Kalof, is further evidence of the connections viewers make with texts based on their gender and their experiences. This study illustrates the selective decoding process when different viewers "read" different interpretations from the same message. These are not revealed by conventional content analysis, even when performed with the trained eyes of the researcher.

In the same vein, Brown and Schulze (1990) conducted a study to find how different young viewers "read" the MTV videos. They chose two videos featuring the rock star Madonna—"Papa Don't Preach" and "Open Your Heart"—as examples of the portrayal of sexuality in music videos. Academic critics see the Madonna presented in music videos as a model that counters "traditional feminine ideals of dependency and reserve" (Lewis, 1987). Shortly after the video was released in the summer of 1986, the Planned Parenthood affiliate in New York condemned it for sending "a potent message to teenagers about the glamour of sex, pregnancy, and childbearing." After the song was released, a spokesperson for Madonna said, "She is singing a song, not taking a stand. Her philosophy is people can think what they want to think" (Holden, 1986, p. H22).

The researchers showed the videos to 186 students, black and white, in undergraduate communication classes at three state universities. These students represent what industry spokesmen claim is the intended target audience for MTV music videos. A majority of the students in this study reported watching music videos at least 15 minutes per day. The open-ended questions about reactions to the videos began with very broad questions, such as how did this video make you feel. They also asked what images stick in your mind, as well as a series of questions assessing how the students understood the video's narrative. The responses varied across gender and race: Almost all (97%) of the white females and 85% of the white males mentioned somewhere in their responses that they thought the girl in the video was pregnant. In contrast, only 73% of the black females and 43% of the black males mentioned or alluded to the girl's pregnancy. Both black and white males were more likely than females to discuss the video in terms of the teen's relationship; few viewers described Madonna's character in the video as an "independent girl." Black males were the most likely group to see Madonna's independence as the video's primary theme, but most viewers (including black males) saw the girl not as issuing an ultimatum but rather as turning to her father for love, support, and perhaps advice. In most of the perceptions studied, significant differences were found among males and females, white and black students. The rock videos, although seen by millions of young people all over the world, do not produce the same impressions and perceptions.

NOTE

1. The co-founders of the Parents Music Resource Center, organized in protest of "pornographic" rock music lyrics, included Susan Baker, wife of Treasury Secretary James Baker; Tipper Gore, wife of then Senator Albert Gore; and Ethelynn Stuckey, wife of Williamson Stuckey, a former representative from Florida. Hoping eventually to see the enactment of a system for rating records similar to the one used for rating movies, the Center won a lesser concession in August 1985 when 19 top record companies agreed to start printing warnings of sexually explicit lyrics on album and music video packaging.

CHAPTER NINE

Portrayal of Groups

W hat do we know about Arabs? Aging people? African Americans? AIDS patients? Police work? Among the major images that mass media create for us are images of various groups of people. For some of these groups, it is only through TV and other media that we meet, learn about, and virtually "encounter." Not only are the mass media our introduction to these people, but the media may be our only source of information about them.

In this chapter, we will examine the mass-mediated images of a variety of groups of people and look at the consequences of such portrayals. It will be impossible to review the media images of so many categories of subpopulations and social groups. Instead, this chapter will review only a selected sample of presentations: the elderly (age group), physicians (professional group), Arabs (ethnic group), African Americans (race group), and people with disabilities (health group). These groups were selected simply because their representations in the media have been studied extensively. Let us look first at the media portrayal of one of the fastest-growing demographic groups in our society, the elderly.

Images of the Elderly

Older people are the most underrepresented group in the media throughout the world (on U.S. television and the elderly, see Davis & Davis, 1985). For example, early in the 1980s, according to U.S. census data, 15.7% of the population was age 60 or over, yet, content analyses of the characters on U.S. television showed only 3% of over 3,500 characters in prime-time series were over 65, with an even lower percentage of older adults in commercials. Early studies examining different types of television programs (see, e.g., Aronoff, 1974; Harris & Feinberg, 1977; Northcott, 1975) have yielded an underrepresentation of the elderly, with figures in the 1% to 5% range. Vasil and Wass (1993) summarized findings of studies done to investigate the portrayal of the elderly in the mass media. They reviewed 28 empirical studies, based on analyses of TV characters and characters in print media, including children's books, magazines, and basal readers series. The elderly, especially older women, were widely underrepresented, with characterizations failing to reflect the size and proportions of the elderly population in the United States. Only daytime soap operas had a higher percentage of older people, 16% judged to be over 55 (Cassata, Anderson, & Skill, 1980). According to a study conducted by the Cultural Indicators team, age is a stable and strong determinant of who appears most and gains or loses most in the world of network television drama (Gerbner, 1993a). In contrast to the distribution of age groups in the American population, the television curve demonstrates a pronounced central tendency; it bulges in the middle years and underrepresents both young and old people. The researchers compared the percentage of age distribution in the actual population and in the "worlds" of prime-time television dramas and commercials. More than half of all television characters in both samples were between 25 and 45 years of age. Those 65 and over, almost 12% of the U.S. population, made up less than 3% of the fictional television population. Commercials tend to further exaggerate these inequities. As the study concludes, "The skewed pattern of age distribution reflects not real life but power, particularly purchasing power" (Gerbner, 1993a, p. 208).

Underrepresentation is only part of the problem: Even that relatively small number of elderly people who did appear on TV were portrayed in a very distorted way. For example, two thirds of the TV elderly were men, as compared with only 43% in the actual elderly population. A disproportionate number of the TV elderly were in sitcoms, with very few in action-adventure or children's shows. More troubling is the stereotypical presentation of the old. Consider, for example, the findings of an analysis of the images of old people in cartoons (Polivka, 1988). The cartoons from U.S. magazines and newspapers were analyzed according to a set of five categories of social roles: sexuality, age-relatedness, power, prestige, and self-sufficiency. The results showed that "older people were portrayed overwhelmingly in a negative light." In terms of sexuality, older people were depicted as impotent, dirty old men, swooning at the sight of the variously displayed anatomy of young females. Old people were depicted as powerless, ineffectual, and resigned to their position of powerlessness. Few cartoons attributed any positive qualities to the elderly. This pattern is revealed in many media contents, and the stereotypes of the elderly can be categorized into the following formats:

1. *Physical and mental weakness and poor health.* Overall, older people on TV are often seen as quite healthy, perhaps even unrealistically so (Davis, 1983; Kubey, 1980). Thus, in their analysis of the old in soap operas, the researchers concluded that the overall assessment was unequivocally positive, with more than 98% of the observations judged as pleasant in appearance and demeanor; 84% agreed that their weight was in "good proportion" to their height (Cassata et al., 1980). Those who are depicted as sick, however, are ailing very badly, often seen as infirm, feeble, and sometimes senile. Moreover, the elderly are usually sexless. The major exception to this was the other extreme, the so-called "dirty old man" (or woman), the older person who is preoccupied with sex and usually is a highly ludicrous character.

2. *Crotchety and complaining.* A frequent image of the elderly is that of a narrow-minded person who is constantly complaining, criticizing, and generally being a nuisance to everyone else. The bitter, crotchety complainer is usually at best a laughable buffoon and at worst an object of scorn and derision.

3. *Stereotyped positions and activities.* Older people are often presented doing relatively trivial things such as playing bingo and sitting

in rockers on the front porch. Such presentations of older people are especially common in advertising.

4. *Physically unattractive.* Unlike most of the very attractive young figures on TV, the elderly are often stoop shouldered, mousy haired, and badly wrinkled, usually wearing long-out-of-style clothing. Such marks may be given to them so that we do not mistake them for younger people. Intentionally or not, it also contributes to their image: Seefeldt (1977) found that elementary school children viewed physical signs of aging as horrifying and saw the elderly as infirm and incapable of doing much.

5. *The "very young" old.* An interesting class of exceptions to the usually negative presentations can be seen in commercials. The elderly in ads often appear as the "young-old," with few of the stereotypic signs of aging, except the gray hair, which is almost always there. Although they suffer more health problems than young people in ads, they retain their vigor. It is as if the producers give the character gray hair so we all realize that he or she is supposed to be older but allow that person to show very few other signs of age, which our society finds so distasteful. Baldness, wrinkles, and general dowdiness are unseemly (Davis & Davis, 1985).

6. *The "new" old people.* In several television programs, older people emerge as affluent, active, and even sexy: Bell's (1992) analysis of five such programs (*Murder, She Wrote, The Golden Girls, Matlock, Jake and the Fatman,* and *In the Heat of the Night*) reveals a "new old man." This might be positive change in the portrayal of the elderly or just a ratings-oriented exception that further emphasizes the routine negative depictions of the elderly.

Even in cases where the elderly are portrayed positively, they tend to be in a rather restricted and stereotyped range of roles. Frequently, they are presented as grandparents and also as antagonists in a relationship with their adult child. We seldom see an older executive or professional. In NBC's *The Golden Girls* (succeeded by its sequel *Golden Palace*), featuring four single women (three widowed, one divorced), ages about 50 to 80, the three were excessively interested in sex and represented various stereotypes of aging (Harwood & Giles, 1992).

U.S. media portrayals of the elderly are not the only ones to have been studied. In the 1970s, a first study of the elderly on Israeli TV was conducted (Shinar, Tolner, & Biber, 1980). All of the 562 television characters in 46 dramatic programs broadcast on Israel Television (then a single-channel) were analyzed. Elderly people (age 60 and over) made up 9.6% of the characters presented. This compares with 31.7% older adults ages 50 to 59, 38.4% ages 30 to 49, and 20.3% ages 15 to 29. The coders also examined the attributes related to old people, distinguishing between positive attributes (e.g., success, lack of prejudice), negative, or neutral. They found 23.6% positive attribute ratings, 10.9% neutral ratings, and 65.4% negative ratings for elderly characters (age 60+). The ratings for older adults (50 to 59) were even more negative, with 9% positive ratings, 2% neutral ratings, and 89% negative ratings. In contrast, the two younger adult groups had 85.4% positive ratings and only 14.5% negative ratings. Considerable percentages of the elderly were found to "live in the past" (31.8%) and to be "unclean and unorderly" (30.4%), "prejudiced" (29.1%), and "conservative" (26.8%). Many were physically ill (27.3%) or mentally ill (25%) or were found to be ugly (23%), mean (22%), not contributors to society (21%), and passive (20%). On the more positive side, many elderly were seen as constructive, honest, realistic, functional, independent, and leaders, within the boundaries of prevailing norms. Older adults were often portrayed as independent and as leaders. The stereotypes of character portrayal appear to be more complex than can be accounted for by simple bipolar distinctions. The finding that negative stereotypes are frequently ascribed to characters over age 50 tells us that on TV, old age begins at 50 . . .

The Impact of the "Media Elderly"

How do these mediated images of the elderly affect the public's attitudes and images of growing old in our society? Research on the users of electronic media reveals that of the overall population, the aged are characteristically the heavier users (Cowgill & Baulch, 1969). Robinson (1989) offered a "Uses and Dependency" interpretation of this relationship. A reduction in the number of friends and family seen regularly, in part perhaps due to decreased mobility caused by health limitations, leads to a proportionately greater reliance on media, especially television. This reliance on the media may mean that the media's portrayal of the elderly has a strong impact on the elderly themselves. (According to Hess, 1974, "Pluralistic ignorance, complemented by the process of the self-fulfilling prophecy, suggests that old people will come to behave in the stereotyped manner while others believe that everyone else does," p. 81). Korzenny and Neuendorf (1980) found a strong relationship between old people's self-concept and exposure to the mass media. Overall, a negative self-concept was predicted by television viewing, especially when viewing was motivated by the "escape" needs and the content was of the "fantasy" genre. Many researchers have found that the myths and distortions of old age are believed by most Americans to be true (see, e.g., Comstock, 1972; Head, 1954; Wober & Gunter, 1982). However, Wober and Gunter (1982), who reported significant association between impressions of old people on TV and in real life, argued that it is not possible to determine the direction of causality between the two.

To study the impact on the public's images of the elderly, Gerbner (1993a) used data from American national surveys, applying measures of television viewing and an index of attitudes on aging. This index included statements asserting that the number, the health, and the longevity of older people are declining. A high score on this index would reflect a belief that old people represent a diminishing rather than growing segment of society. The analysis found a significant positive relationship between the amount of television viewing and scores on this index. The more people watch television, the more they tend to perceive old people in generally negative and unfavorable terms. The correlation is not reduced by controls for education, income, sex, or age, and it is much stronger for younger people. Thus, even with important demographic variables held constant, heavy viewers are more likely than light viewers to believe that old people are a vanishing breed. Other results indicate that heavy viewers are more likely to think that older people are not open-minded and adaptable, are not bright and alert, and are not good at getting things done. All of these relationships are stronger among younger respondents, especially those between the ages of 18 and 29. Finally, no study found watching television to be associated with any positive images of the elderly. Kovaric (1993) raises the issue of the impact on children, arguing that the media portrayal of the elderly may teach young children some rather undesirable lessons concerning old people. The future might not be brighter: modern communication technologies (see Chapter 12) may further promote negative images of the elderly. As Featherstone (1995) argues in his article on virtual reality and aging, the new medium relates to age the image of body decline, illness, disability, and powerlessness.

Media Images of Physicians

Work is one of the most fundamental aspects of life. How do we learn about work? What do we know about various professions? Aside from firsthand experience, we learn about work and professions from friends, relatives, or other sources of personal contact. We also get a sizable amount of information about jobs from the mass media. Media images also provide important information about occupations for their audiences, especially children. Thus, DeFleur and DeFleur (1967) found that children more consistently describe the characteristics of occupations that they see on television than those they are likely to encounter in real life. The researchers suggested that television provides children with a lot of superficial and misleading information about the labor force. Jeffries-Fox and Signorielli (1978) conducted a 3-year longitudinal study of a sample of young adolescents in a rural-suburban area of New Jersey, and found that television was an important source of information about doctors, psychiatrists, paramedics, judges, lawyers, and police officers for these young adolescents. Nearly one half of these children reported that they had seen these occupations portrayed on specific television programs. Although the children also reported that they learned about doctors and police officers from their own personal experiences, such interpersonal sources were much less prevalent for knowledge about these occupations. This study also revealed that descriptions given by these children about these occupational roles were consistent with the image of these occupations on television. Similarly, Wroblewski and Huston (1987) found that early adolescents learned about occupations from watching television and that their future work preferences were related to the kinds of jobs they saw on television. The youngsters in this sample had little knowledge of occupations not seen on television and with which they had no personal contact.

Given the prevalence and importance of occupational roles on television and their potential for providing information about the nature of occupations, it became important to examine occupational portrayals on television to determine whether there were any relationships between television viewing and attitudes toward work and professions. Signorielli (1993d) studied the representation of occupations on prime-time television in the United States. The sample included prime-time network dramatic programs broadcast between 1973 and 1985. It consisted of 14,902 characters (10,576 men and 4,325 women), including 2,932 major characters. Data on the distribution of occupations in the U.S. labor force, as reported in the U.S. Census, were compiled and organized to permit a comparison of the world of work on television with the actual world of work. The analysis revealed that the most overrepresented occupations on television were physicians (both men and women), judges, entertainers, police, and private investigators. The professions most underrepresented included teachers, clerical and secretarial workers, sales workers, and other blue-collar workers. Let us then focus on this extremely popular-on-TV occupation: the physicians.

Television depictions of physicians were consistently positive, offering an idealized view of physicians contributing "to a cultural predisposition to hold the entire medical profession in awe" (Malmsheimer, 1988, p. 1). Early research documented this view: McLaughlin (1975) found television doctors embody the traits of power, authority, and knowledge. Gerbner, Gross, Morgan, and Signorielli (1981c) found that "doctors on television are relatively good, successful, and peaceful, and are perceived as more fair, sociable, and warm than other professionals" (p. 902). Other studies found doctors portrayed as "good, fair, sociable, and warm" (when compared to other professionals), and that this positive television depiction contributed to positive images of physicians. Presentation of physicians and nurses in advertisements (in medical and nursing journals) has changed over the recent decades: medical advertisements have begun dropping some traditional symbols (such as the white coat and stethoscope) in favor of depicting science-in-action and high technology (Krantzler, 1986).

A recent study examined the way prime-time network television programs depict physicians and the medical profession and the influence of these images on public perceptions (Pfau, Mullen, & Garrow, 1995). Three data sets were used: a content analysis of television network programming, which showed television's portrayals of physicians; a telephone survey of area households, which indicated public percep- tions of physicians; and a mail survey of physicians, in conjunction with available sociodemographic data on physicians, which together served as a frame of reference against which to compare television's portrayal and public perceptions. A factor analysis of the TV programs revealed six factors in the presentations of doctors: power, competence, physical attractiveness, interpersonal style, character, and regard for others. Then the researchers assessed the effects of the television portrayals on public perceptions of the physicians' personal attributes (e.g., character, interpersonal style, physical attractiveness, power, competence, and regard for others) and professional attributes (e.g., the proportion of physicians who are female, young, upper class, and involved in family medicine). They predicted that heavier viewers of television medical programs would be more likely to perceive the personal and profes- sional attributes of physicians as they are depicted in these shows:

> The results clearly indicated that television depictions of physicians influence public perceptions. In comparison with the frame of refer- ence provided by physicians' perceptions of their own profession and available sociodemographic data, prime-time network television de- picts physicians, and the general public perceives them, as more likely to be both female and young, and to be more imbued with the personal attributes of interpersonal style, physical attractiveness, and power and less imbued with the personal trait of character. In addition, after controlling for viewer differences in age, gender, and education, the results revealed that the number of medical programs that people watch is positively related to their tendency to perceive physicians as prime-time network television programs depict them. The results thus suggest that network prime-time television images contribute to sec- ondary socialization, even about those professional roles that people directly encounter on a regular basis. (Pfau et al., 1995, p. 454)

These results support the cultivation hypothesis regarding images and value of occupations as revealed by another study. Signorielli (1993d) studied a national U.S. sample of seniors in 125 public and private high schools. She found that television's occupational images influence the perceptions of young people and their aspirations. Television programs overrepresent and glamorize certain prestigious jobs (physicians, lawyers) but not others. Watching more television was found to cause adolescents to desire high-status, prestigious jobs. But as the researcher noted, "television images, however, may be doing our young people a considerable disservice," as "not everyone will be able to have a job with status, prestige, respect and good opportunities for financial compensation or advancement" (p. 337). Thus, the mediated images of physicians may not only breed unreal expectations (even for "miracles," see Chapter 7), but also unreal occupational desires. In a similar vein, Pfau, Mullen, Diedrich, and Garrow (1995) examined the impact of prime-time network television depictions of attorneys on the public's perceptions of attorneys. They found that television's portrayals of attorneys influences the public's perceptions of attorneys, their characters, traits, and persona.

Arabs and Islam in the Mass Media

One of the most unsympathetic and derogatory portrayals of ethnic or religious groups in Western media is that of Arabs. The recent criticism of the action movie *The Siege* demonstrates this distorted and extremely negative portrayal of Arabs.[1] As Shaheen (1979), a leading researcher on the Arab image in the media, argued, "Arabs are often humiliated in novels, motion pictures, editorial cartoons, magazines, and school textbooks" (p. 21). According to Shaheen (1979, 1984a, 1984b), there are several stereotypic ways that Arab men are portrayed, all very negative. One is the terrorist: Although only a small fraction of Arabs are terrorists, many Arabs are portrayed on television and in movies in the terrorist's role. A second stereotype of Arab men is the wealthy oil sheikh, who is greedy and morally dissolute, spending undeserved wealth on frivolities such as marble palaces and fleets of Rolls-Royces. Others are portrayed as madly buying up land in the West and erecting expensive homes in Beverly Hills or London. These two images are often blended in the image of Arabs as cruel, cowardly, and decadent people.

A third stereotype is that of the sexual pervert, often dealing in selling Europeans or Americans into slavery, or taking advantage of young white Western girls. Again, blended images of exaggerated wealth and sick sexual appetites are very typical. Muslim polygamy is often used to either promote the sex-hunger motive or to suggest that Arab marriages cannot be happy and must involve subordination of women. A fourth stereotype is of the Bedouin "desert rat," the unkempt ascetic wanderer far overrepresented on TV in relation to the roughly 5% of Arabs who are Bedouins. Finally, Arab men are generally seen as villains, a stereotype especially rampant in children's cartoons. These barbaric and uncultured villains are not usually balanced by Arab heroes or "good guys."

Shaheen's (1994) examination of the images of Arabs in American comic books from the early 1950s to the present revealed that villains are the dominant Arab characters, falling into one of three categories: the repulsive terrorist, the sinister sheikh, or the rapacious bandit. The caricatures of men and women showed distorted sex roles. Their features were frequently bestial, demonized, and dehumanized. They were portrayed as anti-American, anti-West, anti-Israel, anti-Jewish, anti-Christian. Despising freedom and democracy, they give their allegiance to tyranny and servitude. *Batman* or *Superman* and other comics' heroes are frequently confronted by hostile Arabs, usually in the role of anti-Western terrorists. Another frequent image in the comics is that of the "sinister sheikh": With their dark sunglasses, white headdresses, and scruffy beards, the comic sheikhs vary little in the malevolence of their aspiration to world domination. Sheikh Ahmed Azis is a model example from these comic books: He is a Kuwaiti megalomaniac sheikh obsessed with restoring Egypt's ancient empire: "Soon all the world shall bow to me—or die," he states. Similar evil sheikhs are found in Walt Disney's comic books. The bandit image is also most prevalent in comics: The Arab bandit is a killer, dirty, backward, and anti-West. Such Arab bandits are found in *T-Man, Tarzan,* and other popular comics. The sexual dimension of the Arab image is present in comic books, too. The Arab male's attitude toward females (both foreign and native) as portrayed in comics is almost always negative. If the woman is herself an Arab, she is doomed to one of two depictions, either a belly dancer or a faceless housewife. Voiceless, featureless, and mindless, she is devoid of personality. In fact, as Harris (1994) noted, all over the Western media, Arab women are seen in an oppressed situation and often in highly stereotyped roles such as a member of a harem. Shaheen (1984b) pointed out that in reality, harems were never common and today are nonexistent in Arab countries. The veiling of women is presented as the Arab norm, rather than a characteristic of some Islamic traditions.

How can we explain such a negative and distorted portrayal of an ethnic or religious group? Shaheen proposes several answers: The most important explanation is ignorance. The average Western citizen and the Western media know little about Arabs of the Arab world. The proportion of Arab Americans is relatively small (about 3 million). Hence, unflattering Arab stereotypes are rarely challenged. A third factor is greed. Shaheen argues that the producers of popular media are able to make a profit with negative Arab portraits. There is also the emotional dimension. Shaheen (1979) points to the "Western fear," fear of the unknown Islam, the Arab masses, the "other," fear combined with ignorance. Finally, one must consider the impact of politics. When Israel is considered as the Western ally in the Middle East, media critics may argue that it affects many forms of popular culture:

> Some storytellers perceive U.S. interests as being linked with Israel's. For decades, popular culture's image makers have perpetuated a stale myth: If Arabs are allied against Israel then they are allied against America, and thus Israel's enemies become our enemies. (Shaheen, 1994, p. 130)

The stereotypical images have become part of the folklore, and the process of breaking traditional stereotypes is difficult and slow.

But it is not just Arabs as people but also Islam as a religion which is often portrayed as cruel and vicious, in total contrast to the Judeo-Christian faith and civilization. Edward Said, a well-known critic of the Western media's coverage of Islam, provides a thorough analysis of this coverage and its roots. According to Said (1993, 1997), for most Americans (the same is generally true for Europeans), the channel or cultural apparatus that has been delivering Islam to them for the most part includes the television and radio networks, the movies, the daily newspapers, and the mass-circulation news magazines:

> This powerful concentration of mass media can be said to constitute a communal core of interpretations providing a certain picture of Islam and, of course, reflecting powerful interests in the society served by the media. Along with this picture, which is not merely a picture

but also a communicable set of feelings about the picture, goes what we may call its overall context. By context I mean the picture's setting, its place in reality, the values implicit in it, and, not least, the kind of attitude it promotes. (Said, 1997, p. 47)

Said noted that even in newspapers and on radio and television, there are a host of variations to be observed, as between one editorial line and another, or between different op-ed viewpoints, but despite the variety and the differences, what the media produce is neither sponta-neous nor completely "free": Like all modes of communication, tele-vision, radio, and newspapers observe certain rules and conventions to get things across intelligibly, and it is these, often more than the reality being conveyed, that shape the material delivered by the media. Because the media strive to reach the same audience, which they believe is ruled by a uniform set of assumptions about reality, the picture of Islam (and of anything else, for that matter) is likely to be quite uniform and monochromatic. Because most media are profit-seeking corporations, they understandably have an interest in promoting some images of reality rather than others. They do so within a political context made active and effective by an unconscious ideology, which the media disseminate without serious reservations or opposition. Such aims of the press as objectivity, factuality, realistic coverage, and accuracy, argued Said, are highly relative terms; they express intentions, perhaps, and not realizable goals. The media can represent many points of view, provide many things that are eccentric, unexpectedly original, even aberrant, "but in the end, because they are corporations serving and promoting a corporate identity—'America' and even 'the West'—they all have the same central consensus in mind" (Said, 1997, p. 52). A very serious consequence is that Americans have scant opportunity to view the Islamic world except reductively, coercively, oppositionally. To Western-ers and Americans, Islam represents a resurgent atavism that suggests not only the threat of a return to the Middle Ages but the destruction of what is regularly referred to as the democratic order in the Western world.

Said argued that the term *Islam* as it is used today seems to mean one simple thing, but in fact, it is part fiction, part ideological label, part minimal designation of a religion called Islam. In no really significant way is there a direct correspondence between the Islam in common

Western usage and the enormously varied life that goes on within the world of Islam, with its more than 800 million people; its millions of square miles of territory, principally in Africa and Asia; its dozens of societies, states, histories, geographies, cultures. The media, nevertheless, have "covered" Islam: They have portrayed it, characterized it, analyzed it, given instant courses on it, and consequently they have made it "known." But, as Said argued (1997), this coverage is misleading:

> It has given consumers of news the sense that they have understood Islam without at the same time intimating to them that a great deal in this energetic coverage is based on far from objective material. In many instances "Islam" has licensed not only patent inaccuracy but also expressions of unrestrained ethnocentrism, cultural and even racial hatred, deep yet paradoxically free-floating hostility. (p. 2)

This also affects the Muslims themselves: Many parts of the Islamic world are now inundated with U.S.-produced television shows. Like all other residents of the Third World, Muslims tend to be dependent on a small group of news agencies whose job it is to transmit the news back to the Third World, even in the large number of cases where the news is about events in the Third World. Many Islamic countries have become consumers of made-in-the-West news: "For the first time in history, the Islamic world may be said to be learning *about itself* by means of images, histories, and information manufactured in the West" (Said, 1997, p. 56). This was dramatically in evidence during the Gulf War, when most Arabs, including Saddam Hussein, watched CNN as their principal source on the war.

The reason for the distorted images offered by Western media, according to Said (1997), is the conflict, the real conflict, between the West and Islam:

> The conflict between "Islam" and "the West" is very real. One tends to forget that all wars have two sets of trenches, two sets of barricades, two military machines. And just as the war with Islam seems to have unified the West around opposition to Islam's power, so too has the war with the West unified many sectors of the Islamic world. (p. 65)

Both the Islamic community, according to Said, and the Western or American community as formed mainly by the mass media, have tragically staked much of their energies on the narrow point of confrontation between them, and in the process have ignored what did not concern this confrontation. We have been all too ready to believe the myth about Muslims opposing "satanic" America. Thus, if the Iranian crisis or the Gulf War were rendered by television pictures of chanting "Islamic" mobs accompanied by commentary about "Anti-Americanism" and "Anti-West," the distance, ignorance, fear, and threatening quality of the images limit Islam to these negative attributes. "Since 'Islam' is 'against' us and 'out there', the necessity of adopting a confrontational response of our own towards it will not be doubted" (Said, 1997, p. 48).

Recent historical events have probably encouraged unflattering media portrayals of Arabs: the OPEC oil embargoes of the 1970s, hostage-taking incidents, the Lebanese civil war, the Iran-Iraq War of 1980-1988, the Persian Gulf War of 1991, and continuing Arab-Israeli conflicts. Ironically enough, the media Arabs may have suffered the most from the actions of their fellow Muslims, the non-Arab Iranians, following the 1979 Islamic revolution, especially the holding of U.S. hostages from 1979 to 1981. This protracted tragedy produced a wealth of bad feelings about the Islamic faith in the West, even though the Ayatollah Khomeini was in no way a typical Muslim.

The concern is not that there are some negative portrayals of Arabs and Muslims. The concern is that such portrayals are not balanced by positive portrayals to feed into the perceived mental reality constructed by TV viewers. Historically, argues Harris (1994), Arabs may be the latest villain in a long list of many groups who have been maligned by the U.S. media. The vicious Arabs of the 1980s and 1990s have been preceded by the wealthy but cruel Jews of the 1920s, the sinister Asian villains of the 1930s, and the Italian gangsters of the 1950s. Each of these stereotypes has been tempered and balanced as a result of protests from the offended groups and other concerned citizens. Such media portrayals can provide unwitting social support for racist and discriminatory policies and legislation.

Black Americans' Media Images

In November 1996, the American NBA basketball player, Kareem Abdul Jabbar, came to visit Israel. He asked to meet the Israeli Chief Rabbi, Rabbi Lau. Lau and his brother were liberated from the Nazi concentration camp of Buchenwald by American soldiers. Many of these soldiers were black Americans. Jabbar said this is why he asked to meet Rabbi Lau:

> I had no idea that black troops had fought that extensively because it's never been recorded in American history books, . . . there has been no movies made about it, so this information was fading from sight and it was very important for it to be known, it is certainly a shame how black American history has been neglected like that. (Quoted from Kol Israel broadcasting, July 11, 1996)

The most studied group portrayal in U.S. media has been African Americans. In their review of the studies on blacks in the media, Poindexter and Stroman (1981) concluded that:

1. Blacks have been underrepresented; there has been a trend toward increased visibility; stereotyping and negative connotations of blacks continue; and blacks typically appear in minor roles and in low-status occupational roles on television.
2. Blacks tend to rely heavily on television figures for information, including information about blacks and the black community.
3. Blacks have distinct tastes and preferences in TV programs, are among its heaviest consumers, except for news and public affairs, and prefer to watch shows that feature black characters.
4. Black children tend to believe in the reality of television, to learn behaviors from televised models, and to be influenced by television ads.

Greenberg and Brand (1994) compiled a detailed review of studies on racial and ethnic minorities in the media from the early 1950s to the mid-1990s. Television was not the first medium to be criticized for stereotypical portrayals of African Americans. In the United States, media reflected this prejudiced viewpoint before radio or television were ever conceived (Silk & Silk, 1990). One of the earliest movies was *Uncle Tom's Cabin* in 1903, a film that highly stereotyped African Americans. This trend persisted in films for many years. There are three types of studies on this subject: those that count the presence of blacks in media content and compare these counts with actual figures; those that assess whether the presence of the blacks is of major or minor significance; and, in a relatively new and incisive approach, the extent to which the portrayal of the blacks is like or unlike majority characters in the same content or program, and furthermore, the manner and frequency with which the minority characters interact with the majority characters.

In terms of frequency of appearance or head counts, blacks are indeed underrepresented. One decade-long study conducted by Seggar, Hafen, and Hannonen-Gladden (1981) included 18,000 character portrayals. Across this decade, white males increased steadily from 81% to 88% of the television male character population, and black males fluctuated from 6% in 1971 to 9% in 1980, with no change recorded between 1975 and 1980. The same pattern was found for females. In 1971, 84% were white, and 91% were white in 1980; black females fluctuated at a lower level from 5% to 6% across the decade. Thus, whites expanded their domination in these television content areas whereas blacks were below their population percentages. A second decade-long study was conducted by the Cultural Indicators team. Across the decade, nonwhite characters on U.S. television averaged 11% per year. Later, Gerbner (1993b) reported that for the 1991-1992 season, African Americans constituted 11% of the prime-time program characters, 9% on the daytime serials, and less than 3% on Saturday morning. These studies are in relatively strong agreement. By 1980, 8 of every 100 prime-time television characters were likely to be black. Black females were infrequent, and other nonwhite females were essentially absent. These findings have been consistent across studies, and these levels have not changed over the years.

What about news programs? Greenberg and Brand (1994) concluded a review of studies on news and minorities with the statement that these studies

> indicate clearly an increased presence of blacks and Hispanics in news stories and news presentations. They are far more visible than two decades ago, although questions remain as to the qualitative attributes of their presence, that is how they are being presented and in what context. (p. 274)

Numerous studies revealed that news coverage of blacks is still highly stereotyped (see, e.g., Chaudhary, 1980; Entman, 1990, 1992, 1994; Gray, 1989; Jamieson, 1992; Roberts, 1975) and suggested that news coverage may reinforce a complex of antiblack feelings labeled by some social scientists as "modern racism." Thus, for example, Entman's study (1990) of local TV news in the United States found that in crime stories, local news tends to depict blacks as more dangerous than whites accused of similar crimes. In political stories, local news makes blacks appear more demanding of special government favoritism than whites. And the employment of highly visible black anchors and reporters paradoxically presents white audiences with daily images of black success, messages suggesting that racial discrimination no longer impedes African Americans. An analysis of the images of African Americans on news programs on ABC, CBS, and NBC found that

> network news appears to convey more stereotyped impressions—a narrower range of positive roles—for blacks than for whites. Representations of whites in network news are more varied and more positive than of blacks, not because of conscious bias, but because of the way conventional journalistic norms and practices interact with political and social reality. The findings raise theoretical and normative questions about journalists' ability to "represent" the "reality" of black America. (Entman, 1994, p. 514)

Thus, most network and local news stories involving blacks are related to crime (blacks committing crimes or being victims of violent, drug, and nonviolent crimes) and politics (activities of black politicians and community leaders). Blacks were also shown as victims of social misfortunes other than crime, such as fires, poverty, bad schools, and racial discrimination. The crime plus the victim categories account for 46.4% of the stories; thus, nearly half the coverage depicted blacks as threats to or noncontributing victims of American society. In the case of crime news, 77% of network stories in which a black was accused concerned a violent or drug crime versus 42% of crime stories with whites accused. In other words, the overwhelming majority of black crime stories concerned violence or drugs, whereas these especially threatening forms of crime were a factor in a minority of stories about alleged white criminals. This disparity could reflect a true racial difference in the focus of criminal activity, but as Entman (1994) argued, these differences do not reflect actual differences in reality. With regard to politicians and leaders, Entman found that network news implicitly constructed an unfavorable contrast in black-white leadership behavior. Black leaders frequently complained of racial discrimination and often criticized government policy; yet, not once in this sample was a black leader quoted praising the government. This finding suggests the prevalence of images in which black leaders attack government and rarely support it.

Another popular role assigned to blacks in media reality is that of poverty. As numerous studies revealed, the black urban poor have come to dominate public images of poverty. Surveys show that the American public dramatically exaggerates the proportion of blacks among the poor. In a study of advertisements, Humphrey and Schumann (1984) found that 10% of the blacks shown in these ads were portrayed as poor whereas none of the whites in these ads were shown as poor. Gilens's (1996) study of the American news media found that network TV news and weekly news magazines portray the poor as substantially more black than is actually the case. This study content-analyzed every story on poverty in three leading American magazines (*Time, Newsweek,* and *U.S. News and World Report).* There were 635 poor people pictured in these stories, with 560 pictures of determinable race. Out of these 560 poor people, 345 were blacks (that is, 61.6%). But in reality, the majority of the American poor (66%) are nonblack. Moreover, the coverage of the black poor is very distorted because it focuses on the most unsympathetic subgroups of the poor, such as the unemployed, while misrepresenting the more sympathetic groups (elderly and working poor). These findings led Gilens (1996) to relate the revealed patterns of portrayal to racial stereotyping:

> It is the pattern of racial misrepresentation that most clearly signals the impact of negative racial stereotypes on the portrayal of poverty. The absence of blacks among pictures of the working poor, the elderly poor, and poor people in employment programs; the abundance of blacks among pictures of unemployed working-age adults; and the association of blacks with the least favorable poverty topics indicate the operation of a consistent prejudice against poor African Americans. (p. 532)

There is one genre in which blacks enjoy both status and viewership of whites—the sitcom. Two of the most successful U.S. sitcoms of all time have been shows about black American families, *The Jeffersons* (1975-1985) and *The Cosby Show* (1984-1992). In one sense, both are unstereotyped and atypical of African Americans; both families were quite well off economically, although not among the super rich. However, some critics have argued that *The Jeffersons* retained some earlier racial stereotyping in a more subtle way. The black characters were mostly rather loud and brassy, not very bright, and often acted rather foolishly. Cliff Huxtable and his family, on the other hand, are the epitome of upper-middle-class gentility. In fact, some critics have argued that their wealth and high status are so atypical of African Americans that it is inaccurate and even offensive to consider *The Cosby Show* an African American show at all (Harris, 1994). Some have argued that the show is a sort of neo-tokenism in that it is a show at heart about whites with black faces.

Another aspect of the portrayal of blacks is role assignment: Seggar and his colleagues (1981) examined the roles played by black and white characters on television. Over the years, white men showed sizable gains in both major and supporting roles and had trivial changes in minor and bit parts. Black males gained only slightly in the latter two categories and dropped more than 50% in major and supporting roles, from 9% to 4.4% and 12% to 4.5%, respectively. White women gained 10% in major roles, whereas black women decreased in major and supporting roles even more sharply than black men. Blacks were found in situation comedies or in less serious roles: Black characters were consistently less serious than whites in prime-time drama; two thirds of the white characters were portrayed in serious roles, compared to half of all nonwhite characters and less than half of the nonwhite females. Signorielli (1985) concluded that "minorities . . . generally were in nonserious and/or family-centered roles, limiting their opportunities for action and diminishing their symbolic power" (p. 110).

Role analyses frequently focus on the characters' aggressiveness. Blacks were certainly more related to violence, both as victimizers and as victims. Gerbner's studies show that violence was committed by half of all white Americans and two thirds of the nonwhites; nonwhites were more likely victims, and the killer-to-killed ratio for whites was 4:1 whereas for nonwhites it was 1:1 (see Chapter 5). Gerbner reported that blacks were more likely to kill than be killed, with whites, Asians, and

Hispanics more likely to be killed than to kill. These rates differ significantly from the real rates reported in FBI statistics. In occupational roles, blacks were less often portrayed in white-collar and professional roles, but they were overrepresented in these roles when compared to U.S. census data. This is certainly the case with Bill Cosby's TV family, the Huxtables. Cliff Huxtable and his family were clearly positive role models, but they also enjoyed a lifestyle that is beyond the reach of most African American families (and, for that matter, most Caucasians and other races as well). In fact, a recent study of the U.S. media's presentation of the black male (Page, 1997) found that it encourages the viewing public to believe that only a few exceptionally embraceable African American men are capable of succeeding and that the remainder should be contained due to their tendency to fail even when offered a chance.

The portrayal of blacks in various media contents was also studied by examining within-show or within-program characterizations of two races. Reid (1979), for example, compared the behaviors of black and white characters on 10 situation comedies and found black characters sought recognition for their deeds more often than white characters. Further analyses by sex of the characters indicated that black women were less achieving (e.g., in initiating plans), less likely to help in crisis, and more boasting—all indicative of a continuing black female stereotype. And black females appeared almost exclusively on the black-dominated shows. Brown and Campbell (1986) looked at music videos, with one sample from MTV and the second from *Video Soul* on the Black Entertainment Network. The MTV collection had 3% black male leads and 1% black female, compared with 54% and 19% on the minority-centered channel. They concluded that "white men . . . are the center of attention and power and are more often aggressive and hostile than helpful and cooperative. Women and blacks are rarely important enough to be a part of the foreground" (p. 104). Cross-racial relationships are infrequent and relatively formal. Blacks and whites can work together but do not maintain the same degree of voluntary, individualized relationships that whites do. For the most part, blacks and whites appear on different shows; when they do appear together, they largely maintain that separateness. In a recent study conducted in Canada, televised and newspaper coverage of portrayals of African American basketball players in Toronto was analyzed (Wilson, 1997). The results (based on the 1995-1996 season) revealed that they tended to stereotype African Americans as either "good" or "bad" blacks.

Another important media content is advertisements and commercials. The issue of portraying blacks (and other minorities) in advertising has long interested social scientists. Numerous content analyses were conducted to examine how commercials and ads depict blacks, when compared to other groups (see, e.g., Stevenson, 1992; Zinkhan, Qualls, & Biswas, 1990). The findings highlighted the underrepresentation of blacks in advertising, when compared to population statistics. The studies of print advertising found not more than 3% usage of blacks in major magazine advertising, with their few appearances as entertainers, athletes, and servants. Numerous studies of newspapers and magazines found the same pattern: very few blacks and few if any in central roles. For example, examining 962 ads in *Cosmopolitan, Glamour,* and *Vogue* fashion magazines from 1986 to 1988, Jackson and Ervin (1991) found that only 2.4% showed black women, whereas 12.5% of the U.S. female population in the late 1980s was black—as were 15% of subscribers to these magazines. Moreover, 83% of the ads showing black women portrayed the full body, whereas 9% portrayed only the face conveying, the authors note, that black women are usually portrayed from a distance if at all. A study of blacks and whites in cigarette and alcohol ads added new dimensions to the activity portrayal of the races (Reid, Whitehill King, & Kreshel, 1995). An analysis of 418 cigarette and alcohol ads appearing in 11 magazines (e.g., *Time, Esquire, Newsweek, Life*) in the 1990s revealed a world in which blacks and whites smoke and drink separately, seldom encountering one another. Their activities differ significantly: Blacks are more often portrayed in leisure activities whereas whites are portrayed at work.

Finally, studies of children's television programs found that blacks were only 3% of television characters on these shows and were more likely to be children than adults. Black characters on weekend programming for children were consistently younger than white characters. More than 40% were teenagers, compared with 25% among white characters. Special attention should be given to cartoons: "Cartoon comedy programs contain the most blatant ethnic stereotypes. These programs . . . frequently provide cruel stereotypes of ethnic minorities. And cartoon comedies alone amount to nearly one half of all program time in children's TV" (Barcus, 1983, p. 115).

Blacks' Criticism of Their Portrayal

African Americans' relationship with television has been labeled correctly as ambivalent. Although African Americans have been and continue to be high consumers of television programming, many African American educators, journalists, entertainment personnel, and activists have been and continue to be very critical of African American representations in entertainment programs. Usually their assessments result in requests for more diverse—meaning less comedic—characters and situations as well as positive role models (Bradley, 1987; Clark, 1969; Coleman, 1983; Dates & Barlow, 1990; Gray, 1989; Michaelson, 1987; Sanoff & Thomton, 1987; Smith Hobson, 1974; Staples & Jones, 1985). What do ordinary African Americans, those who are not called on nor prone to disseminate information through the mass media, think about African American representations on television? This was the research question guiding a survey of African Americans, investigating the "ways in which people encounter, use, interpret, enjoy, think and talk about television" (Abernathy-Lear, 1994, p. 830). The study, entitled "African Americans' Criticisms Concerning African American Representations on Daytime Serials," used an open-ended, semistructured questionnaire to gain information about specific viewing practices and to solicit personal responses about the interviewee's relationship with the genre.

The findings highlight the dissatisfaction of blacks with their television images. Although numerous African American characters populate the daytime serials, for many viewers in this study, quantity does not equal quality. Blacks are certainly heavy viewers of daytime television serials: According to A. C. Nielsen surveys, blacks' daytime serial viewing is 55% higher than that of the general audience, and their share of this genre's audience is 17% to 37%, the largest share across all genres. Although many blacks are daytime serial fans, they do not necessarily condone African American representations in the serials. These black fans of daytime serials desire more realistic and diverse African American roles. Specific criticisms included (a) the desire for more black characters who do not "act white"; (b) the lack of a realistic "black perspective" or "situations that I would relate to as a black person"; (c) the forced assimilation of the African American characters' story lines/representations, such as African American female characters marrying non-African American male characters; and (d) the lack of diversity of positive role models. Research on African American audiences that includes expanded comments about blacks' representations in the mass media is scarce. Such audience research yields knowledge that is constructed from the point of view of actual audiences as opposed to that which is offered by designated professionals, such as black academics, media analysts, leaders, and activists.

The Effects of the Mediated Portrayal of Blacks

So what are the effects on audiences of this stereotyped, biased, and selective presentation of blacks? One should note the potential effect of television on blacks' self-images because they watch more television than others. Studies also found that black viewers prefer blacks-dominated programs and are more than three times as likely to identify with black characters (Greenberg & Atkin, 1982). Studies among blacks continue to confirm the reality perception theme: Black youths consistently believe that the television portrayals of blacks and nonblacks are more real-to-life than whites believe. Typically, 40% of the blacks agree that television's presentation of black men, women, teenagers, dress, and language are realistic, compared to 30% for whites. This might be due to the tendency of black youngsters to approach television with the stated motivation to learn something they can apply in their daily lives. In a survey, black preteens and teens claimed that television taught them most of what they know about jobs (47%), how men and women solve problems (42%), how parents and children interact (57%), how husbands and wives interact (45%), and how teenagers act (48%). Corresponding percentages for white respondents averaged 33% (Greenberg, 1972). Whites learn more about blacks from television; blacks claim to learn about both whites and themselves. Moreover, a study found that black youngsters use the televised portrayals to reflect on themselves (McDermott & Greenberg, 1984). Similar effects on blacks' self-concept, mainly for young black women, were reported by Stroman (1986).

What do white youth who choose to watch black television programs on a regular basis learn? From a sample of fourth-, sixth-, and eighth-grade white children, Atkin, Greenberg, and McDermott (1983) explored the consequences of exposure to black programs on a variety of belief areas. Frequent exposure to programs starring blacks was significantly associated with self-reports that television teaches them most of what they know about blacks. Studies on white children have shown that prolonged exposure to television comedies or *Sesame Street* with regular African American and Hispanic cast members influences the attitudes of these children in a more accepting, less racist direction. However, even a very positive portrayal developed with the best intentions may contribute to misconceptions. For example, some white viewers of *The Cosby Show* cite the Huxtables as examples of why affirmative action is no longer necessary (Jhally & Lewis, 1992). If the affluent Huxtables have attained their share of the American dream, and they are assumed to be representative of African Americans, then African Americans who "haven't made it" must not be trying very hard. More recent attempts to link media exposure to beliefs about blacks and whites suggests that heavier exposure to television entertainment by white university students is associated with beliefs that blacks enjoy a relatively higher income, social class, and educational achievement than census data reveal (explained by the television portrayal of unreal blacks' occupational structure, such as the Huxtable family; see Armstrong, Neuendorf, & Brentar, 1992). Conversely, heavier exposure to TV news is associated with the belief that blacks are worse off than whites, again reflecting the "reality" of news with its overrepresentation of blacks' poverty, crime, victimization, and violence.

A clear pattern of media impact on public perceptions of the blacks is found in the poverty domain. As shown earlier, blacks are presented as poor in a frequency that is far beyond their real proportion of the poor population (they were found to be 66% of the poor in news magazines' stories whereas in reality 61% of the poor are not blacks; see Gilens, 1996). This overrepresentation affects the public images of race and poverty: National surveys in the United States find that the public overestimates the percentage of blacks among the poor (averaging the answers for blacks among the poor yielded 50%, compared with the real proportion of 29%, according to U.S. Bureau of Statistics). Despite the fact that in reality most poor are not black, the public seems to follow the media's distorted presentation: When asked "are there more blacks or more whites among the American poor," most of the respondents in an American national survey chose blacks (55%) whereas only 24% chose whites. The media portrayal of race and poverty affects the public not only in terms of "statistical misperceptions" but also in terms of attitudes: "Whites who think the poor are mostly blacks are more likely to blame welfare recipients for their situation and less likely to support welfare than are those with more accurate perceptions of poverty" (Gilens, 1996, p. 516). In one national survey, 46% of the white respondents who thought blacks make up more than half of the poor wanted to cut welfare spending. In contrast, only 26% of those who thought blacks compose less than one quarter of the poor wanted welfare spending cut (*Los Angeles Times* Poll No. 96, April 14, 1985, p. 86). Thus, Americans' exaggerated association of race and poverty, following the mediated portrayal of this association, perpetuates long-standing stereotypes of blacks as poor and lazy.

There is the tendency of the media to reinforce existing stereotypes. For example, more bigoted white viewers tended to identify with Archie Bunker of *All in the Family* and accept his racist views, whereas less prejudiced people decried these views and found Archie's attitudes offensive or laughable (Vidmar & Rokeach, 1974). Although the revealed correlations between media consumption and perceptions of blacks may result in part from selective distortion of the media portrayals, it is likely that the incoming perceptions exert a stronger influence. Thus, for some sets of beliefs, content is important; for others, predispositions clearly have a greater role. In this manner, television both serves to reinforce what is learned outside the television situation and offers the possibility of new information, where little or none was available.

Images of People With Disabilities

The last group we will look at is that of people with disabilities. An early systematic analysis of media coverage of "handicappers" (undefined) was reported by Donaldson (1981). Sampling 85 half-hour network prime-time programs, 1% of the characters were handicapped, 3% among major characters. Handicappers in Donaldson's study were seldom portrayed positively. For most of the characters, their disability was a central feature of their lives. Elliot and Byrd (1982) found that

57% of the comic book characters with disabilities were found to be villains, whereas only 11% were heroes. They also noted that prime-time television portrayals of people with disabilities depict this group predominantly in lower social classes, unemployed, single, victims of abuse, and more likely than able-bodied characters to enjoy a positive outcome at the end of the show. In a study of newspapers and prime-time television over a 3-week period, Gardner and Radel (1978) found that 68% of disability portrayals depicted physical handicaps and 22% mental retardation and mental illness. The kinds of physical disabilities included people who were paraplegic, quadriplegic, blind, deaf, with cerebral palsy, epileptic, diabetic, and physically deformed. Only one third of the characters with physical handicaps were depicted as independent and capable contributors to society or their environment. People with disabilities were found more often in entertainment than in news or informational content: In 19 television entertainment programs with portrayals of people with disabilities, 42% were depicted as dependent, 21% were abusers or in some way socially deviant, and 5% were victims of abuse. Major themes in these shows portrayed 48% of the people with disabilities dealing with problems adjusting to the majority world and 26% projecting strange, bizarre, antisocial, or otherwise deviant attributes of such people or groups. Byrd (1989) looked at the role portrayals of 67 characters with disabilities in the movies between 1986 and 1988 and found that 73% had abnormal personalities; two thirds were normal in appearance, but more were unattractive (22%) than attractive (12%); 55% were victims in the story, and more (45%) experienced negative consequences than either neutral or positive conclusions.

News coverage of and themes related to people with disabilities were very different for television and for newspapers. Gardner and Radel noted that newspapers dealt with the theme of special services (44%) for people with disabilities significantly more than did television (11%). Difficulty in adjusting to the majority world was found in 8% of the newspaper stories and 37% of the television programs. The theme of abuse of those with disabilities was carried in 14% of the press stories and in no television coverage. It appears that television news portrayal of people with disabilities was much less favorable than that of the press. However, images in newspapers were neither as positive nor as realistic as the thematic coverage. Half the articles portrayed dependency whereas only 22% depicted people with disabilities who were nevertheless independent. Newspapers represented handicappers as objects of abuse in 19% of the stories and as social outcasts or deviants in 9%. Sampling national daily newspapers, a research team analyzed articles covering disabilities to determine whether disabilities were the prominent focus of each article and what types of disability were covered, in what article genres, and with what impact to the subject or subjects of the disability (Keller, Hallahan, McShane, Crowley, & Blandford, 1990). They found very few articles in which disabilities were either a major or minor focus of the story. In 63% of those, the disability was the major focus of the story. However, half the stories were soft news features "tending to be more emotionally charged." About half the articles did not discuss the effect of the disability on the life of the story subject, but 48% were negative about the disability's impact, whereas only 1% portrayed positive impact. Most articles (52%) featured no details about potential for improvement in the person with disabilities, although 44% of articles portraying the negative impact of the disability indicated potential for improvement, and 4% portrayed the disability as unimprovable.

In England, Cumberbatch and Negrine (1992) conducted a thorough analysis of the images of disability on television. Their first inquiry was designed to examine the extent and the manner of television's portrayal of people with disabilities. The second inquiry was designed to assess reaction to this portrayal and to provide a commentary on it. For the content analysis, all appearances of people with disabilities were counted and classified; the tallies were then compared with what is known about the actual incidence of people with disabilities in the U.K. population, based on a recent survey carried out by the Office of Population Censuses and Surveys (OPCS). The findings indicated that people with disabilities were portrayed in fictional programs, but they represented a mere 0.5% of all the characters portrayed. When only major and minor (that is, speaking) characters are considered, the percentage rises to 1.4%. This contrasts strangely with the evidence of the Office of Population Censuses and Surveys that 14% of the adult population of Britain has disabilities of one kind or another. The researchers also found that the most common focus for factual reporting that involved people with disabilities was that of medical treatment. The emphasis on medical treatment was even greater when news programs alone were examined. Very few focused on the special achievement of people with disabilities. The characters depicted as having some disability or other are overwhelmingly shown to have behavioral or disfigurement disabilities. The range of disabilities portrayed is conspicuously narrow: "It is not so much the real world that is being portrayed as the readily screenable world," argued the researchers (p. 36).

In feature films on television, the portrayal of characters with disabilities was stereotypical: The most commonly used stereotypes were those of a criminal or someone only barely human or someone who is powerless and pathetic. The overall conclusion was that characters with disabilities are included in the story lines of feature films for ulterior motives; that is, not because they are ordinary people whom one might expect to encounter in an ordinary society; to the contrary, they would appear to be brought in to enhance an atmosphere of depravation, mystery, or menace. When the portrayal of characters with disabilities is compared and contrasted with the portrayal of able-bodied characters, it is immediately apparent that the characters with disabilities are of lower status. They are less likely to be in professional or white-collar employment and more likely to be unemployed and over 60. The attitudes displayed toward characters with disabilities are also markedly different from those shown toward able-bodied characters. Characters with disabilities are much more likely to evoke sympathy, pity, sadness, fear, or a patronizing attitude. In contrast, able-bodied characters are much more likely to evoke respect or attraction. The lowly character with disabilities is lowered again through the attitudes and behavior of the able-bodied. The characters with disabilities are portrayed even more negatively: They are much more likely than able-bodied characters to be portrayed as villains and also more likely to be portrayed as "difficult to get on with," moody, introverted, unsociable, or sad. Furthermore, characters with disabilities were far more likely than their able-bodied compatriots to be either aggressive or the victims of violence; and they were more than three times as likely as able-bodied characters to be dead by the end of the program.

What is the impact of these media images of people with disabilities on the public's perceptions? An experiment by Elliot and Byrd (1983) determined how televised portrayals affected participants' attitudes toward this minority. Using 101 eighth-grade students divided into three groups, they exposed one group to an episode of *Mork and Mindy* featuring a blind actor, a second group to a professional informative film that discussed meeting blind people, and a control group to an episode of *Mork and Mindy* without characters with disabilities. The first group did not have significantly more positive attitudes toward blind people than the control group, but the second group (informational film) emerged with more positive attitudes. In a replication with 46 college males, Elliot and Byrd (1984) found, again, that the informational film produced significant attitude change. The researchers concluded the set of experiments by stating that the mass media reinforce negative attitudes toward handicappers through misinformation and stereotypes.

NOTE

1. In the movie *The Siege,* Arab Americans and American Muslims are arrested in reaction to a Muslim bombing in New York City. The Council on American Islamic Relations (CAIR) and other groups demanded that 20th Century Fox either re-evaluate and reshoot the main plot line or insert disclaimers and eliminate all religious symbolism.

CHAPTER **TEN**

Images of America

*Those movies were the real cause . . . they described life in
America as a legend: big cars, rock music, dancing parties,
plenty of everything. . . . I believed that this is the way of life
of everyone who lives in America.*

—Joe Nakash (Israeli emigrant living in the
United States, creator of Jordache Jeans)

I come from a relatively small country, Israel. Despite its size, Israel is
a frequent "item" in world news and is considered as a major newsmaking arena. However, most of the people of the world have never
met someone from Israel in person. In such cases, the media portrayal
of Israelis may be the source of strange and even distorted images. In
Perl, a village in southern Germany, I surprised a hosting German family
who expected a rabbi, "the way an Israeli Jew from Jerusalem looks on
television news." In Singapore, my new students at the National University of Singapore were disappointed to find that their Israeli guest
professor does not resemble the Rambo type of the "Israeli soldiers from
the movies." Rabbi and Rambo were both images created by the mass
media: As a study reported in the 1960s, children said that most of their
information about people from different nationalities came from their

parents and television, with TV becoming increasingly important as the child grew older (Lambert & Klineberg, 1967). In this chapter we will examine the images of the United States as portrayed in various countries and various media contents. We will also look at the impact of these mediated images on various audiences all over the world. The choice of American images was guided by the dominance of the American media in the international flow of news and entertainment, the impact of U.S.-made media on world media, and studies of the impact of American media in various societies.

Who Are the "Lords of the Global Village"?

Most nations in the world are exposed to American media products either by importing American programs or through home-style imitations of American formulas.[1] In his survey of the cross-national flow of television programs and films, Varis (1974, 1984) found that the United States is the biggest program exporter in the world; in most countries of the world, American TV programs compose a major part of all the imported programs. This has led some critics to suggest that the "free flow of communications" has turned into a one-way trade, reflecting the uneven distribution of cultural power in the world and threatening the cultural independence of other societies with the massive influence of the American media. Many communication scholars have ascribed special importance to the impact of America throughout the world. Some related to it a conspiracy motive: Herbert Schiller (1969), in his *Mass Communication and American Empire,* argued that American television exports are part of an attempt by the American political-military-business complex to subjugate the world. Alan Wells's (1972) *Picture Tube Imperialism?* pursues the television imperialism thesis in Latin America.

The great expansion of American television into the world around 1960, and the American dominance in exporting equipment, programming, and advertising, is seen by Schiller (1969) as part of a general effort of the American military-industrial complex to subject the world to American control and homogenized American commercial culture.

American television program exports, through their close connection with the manufacture of television receiving sets and American advertising agencies, are also seen as the spearhead for an American consumer goods invasion of the world. This export boom has, and is intended to have, the effect of muting political protest in much of the world; authentic local culture, in many countries, is driven to the defensive by homogenized American culture. As Tunstall (1977) summarizes, "So powerful is the thrust of American commercial television that few nations can resist. Even nations that deliberately choose not to have commercial broadcasting find their policies being reversed by American advertising agencies" (p. 38).

If one looks beyond the American conspiracy argument, which was more ideological than empirical, one can find powerful cultural, economic, and political factors that combine to promote American culture worldwide. Stevenson (1994), for example, argues that neither U.S. foreign policy nor British colonialism explains why U.S. media are growing in influence at the end of the 20th century and are the model for media in most other countries. Several other factors to be considered include:

1. *American cultural values:* Initiative, ambition, and creativity are encouraged, and individual eccentricity is tolerated. Combined with the lure of financial and popular success in the global market, these values are powerful, attractive features of Western, and especially American, cultural products.

2. *The economy of the global media market:* A publication in English has, in theory, a potential audience of up to one quarter of the world's population. A similar advantage accrues to broadcast and film, which can be shipped around the world without dubbing or subtitling. This situation provides U.S. media organizations with a significant advantage in accessing audiences and information content consumers worldwide.

3. *The competitive, market-oriented structure of most American media:* Regardless of its artistic and cultural merits, a TV series that survives the ratings gauntlet of American networks has already been tested for its popular appeal. With few exceptions, these American hits become hits in other countries as well.

4. *Western dominance in other areas of global communication:*
Hegemonic Western media organizations, with subsidiaries involved in
numerous communication media formats, enjoy a synergy or mutually
supporting embrace of all aspects of global communication. Dominance
in news supports dominance in popular culture, which supports dominance in technology, which supports dominance in journalistic style,
which supports dominance in the English language, and so on.

The American dominance in the global communication flow is less
powerful today than it was in the past. A growing concern is not the old
complaint of excessive American cultural influence around the world,
but the astonishing speed with which the United States is selling off its
popular culture industries to foreign buyers. New Lords of the Global
Village emerge, and most of them are not American. Moreover, some
countries now apply special laws limiting the import of American media
products. These trends do not match McLuhan's "universal understanding" or the original claims against American cultural imperialism.
The driving force for these media giants is profits. The political-ideo-
logical motives behind the alleged media imperialism of the early 1960s
and 1970s have given way to more business-oriented goals among the
new lords of the media village, but ideological motives should not be
overlooked. Moreover, whereas Rupert Murdoch is relatively well-
known, many of the other modern moguls are not. Silvio Berlusconi in
Italy, the late Robert Maxwell in Britain, the Japanese Sony Corporation, the Hachette organization in France, and Bertelsmann in Germany
have played down their dominance of multinational multimedia ownership. All are taking advantage of new technology, global management
strategies, and a tide of hands-off government policies to extend their
operations and influence beyond national and regional borders. Despite
the wide array of national memberships they represent, the new lords
of the village do have political and cultural impact, as noted by Bagdikian (1984):

> The lords of the global village have their own political agenda. All
> resist economic changes that do not support their own financial
> interests. Together, they exert a homogenizing power over ideas,
> culture, and commerce that affects populations larger than any in
> history. Neither Caesar nor Hitler, Franklin Roosevelt nor any Pope,

has commanded as much power to shape the Information on which so many people depend to make decisions about everything from whom to vote for to what to eat. (p. 2)

As the world heads into the 21st century, the notion of media domination assumes new dimensions and new meanings. But despite the decline of American dominance in media ownership, the new media empires still consume and diffuse mainly American media products—from movies to pop music and American television programs. The factors listed above still guide the new lords of the village to buy, produce, and sell the American media products.

Cultivation and International Images

The United States continues to be the major exporter of media contents, movies, and television programs to the rest of the world. In the 1980s, imported programs constituted about one third of total programming in more than 70 counties. The United States was the source of about three quarters of imported programs in Latin America, 44% in Western Europe, and 33% in Asia and the Pacific. To many foreign audiences, American television is the only or main source of information about American culture and people. It is important therefore to understand how American television is consumed by its foreign audiences and to determine the images of Americans that American programs are projecting abroad. The notion of cultivation can be applied to reconstructed, mediated images of nations and societies. Introducing the concept of cultivation, Gerbner and Gross (1976) claimed that

> the dominant stylistic convention of Western narrative art—novels, plays, films, TV drama—is that of representational realism. However contrived television plots are, viewers assume that they take place against a backdrop of the real world. Nothing impeaches the basic reality of the world of television drama. It is also highly informative. That is, it offers to the unsuspecting viewer a continuous stream of "facts" and impressions about the way of the world. . . . The promise of realism is a Trojan horse which carries within it a highly selective, synthetic, and purposeful image of the facts of life. (p. 178)

The interweaving of entertainment and information in the same TV program cultivates a knowledge of reality based on "facts" that are often learned from fictional dramas or selective news stories. Does this apply to the flow of international images? The theory and methods of cultivation analysis were applied mainly in the context of the political, cultural, and media systems of the United States. However, the original concept of cultivation has been adapted by scholars from various countries and cultures. In his review of the international dimension of cultivation research, Morgan (1990) provides convincing evidence of the validity and usefulness of the cultivation paradigm in various societies, countries, and cultures. Modern media and especially television have transformed the sociocultural landscape of most countries around the world. In almost every corner of the globe, it has become an integral part of daily life for young and old, rich and poor, male and female, and urban and rural populations to a degree not matched by any cultural institution since preindustrial religion. At the same time, many countries in all "three worlds" are becoming ever more interdependent while trying to uphold their own traditions, interests, values, and cultural identities. This dual nature of global culture led to the linking of international cultivation analysis with arguments and debates concerning cultural imperialism. There is no question that the U.S. media industries export more of their product and to more places than does any other country. Often, these programs present values, lifestyles, and ideologies that are contrary to those of the host culture and that are in conflict with those presented in the host country's programming. Moreover, Morgan argues that structural differences among systems may be exaggerated by differences in how much of the programming is imported and by the degree of cultural inconsistency between domestic and imported programs. Although no two cultures are identical, U.S. programs may "fit" better in some cultural contexts than in others.

In the Philippines, Israel, Taiwan, Mexico, Iceland, Jordan, Korea, and other societies where most of the television programs come from the United States, several scholars studied the impact of Americanized television on values associated with Americans, images of America and Americans, and the perceived "American Dream." Kang and Morgan (1988) analyzed the contribution of exposure to U.S. programs to the attitudes of 226 college students in Korea. (For a comparison of cultivation patterns among college students in Korea and Taiwan, see Daddario, Kang, Morgan, & Wu, 1988.) American television presents some sharp contrasts with traditional Korean values concerning "proper" roles of men and women, family values, and respect for parents and elders. In general, exposure to U.S. TV is associated with more liberal perspectives among women; women who watch more are less likely to endorse traditional notions of filial piety, less likely to want a traditional match-making marriage, more likely to wear jeans and like rock 'n' roll music, and more likely to see Confucianism as old-fashioned and irrelevant. In contrast, greater viewing of U.S. TV among Korean male students goes with more hostility toward the United States and greater protectiveness of Korean culture. This suggests a possible outcome rarely considered—that U.S. TV may have a backlash effect, engendering opposition to an imported culture and raising nationalistic cultural consciousness, at least among some politicized college students.

A study of media use and images of the United States in Jordan was conducted by Van Tubergen and Boyd (1986). First, they asked the Jordanian respondents to rate their information sources about the United States. Their analysis revealed three types of media users: Type 1 Jordanians form their images of America and Americans almost solely on the basis of interpersonal sources. Type 2 Jordanians form their images and perceptions of the United States based on mass media, mostly Jordanian and American (these were the older and better educated respondents). Type 3 relied only on American sources to form their images of America. Although this study did not explore the images themselves, it did reveal the various patterns of media use. Whereas American media were most likely to shape images among the more educated individuals, the less educated Jordanians relied on interpersonal sources. As the researchers conclude (1986), "No matter how dominant American media might be in a society, the cultural traditions of the society must be considered as a mitigating factor when possible effects of media contents are at issue" (p. 611).

In Iceland, Payne and Peake (1977) tested the cultural imperialism hypothesis. They focused on three questions: first, that viewing U.S. TV affects Icelanders' attitudes toward the United States; second, that watching U.S. TV conveys political information to Icelanders about the

United States; third, that watching U.S. TV creates attitudes in Icelanders that they claim are characteristic of American culture. Data analyzed
in this study were taken from a larger survey on the effects of TV in
Iceland. Only children ages 11 to 14 were sampled. There are four basic
indicators of exposure to U.S. TV (independent variables). The first was
the city of residence (those in Akureyri received no U.S. TV and were
classified as nonwatchers; those in Vestmannaeyjar and Reykjavik received U.S. TV and were classified as watchers). The second measure
was length of time that the respondent's family had owned a TV. The
third measure was a self-report of how often the respondents watched
TV in their homes. Finally, the survey included a message discrimination
measure, measuring the number of U.S. TV programs the respondents
could name.

There were three basic dependent variables: favorable attitude
toward the United States, political knowledge of the United States, and
adoption of attitudes considered characteristic of U.S. culture. Favorable attitude toward the United States was measured by asking respondents to indicate the one country to which they would like to migrate
if they had to. Political knowledge of the United States was measured
by asking for identification of the chief executive of various countries
including the United States. The final dimension was that of attitudes:
The authors argued that American culture was often characterized by
an atmosphere of fear, anger, and sadness. These feelings were measured
by a closed response question asking if respondents had ever had such
feelings from watching TV and a second question asking if these came
from U.S. TV, Icelandic TV, or both.

The analysis revealed a fairly consistent increase in desire to migrate
to the United States by TV viewing. TV watching was directly associated
with recognition of American leaders. The researchers also examined
the notion popular in Icelandic circles that U.S. culture is characterized
by fear, anger, and sadness and that U.S. TV transmits these general
attitudes to Icelandic viewers. TV was a primary cause of respondents'
feeling frightened, angry, or sad, and it seemed likely that those who
frequently watched it would more frequently report having those feelings than those who rarely watched it. Indeed, amount of TV watched
was associated significantly ($p < .05$) with feelings of fear, anger, or
sadness, but these correlations were rather weak.

Images of the "Land of Promise" in the "Promised Land"

In the early 1980s, I conducted a research project attempting to relate the American content on Israeli TV to images of American reality (Weimann, 1984). It was based on a comparison of perceptions of heavy and light Israeli viewers, following the cultivation concept and methodology. The dominance of American TV then was clear: Israel had at that time (and for 25 years!) only one TV station, which was government-supported and -operated and enjoyed a regular audience of 90% to 95% of the population. The fact that this station was noncommercial imposed severe limitations on its budget, equipment, and skilled manpower and thus on its ability to produce quality programs. The reliance on imported programs was considerable: More than 60% of broadcasting time was allocated to imported content (Varis, 1984, reported a rate of 55% in the 1970s, whereas our own survey of the period January 1979-December 1981 revealed a rate of 65%). Most of the imported programs were American.

During the 3 years 1979 through 1981, Israeli viewers were exposed to various American comedies from *Archie Bunker's Place* to *Love Boat*, detective series such as *Starsky and Hutch* and *Hawaii Five-O*, and TV serials and miniseries such as *Roots* and *Dallas*. This rich diet of American programs was even more significant because no alternative Israeli channels were available. Consequently, these programs got very high ratings, reaching a peak of 81% for *Dallas*. According to a survey of TV viewing in Israel conducted by the Israel Institute of Social Research in June 1981, 81% of the Israeli population watched *Dallas*, 52% reported regular viewing of the program, and 77% of the viewers enjoyed the program.

Almost two decades later, in 1997-1998, we replicated the study in the same schools, with similar samples (high school students, university students) and the same procedure. The setting, however, had changed drastically: Cable TV has come to the Holy Land. Television had been a single-station medium in Israel since 1968, when the Israeli Broadcasting Authority started airing television programs. However, the 1990s brought a dramatic change. The Israeli parliament approved two significant changes that altered the media environment: the introduction of cable television and the establishment of a second national channel, which unlike the first, would be a commercial channel. Cable television in Israel is privately owned and operated. According to the regulations, Israel was divided into 31 concession areas, and the operator in each area was determined by an open tender. During 1992, most of these cable operators started their operation and did so with a fast penetration rate that reached an average of 40% of the Israeli households in the "cabled" areas. By the end of 1992, 400,000 households subscribed to cable TV, with a total of 1.6 million viewers (out of a total Israeli population of 1,290,000 households, a third of which were in areas where cable was still unavailable). By the end of 1994, 800,000 house-holds (of 1.2 million households reached by cable) subscribed to cable, bringing the subscription rate to 67%. The cable services offered the subscribers about 40 channels, mainly foreign stations received through satellite dishes in the cable station and transmitted through the cables to the subscribers. Cable channels included Sky News, Sky One, and the Super Channel from Britain; CNN International; MTV Europe and MTV Asia; the German SAT1 and SAT3; RTL from Luxemburg; BBC Asia; three Turkish channels; two Russian channels; the Spanish channel TVE; an Italian channel; Eurosport; the French TV5; Star TV and Star One from Hong Kong; Arab channels from Jordan, Lebanon, Morocco, and Egypt; and two Israeli stations. The Israelis were also exposed to the Christian Broadcasting Network (CBN) through the Middle East Network located in southern Lebanon. The cable services also provide five special channels: movie channel, sports channel, children's channel, family channel, and nature/documentary channel. The introduction of cable and the multichannel environment had a dramatic impact on the Israelis' viewing habits and allocation of leisure time. But did it also affect their images of other "realities"?

The analyses were based on data collected from two samples of adolescents and undergraduate students. In the first study, the first sample was drawn from five secondary schools in urban areas, Tel Aviv, Haifa, and Jerusalem ($n = 310$), and one school in a rural area, mainly serving the neighboring kibbutzim (rural and collective communities, $n = 58$). The second sample included 93 undergraduate students enrolled at the University of Haifa. Thus, the total sample comprised 461 respondents. In the second study, almost 16 years later, we returned to the same schools, sampling again 540 high school students from the urban schools, 70 from a rural school, and 160 students from Haifa University (a total of 770 respondents). Each respondent filled out a questionnaire structured to study TV viewing habits and various perceptions of "living in America." (Respondents were asked to estimate the percentages of Americans who own two cars, a five-bedroom house, etc.)

We compared the estimates given by the respondents with the actual percentages drawn from the Statistical Abstracts 1980 for each sample and across demographic variables separately. The differences between the perceived and real reality were then compared for heavy and light viewers (the levels of viewing were determined by a median split of each sample). The resulting "difference of differences" serves as the Cultivation Differential or CD (average error of heavy viewers minus average error of light viewers within each comparison group). Four measures were calculated for each question:

1. The real measure, drawn from the American Statistical Abstracts
2. The average estimate of light viewers
3. The average estimate of heavy viewers
4. The Cultivation Differential (CD), where $CD = (1 - 3) - (1 - 2)$.

These measures were computed for each of the estimates, covering various aspects of living in the United States—occupational structure, consumption, earnings, sources of personal income, personal wealth, and housing. The measures for the entire sample are presented in Table 10.1.

Table 10.1 reads as follows: If we take, for example, the first measure of wealth (percentage without a car), the reality according to the Statistical Abstracts is that 15.9% do not have a car. The light viewers' average estimate of this percentage was lower (8.2%) whereas the heavy viewers' average was even lower (2.6%). Although both groups underestimated the percentage of Americans without a car, the heavy viewers' estimate was the lowest, yielding a CD of −5.6 (between the 8.2% of the light viewers and the 2.6% of the heavy viewers). In the second study, conducted in 1998, the revealed CD was −7.8, indicating a somewhat more powerful cultivation impact.

The estimates of both light and heavy Israeli viewers clearly differ from the real measures. Note that in most cases, both light and heavy

TABLE 10.1 Israeli Perceptions of "Living in the United States": Light Versus Heavy TV Viewers

		Average Estimates of:[a]			
	Reality[b]	Light Viewers	Heavy Viewers	Cultivation Differential, 1982	Cultivation Differential, 1998
Personal wealth:					
Percentage with no car	15.9	8.2	2.6	−5.6	−7.8
Percentage with one car	47.5	25.2	16.3	−8.9	−8.4
Percentage with two cars	28.8	36.4	46.8	−10.4	−9.7
Percentage with three cars or more	7.8	30.2	34.3	+4.1	+6.3
Percentage of cars under 3 years old	26.9	65.2	82.3	+17.1	+19.2
Percentage of cars 3 to 5 years old	24.1	16.3	9.2	−7.1	−8.7
Percentage of cars 6+ years old	49.0	18.5	8.5	−10.0	−9.3
Percentage owning air conditioners	55.5	61.2	74.3	+13.1	+15.2
Percentage owning blenders	52.4	82.3	85.4	+3.1	+1.9
Percentage owning electric can openers	63.6	78.4	84.6	+6.2	+2.4
Percentage owning dishwashers	43.0	52.3	61.8	+9.5	+8.9
Percentage owning food waste disposers	43.0	49.6	54.3	+4.7	+5.7
Percentage owning clothes dryers	61.5	60.8	68.3	+7.7	+7.4
Percentage owning freezers	44.7	65.2	82.2	+17.0	+19.3
Percentage owning microwave ovens	7.6	25.3	31.6	+6.3	+7.9
Occupational structure:					
Percentage of white collar workers	60.5	52.4	65.7	+13.3	+16.1
Percentage of blue collar workers	39.5	47.6	34.3	−13.3	−16.1
Weekly earnings:					
Average for all workers ($)	244	312.8	341.6	+28.8	+27.2
Average for males ($)	298	337.4	380.9	+43.5	+37.6
Average for females ($)	186	273 .2	258.6	−14.6	−11.2
Family annual income:					
Percentage over $50,000 per year	5.2	11.8	18.8	+7.2	+11.4

TABLE 10.1 Continued

		Average Estimates of:[a]			
	Reality[b]	Light Viewers	Heavy Viewers	Cultivation Differential, 1982	Cultivation Differential, 1998
Sources of personal income:					
Percentage of wage/ salary/labor	69.8	64.6	58.3	−7.3	−7.7
Percentage of rental/ dividends/interest	11.9	21.3	29.7	+8.4	+7.5
Housing:					
Percentage of units with:					
1 to 2 rooms	4.0	5.3	5.8	+0.5	−5.4
3 to 4 rooms	29.0	16.2	14.3	−1.9	−4.6
5 rooms	23.0	41.6	34.8	−6.8	−1.3
6 rooms	20.0	28.6	24.3	−4.3	+3.3
7 or more rooms	24.0	8.3	20.8	+12.5	+9.7
Percentage of second-home owners	4.1	11.8	21.3	+9.5	+9.2
Percentage of houses built prior to 1940	31.5	20.4	11.7	−8.7	−8.6
Personal consumption expenditures:					
Percentage for food, beverages, tobacco	21.3	22.3	26.8	+4.5	+3.5
Percentage for clothing, accessories, jewelry	7.8	18.8	24.9	+6.1	+5.8
Percentage for housing, household	20.5	16.3	8.7	−7.6	−6.4
Percentage for recreation	6.7	15.2	18.2	+3.0	+7.2
Percentage for transportation	14.1	11.3	10.8	−0.5	+0.8

a. Based on the average percentages given by the respondents answering the question: "About what percent of all people living in U.S. have/own/are . . . ?" Estimates presented in the table are from the 1982 study.
b. The reality measures are drawn from the Statistical Abstracts of the United States, 1980, Tables 696, 704, 733, 744, 1123, 1404, 1411, and 1415. The same measures for the 1998 study were drawn from the Statistical Abstracts of the United States, 1996.

viewers overestimate the actual rates of wealth and income. Both groups tend to visualize Americans as earning and possessing more than they actually do. Although this idealization of life in America may be traced to various sources, our interest is in the part played by the media. Hence, we focus on the differences between the estimates given by light and heavy viewers, or the CD. These measures, presented in Table 10.1, reveal that heavy viewers are more likely to overestimate the various indicators of wealth than light viewers. Let us briefly review some of the differences.

Heavy viewers tend to overestimate and light viewers to underestimate the percentage of Americans employed in white-collar occupations. Heavey viewers perceive average weekly earnings to be significantly higher than in reality (a $100 per week difference), and this overestimation is higher among heavy viewers than light viewers. In regard to the sex of the worker, our analysis reveals an interesting difference: Heavy viewers overestimate the weekly earnings of male workers more than light viewers do. The opposite holds for female workers: The overestimation of light viewers exceeds that of heavy viewers. This finding may be the result of the impact of the home-making role played by women in most TV dramas, as revealed by several studies (see Chapter 6). Both light and heavy viewers tend to overestimate the proportion of top earners; light viewers' estimates of the proportion of families with an annual income of over $50,000 was 11.8% (an overestimation of 6.4%) whereas the equivalent estimate of heavy viewers was 18.8% (an overestimation of 13.6%, double that of light viewers). This difference related to TV viewing was even larger in the 1998 study. Regarding sources of personal income, heavy viewers tend to overestimate nonwork sources of income and underestimate wage, salary, and labor income (smaller errors of estimate are made by light viewers). As to personal wealth, heavy viewers are more inclined to overestimate the ownership of electrical appliances and cars, especially the number of people owning several cars. Their overestimates, ranging from 6.8% to 31.8%, are higher for every item than those made by light viewers. As to housing, the same pattern is revealed: Heavy viewers are more likely to overestimate the number of rooms per unit and to underestimate the percentage of old houses (built prior to 1940).

Finally, when respondents estimate personal consumption expenditures in the United States, they tend to overestimate expenditures on recreation, food, beverages, cigarettes, clothing, accessories, and jewelry while underestimating housing, household, and transportation expenditures. Once again, the overestimates of heavy viewers are higher than those of light viewers, but heavy viewers clearly underestimate cost-of-living expenditures even more than light viewers do. To sum up, the comparisons in Table 10.1 reveal that young Israelis seem to have an idealized perception of life in America. Focusing on the differences between heavy and light viewers, the impact of TV-cultivated images is clearly evident: Heavy viewers demonstrate a strong and consistent tendency to overestimate, thus painting a rosier picture of reality. These findings provide considerable support for the claim that heavy television viewers perceive life in the United States differently from light viewers. Another interesting finding is that the impact of television viewing was stable: The CD coefficients did not diminish despite the changing media environment in Israel. In fact, most of the coefficients were higher in 1998. This might have been a surprising finding if we consider the rich variety of TV channels in modern Israel.

At this stage, the data reveal an interesting relation between amount of TV viewing and the level of overestimating wealth in America. According to the cultivation concept, this relation should be interpreted in terms of causality rather than simple association. Although one can never directly demonstrate causality from correlational data, it is possible to make causal inferences concerning the adequacy of specific causal models using partial correlations. This method involves testing the fitness of various models by means of partial correlations. We computed zero-order correlation between amount of TV viewing, level of overestimation (in four different estimates), and background variables— age, parental education (years of schooling), and location of residence (rural-urban), and gender. The analysis of the partial correlations reveal that none of the control variables is affecting the impact of viewing on the dependent variable (level of overestimation). Moreover, the fit of the causal model is evident for every type of estimation, under every control variable, and for both studies.

These findings highlight the impact of American TV on Israeli viewers: Unaware of the fictitious nature of television drama, unable to distinguish fantasy from reality, heavy viewers tend to absorb and retain overidealized perceptions of the American way of life. These images are diffused through other channels as well, including movies, the popular press, literature, and interpersonal communication. It is interesting to note that the replication of the study in 1998 resulted in almost the same findings. Despite the rising number of channels and of people who had visited the United States, television's impact on images still has retained its power.

American TV in the Philippines and Its Impact

The Philippines is an ideal location to test the cultural impact hypothesis for several reasons. First, television is an established medium in the Philippines. Already in 1980, there were more than 30 stations and more than 1 million sets. Television is available in most urban areas and in many rural communities through a domestic satellite system. Second, American television programs are available and popular in the Philippines. In 1983, about 60% of all TV programs in the Manila area were imported from the United States. Third, English is a second language to many Filipinos. American TV programs are shown in their original versions; dubbing in the native language is not required.

A study conducted in the Philippines examined the possible influences of American television on two manifestations of culture—the value system and aspirations (Tan, Tan, & Tan, 1987). Most definitions of values consider them to be enduring and central clusters of beliefs, thoughts, and feelings that influence or determine important evaluations of choices regarding persons, situations, and ideas. Compared to attitudes, values are fewer in number; more general, central, and pervasive; less situation-bound; and more resistant to change. The measures of value system used in this study are based on Rokeach's conceptualization of values. According to Rokeach (1968), there are two general categories of values: instrumental and terminal. Instrumental values are preferred means, measured in terms of importance to the respondent as "guiding principles in your life." Terminal values are preferred goals, measured in terms of important end states to the respondent. The researchers expected heavy viewers of American television to place more importance on those values (as measured by the Rokeach Value Survey) emphasized in American programs and less importance on those values that are de-emphasized, compared to light viewers. They also looked at how American television might affect the aspirations of Filipinos. Assuming that American television emphasizes pleasure from material comforts, they expected that heavy viewing of

American television would influence the respondents to aspire to higher education (because higher education is a means to economic prosperity) and would influence them to want to go to the United States.

Using a questionnaire administered to Filipino high school students, television use and value systems of Filipinos were measured. Respondents were asked how often they went to the movies and how often they watched individually listed American and Filipino television programs that were being aired at the time of the study. The respondents were then asked to indicate the frequency with which instrumental and terminal values from Rokeach's Value Survey were portrayed in the American television programs that they watched. They were asked to estimate these frequencies on a 4-point scale, from *all the time* to *never.* The sample consisted of 225 seniors in three Philippine high schools (mean age was 16.09 years). Respondents watched television an average of 3.8 hours per day; 72% owned a television set. American television programs were watched frequently by the sample. Of the 10 most popular programs, six were American (e.g., *Different Strokes, The Price Is Right,* and *The Incredible Hulk*).

Viewers said American television emphasized the following terminal values, listed in order of frequency: pleasure, an exciting life, freedom, true friendship, happiness, and others. The least emphasized terminal values were salvation, inner harmony, and self-respect. The instrumental values considered to be reflected in American television were, in order of importance, loving, independent, intellectual, ambitious, imaginative, and others. The least emphasized instrumental values were polite, clean, forgiving, and honest. The researchers noted that "American TV rarely emphasizes the instrumental values politeness, forgiveness, and obedience, which were important to those in our sample" (Tan et al., 1987, p. 71).

An analysis of covariance regression model showed that, controlling for various variables (e.g., number of American friends), the average frequency of watching all available American programs significantly predicted intention to visit the United States ($\beta = .262, p = .005$). This suggests that heavy viewers of American TV were more likely than light viewers to wish to go to the United States. American TV viewing was found to be related to the respondents' ratings of instrumental and terminal values. This analysis shows that ratings of several terminal and instrumental values were influenced by frequency of watching American

TV programs. Thus, for example, heavy exposure of Filipinos to American TV led them to rate pleasure as a more important terminal value (controlling for other variables, beta = .341). The interesting pattern was that although several values were not rated by the general Filipino sample as important, those who viewed a lot of American programs tended to adopt them and rated them as more important.

Stereotyping Americans in Taiwan and Mexico

Images of other societies include not only values but stereotypes as well. To study the impact of American television programs on stereotypes of Americans in Taiwan and Mexico, Tan (1987) conducted surveys in these countries. Identical questionnaires were administered to purposive samples in Taiwan and Mexico. Respondents were presented with a list of all American television programs that were then being aired in their countries and were asked how often they watched each program on a 5-point scale. Respondents were also asked how many hours they watched television daily, which American television programs they thought most accurately portrayed American culture and people, and how accurately they thought American television programs (in general) portrayed "what the United States is like" and "how Americans act."

Then, the Chinese and Mexican respondents were given a list of 37 adjectives describing (or not) the Americans (e.g., aggressive, artistic, athletic, arrogant). They were asked to pick the 10 adjectives that were most descriptive of Americans in general and then to rank the top ten from 1 (the most descriptive) to 10 (the least descriptive among the top 10). The list of adjectives and the procedure for scoring to approximate interval scaling were derived from previous studies of social stereotypes. Among the Chinese sample ($n = 788$), 96.7% had at least one television set at home; 95% had never been to the United States. Interpersonal contact with Americans was infrequent: 22% did not have any contact at all with Americans, 38.9% had *very little* contact, and 16.8% had *some* contact. In the Mexican sample ($n = 150$), all the respondents had television sets.

The most often watched American television programs in Taiwan were *Three's Company* (76.9% of the sample watched it every week) and *Hawaii Five-O* (50.7% watched it every week). The most popular American television programs in Mexico were *Love Boat, Magnum P.I., Hotel,* and *Dynasty*. The Chinese respondents considered *Dallas* and *Three's Company* to be the programs that most accurately depicted American culture and people. The programs listed most often by our Mexican sample to be accurate depictions of the United States were *Dynasty* and *Dallas*. Most Chinese (66.6%) felt that American television programs were "somewhat accurate" portrayals of Americans and the American culture, whereas most Mexicans felt that American television programs portrayed the United States either "quite accurately" or "very accurately." The adjectives used most often to describe Americans by the Chinese and Mexican samples are shown in Table 10.2.

The Chinese described Americans as individualistic, conceited, practical, athletic, ambitious, scientifically minded, straightforward, pleasure loving, mercenary, courteous, materialistic, artistic, argumentative, sensual, aggressive, and passionate. The adjectives used most often by the Mexicans were materialistic, ambitious, artistic, practical, industrious, efficient, individualistic, pleasure loving, intelligent, athletic, aggressive, and arrogant. Several adjectives appear in both the Mexican and Chinese lists of most descriptive adjectives. These are individualistic, practical, athletic, ambitious, pleasure loving, materialistic, artistic, and aggressive.

To find out whether the viewing of American television programs is related to a particular social stereotype of Americans, the researcher identified the programs considered by our samples to be the most accurate portrayals of Americans. Then he ran partial correlations between frequency of viewing these programs and the ratings of individual adjectives used to describe Americans in the real world, controlling for demographic variables and frequency of contact with Americans. The predictive programs used in the analysis, considered by the respondents to most accurately portray Americans, were *Dallas* and *Three's Company* in Taiwan, and *Dallas* and *Dynasty* in Mexico. These programs were also among the most frequently watched by the Chinese and Mexican samples. Although there was no formal analysis of the contents of these three programs, media critics have agreed that *Dallas* and *Dynasty* depict materialism, wealth, aggression, dishonesty, and the pursuit of pleasure, and *Three's Company* depicts the pursuit of pleasure and sex.

TABLE 10.2 Images of Americans Among People in Taiwan and Mexico

	Adjective	Rank	Mean Score
Taiwan			
	Individualistic	1	3.797
	Conceited	2	3.748
	Practical	3	3.701
	Athletic	4	3.563
	Ambitious	5	2.991
	Scientifically minded	6	2.562
	Straightforward	7	2.283
	Pleasure loving	8	2.053
	Mercenary	9	1.972
	Courteous	10	1.954
	Materialistic	11	1.776
	Artistic	12	1.775
	Argumentative	13	1.668
	Sensual	14	1.626
	Aggressive	15	1.499
Mexico			
	Materialistic	1	4.621
	Ambitious	2	4.266
	Artistic	3	4.089
	Practical	4	3.815
	Industrious	5	3.460
	Efficient	6	3.210
	Individualistic	7	2.653
	Pleasure loving	8	2.339
	Intelligent	9	1.895
	Athletic	10	1.750
	Aggressive	11	1.532
	Arrogant	12	1.218

In the Chinese sample, the frequency of viewing *Dallas* was positively related to characterizations of Americans as materialistic ($r = .158, p < .01$), and negatively related to characterizations of Americans as honest ($r = -.179, p < .01$). These partial correlations controlled for frequency of contact with Americans, frequency of movie going, age, and education of respondents. Also in the Chinese sample, frequency of viewing *Three's Company* was negatively related to characterizations of Americans as faithful ($r = -.171, p < .01$), and positively related to perceptions that the divorce rate is high in the United States ($r = .083$,

$p < .05$). In the Mexican sample, frequency of watching *Dynasty* was positively related to perceptions of Americans as individualistic ($r = .159, p < .05$) and pleasure loving ($r = .169, p < .05$) and negatively related to perceptions of Americans as honest ($r = -.189, p < .01$). Frequency of viewing *Dallas* was positively related to perceptions of Americans as aggressive ($r = . 178, p < .05$) and cruel ($r = .1612, p < .05$) and negatively related to perceptions of Americans as honest ($r = -.2349, p < .01$), industrious ($r = -.1796, p < .05$), and scientifically minded ($r = -.2331, p < .01$). These findings led Tan (1987) to conclude:

> While these correlations are modest, a pattern of relationships is apparent in both samples. The images of America depicted in the three programs considered by our respondents to be the most accurate portrayals of Americans are projected to some extent to Americans in general by heavy viewers of these programs. And, for the most part, these images are negative, consisting of characterizations of Americans as dishonest, materialistic, pleasure loving, aggressive, and cruel. (p. 814)

Enemy Turned Friend: U.S. Images in Russian Media

Rapid changes in Soviet society and its political system changed the Soviet attitude toward the United States. These changes affected the mediated image of American society in Russia. Several studies focused on the changing image of America in the Soviet media. One of these studies examined the portrayals of the United States in *Novoye Vremya* (New Times), a Soviet weekly newsmagazine (Richter, 1991). The method used for this study was content analysis. All the articles with corresponding content were divided into three large groups. The first group consisted of reports and features concentrating on American internal affairs. The second group included stories covering foreign policy. Articles in the third group dealt with military issues such as the armed forces of the United States, its activities within the limits of the North Atlantic Treaty Organization, balance of power, arms control talks, and the peace movement. The analysis of the Soviet magazine revealed that compared to 1985, a slight increase of space given to news and features about life inside the United States took place at the expense of reports concentrating on foreign affairs, with a stable proportion of military issues.

Dealing with the domestic life in the United States, *Novoye Vremya* conjures up three different images of the country. In 1985, it allotted only 9% of its total space to America, which was portrayed as a society where human rights were violated and people suffered in the grips of Reaganomics and ecological problems. In 1987, the main topic of the reports was "Irangate" and other political scandals. Coverage of human rights abuses was half as much as in 1985 and dealt mainly with a historical view on them: More was written about Dr. Martin Luther King than about Dr. Charles Hyder. The grip of Reaganomics was replaced with "the hangover of Reaganomics." More prominence was given to literature and art. Moreover, whereas in the first 11 issues of *Novoye Vremya* just one article on literature and art was published (a story on anti-Soviet movies and books in the United States), in the next 15 issues, there were six articles about various aspects of American culture, but none about anti-Soviet or antiwar art. The most important changes in presenting reports about the United States occurred in 1989. A new heading, "Experience," appeared. Different sides of American life such as the way the Congress works, the conversion of defense industries, copyright protection, methods of combating disaster effects, and others were favorably discussed. The idea was how to apply the American experience to Soviet realities. Human rights was a topic for just one report, about the necessity of parliamentarian cooperation in this field. More space was provided for the coverage of cultural life in America, but this was mainly attributable to the increased number of reports about American Russians, such as artist Ernst Neizvestny.

The best way to show the transformation of the U.S. image in the pages of *Novoye Vremya* is to compare two covers devoted to the life of Americans (there were only two such covers in the examined period). The cover of the 1985 issue showed a youngster at a crossroad with pointers reading "drug addiction," "unemployment," "crime," and "poverty." Above the picture is the heading "U.S. Youth: Grim Problems, Gloomy Prospects" (issue No. 26, 1985). Young Americans can also be seen on a 1989 cover, but here they are in a multicolor photo with a view of the Statue of Liberty. The heading reads: "Room at the Top: How to Make Good in America" (issue No. 2, 1989).

Political, social, and economic issues of U.S. foreign policy as covered by *Novoye Vremya* in 1985 included various plots of the CIA, interference in the affairs of Third World countries, subversion of international organizations (UNESCO), ecological terrorism (Bhopal, etc.), and cooperation with the USSR during World War II. Such descriptions of aggressive policies with a tint of yearning for the bygone friendship could only strengthen the image of enemy-traitor. The tone of *Novoye Vremya* reports fitted the image. Here, for example, is a typical quotation: "The United States and its monopolies plunder the Latin American continent. Their puppets—local rulers—plunder the peoples of the countries they govern. Such a situation suits both Washington, and its puppets—heads of reactionary regimes—perfectly" (*Novoye Vremya*, 1985, No. 3, p. 19).

In 1987, this image changed somewhat. When reporting world events, *Novoye Vremya* didn't mention U.S. "wrecking activities" in every item and gave less space to reports about U.S. state terrorism and CIA intrigue. The greatest changes in American-related content occurred in 1989. References to the "American aspect" appeared less and less often in reports about different countries. What used to be called *neocolonialism* became "a rather complicated relationship between the industrialized and developing nations" (*Novoye Vremya*, 1989, No. 26, p. 13). Most of the attention was paid to "peoples' diplomacy," that is, the movement of common people toward mutual understanding and cooperation between the two countries. In short, *Novoye Vremya* in 1989 gave the United States an image of a friendly nation from which there is much to learn. The absence of negative information about unemployment, abuses of human rights, and CIA activities added idealistic features to the image. Pro-American enthusiasm compensated for the grim perception of the United States in earlier days.

Another study, conducted by Lukosiunas (1991), examined the well-known Soviet newspaper, *Izvestia*. Eleven million copies of *Izvestia* are distributed daily, with 30 million people reading it. In 1989, the number of editorial reports covering the domestic affairs of the United States decreased 20 percentage points from the year 1985: The number of reports concerned with economics, social relations, and human rights decreased. Compared to 1985, editorial reports on these topics in 1989 decreased by 16.1, 6.0, and 33.4 percentage points, respectively. What explains this decline? According to Lukosiunas, in 1985, there was a more critical attitude toward American society. In 1989, the USSR was faced with some serious problems of its own in the above-mentioned categories, and the crises had still not been overcome, thus the newspaper did not call its readers' attention to these topics. This, argues Lukosiunas, reaffirmed the conclusion of American scholars that one of the social functions of mass media is to serve as an instrument of social control to help maintain social stability. The second possible reason for the decrease in editorial space devoted to economics, social relations, and human rights is the stable development of these topics in American society. Thus, journalists' attitudes had changed along with the reality in the United States. The third reason concerns the changes not only in Soviet ideology but also in the practice of journalism. These changes can be illustrated by *Izvestia*'s characterizations of American entrepreneur Ted Turner, owner of the Cable News Network. On May 4, 1985, the newspaper wrote that "the right-winger Ted Turner wants to buy CBS." On May 15, Turner was named "an aggressive, conservative businessman." By 1989, he had become one of the Soviet Union's best friends and was no longer called right-wing or aggressive.

Lukosiunas (1991) noticed changes and decreases in stereotypes concerning human rights problems in the United States. In 1985, 75% of *Izvestia*'s reports were devoted to the problem of racism. In 1989, the problem, as well as the word *racism,* disappeared from its pages. In 1985, Soviet newspapers presented the United States as a semifascist state. In *Izvestia,* 40% of the reports and more than half of the editorial space were devoted to the increasing influence of fascism in the United States. In 1989, the main political reports concerned the work of Congress, the Supreme Court, and other political institutions and the relations between the government and the citizens. The reports now, after the change, attempted to convey a positive image of American society to Soviet citizens. Separate analysis of the editorial space in every category in 1985 and 1989 revealed that neutral coverage increased 78 percentage points, positive coverage increased by 7 points, and negative coverage decreased by 85 percentage points (see Table 10.3).

The increases and decreases in Table 10.3 are quite sharp. The neutral coverage in 1989 occupied more than two thirds of the editorial space of *Izvestia,* which was similar to the rate the study found in the *Christian Science Monitor.* This finding, argues Lukosiunas (1991),

TABLE 10.3 Neutral, Positive, and Negative Coverage of the United States in *Izvestia*

	1985		1989	
	Number of Reports	Percentage of Space	Number of Reports	Percentage of Space
Neutral	4	4	22	82
Positive	3	9	2	16
Negative	38	87	1	2
Total	45	100	25	100

NOTE: Table based on data included in Table 11.4 in Lukosiunas (1991).

confirmed that the rules of selection and evaluation of facts in the editorial offices were becoming more similar:

> The style of coverage by both American and Soviet journalists is becoming more similar, and the neutral category is becoming the dominant one. But the dynamics of this process are not the same. The *Izvestia* editorial policy changed more radically. On the one hand, the truth about domestic affairs in the United States is seen through rose-colored glasses. Yet on the basis of the ideals embodied in different aspects of U.S. social life (which are being propagandized by *Izvestia*), the newspaper is forming the necessary model of a possible interior structure for the Soviet Union. (p. 109)

Looking Over the Great Wall: Images of the United States in China

China, too, underwent major political changes that affected the media. How is the United States portrayed in the "new China"? Liqun (1991) conducted a study of the Chinese daily newspaper, the *People's Daily*, for the purpose of assessing the image of the United States in present-day China. The *People's Daily* is in some sense a *Pravda* in China, an official organ of the Chinese Communist party (CCP) and a typical, representative, and authoritative newspaper. Liqun sampled three complete volumes of the paper for the month of May in 1987, 1988, and 1989 to see what kind of images the newspaper presented of the United States. In addition to the analysis of the *People's Daily,* he examined the major Chinese media.

Sino-American relations went through a very tense and hostile period after the end of the civil war in China, with the victory of the CCP over the Kuomindang in 1949. After the United States and China established normal diplomatic relations in 1979, the relations between the two countries changed greatly. Since then, the Chinese media have not only increased their coverage of the United States, but they have also become more positive and even favorable in their coverage. In the *People's Daily* the number of foreign news items was 960, 1,029, and 756, respectively, in 1987, 1988, and 1989. More important, the quality of the coverage of the United States by the *People's Daily* improved with the increase in quantity. The paper tried to portray a balanced and sometimes favorable picture of the United States to the Chinese public. For example, an article entitled "A Talk With 10 American Heroic Kids" was carried on the front page of the *People's Daily* on May 8, 1988, and put in a column called "Forum of the Week." The piece praised the heroic deeds of 10 American youngsters who rescued a man from the icy water of a partially frozen pond. The paper even called its readers to select 10 similarly heroic Chinese youths to promote spiritual culti-vation among the Chinese young people. For once, the powerful party organ devoted the most important front-page column, the "Forum of the Week," to present American heroism to China. "This would have been unimaginable 11 years ago," argued Liqun (1991).

However, despite the growing sympathy to the United States in Chinese media, a new trend emerges, too: Liqun (1991) refers to it as a new propaganda campaign to criticize the United States for interfer-ence with internal affairs of China. This propaganda has certainly led the media, in some respects, to create a negative image of the United States. This campaign included articles criticizing the Voice of America (VOA) for broadcasting an "utterly groundless" report about Gor-bachev's wish to speak at a university in Beijing, arguing that VOA was "rumor mongering" during the student unrest and later "the counter-revolutionary rebellion" in Beijing. The criticism's targets expanded to other American media, such as the Assoicated Press and United Press International. Another feature of this propaganda campaign was to show old films, especially war stories, on television. The main theme that the officials wanted viewers to pick up from these films was that the only saviors of China were the CCP and the socialist system. One of the most popular films shown on Chinese TV was *The Battle of Sangluorung*. Over the past 40 years, this film has played a role in shaping a negative image of the United States, and almost every Chinese citizen on the mainland remembers the film's theme song, "My Motherland," which ends with the words, "If friends come, we have good wine; but we also have hunting guns if the enemy comes." The enemy is, of course, a reference to the "American aggressors."

The attitude of the Chinese young people toward VOA may serve as an indicator of their response to the official media in China. During the student unrest and later the "counterrevolutionary rebellion," it was reported that radio sets with shortwave bands had been completely sold out in shops and that the salesclerks were telling the customers how to find VOA frequencies. In addition, people in Beijing would go to loudspeakers on university campuses, on buildings in the streets, and in Tiananmen Square to broadcast tape recordings from VOA's Chinese service. These loudspeakers and recordings were installed and taped mostly by the young people.

What is the U.S. image in the eyes of the younger Chinese generation now? What effects have the "new propaganda campaign" and the mixed mediated images had on those young people? The long queues of young students outside the TOEFL offices (Test of English as a Foreign Language) in Beijing, trying to register for this test in order to go to the United States, provide a simple but eloquent answer to the above questions. But,

> If we believe that the mass media are powerful instruments for influencing opinions and creating images and that over the last 11 years the Chinese media have portrayed a more accurate, balanced, or even favorable picture of the United States to the Chinese audience, then we should also realize that the Chinese media are both dominated and benefitted by China's open-door policy. (Liqun, 1991, p. 121)

In many ways, the mass media served as a communication channel between China and the United States. The mediated messages and images were part of this open-door policy. It was this policy that helped China establish cooperation with the United States in economic, cultural, educational, scientific, diplomatic, military, and tourist exchanges. These exchanges combined with the media images to bring colorful, three-dimensional images of the United States to the Chinese people. The cultural exchange, for example, especially the introduction of U.S. pop culture and its images to the Chinese audience, has had a penetrating and magical effect. For example, American pop culture is so pervasive in China that people's images of the United States cannot help but be influenced by it. Watching Chinese TV news reports carefully in 1989, one could have observed that military troops, crushing the students' demonstration in Tiananmen Square, were praised and treated with cans of Coca-Cola. One scene showed some soldiers celebrating their victory by disco dancing; in others, military trucks and armed soldiers on duty formed a line in front of a Kentucky Fried Chicken restaurant in Beijing. It was said that for some time, one of these restaurants in Beijing provided martial-law soldiers with 2,000 buckets of Kentucky Fried Chicken every day.

The invasion of foreign advertising, mainly American or American-style, into China is well documented in a recent study (Wang, 1997). The two-part study addressed two aspects of foreign advertising in the rapidly growing Chinese market, namely, types of foreign ads in the advertising environment and Chinese reception of foreign advertising. It used multiple methods of content analysis, survey, and focus groups to present some preliminary indications about the development and reception of foreign advertising in China. As the study demonstrated, a wide array of international brands are advertised in Beijing. The vast majority of ads were for consumer goods, and this was more pronounced in foreign advertising than in domestic advertising. There were more foreign ads than domestic ads in subway and billboard advertising, but fewer in newspaper and TV advertising. Products from the United States appeared most frequently.

The study also indicated that, in terms of creative concepts, foreign ads were perceived as better than domestic ads by some young Chinese consumers at a Shanghai vocational school. They appeared to be most impressed by the use of visuals and soundtracks in foreign ads, such as those in the Marlboro Country commercials. Chinese domestic ads paled in comparison to the "makebelieve" quality in foreign advertising. "In summary," argues Wang (1997), it is important to note that aside from the overall superior production quality of foreign ads, what underlies these young Chinese consumers' overwhelming preference for foreign ads seems to be their curiosity about and yearning for the exotic and the affluent Western Other, which is embodied by the stylized representations of lifestyle in foreign ads in that country. (p. 39)

These results echo earlier research on Chinese attitudes toward foreign advertising. According to a 1987 survey, foreign ads were perceived by Chinese consumers as "more honest, more artistically designed and a more pleasant experience," and "more memorable and more convincing" (Pollay, Tse, & Wang, 1990). A survey by the Chinese People's University and CCTV in Beijing in 1987 indicated that 29.8% of the residents liked foreign advertising and 12.7% liked it very much (with 38.2% with no opinion; see Huang, 1992). Other surveys also showed that people with higher income and higher levels of education, or the younger generation, tended to like foreign advertising more than those with less income and less education, or the older generations. The main reason Chinese consumers liked foreign advertising was their belief that foreign advertising could increase their knowledge about foreign cultures and society. Foreign ads were also perceived as more entertaining and creative than domestic advertising. Chinese consumers are not apparently critical of foreign advertising. When Wang's (1997) focus group was asked about any negative aspect of foreign advertising, participants replied they simply enjoyed foreign ads and had no objection to them.

It is interesting to note that only a few people viewed foreign advertising as a stimulus of consumerism, a challenge to Chinese traditional values, or a form of cultural invasion. Instead, Chinese consumers seem to admire the subtle Western style of advertising and welcome the sophisticated advertising techniques practiced by multinational ad agencies (Stross, 1990). In short, foreign advertising appears to be preferred over domestic advertising among Chinese consumers. Foreign advertising has generally been successful in cultivating brand names and images in the minds of Chinese consumers. A 1994 Gallup survey of Chinese consumers (the first national consumer survey by a foreign research company in China) showed that, among the top 10 brand awareness leaders, 9 were foreign brands. The only Chinese entry was Tsingdao beer. The top foreign brands were (in the order of ranking) Hitachi, Coca-Cola, Panasonic, Toyota, Mickey Mouse, Marlboro, Suzuki, and Honda (Li & Gallup, 1995).

There is an old Chinese saying: It is easier to draw a picture of a ghost than a man. This is because nobody knows what a ghost really looks like. The same might be true for the Chinese images of the West: When information obstacles or news blockades existed, Chinese people tended to form the image of an alien country by relying heavily on manipulated, politically shaped messages. When the obstacles were removed, when the flow was enriched and more balanced—they got rid of the old, inaccurate, or stereotyped pictures in their minds and drew new ones. American TV series are now being shown in China. The radio language-teaching programs are also being broadcast. During the Cultural Revolution, learning or teaching English was regarded as something bourgeois or even taboo. Today, martial law in Beijing has done nothing to stop the teaching of English on radio or TV. This new flow of messages through the media affects the younger Chinese: According to Liqun (1991), the younger generation tends to see the United States as a rich, modern, open, and democratic country with hardworking, independent, open-minded, carefree, and easygoing people.

"Decent People Should Not Live Here": Media Images of American Cities

One of the most popular settings for American movies, TV programs, and series is the American city. The impressions, the images, the rhetoric, the "noises" of the mediated cities provide the frequent contact people all over the world have with America and its cities. Muzzio (1996) studied these images of mediated cities, or the comparison of "reel cities" to "real cities." He argued that movies do not merely reflect audiences' worldviews but also help to shape them. Part of the power of film (and media contents in general) is that it structures, shapes, and reflects popular attitudes and memory. The resonances of an image of the city are reinforced by filmmakers' and viewers' own experiences of city life, whether real or imagined. Images of the reel city represent to the world the life in American cities. The study of cinematic images of the city thus raises the inescapable issue of the "correspondence between an urban reality (one that exists or is presumed) and the image of that reality" (Rodwin & Hollister, 1984, p. 12). The relationships between the real city and the reel city appear to be indirect and complex. Film, argued Muzzio, is always a very partial reproduction of external reality: The visual information is selectively recorded and structured to create a pictorial message, whether the film is realistic or fanciful. What passes for reality, in fact, is itself a melange of techniques and signs and conventions (graphic depictions of sex, violence, and despair).

The analysis revealed that the dominant images of the generic U.S. city and of specific cities in movies of the 1970s, 1980s, and 1990s have been grim, almost irrespective of genre, location, and director. How can this be explained? Films set in the city have become bleaker as cities themselves have become bleaker, as the American city has become a "much more menacing place in fact and especially in fantasy" (Schickel, 1989, p. 284). What seemed to explain the negative images of media cities are two phenomena: the growth of the suburbs and the live televised viewing of the great urban riots of the 1960s and of Los Angeles in 1992. From the safe distance of the suburbs, audiences could view the degraded and perilous places they had fled. The riots brought the cities to the forefront of the national and international consciousness with a power and vividness that was compelling. What are the most frequent images of American cities as studied by Muzzio?[2]

The city as a jungle: The U.S. city in cinema is a jungle, densely packed, with a stunning variety of human fauna and brimming with danger, seen and unseen. In the jungle, each person is confronted with strangers who may be menaces. The public of the city is a public of strangers, of individuals, classes, and races fighting for territory, power, money, and respect.

The city as mean streets: The streets of the U.S. city in American movies of the last quarter century have been mean, sometimes inhumanly so. City streets are shown with a metaphorical malignancy symbolizing "all the environmental forces massed to degrade its residents, destroy their potentialities, and prevent their rising to better status" (Strauss, 1968, p. 17). The malignancy of the streets was depicted in films such as *West Side Story* (1961) and *Midnight Cowboy* (1969). Urban crime films, movies that relate the careers of criminals to the life of cities, flourished in the last quarter century. Crime (organized and otherwise), corruption, degradation, and deprivation characterize the mean streets of U.S. cities in most movies, cutting across all genres. The streets were mean for all nationalities and races: the Italian hoods in New York's Little Italy (e.g., the *Godfather* films 1972, 1974, 1990, and the wiseguys of *Goodfellas,* 1990), the Irish mob in New York's Hell's Kitchen (e.g., in *State of Grace,* 1990), blacks (e.g., in *New Jack City,* 1991), the Latinos in the barrios of Los Angeles or the penthouses of Miami (in *Scarface,* 1983), the Jewish gangsters on the Lower East Side of Manhattan (e.g., *Once Upon a Time in America,* 1984), the criminal Chinese in Chinatown (*Year of the Dragon,* 1985). In these reel cities, notes Muzzio (1996), not only are the people dangerous but so are the cars and subways. The movies also expose the labyrinthine character of the city, a city of subway tunnels, sewers, and parking garages. Thus, as Kevin McCallister described the big city streets in *Home Alone 2:* "It's scary out there."

The city as living hell: City films have often portrayed the city as "a seething human hell" (Mast, 1986, p. 426). The first line of director Tim Burton's script for *Batman* reads: "Hell has erupted through the pavements and carried on growing." *Batman*'s opening shot of Gotham City shows a dark smoggy wasteland, a nightmare version of megalopolis, an urban landscape without sun, seen through a smog of pollutants and despair where "gray and anonymous people scurry fearfully through the shadows" (Ebert, 1993, p. 54). Martin Scorsese's *Taxi Driver* (1976) is a "nightmare vision of New York City as one of the middle levels of Dante's Inferno" (transcribed from movie). The film opens with a taxi emerging from the steam billowing from the street. It is a vision of a hellish netherworld. *Taxi Driver,* according to Scorsese,

> is very much based on the impressions I have as a result of growing up in New York and living in the city . . . The overall idea was to make it like a cross between a Gothic horror and the New York *Daily News* . . . We shot the film during a very hot summer and there's an atmosphere at night that's like a creeping kind of virus.

The city as killing fields: Many films offer especially grim portraits about the fate of U.S. cities and those living in them. *Boyz 'n the Hood* (1991) and *Menace II Society* (1993), with their long helicopter shots of urban wastelands, offer devastating indictments of the city, depicted as a crime-ridden area, or "misery magnet" (Waste, 1995). The police are presented as an occupying force in an "internal colony." *Boys 'n the Hood* depicts the inner city, the violence of everyday life in the streets of the ghettoized black neighborhood where drive-by shootings are a fact of daily life. *Menace II Society* portrays inner-city black neighborhoods where "the ubiquity of fire arms, the violence of television and video games, and an insanely inflated macho ethic combine with boredom and hopelessness to create a combustible atmosphere that can explode at any time" (Holden, 1993, p. C13).

The city as center of racial riot: Movies such as Spike Lee's *Do the Right Thing* (1989) present the city as the site of constant racial conflicts, ethnic wars, and killings. These films explore the black underclass, the interracial animosity that explodes in violent forms: Blacks slam Italians, Italians slam blacks, Latinos slam Koreans, whites slam Latinos, Koreans slam Jews. Cities are the place for riots, for violent struggles, and not for co-existence and social integration.

The city as guided by corruption: In *City of Hope* (1991), the fictional Hudson City, New Jersey, is presented as a sick, corrupted organism. This city, as many reel cities, is portrayed as a declining rust belt city faced with disinvestment, deindustrialization, and racial/ethnic change and conflict, beset by poverty, drugs, substandard schools, street violence, corruption, and government's abuse of power. These cities are "growth machines," used for real estate and financial interests and private capital accumulation, a place where greed combines with corruption. In *Chinatown* (1974), the city is projected as a cesspool of corruption. Los Angeles in *Chinatown* is a "moral wasteland," where political corruption permeates every level of the government and the public. As Davis (1991) describes this image of American cities in the movies:

> There is this idea that inner cities are just going to be abandoned, that the money is going to be stripped from them, and whoever wants to

deal with them can deal with the problems. And that people are going
to have their little enclaves and take out of their pocket to buy a police
force, or good schools and, in a perverted way, that's the American
dream: I'll take care of my own and fuck the rest of you. (p. 21)

The city as Apocalypse: The cinematic city of the future is even
bleaker than the ones of the present and the past. The city in *Blade
Runner* (1982) is set in a hellish, claustrophobic city, dark and polluted,
and with a continual drenching rain, the Los Angeles in 2019. In *The
Crow* (1994) a postapocalyptic Detroit is a desolate urban wasteland
with dark, rain-slicked, steaming streets that are the scene of random
brutality and wanton murder. The city as apocalypse is also vividly
portrayed in the opening scene of *Terminator 2* (1991), where killing
machines seek out and destroy human foes in a 1997 Los Angeles
incinerated by a nuclear holocaust. Los Angeles is also a war zone in
Demolition Man (1993). The Hollywood sign is on fire, and the rest of
the city is in worse shape. *Predator 2* (1992), also set in future Los
Angeles, opens with shots of a sweltering city lacerated by a pitched
battle between drug dealers and police, with a loudmouthed news
reporter fuming, "It's like Dante's hell down here."

The city as two cities: One of the prevailing metaphors of movies
has been the American city as "two cities" divided by class, race,
ethnicity, and culture. The two cities are the city of power, wealth, and
culture facing the city of the underclass. The two cities imagery is
explicitly presented in *Grand Canyon* (1991) and *Bonfire of the Vanities*
(1990) with their scenes of upper class white men getting lost in their
cars in the black and Latino underclass haunts of Los Angeles and the
Bronx. The two cities also are found in other popular movies: The New
Yorkers of Lee's *Do the Right Thing* and Allen's *Manhattan* are truly
brothers and sisters from other planets: Manhattan versus Brooklyn,
Harvard classes versus underclasses, rich versus poor.

The American urban cinematic landscape has not been exclusively
dreary, however. Some movies have portrayed the city positively as a
center of culture and civility, as mosaic, as center of freedom and
opportunity, as a feast/bazaar/place of excitement, and as a place of
romance, love, and friendship. However, the most frequent themes—

the popular images—are the negative ones. Muzzio (1996) found that 24 of the 39 movies analyzed offered overall negative portrayals (while some of the other movies present a mix of positive and negative images and motifs). A simple comparison of the cinematic images of the American city with the findings of social scientists about the objective state of the cities, or the real versus the reel city, will reveal the overemphasis of movies and TV series on the mean, cruel, aggressive, and apocalyptic nature of the cities. Moreover, the images projected by movies join other forms of cultural communication, the flow of news and the popular urban legends and folklore. Cinematic images react with other elements of culture, including television, music, legend and folklore, and literature, to produce metaphors and systems of metaphors about the U.S. city. These dominant images are rarely the product of single works, no matter how popular and acclaimed they may be. The media, and especially movies and television, contribute to this image-forming process the notion of "evil cities," places in which "decent people don't live."

NOTES

1. On the export and flow of American media products, see Guback, 1974; Schiller, 1969, 1973, 1977; Shayon, 1977; Turnstall, 1977; and Varis, 1974, 1984.

2. One should note that this analysis is based on a very different approach than all the other studies included in this book: It is a somewhat subjective collection of impressions by Muzzio (1996), with embedded personal assumptions. Nevertheless, it may reflect the messages many of us see in the mediated images of American cities.

CHAPTER ELEVEN

The Unreal War

*The Gulf War was like going to a movie: we paid our money,
we went to the theater, we laughed, we cried, the movie ended
and an hour later we had forgotten about it.*

—Saudi financier Adnan Khassoghi (quoted in Masland,
1991)

*In this war truth was more than a casualty. Truth was hit over
the head, dragged into a closet, and held hostage to the public
relations needs of the United States military.*

—Deborah Amos, who covered the Gulf War for National
Public Radio (Amos, 1991)

In the late night hours of January 17, 1991, I woke up to the first Scud
missile attack on my hometown, Haifa, Israel. The first Iraqi missiles
slammed into Haifa and Tel Aviv at 2:15 a.m. local time. The entire
Israeli population, about 5 million people, was wakened by a piercing
alarm. Following the instructions of the Civil Defense authorities, we
all rushed into our "sealed rooms," wearing gas masks and watching
television or listening to the radio. Most of us switched between the

Israeli stations and CNN. Very often, on the following nights, we were informed by CNN from Atlanta about Scud landings in our own streets. Seconds after we heard the noisy landings outside, we watched CNN to learn about the victims and "see" the damage. For those scary hours in the sealed rooms, the media were our umbilical cord to the world outside. As this chapter will explain, this cord fed us, all over the world, a rather reconstructed image of war, an unreal war.[1]

On August 2, 1990, President Saddam Hussein of Iraq sent his troops into Kuwait, and within a week, U.S. President George Bush was sending American troops to Saudi Arabia to prevent an Iraqi invasion there and to prepare for a military confrontation with Saddam. What followed was "a war by appointment," one carried out on the precise date set by Bush: January 16, 1991. An air war began on the date set just at prime time for television in the Eastern Time Zone (it was early morning, January 17, in Iraq) and, on February 23, a ground war that lasted less than 5 days, called the "100-Hour War" by some. With a speed that eclipsed even that of Israel's 1967 Six-Day War, the coalition forces swept over Saddam's overestimated but quickly overcome forces, and a surrender was issued from Baghdad. Who lost this war? According to Small (1994),

> The big loser was Saddam Hussein. The other loser was traditional American journalism, which also found itself outmatched by the Bush forces and while not surrendering its First Amendment function, independent reporting, found that function seriously compromised. As for the global press, it was even more seriously handicapped. Too much of the domestic American and the world press relied too much on the output of cable's 24-hour news service, the Cable News Network (CNN), and far too often on a carefully orchestrated news management by military and White House sources. It was not journalism's finest hour. Worse yet, in the United States, at least, the public didn't seem to care. (p. 4)

A Princeton Survey Research Associates poll for the Times-Mirror Company showed that over three quarters (76%) of Americans knew that Gulf War news was being censored by the American military, and a larger number (79%) thought that was a good idea. As Small (1994) noted, the public seemed perfectly happy with the news they got, even if they felt that the media were being spoon-fed by the military. An

NBC-*Wall Street Journal* poll said three out of four Americans thought that the military gave the public sufficient information (Stone, 1991).

The Made-for-CNN or Made-by-CNN War?

The coverage that got the most attention, all over the world, was that of the Cable News Network. Bush and American leaders acknowledged their reliance on CNN for early developments in the conflict. Both Secretary of Defense Dick Cheney and Joint Chief of Staff Colin Powell dubbed CNN the best source for discovering the extent of the Baghdad bombing. Air Force Lt. General Charles Homer, the architect of the air war, confessed that because of the detail of CNN reports, he installed a television at his command post. Peter Tarnoff, president of the Council on Foreign Relations, was quoted as saying that CNN was "the most efficient way for one government to speak to another during the crisis" (Cooper, 1991, p. 44). Saddam Hussein also watched the war on CNN in his headquarters. Iraqi officials often delayed press conferences until CNN reporters arrived. The network enjoyed special treatment and access to Iraqi officials, events, and city locations. CNN reporters were the only ones allowed to stay in their hotel rooms early in the conflict: Peter Arnett, the CNN reporter in Baghdad, became the world's window on Iraq. On January 28, 1991, in the middle of the war, CNN became the world's first truly global television network. CNN began its international triple feed, a technology that allowed CNN's Atlanta headquarters to send out three simultaneous feeds of news and information (and advertising) and reach literally every part of the globe. Previously, CNN was available in all parts of the world, but some of the contents received a relayed feed of the domestic CNN transmission, whereas the rest of the world received a "true" CNN International (CNNI) feed. Now, every part of the globe was able to receive the CNN International transmission.

The whole world was watching CNN.[2] In their wildest dreams, the CNN people could never have imagined this "perfectly made-for-CNN war."[3] This war seemed to be tailor-made for this 24-hour news service. CNN could bring blanket coverage, including live coverage of briefings in the Pentagon and by military officers, both U.S. and British, in the

Gulf. The volume was immense. It also was exclusive in Baghdad for many weeks. CNN was the only one capable of broadcasting from the scene on January 16 when the first air raids began over Iraq. Media critic Edwin Diamond (1991) said the CNN team had what every other news organization wishes it had: "implicit recognition on the part of Iraqi authorities that it is the preeminent news-gathering force in the world" (p. A36). In the opening hours of the war, CNN's usually modest audience swelled 10-fold to nearly 11 million viewers. With exposure to just over 60% of American television homes, on January 16, CNN was getting audiences in prime time as large as the three networks, with their 98% reach. Everyone with access to CNN, including the president, was receiving the news of the beginning of the war from the very target, at the very same instant. However, many more people probably would have tuned to CNN as a cable network if it was not so easy to find the CNN coverage on many broadcast stations at the same time:

> Not only did the world watch the beginning of a war in real time for the first time, but the CNN monopoly on the activity resulted in an extraordinary night of "borrowing" CNN's coverage by local TV stations, many of them affiliates of the three major broadcast networks. (Gustadt, 1993, p. 400)

Some of this usage was legal, through a variety of contracts made by CNN and hundreds of local TV stations. However, so compelling was the coverage that much of the CNN usage was pirated, simply taken off the local cable feed by the stations. Based on some actual reporting of CNN usage by stations in metered markets, as well as anecdotal stories of pirated coverage, Gustadt estimated that audiences to CNN were actually 40% to 50% higher than pure cable ratings indicated. During the first week of the air war, not only did CNN break records for itself and for cable viewing overall, but it also outperformed all three groups of broadcast network affiliates (ABC, CBS, and NBC) in its own universe on a 24-hour basis. Clearly, the claims of CNN's chairman and founder, Ted Turner, that his network was the world's most important was getting a degree of support that even he might not have envisioned. In a fitting and perceptive tribute, *Time* magazine named Ted Turner its Man of the Year for influencing the dynamics of events and for making viewers around the world instant witnesses of history. Zelizer (1992) indicated that CNN's coverage was ubiquitous; early in the war "over 200 news directors at local affiliates abandoned their own network's feed to acquire CNN material" (p. 81).

Before the war, CNN launched a new nightly program, *Crisis in the Gulf*, that quickly became the most popular (and militarist) program during the first months of the confrontation. The Gulf war brought CNN into international prominence, producing higher name recognition, ratings, and advertising revenues. CNN had begun service 10 years earlier as the first cable news channel on the air 24 hours per day. Within a decade, it had developed the largest news operation in the world with a staff of 125, compared with 60 to 80 for the major networks, and with news bureaus throughout the world. In particular, CNN had established itself in the Middle East with news bureaus and broadcast outlets connected to the United States via satellite feed and thus was well positioned to provide coverage of the crisis in the Gulf and then the Gulf War. CNN's *Crisis in the Gulf* program began as a half-hour segment on August 13 and 4 days later was expanded to an hour, preempting CNN's prime-time news program for news on the crisis. As Kellner (1992) noted,

> Night after night, CNN, and the other networks as well, broadcast an incessant flow of pictures of troops, airplanes, ships, tanks, and military equipment, with interview after interview of the troops and their military spokespeople. Footage of the U.S. military was frequently supplemented on CNN by footage from the British and other allies' military establishments, resulting in seemingly endless images of military hardware and personnel. Interviews with the U.S. soldiers "humanized" the coverage, picturing "our boys" (and some military women as well) as innocent and heroic protectors against Arab greed and aggression. (p. 87)

The continuous live reports provided by CNN prompted some observers to call the conflict "The CNN War." Some even called the Gulf War a "critical incident" for television journalism because of the challenge CNN posed to the networks (ABC, CBS, NBC). But along with the praise and legitimacy conferred on CNN came ample criticism (Dobkin, 1992). The charges included questions about "packaging the news into stories," media bias, the perceived inadequacy of information due to manipulation by political and military authorities, and the potentially adverse effects of television news on public understanding of political events. An examination of CNN's *Headline News* reveals the extent to which conventions of television news presentation constrained CNN's packaging of events in ways similar to the three American networks. Television news relies on dramatic visual presentations. Its need to captivate viewers leads to condensation of information into brief segments and an emphasis on immediate and technologically sophisticated coverage. Numerous studies have found that news formats among the networks ABC, CBS, and NBC are consistent and almost similar. CNN may not follow the same conventions: CNN's status as an international news service, with live reports and journalists behind enemy lines, has raised questions about its uniqueness. As Walker, Wicks, and Pyle (1991) noted in their study of CNN's live coverage during the Gulf War, CNN presented accounts of action taking place without much simultaneous analysis.

Mainstreaming the Media

The White House and the military were ready for this televised war. Since Vietnam, war colleges have trained officers to become more media-savvy. Even young officers receive training in media and community and public relations. At the Pentagon, detailed plans for handling the media were developed and awaiting implementation. The military needed television to build and sustain public support for the war. They realized pictures were powerful weapons and could easily help the enemy and lower morale of the troops as well as the general public. After the war, many journalists, media experts, and scholars argued that the media were managed, before and during the war, to serve as a mouthpiece and amplifier for the U.S. administration and military (Kellner, 1993). Thus, they argue, the media failed to serve the public interest by providing a wide range of opinion on issues of public importance, and they failed to inform the public of what the war was really like, its true nature and consequences. The media coverage of the crisis and the war, orchestrated by the Bush Administration and the Pentagon, helped promote the eventual military attempt at solving the crisis. It certainly created massive public support in the United States and all over the world. Throughout the months of the crisis, media coverage, and TV in particular, favorably portrayed all U.S. policy actions, presented the U.S. military intervention in an extremely positive light, and privileged those voices presenting the success of the war. Before the war, the media rarely criticized the Bush Administration's failure to negotiate a diplomatic settlement to the crisis in the Gulf. During the war, the coverage was biased, selective, and very supportive of the mainstream positions. As Kellner argued, no significant antiwar voices were allowed in the media during the first months of the troop buildup in Saudi Arabia, and there was almost no public debate and little criticism of his policies from the time that Bush first sent troops to Saudi Arabia on August 8, 1990. A study by the media watchdog group FAIR reported that during the first 5 months of TV coverage of the crisis in the Gulf, ABC devoted only 0.7% of its total Gulf coverage to opposition to the military buildup. CBS allowed 0.8%, whereas NBC devoted 1.5%, a hearty 13.3 minutes, to all stories about protests, antiwar organizations, conscientious objectors, religious dissenters, and the like. Consequently, of the 2,855 minutes of TV coverage of the Gulf crisis from August 8, 1990, to January 3, 1991, FAIR claimed that only 29 minutes, roughly 1%, dealt with popular opposition to the U.S. military intervention in the Gulf.

From the beginning of the U.S. deployment, the press was prohibited from having direct access to the troops. Journalists were divided by the military into pools that were taken to sites selected by the military itself, and then reporters were allowed only to interview troops with their military "guides" present. Press and video coverage was also subject to censorship, so that, in effect, the military tightly controlled press coverage of the U.S. military deployment in the Gulf and subsequently the Gulf War itself. Reporters who ventured out on their own were detained or told to leave if they arrived at bases without an escort. Such control of press coverage was unprecedented in the history of American warfare. Historically, journalists had been allowed direct access to combat troops and sites, and frontline reporting had been distinguished during World War II and Vietnam. The pool system was established, however, because it was perceived by the military that reporting had been too critical in Vietnam. The military blamed the press for helping erode public support for that war. Following British censorship of the press during the Falkland Islands war, the United States controlled press access during the Grenada invasion and instituted the pool system during the Panama Invasion. The pool system allowed the U.S. military to keep the press away from the battle action in Panama completely during the decisive first day of the invasion and to keep most of the press on a U.S. military base during the next days. Because the press was not able to discern the extent of civilian deaths or the destructiveness of the invasion, it was deemed a great success in the management of information by the military, which used the same strategy during the Gulf War.

There were essentially three strands to the system established by the coalition forces for releasing information to the media actually present in Saudi Arabia: the Joint Information Bureau in Dhahran, the arrangements made for daily press briefings in Riyadh, and the news pool system for journalists attached to the armed forces at the front (Taylor, 1992). The pool system was supposed to work as follows: With the troops at the front, journalists were formed into Media Reporting Teams (MRTs). The Americans were to be supervised by censors from the Public Affairs Office (PAO) and the British by the Multi User Domain's (MUD's) public relations officers (PROs). There were eventually about 200 places in the pools for the 1,500 or so journalists who had flocked to the region, although in the first half of the war there were only about 50 correspondents with the troops. The pools consisted of reporters from all the media whose reports were to be made freely available to all news organizations. In an attempt to negate recent developments in satellite communications technology, however, American television companies were refused permission to operate satellite dishes with the U.S. military, which not only slowed down the transmission of their taped reports but sometimes forced them to use British TV pool reports for more rapid transmission.

The management of news and information was one of the key pillars of Pentagon policy. The military tightly controlled both access to and content of the news in one of the most thoroughgoing exercises in news management and manufacture of public opinion in history. Members of the press corps were virtually totally dependent on the series of daily briefings organized for them by the American, British, and Saudi military authorities. When the military was able to retain such virtual total control over the flow of information, it could shape the overall view of the war. It was generally thought, however, that the briefing system operated quite smoothly: A series of briefings were held throughout the day, culminating in an American briefing in time for European and American newspapers and television. As in the pools, there was a price to be paid for this. David Fairhall of the *Guardian* wrote, "In Riyadh, the relationship between press and military was a familiar one, in which one traded operational information and access for the opportunity this inevitably gave the military to present their own version of the events" (quoted in Taylor, 1992, p. 64). Moreover, any information that might raise questions concerning the Bush Administration's policies was considered off limits. Reporters who were critical of U.S. policy found themselves without access to sources or sites. For 2 months, *New York Times* reporter James LeMoyne requested an interview with General Schwarzkopf, but it was denied because his articles "were not liked" by the U.S. military (*New York Times,* February 17, 1991). Some television reporters also found themselves blacklisted. ABC's John Laurence was refused access to the troops after he helped produce a segment that detailed heat and sand problems with equipment in the desert and described ammunition shortages.

Thus, the military was able to control the flow of information coming from the press in the field by allowing access only to those favorable to the military and by exercising a security review of reports and video that were produced by the pools. *New York Times* reporter Malcolm Broome wrote, "I've never seen anything that can compare to it, in the degree of surveillance and control the military has over the correspondents" (cited in *The Village Voice,* February 5, 1991). Consequently, the lack of any critical voices in the media during the early stages of the crisis resulted in a massive mainstreaming of public opinion. As Kellner (1993) concluded,

> The lack of an adequate critical discussion in the media concerning the Bush Administration Gulf policy enabled Bush to prepare for his eventual war and triumph by giving him time to slowly but inexorably build up his war machine and military strategy. The mainstream media aided Bush by employing forms of popular culture to demonize Saddam Hussein and the Iraqis, by glorifying American troops and technology, and by submitting to the pool system that allowed the military to control images and information. Saddam Hussein was presented so negatively and the massive U.S. troop deployment so positively that the only logical solution to the crisis was decisive

military action and unquestioning support for the U.S. troops. The
nightly images of the U.S. troops in the desert bonded viewers to the
soldiers and created a basis of support. (p. 45)

Manipulating the Media

From the earliest days, prominent journalists expressed concerns about
manipulation. The editor of *U.S. News and World Report* argued that
the common images Americans had about what happened in the war
were no longer being provided by the networks, either by the anchor-
men or by the correspondents. They were increasingly the releases of
the government (Gould, 1991). Since Vietnam, military sources had
clearly become more sophisticated in managing the news. One senior
military officer wrote (to the *Wall Street Journal* in an article entitled
"U.S. Used Press as Weapon"): "Some people say the media is the enemy
but in fact the media is really a battlefield and you have to win on it."
The article went on to give examples of how the press was "used" in
military briefings that served up contradictory or confusing figures
about battle damage, about Iraqi ships declared out of action and later
reemerging as targets, and—most of all—about leaving the impression
that a Marine landing was planned when in fact it was a means to
convince Iraq that it had to deploy troops to block an invasion from the
sea. As Pentagon press officer Pete Williams put it, "We were not trying
to deceive the press. We were trying to fool Saddam Hussein" (quoted
by Mossberg, 1991).

Hodding Carter, a former State Department spokesman, has noted,
"Our government is in the business of propaganda, which is not the
same thing as lying, but definitely not the same thing as truth" (quoted
by Gould, 1991, p. 11). Pentagon-released pictures of precision-guided
"smart" bombs going down chimneys of Iraqi targets left an impression
that they rarely missed, but these were a small part of the total bomb
load dropped in 43 days of aerial attacks. Some 82,000 tons of unguided
bombs were dropped, and their accuracy rating was 25%, not the 90%
of the smart bombs. Of 88,500 tons of bombs dropped, 70% missed
their targets (Wicker, 1991, p. A29). That was not the impression left
by the handout videotapes.

The media were not totally unaware of the manipulation. Many in journalism, from the start, felt that the output of the media was too jingoistic and not critical enough. The *Wall Street Journal* ran a story titled "TV Faulted as U.S. Cheerleader in Gulf." Sam Donaldson of ABC News said, "I'm worried the networks are whooping up war fever. I was surprised and dismayed by the jingoistic tone of some of my colleagues. The public didn't object." In contrast, when Dan Rather and Ted Koppel reported from Baghdad in the prewar period, *Newsweek* reported that the president was angry at "Iraqi cheerleading by television newspeople." The Pentagon imposed pools on reporters, laid down ground rules, ignored journalistic protests, and found its reward was news as the administration would have it and popular reception by readers and broadcast audiences. The German weekly, *Die Zeit,* in an article "Reporters in the Gulf Rally Around the Flag," wrote of the U.S. Defense Department success "in launching a surprise attack on the public" and complained that German newscasters had fallen "under the spell of Cable News Network (CNN) and video clips from the Pentagon." Throughout the air war phase in January and most of February, media complaints were dismissed. The chief Pentagon spokesman, Assistant Secretary of State for Public Affairs Pete Williams, told Congress on February 20 that pools were needed because "over 1,400 reporters, editors, producers, photographers, and technicians" were registered with Joint Information Bureaus in Dhahran and Riyadh; in contrast, during the 1983 U.S. invasion of Grenada, journalists were kept away until the fighting was over. The journalists and reporters were fed with visuals, statistics, videos, pictures, selected interviews, maps, and numbers. They all used still photos and videotapes handed to them by the Pentagon. Even before the air war ended, the *New York Times* reported on angry protests by reporters who were held for up to 8 hours for trying to cover the war on their own without military escorts. (These and many other relevant media stories are cited in Chomsky, 1992.)

When PR People Feed the Media

One of the most outrageous propaganda ploys by the American authorities and the Kuwaiti government concerned fallacious stories about Iraqi atrocities in Kuwait, stories manufactured and fed to the media by a public relations agency, Hill and Knowlton. In October 1990, a tearful teenage girl testified to the House Human Rights Caucus that she had witnessed Iraqi soldiers remove 15 babies from incubators and had seen them left to die on the floor of the hospital. The girl's identity was not revealed, supposedly to protect her family from reprisals. This shocking baby-killing story helped mobilize support for anti-Iraq actions. President Bush mentioned the story six times in 1 month alone and so did Vice President Quayle, General Schwarzkopf, and other military spokespeople. Seven U.S. Senators cited the story in speeches supporting the January 12 resolution authorizing war. However, in a January 6, 1992, op-ed piece in the *New York Times,* the publisher of *Harper's* magazine revealed that the unidentified congressional witness was the daughter of the Kuwaiti ambassador to the United States. The girl had been brought to testify to Congress by the PR firm Hill and Knowlton, who had coached her and helped organize the Congressional Human Rights hearings. The Kuwaiti account was one of the most expensive PR campaigns in history, costing $5.6 million from the period from August 20 to November 10; eventually it was estimated that the total account was $11 million (Ruffini, 1991, p. 22). Hill and Knowlton organized a photo exhibition of Iraqi atrocities displayed at the United Nations and the U.S. Congress and widely shown on television, assisted Kuwaiti refugees in telling stories of torture, lobbied Congress, and prepared video and print material for the media. There were also reportedly six other U.S. PR firms working for the Kuwaitis.

Hill and Knowlton put out over 30 Video News Releases (VNRs) that were distributed free to television stations. One video, based on a film of destruction in Kuwait, reached 61.4 million viewers, whereas another on human rights violations in occupied Kuwait reached 35.3 million. Viewers had no way to tell that the source was a PR firm. CNN, in particular, frequently played these tapes. For instance, on October 28, CNN played a tape in which a Western man in hiding told of Iraqi atrocities, including the baby incubator story, and called on the United States to intervene militarily. In retrospect, this appears to be part of the Hill and Knowlton/Free Kuwait propaganda campaign that duped CNN and the other networks. On January 17, 1992, ABC's *20/20* disclosed that a "doctor" who testified that he had "buried fourteen newborn babies that had been taken from their incubators by the soldiers" was also lying. The doctor was a dentist who admitted that the story was a fake. ABC also disclosed that Hill and Knowlton had commissioned a focus group survey, which gathers groups of people to find out what stirs or angers them. The focus group responded strongly to the Iraqi baby atrocity stories, and so Hill and Knowlton featured this in their PR campaigns for the Free Kuwait group.

Furthermore, Hill and Knowlton also used the wife of Kuwait's Minister of Planning, who was herself a well-known TV personality in Kuwait, in the UN hearings. The woman, Fatima Fahed, appeared just as the United Nations was debating the use of force to expel Iraq from Kuwait, and she provided "harrowing details of Iraqi atrocities inside her country." Fahed claimed that her information was firsthand, stating, "Such stories . . . I personally have experienced." But when the woman was interviewed before the UN appearance, she said that she had no firsthand knowledge of the events she was describing. After her Hill and Knowlton coaching, however, her story changed and became a "personal testimony."

Hill and Knowlton were manufacturing stories, testimonies, VNRs, and tapes and feeding them to the media, which accepted and published the material without any questions or doubts. The Hill and Knowlton campaign focused on two motives: the Iraqi "rape" of Kuwait and the baby atrocity story. "Rape and the murder of babies," argued Kellner (1993), "are two primal images of evil that have frequently been employed in propaganda campaigns" (p. 45). Hill and Knowlton realized that the rape metaphor was powerful and carried through a "rape of Kuwait" campaign replete with a book, newspaper articles, packaged videos, pictures, press releases, news conferences, and demonstrations. There were frequent staged media events such as National Free Kuwait Day, National Prayer Day (for Kuwait's liberation), and National Student Information Day. Thus, for example, the UN testimony was accompanied by a photo exhibition of torture victims and other exhibits staged just before the United Nations was to vote on whether to legitimate the use of military force against Iraq.

Shaping Reality by Discourse

What we knew about the war was shaped in many ways by what we saw, heard, and read. In the media coverage of the war, many terms, icons, and metaphors were used to distance the viewer, listener, and reader from war's brutal and bloody effects. Terms such as *collateral damage,* used to refer to civilian death and destruction on the enemy side, function to dehumanize the war, making it seem less real and less fearful. Many such terms were first adopted by the military and then picked up by the media. Cheney (1993), for example, noted that "you got to love a missile called 'Patriot,' but who can feel good about a missile named 'Scud'?"

After the war, several journalists and researchers noted the militarization of language and discourse. In the novel *1984,* George Orwell developed the term *Doublespeak* to connote language that makes the bad seem good, the negative appear positive, and the unpleasant appear attractive, or at least tolerable. Orwellian *Warspeak,* as Kellner (1993) referred to it, was "the production of neologisms and language to sanitize unpleasant realities" (p. 238). Thus, the coalition forces "engaged" the enemy rather than attacking it. Instead of dropping bombs or firing weapons, planes "dropped ordnance." If the bombs missed their targets, "incontinent ordnance delivery" resulted, which produced "collateral damage," a neologism used to sanitize the destruction of civilian targets and civilian deaths as accidental damage. Targets were referred to as "assets," and warplanes were described as "force packages." Targets were not destroyed, but "visited," "acquired," "taken out," "serviced," or "suppressed." Tanks and equipment were "neutralized" rather than blown up. "Cluster bombs" became "area denial weapons." Rather than destroying the Iraqi military, the goal was "assertive disarmament," to be achieved through "discriminate deterrence." Instead of descriptive terms such as "bombing targets," the military and the media spoke of "servicing the target," "neutralizing targets," "suppressing assets," or "visiting enemy."

In reports about the war, one easily finds many euphemisms, including "friendly fire" and "smart bomb," or "soften up," which describes the bombing of concentrations of enemy troops prior to a ground attack. Thus, even ordinary language was used as a propaganda apparatus. Such discourse concealed the lethality of the destruction and the effects of the bombing and provided a false picture of surgical, precision bombing. "Warspeak," argued Kellner (1993), "abstracts and sanitizes military activity and substitutes familiar and friendly terminology for the unpleasant activities being undertaken" (p. 239). The Danish paper *Poli-*

tiken examined the English-language press and documented some of the ways in which language had been molded to fit the desired reality. The document (reproduced in *In These Times,* Feb. 13, 1991, p. 5), reveals the linguistic distinctions shown in Table 11.1.

Metaphors were used to attach specific meanings, often taken from nonwar worlds, to the violent inhuman acts of real war. The metaphors prevailing in the media coverage of the Gulf War included the football game (e.g., "our post-game plan" and "Patriots blast Scuds"), the video game (e.g., the "Nintendo War" and "We hit the target with video-game precision"), the poker game ("We can't show Saddam all of our cards"), and of course, the Super Bowl (see below). The use of the term *Operation Desert Shield* to describe the decision to send U.S. troops to the desert of Saudi Arabia was a use of a metaphor: Bush claimed that he was drawing "a line in the sand" and providing a "shield" against Iraq's invading Saudi Arabia (although it now appears that Iraq had no intention of invading Saudi Arabia). The use of the word *operation* rather than *war* was suggesting the surgical removal of malignant matter. The medical discourse pervaded the war with its rhetoric of *surgical strikes,* a term that connotes both a precise, clean mode of bombing and the beneficial removal of disease and malignancy.

The code for the war itself, Operation Desert Storm, also created the impression that the Gulf War was a natural event, occurring as a force of nature. The war "erupted" with "waves" of attacks. Bombs continued to "rain" on their targets, and planes "thundered" through the night. Scuds "showered" their debris below, Baghdad was "awash" in sounds and lights as the bombs exploded, and there was, of course, the "fog of war." The discourse also mythologized technology and related it to mythologies of the American West, such as the Apache helicopter and Chieftain, Sidewinder, and Tomahawk missiles. CBS used the Western mythology in its nightly logo "Showdown in the Gulf," reducing the war to a struggle between good and evil, as in the most common Western.

Sports metaphors were also very common: "Our team has carried out its game beautifully," exulted a military expert on NBC. "We ran our first play, it worked great," said a pilot interviewed on CBS. "We scored a touchdown." On December 19, Lt. Gen. Calvin Waller told the press, "I'm like a football coach. I want everything I can possibly get and have at my side of the field when I get ready to go into the Super

TABLE 11.1 Linguistic Distinctions Used in War Coverage

The Allies have:	*The Iraqis have:*
Army, Navy, and Air Force	A war machine
Guidelines for journalists	Censorship
Briefings to the press	Propaganda
The Allies do:	*The Iraqis do:*
Eliminate	Kill
Neutralize	Kill
Hold on	Bury themselves in holes
Conduct precision bombing	Fire wildly at anything
The Allied soldiers are:	*The Iraqi soldiers are:*
Professional	Brainwashed
Cautious	Cowardly
Full of courage	Cannon fodder
Loyal	Blindly obeying
Brave	Fanatic
The Allied missiles:	*The Iraqi missiles:*
Do extensive damage	Cause civilian casualties
George Bush is:	*Saddam Hussein is:*
Resolute	Intractable
Balanced	Mad

Bowl" (United Press International, December 20, 1990). An American soldier in a January 23 report on CNN said that "Saddam Hussein doesn't have much of a team; in comparison with football, he'd be the Cleveland Browns." Army Chief Warrant Officer Ron Moring stated on the eve of the war: "It's time to quit the pregame show. We're a lot more serious about what we're doing. There's a lot more excitement in the air." Football metaphors were also used in war rhetoric when Bush said that Tariq Aziz gave them a "stiff arm" after the unsuccessful Geneva meeting on the eve of the war. Helen Thomas asked Bush in a January 18 press briefing if the Gorbachev peace initiative was perceived as an "end run" (around Bush's desire to start the war). A Canadian Broadcasting Corporation (CBC) Radio headline indicated that the Canadian armed forces in the Gulf were given "the green light to tackle the Iraqis." ABC's *Nightline* (January 17, 1991) quoted fliers just back from the first missions of the war: "It's just like a football game once you get airborne and you get the jet under you and you start feeling good, then you just start working, working your game plan." Another pilot exclaimed,

> It's like being a professional athlete and never playing a game. Today was the first game and the enemy didn't show up, the opponent didn't show up. We went out there and ran our first play and it worked great, we scored a touchdown, there was nobody home.

In addition, the military planners talked of making an "end run" around the Iraqi troops massed on the Kuwaiti border. Scud missiles were "intercepted" by Patriots, and Col. Ray Davies described the U.S. air team as "like the Dallas Cowboys football team. They weren't a real emotional team" (*Washington Post*, January 19, p. C1).

Another dimension of the discourse of coverage was the state-as-person metaphor. As President Bush put it, "Our quarrel is with Saddam and *not* with the Iraqi people." The Bush administration and media personalized the crisis as the result of the actions of one man, Saddam Hussein, the Iraqi president, who was identified with his country throughout the war. It should be noted that during the Iran/Iraq war, the media invariably referred to "Baghdad" and "Iraq" as the agents in the war, but during the Gulf crisis and war, the dominant mode of reference was to "Saddam Hussein," who was presented as the sole agent of all Iraqi actions, thus collapsing Iraq into Saddam. Two quotations from NBC News give some sense of the importance of the personal figure of Hussein to the narrative structure of the war story. The day of the UN deadline, NBC's anchor Tom Brokaw said, "Good evening. Two men, one in Washington and one in Baghdad, backed by two mighty military machines, are now in a short countdown to a showdown." The day the war ended, Brokaw began the broadcast, "His men and military machines crushed, Saddam Hussein finally surrenders." This was misleading and dishonest, as the Iraqi people were themselves victims of Saddam Hussein and his regime, but the media images of the evil Hussein reduced the Iraqis to an evil essence embodied in the Iraqi leader.

> Yet constructing Saddam Hussein as an absolute villain, as a demon who is so threatening and violent that he must be destroyed and

eradicated, precluded negotiations and a diplomatic solution, . . . one must exterminate such evil to restore stability and order in the universe. (Kellner, 1992, p. 64)

Focusing the conflict on the person of Saddam Hussein blinded the world to the fact that during the war, it must be the case that many Iraqi soldiers and civilians would die. When war becomes a personal matter with one man, one evil ruler, it is easy to ignore the victims either by focusing on him only or by blaming the "price of war" on him ("We told you many times to stop that, and you didn't listen"). Media coverage of the crisis in the Gulf tended to personalize the crisis as a conflict between George Bush and Saddam Hussein. Whereas Hussein was presented in purely negative terms, Bush's actions were praised as "decisive," "brilliant," and "masterful."

A frequent element of the war discourse in the media was the use of *we, our,* or *us.* Lee and Solomon (1991) discussed the propensity of the mainstream media to use *we* in such a way as to identify the media spokesperson with the government or military, and both this form of discourse and the use of *our* ("our troops," "our country") were very frequent in the Gulf War coverage. As Kellner (1992) noted, the military "experts" in the media almost always used the term *we* to describe U.S. military policies or action, and this was perfectly appropriate as they actually identified totally with the military. TV "journalists" such as Barbara Walters, Tom Brokaw, and Dan Rather also used *we* and *our* to bind themselves to the military and the nation. *We* and *our* also bind the audience into an intimate relation with the troops and nurture a sense of shared national purpose.

The use of pseudo-technical language made the distance from real war even larger. Coverage of the Persian Gulf War, the first "live war" as it has been called, can be characterized overall as having had an aura of technological wizardry. As a *New Yorker* editorial said, "For those of us riveted to our televisions in the United States, the war in the Persian Gulf for the first day or so had an eerie, remote-control quality" ("Talk of the Town," 1991). Cheney (1993) argued,

This war was a spectacle. In Vietnam, a war fought predominantly on the ground and in the jungle, looked like the films *Platoon* and *The*

Deer Hunter. The Persian Gulf War appeared to us—especially during
the air campaign—as *Top Gun* and *Star Wars.* (p. 63)

The mass-mediated discourse relied heavily on numbers and statistics, thus further sterilizing the war and its consequences. However,
whereas in the Vietnam War, the numbers were enemy casualties, the
numbers game in the Gulf war focused on the number of sorties, planes
shot down, and equipment destroyed. During the last days of the war,
there was a daily count of remaining Iraqi tanks, artillery, and ground
vehicles rather than body counts. The American authorities provided
running tallies, reproduced in graphics and charts by the media. So, for
example, Schwarzkopf's opening statement during the briefing on
January 18 indicated that the U.S.-led coalition was flying "about 2,000
air sorties of all types each day" and "more than 80% of all of those
sorties have successfully engaged their targets."

One must also note the rhythms of the coverage, which turned into
a language of its own: Live broadcasting from various arenas with live
shifting from one site to another created a special effect. Here is a report
from Tel Aviv on the casualties from an Iraqi missile attack; cut to a
prediction about the effects of the war on the price of oil at home; cut
to the press conference in a desert camp in Saudi Arabia; cut to the
White House, where officials brief the press; cut to an interview with a
pilot returning from a bombing mission; cut to a local ad about escaping
stress at a mountain resort. Cheney (1993) claimed that there is a
"leveling" effect in this type of mediated imagery, whereby all of these
well-crafted images seem to share the same degree of significance: They
blend together in one big montage of symbols, a "Theater of the Absurd"
in which the sacred and the banal become one in a way that strangely
seems to make sense or in a way that at least seems familiar and
comfortable.

The Visuals of Unreal War

We discussed the use of language and metaphors in the reconstruction
of the reality of war. Let us now examine the visual depiction of the war.
A study conducted by Griffin and Lee (1995) surveyed and analyzed

1,104 war-related pictures appearing in *Time, Newsweek,* and *U.S. News & World Report* during the Gulf War. As the title of the reports indicates ("Picturing the Gulf War: Constructing an Image of War"), the analysis found a narrowly limited range of images, with a special emphasis on cataloguing military weaponry and technology, dominated the pictorial coverage.

What images of the conflict did the public actually see? Several questions directed the analysis of the photojournalistic coverage. A primary interest was to see how much of the pictorial coverage actually depicted wartime events and combat-related military activity. Categories were designed to discriminate between depictions of actual warfare and depictions of noncombat army life, training exercises, and catalogues of weaponry. Thus, a central research question concerned whether the photojournalistic coverage in U.S. news magazines was characterized more by candid, on-the-scene, visual reporting of events or by pre-existing, staged, or symbolic representations of nations, political actors, and military power. A second concern was to compare the coverage of U.S. and Iraqi military forces and political leaders. Were pictures used to exaggerate the strength of Iraq's army, to symbolize the war as a personal conflict between Saddam Hussein and George Bush, or to emphasize the United States' centrality? Finally, the researchers wanted to examine the attention given to civilian casualties and damage.

After coding the pictures in each of the three news magazines, Griffin and Lee (1995) found that six categories constituted more than half of all the 1,104 pictures coded. The dominance of a narrow range of picture types was striking: The three most frequent categories of pictures were of military hardware, noncombat scenes of troops, and photos of political leaders. The most numerous types of pictures in all three magazines were photographic records of the "Arsenal" of military hardware in noncombat situation (planes, ships, tanks, missiles, or other weapons systems were included in this category but depictions of weapons and military hardware being used in scenes of actual combat were coded "Combat"). The Arsenal pictures included Department of Defense and photo agency file photos, illustrations provided by arms manufacturers (McDonnell Douglas Raytheon, etc.), and photos reproduced from arms catalogues, and so on. These catalogue-style pictures made up 26% of the total. In *Newsweek* (32%) and *U.S. News and World Report* (31%), almost one third of all pictures were of this type. In many cases, all three magazines reproduced the same pictures from the same sources. This prevalence of weapons illustrations in the war coverage has been found in the analysis of warspeak and images (see above): Kellner (1992) referred to "images of techno-war"; Gerbner (1992) identified it as part of "Gulf War—the movie" and Katz wrote (1992),

> We saw portraits of the technology—advertisements for smart planes, tanks, missiles, and other equipment in dress rehearsals of what they are supposed to do in combat, but we rarely, if ever, saw them in action. Indeed, it was as if there was no other side. (p. 11)

The analysis supported these claims: For every picture of actual combat (3% of the total), the newsmagazines printed about nine non-combat holographs of American military hardware. In place of images of warfare, there were images of American military technology and power. This pattern becomes even more pronounced when one looks at the second most popular category, "U.S. Troops." The results reveal virtually no pictures of troops other than American. Of the 163 pictures of troops (that is, soldiers in noncombat situations), 154 (95%) show U.S. soldiers, 4 (2%) show Saudi or Kuwaiti pilots or soldiers, and 5 (3%) show Iraqi soldiers. Two aspects of the troops pictures are most salient: (a) the wholesale substitution of photos of soldiers in noncombat situations for any actual combat coverage and (b) the completely one-sided focus on U.S. forces.

Pictures of actual combat activity constituted only 3% of news magazine pictures during the war. Depictions of wartime destruction were 6% of the total: 37 in Iraq (3%), 27 in Kuwait and Saudi Arabia (2%), and 7 in Israel (0.6%). As to casualties, there were almost no pictures of victims. The relative absence of images of U.S. casualties might be attributed to the extremely low number of actual casualties among U.S. forces, but the relatively large number of Iraqi casualties is even more invisible. This supports the charge made by many commentators that the U.S. media cooperated with the military to eschew images of bloodshed and present the American public with a "clean, victimless war."

Another interesting facet of the pictures was the "Pictures Not Seen," or the absence of certain visuals. Categories for which there were no pictures in any of the three magazines included Iraqi military leaders and individual Iraqi soldiers. Griffin and Lee (1995) also found that Iraqi POWs were only shown in large groups. The conflict was personalized in the visual juxtapositions of Bush and Saddam, but all other Iraqis remained part of an anonymous, or even unseen collective. Other absent pictures included pictures of non-U.S. Allied military casualties or public demonstrations against the war in coalition member nations.

The conclusions of the analysis of the photojournalistic coverage of the war highlights very little actual combat activity of any kind. "Catalogues of military hardware and generic military illustrations stand in for images of actual events," argued Griffin and Lee (1995), "and the massing of a powerful U.S. military machine becomes the central signifying image of the war" (p. 821). The photographic portrayal of the war seems to promote American technological superiority as a central theme. The overall image of the war that emerges from the analysis is extremely U.S. centered. The focus of photographic coverage neglected several important aspects of the war, particularly those involving the human cost of the conflict. There are very few images of casualties or human suffering due to the war. Several factors contributed to this selective visual presentation: constraining photo opportunities, including the press pool system, limited access to areas of military activity, the censorship imposed by the military, and the self-regulation maintained by news media. It appears that the mass-mediated war discourse, both visual and linguistic, was replacing the horrors and prices of war with reconstructed realities of surgical, clean, almost enjoyable unreal war. Hallin and Gitlin (1993) noted this absurd beauty of the "unreal war": "But there was something else distinctive about many of these images: they were beautiful" (p. 417). During the Gulf War, they argued, the separation between the news and the commercials was much less clear. Probably the most striking similarity was in the lighting. One of the things that gives the images in commercials their romantic quality is strong backlighting, often with a light source shining from behind the scene into the eye of the viewer. Many of the scenes in Gulf War coverage were lit in this way. One of the most common images was that of the fighter-bomber taking off or landing at sunrise or sunset. About 38% of film reports from Saudi Arabia in Hallin and Gitlin's (1993) sample had at least one sunset shot, as did 7 of 19 stories that closed broadcasts and 4 of 5 of the sequences of images CNN used to close segments of its broadcasts. The Gulf War coverage demonstrated that television has the capacity to make war aesthetic, and it did this by emphasizing images that conveyed awe and beauty.

The Triumph of the Images

The Gulf War was presented in the media with a rich variety of metaphors and images. In fact, they were so appealing, so well tailored to television and film genres, that they replaced the war as war (Gerbner, 1992). The Gulf War was the first major global media crisis orchestration that involved media image manipulation on a global scale. What were the most dominant images of the war?

A "crusade against the evil empire": In the media, the Iraqis were portrayed as brutish bullies whereas Bush and the United States were presented as the honorable defenders of international law and order. *Newsweek* proclaimed that "the president's grand plan for the post-cold war world can be summed up simply: Stop International Bullies" (September 3, 1990). Many newspapers and TV commentators praised the United States as the only superpower able to stand up against aggression and enforce international law. As Asu and Robins (1992) argued, the war was cast as a global confrontation between humanity and bestiality, a battle between civilization and barbarism. This was a war to defend the principles of modernity and reason against the forces of darkness.

When Hussein invaded Kuwait, gruesome atrocity stories filled the media. After the war, the *New York Times* reported (on December 20, 1991), "the discovery that the country suffered less damage than originally estimated." The war was also presented as the only way to stop Hussein from marching into Saudi Arabia, although there was no evidence he intended to do so. It was in this cause that the West was using what was projected as a moral kind of violence. In this cause, "the angels became exterminators." The United States was "on the side of God" whereas Saddam Hussein was demonized as a "new Hitler" poised to take over the world. Hans Magnus Enzensberger (1991) put it most bluntly:

The description of Saddam Hussein as the new Hitler is not merely
journalistic license, not the hyperbole of propaganda, but is actually
deadly accurate. . . . The behavior of the new enemy of humanity is
no different from that of his predecessor." (p. 13)

Such an aggressor—this "enemy of the human race"—had to be
"removed from the surface of the earth." As Margaret Thatcher put it,
the assault had to go ahead in the name of making the world a better,
safer place. Those who were opposed to this mission could be seen only
as the "indecent" supporters of fascist rule. Saddam Hussein was the
Great Satan: President Bush referred repeatedly to Saddam's immoral
and unconscionable brutality; to rape, assassination, cold-blooded murder, and rampant looting; and to the violation of every civilized princi-
ple. Saddam was a violent monster who was a mass killer, whether it
was the victims were Iranians or Kurds, Saudis or Palestinians, Kuwaitis
or Israelis, or even his own unfortunate people. According to Bush and
his publicists, Saddam's troops were supposed to have killed at least 300
premature babies by removing them from their incubators (although this
accusation was subsequently proved to have no foundation). Asu and
Robins (1992) argue that so convinced were the Western forces of the
moral justness of their mission to neutralize Saddam that they were
prepared to put no limits on the drive to accomplish this objective.

The "clean" against the "dirty" war: In this just war against this new
evil empire, all kinds of advanced weapons would be enlisted. These
included the "daisy cutter," fuel-air explosives, the cluster bomb, the
Stealth bomber, the Tomahawk cruise missile, the multiple-launch
rocket system, and more conventional weapons such as B-52 bombers.
Saddam Hussein's violence was always seen as vicious and brutal. His
weapons appeared to be imprecise and undiscriminating as they were
blindly launched against Israel and Saudi Arabia. In contrast, the allies
were, paradoxically, able to project their bloody assault as clean and
clinical. The desert was to be a theater in which the Western forces
would play out the fantasy of a war made bloodless through scientific
and technological expertise. The Coalition forces' aim was to "take out"
legitimate targets through "professionally executed strikes" by allied
aircraft using precision-guided munitions. These "supersophisticated
systems"—stealth weapons, smart bombs, precision missiles—were pre-

sented as saving the lives not only of allied pilots but also of Iraqis because they enabled precision attacks that limited civilian casualties. Even when it became clear that the "phenomenally accurate" weaponry killed civilians by the hundreds and thousands, as with the bombing of an air raid shelter in Baghdad, the American sources argued that Saddam Hussein would have to take the blame for it.

War and the Super Bowl: An interesting analysis of the themes and images of the Gulf War in the media revealed the Super Bowl image (Rabinovitz, 1994). Televised professional and college basketball and football games were quick to incorporate the Persian Gulf War. The juxtaposition of new emblems of flags and yellow ribbons on the teams' uniforms signified that these were the warrior-heroes, not only for school or geographic community, but also for the state. The singing of the national anthem (already a part of sporting events but now accompanied by standing ovations and announcers' voice-over commentaries as well as team prayer huddles) brought patriotism, God, and country together into new ritualistic elements. The Twenty-fifth Anniversary Super Bowl telecast, whose January 27, 1991, broadcast coincided with the first crisis-ridden days of the Persian Gulf War bombings, became repositioned as a patriotic extravaganza. The explicit linkage of soldier patriots and football heroics was repeated at the end of the pregame ceremonies when pop singer Whitney Houston, dressed in a red, white, and blue sweat suit and headband, sang "The Star-Spangled Banner." Her appearance was crosscut with a montage of U.S. flags and athletic-looking, young male representatives of U.S. combat units (Marines, Army, Navy, Air Force) who stood at attention in salute.

As Rabinovitz (1994) argued, linking the war to the beginning of the Super Bowl as an event that was produced as spectacle for the fans in the stadium and at-home viewers repositioned the battle from the gore of the battlefield—with its destruction, dead, wounded, and displaced victims—to the allegory of a football game of equally matched masculine superheroes who meet for the glory of the game, hefty paychecks, and the spectacle of individual and team accomplishment. For the first time, football spectatorship itself became identified as patriotic and heroic (the frequently used logo at beginning and end of every break was The Gulf War/Super Bowl). During the halftime break, a narrator announced the 2,000 sons and daughters of Persian Gulf military personnel, who then marched onto the field. Each wore a yellow ribbon and carried a small U.S. flag. Well-scrubbed and groomed, they filed past the camera, and the camera cut to close-ups among them, stressing their racial and ethnic diversity. Even President and Mrs. Bush, who appeared in medium shot at the White House domestic setting, dedicated the Super Bowl to the soldiers in the Persian Gulf. The halftime pageant reached its pinnacle as a high-angle extreme long shot showed the marchers on the football field spelling out the letters *USA*. Behind them was a Disney World Magic Kingdom castle, as the representation of "home" in North American commodified leisure images. Thus, argues Rabinovitz (1994),

> The coverage of the Super Bowl—especially its halftime show—constructed through its simultaneity, liveness, and spectacle a "national family" of viewers, specifying the soldiers' places in the family as sons and daughters, brothers and sisters. Being a loyal family member became synonymous with being a patriot. (p. 191)

Defending civilization: The frequent use of the Saddam-as-Hitler theme especially prejudiced the public against a negotiated, diplomatic solution and justified any use of aggression. Obviously, one cannot negotiate with a Hitler who is such a threat to world peace that he must be destroyed. Thus, the extremely negative framing of Hussein and the Iraqis created a climate in which only military action could resolve the crisis. The media scenario of the confrontation as a struggle between good and evil, with the evil Hussein unwilling to negotiate and threatening the allies, produced tension and the need for a resolution that war itself could best provide.

What emerged in most of the Western commentaries on the war was the belief that there was a profound moral difference between the violence of Saddam and that of Bush. After the war, Bush could declare that it had been a victory for the United Nations, mankind, the rule of law, and what is right. Bush's deeds of violence were always assumed to be morally defensible, to be self-evidently just acts in defense of civilization, reason, and sanity and against the "dark practices" of an alien force. The key to this image was the polarization between Western civilization and its counterpart, represented in this case by the endemic barbarism of Saddam's evil regime of terror and violence. It was the contrast between Western enlightened modernity and the benighted dark ages. "Their twentieth century is not ours," wrote Alain Finkielkraut (1991), "They have allowed honor to prevail over democracy, and force and machismo over freedom" (p. 24). Associated with this confrontation is a false dichotomy between the rational and the irrational. The choice, quite simply, is between reason and unreason. And then the choice is implicitly made between the moral and the immoral, for it is on the power of its reason and rationality that Western morality is reputedly grounded. The symbolic damnation of Saddam reflected this logic. In positioning Saddam as representing the barbarity of "medieval practices," the Western forces sought to legitimize their rationalized violence in the name of civilized reason and progress.

The aesthetic techno-war: The sterilization of the war was accomplished by the absence of victims (see below) and by the illusion that only machines and not people were involved in this new high-tech warfare, which was bloodless and antiseptic. The targets of the released footage were always ugly buildings, usually bunkers or structures serving military functions. These buildings were seemingly always deserted, devoid of humans, so the bombing was coded as a positive surgical operation that was removing methodically the instruments of evil Iraq. This image proved to be quite untrue, yet the constant replaying of these tapes, and their power to produce images of a clean and precise techno-war, created the impression of "mechanical war," involving machines, not living people. Images of the bombing of Baghdad taken by night cameras produced an eerie, surreal, and even aesthetic vision. Images of buildings, bridges, and military targets being destroyed by laser-guided bombs were photographed by cameras on the planes and on the bombs themselves, which conveyed the images to satellites, where they were downloaded and recorded on videocassette and then shown to a captivated audience. Kellner (1992) noted the impact of such high-tech special effects:

> These images literally took the TV viewers into a new high-tech cyberspace, a realm of experience with which many viewers were already familiar through video and computer games, the special effects of Hollywood movies, and cyberpunk fiction. Fascination with video and computer images provided an aura of magic and power for the

military that produced such spectacles and enhanced their credibility with a public eager to believe whatever they would claim. Not surprisingly, the media themselves were mesmerized by these images, which they played and replayed repeatedly. (p. 157)

The television networks circulated images that were high-tech visuals of an aesthetic war, of a techno-war or a video game spectacle. In this technological war, argued Hallin and Gitlin (1993), the machines were no less central as "characters" of the television drama than the soldiers. They were in fact often spoken of as if they were human actors. In their analysis of the war coverage by CNN and network television, Hallin and Gitlin found that most prominent were images of machines and related technical images. The image of techno-war was more sharply defined during the numerous press conferences and briefings held by General Schwarzkopf and other military spokesmen. In these briefings, the media were provided with videotapes of the high-tech precision bombings, the sophisticated machines, and the computerized attacks. The highlights of the briefings were always the spectacular videos, the planes, the missiles, the technology. Schwarzkopf's videos were always showing how U.S. bombs hit their targets, do not cause "collateral damage," and only take out nasty military targets. This was intended to change the public perception of war itself: The new techno-war was clean, precise, and surgical, and the very nature of war had changed. War was thus something that one could enjoy, admire, and cheer about. The media could not resist falling prey to the visual images, spectacular videos, and the imagery of techno-war. The high-tech weapons were endlessly praised by network commentators, reporters, and analysts. CBS's Charles Osgood acclaimed the high-tech bombing of Iraq as a "marvel," while NBC's Tom Brokaw explained, "So far the U.S. has fought this war at arm's length with long-range missiles, high-tech weapons. This is to keep casualties down." *Newsweek*'s February 18 cover read, "The New Science of War," with a subheading, "High-Tech Hardware: How Many Lives Can It Save?" This myth of techno-war continued to dominate the media discourse for days and helped fix the public's image of a new era of high-tech warfare.

A victimless war: The very distance of the media from the battlefields made it almost impossible to realize the awful truth of the carnage.

The Iraqis at first seemed intent on avoiding images of damage to their civilians and soldiers, and viewers thus saw very few images of the suffering, mutilation, or death caused by the U.S.-led multinational forces' daily bombing runs. The Gulf War at first appeared to be peculiarly antiseptic, a victimless war. We know now that the war caused 60,000 to 100,000 deaths in direct casualties alone. The kill ratio of about 100,000 to 150 U.S. soldiers, at least 35 of them, as it later turned out, killed by "friendly fire," was not revealed for a long time. We did not see the victims, the suffering at the other end, which made it all seem like a war with no victims. The enemy was "targets," far removed from us, and the remote-control images of war had no blood, no killing, no dead, no wounded. The images of "clean" bombing seemed to give credence to military claims that they were avoiding civilian casualties. The main facts of casualties and damage were carefully kept out of the briefings and were censored from the reports. NBC first commissioned, then refused to broadcast, uncensored footage of heavy civilian casualties. The video was then offered to CBS. The night before it was to air on the *CBS Evening News,* the show's executive producer was fired and the report was canceled.

During the brief land war launched by Washington, the allies shot thousands of fleeing Iraqi soldiers and civilians. The shooting, absent from most media reports, was described as being like "a giant hunt." After the bombing of the fleeing Iraqis, a U.S. officer said that he found it distressing to describe the scene on the main road between Kuwait City and the Iraqi city of Basra: "Dead, mutilated, and charred bodies were everywhere"; and in another account, it was reported that

> for sixty miles, on the road to Umm Qasr, hundreds of Iraqi tanks and armored cars, howitzers and anti-aircraft guns, ammunition trucks and ambulances were strafed, smashed and burned beyond belief. Scores of soldiers lay in and around the vehicles, mangled and bloated in the drifting desert sand. (*Guardian,* March 11, 1991)

However, during the war, these facts were ignored, over-ridden by smart bombs and video-game images from remote cameras.

Although the popular imagery of war may revolve around killing, in the case of the Gulf War, only a few media items portrayed the results of military action in terms of human casualties. A content analysis of television coverage in England (including BBC1, BBC2, CNN, ITV, and Channel 4) revealed that only 3% of the total Gulf War coverage was devoted to casualties and injuries. One half of this 3% was in Iraq, one quarter was in Israel, 10% was in Saudi Arabia, and 9% was in Kuwait. As Morrison (1992) concluded, "Considering that the sample period covered a range of attacks and full-scale battles, the number of people shown to be injured is remarkably low" (p. 90).

Smart bombs do not kill: TV images of missile attacks were always reported with a detailed description of their almost human qualities. If these weapons were so smart, they did not kill civilians. We were continually told about the marvelous intelligence of the new high-tech weapons. We were impressed with the Stealth fighter-bomber's sleek invisibility and its smart bombs that could be guided "down the air shafts" or "through the front doors" of targeted buildings. We were amazed at how the Tomahawk missile had "a mind of its own" and at how it could find the intelligent way to its "terminal end point." The clear message was that smart was good, and brilliant was virtuous. Smart weapons, it was being claimed, could actually save the lives of soldiers and civilians alike in the Gulf. On this basis, it became possible for the allies to dissociate themselves from the pain and death that their modern weapons brought about. Because the weapons were so smart they functioned to desensitize the troops and to disconnect their actions from their human consequences. Smart technologies allowed action "at a distance." As Bauman noted (1990), "Distance technologies . . . eliminated face-to-face contact between the actors and the objects of their actions, and with that naturalized their morally constraining impact" (p. 7). The causal connection between the act and its human consequences was broken, and the ultimate effects of actions remained invisible to the spectators.

After the war, it was revealed that U.S. bombing was highly imprecise and overwhelmingly low-tech. In a March 15 press conference after the war, Air Force Chief of Staff General Merrill McPeak admitted that only 6,520 out of 88,500 tons of bombs dropped by U.S. planes on Iraq and occupied Kuwait were precision bombs, merely 7% of the total. A senior Pentagon official told *Washington Post* reporter Barton Gellman that only 25% of the conventional bombs hit their targets and that cumulatively U.S. bombs missed their targets at least 70% of the time

(*Washington Post*, March 16, 1991, p. A1). Shortly thereafter, General McPeak admitted in an interview with *USA Today* that the United States made targeting mistakes in its massive bombing campaign against Iraq, "indicating that U.S. pilots hit and destroyed civilian targets" (March 19, 1991). Furthermore, the U.S.-led coalition dropped a large variety of "area-impact munitions" that were imprecise and extremely lethal. The smart bombs were not that smart.

Patriots save lives: When the Patriots were positioned in my hometown, Haifa, people rushed to greet the American soldiers, giving them cakes, drinks, fruits, and candies. Each night, when the Scuds were approaching us, we heard the Patriots launched to meet the incoming missiles. We were told that the Patriots saved us. So the story was told worldwide. But the Patriot missiles, costing $700,000 each, missed 8 out of 10 times. When they found their targets, the resulting debris caused more destruction than the Scuds might have done. Thirteen Scuds that fell unchallenged near Tel Aviv caused no deaths, fewer injuries, and less than half the property damage than the 11 Scuds in the same area that were intercepted by Patriots.

After the war, it was revealed that many of the missiles that the military said had been intercepted by Scuds were only partially hit, with the warhead crashing to earth. Many Patriots hit the fuel storage part of the Scud, causing spectacular explosions, while the warhead continued toward earth unimpeded. In one case, in Haifa, a Patriot missed the Scud: The Scud landed in the sea, but the Patriot landed in Bat Galim, a densely populated neighborhood, causing damage but no fatalities. Out of four Patriots launched against incoming Scuds over Tel Aviv on January 25, one self-destructed in midair while two others crashed into residential areas and the fourth climbed and then dived into a warehouse district. However, for weeks during the war, in Israeli media as well as world media, experts and commentators praised the Patriots' 100% intercept record, creating the deceptive impression that the Patriots constituted a shield of total security. For example, on January 21, *NBC Nightly News* correspondent Katherine Couric commented, "Every war supplies a hero above all others and this one has produced the Patriot missile." In an episode titled "The Protector," she argued that the Patriot is "10 for 10" and that "every Scud missile that threatened Saudi Arabia ... has been smashed to bits by the Patriot," which she eulogized as "the king of air defense systems." The segment concluded by noting that "star wars technology is expected to be revitalized, thanks to the Patriot's success."

It is clear now that the Patriots were more of a propaganda weapon than a military one. In his January 21 briefing, General Schwarzkopf claimed that the Patriot had intercepted 10 out of 10 Scuds fired at Saudi Arabia. During a February 15 visit to the Raytheon Patriot missile factory, Bush claimed that the Patriots had destroyed 32 of 33 Scuds fired. Yet, after the war, it was admitted that only 49 of the 60 Scud missiles launched by Iraq had been destroyed by Patriot missiles. Furthermore, at an April 16, 1991, briefing, it was revealed that the Patriots in Israel and Saudi Arabia may have caused more damage from debris than would have occurred if the system had never been deployed. In the case of Israel, before the Patriots were used, 13 Scuds fell near Tel Aviv; they wounded 115 people and damaged 2,698 apartments. After the Patriots were deployed in Israel, another 11 Scud attacks occurred, killing 1 person, injuring 168, and damaging 7,778 apartments. So although the number of attacks dropped 15%, the figures show that Israeli casualties per Scud fired increased by 50% after the Patriots started "defending" Israel. The number of buildings damaged per Scud tripled. No wonder that it was argued that Israel might have been better off if the Americans had never fired any Patriots at all (Postol, 1992). However, the Patriots were successful in targeting public opinion. Serving mainly as psychological weapons, they fooled us, in the "protected by Patriots areas" and the world public. Their success was shown in surveys (81% of American respondents knew about the Patriots, whereas only 42% could identify Colin Powell).

The Effects on Public Opinion

The public was not troubled by the media coverage of the war and, in fact, was rather satisfied with it, as revealed in surveys conducted in various countries. The American public was clearly satisfied with the media coverage of the war. In the data collected by the Roper Center for Public Opinion Research, the following findings were revealed:

1. Most people gave the press high marks for the coverage of the Gulf conflict.
2. Most respondents favored censorship of the media in the Gulf crisis.
3. Two thirds thought reporting of the war was unbiased. (Dennis et al., 1991)

During the operation's second week, nearly 8 out of 10 believed that the censors were not hiding bad news; 57% wanted increased military control over reporting.[4] Two months after the war, the public rated the coverage, military censorship, and general information about the war even higher. The *Times Mirror* poll found that the percentage of "very favorable" rating of the military rose 42 points from 18% to an unprecedented 60%. Desert Storm commander Norman Schwarzkopf's 51% was the highest "very favorable" score in more than 150 *Times Mirror* public favorability surveys conducted since 1985.

The public opinion was mainstreamed by the mass-mediated flow of "facts," images, metaphors, and language of the unreal war. The lack of knowledge among the American people represented an opportunity for effective image management. Gerbner (1992) argued that "once the saturation bombing had started, dissent had been marginalized, challenge had been suppressed, and the tide of saturation coverage had risen" (p. 260). Evidence of cultivation was found here too: The Morgan, Lewis, and Jhally survey showed that less than half (47%) of light viewers, compared to three quarters (76%) of heavy viewers, "strongly supported" President Bush's decision to use military force against Iraq (Chapter 18 in Mowlana, Gerbner, & Schiller, 1992). Heavy viewing also boosted the percentage of those who would vote for George Bush, especially among those who were otherwise the least likely to vote for him: Only 31% of low-income light viewers but 51% of low-income heavy viewers expressed an inclination to vote for Bush in 1992. And as Morgan, Lewis, and Jhally demonstrated, the more viewers saw, the more they remembered the misleading imagery, but the less they knew about the background and facts of the war.

John Mueller (1994) argued that the substantial increase in support for the U.S. Gulf War policy can be explained wholly as an example of the "rally around the flag" phenomenon. This hypothesis has been characterized by Brody (1991) as "a way of accounting for otherwise inexplicable rises in support for the President in the face of surprise and threat" (p. 58). Mueller (1994) explains that the public "did not want to hear anything critical" during the Gulf War, and the media complied by reacting "with predictable boosterism, even sycophancy" (p. 208). Advocates of the rally around the flag hypothesis further argued that the White House controlled information in the early stages of an international crisis, leading opposition elites to suppress their disagreement with the president in public forums, resulting in the appearance of elite consensus. Lacking independent information and fearing they will be perceived as foolish, intemperate, or even unpatriotic, rival politicians who normally challenge the impression of consensus are silent. As the boundaries of public discourse are constricted by self-censorship, media find it more difficult to voice the alternative views necessary for debate. Without the usual challenges from political elites, reporters covering elite opinions during this stage of an international crisis are left to repeat information that amplifies support for whatever action the president takes. Journalists thus become conduits of one-sided, supporting messages.

Because an international crisis provides inherent excitement and emotional intensity, the media need only engage in reporting these events themselves, Brody (1991) argues. The intrinsic drama of international conflict overrides the media's tendency to emphasize the news value of other types of conflict, including disagreement among political elites. During an international crisis, a rally materializes because the public wishes to support its leaders' actions, rival elites see no political advantage in expressing public dissent, and the media have vivid, compelling copy and visuals without disrupting this equilibrium.

Although the research inspired by the rally hypothesis identifies the results of the media's role in supporting consensus and media's self-censorship, it does not cover all the other aspects of public opinion or how public opinion develops and changes. The rally hypothesis was argued to oversimplify and underestimate the role media play in opinion formation (Kelman, 1993). Another important reservation is that media coverage interacted with other factors to create the public support. Some of the better educated and informed Americans understood that this was a war more about oil than about saving the Kuwaiti government, which was seen by many as an authoritarian system. Some of them also understood that the government-media construct of "good" versus "evil" was just that, a construct. But they supported Bush and his policy because of other reasons. Some supported Bush because they too cared more about oil prices. Some hoped that the war would put an end to Saddam Hussein, whom they saw as a dangerous leader in a dangerous neighborhood.

There were also those who opposed the war, either because they cared about human rights and wanted a negotiated settlement (e.g., the Ramsey Clark group) or because they did not want American soldiers to be killed for this remote conflict (e.g., the Buchanan conservatives). Thus, when considering the rally around the flag phenomenon, one must distinguish among subpopulations. This is particularly necessary when it comes to identifying those who recognized the level of propaganda and Bush's true motivation and either went along or found venues in which to express their disagreement.[5]

Reconstruction of Public Opinion: The Spiral of Silence Effect

In Chapter 2, we discussed the effect called the Spiral of Silence. According to this concept, people's perception of the distribution of public opinion motivates their willingness to express political opinions. The mass media play a central role in this process by creating the climate that shapes perceptions, influencing choices of debate or self-censorship (Noelle-Neumann, 1974, 1984, 1989, 1991). The prominence of the news media in the United States was very evident from the outset of the Gulf War, and those many individuals who looked to the news media for factual information and cues to public opinion about the war encountered relatively consonant images of support.

The Spiral of Silence hypothesis was tested by a study that analyzed actual and perceived support for the Persian Gulf War in the United States (Eveland, McLeod, & Signorielli, 1995). Data were collected from 292 residents of New Castle County, Delaware, during the 1991 Gulf War. Results showed that support for the war was not the strong consensus reported in mainstream media. The amount of support for the war exhibited by respondents in this study was not consistent with the media image of tremendous public support for the war: In fact, most respondents fell within the *neutral, disagree,* or *strongly disagree* ranges of support for the war scale. Only 6.6% of the respondents were in the strong support range. However, the U.S. news media, through naive reporting of public opinion poll data and other direct and indirect representations of public opinion, presented a consonant image of bipartisan support for the war. The results of these analyses lead to two primary conclusions: (a) perceptions of public opinion about the Gulf War were inaccurate and biased toward perceptions of support for the war, and (b) at least to some degree, news media use influences perceptions of public opinion, and these perceptions in turn influence individual opinions. The results of this analysis, then, provide qualified but compelling support for the basic predictions of the Spiral of Silence theory. Also consistent with the Spiral of Silence was the finding that one of the best predictors of support for the war was the perception that most people supported it. Thus, in the case of the Persian Gulf War, it seems that instead of just telling us what to think about, the news media told us what others thought, which influenced how we thought.

Agenda Setting, Framing, and Priming Effects in the Gulf War

Not only was the Gulf War the subject of extensive news coverage, there is ample evidence that Americans paid attention to this coverage. In January 1991, for example, 70% of the public reported that they followed news about the Gulf "very closely." Television news viewing in general surged during this period, and nearly 80% of the public reported "staying up late" to watch news of the conflict (according to Gallup surveys, 1991). Another symptom of this surge in viewer interest was the transformation of CNN into a major source of information, with ratings points in the double digits. The events leading up to the Gulf War provide a powerful "natural experiment" for examining the effects of news on the crystallization and development of public opinion. The first effect, agenda setting, is generally defined as the ability of the news media to define the significant issues of the day. We can study this effect by tracking the proportion of the public considering the Gulf crisis the nation's most important problem. The second effect, priming, concerns the relationship between patterns of news coverage and the criteria with which the public evaluates politicians. This is demonstrated by examining if the public weighted their opinions concerning foreign policy more heavily when evaluating President Bush in the aftermath of the Iraqi invasion of Kuwait. Finally, framing is the connection between qualitative features of news about the Gulf (in particular, the media's pre-occupation with military affairs and the invariably episodic or event-oriented character of news reports) and public opinion.

Whereas the term *agenda setting* reflects the impact of news coverage on the importance accorded to issues, the term *priming effect* refers to the ability of news programs to affect the criteria by which political leaders are judged (Iyengar & Kinder, 1987). Priming is really an extension of agenda setting and addresses the impact of news coverage on the weight assigned to specific issues in making political judgments. Priming by television news has been established in several studies for a wide range of political judgments, including evaluations of political performance and assessments of political leaders' personal traits. In general, news coverage of political issues induces stronger priming effects in the area of performance assessments and weaker priming effects in the area of personality assessments. In the context of the Gulf War, we expect increased media coverage of the Gulf War to increase the weight that respondents accord the foreign policy domain relative to the economic policy domain when they evaluate the president.

The concept of framing has both psychological and sociological dimensions. Psychologists typically define framing as changes in judgment engendered by alterations of the definition of judgment or choice problems. The sociological perspective on framing focuses on the use of story lines, symbols, and stereotypes in media presentations. Attributions of responsibility for political issues are of interest for a variety of reasons: The manner in which individuals attribute responsibility may be affected by media coverage of events (Iyengar, 1991). Attributions of responsibility are generally divided into causal and treatment dimensions. Causal responsibility focuses on the origin of the issue or problem, whereas treatment responsibility focuses on who or what has the power either to alleviate or to forestall alleviation of the issue.

Several studies set out to examine these effects. The first one was conducted to measure all three types of media effects that operated on public opinion during the Persian Gulf crisis and war (Iyengar & Simon, 1993). First, the level of network news coverage was found to match the proportion of Gallup poll respondents naming the Gulf crisis the nation's most important problem (agenda setting). Second, use of data from the 1988, 1990, and 1991 National Election Studies (NES) shows that the weight respondents accorded foreign policy performance when evaluating George Bush significantly increased (priming) in the aftermath of the Gulf crisis. Third, content data (showing that network news coverage was preoccupied with military affairs and highly event oriented) and survey data were coupled to show that respondents reporting higher rates of exposure to television news expressed greater support for a military as opposed to a diplomatic response to the crisis (framing). In conclusion, it is suggested that these effects, in combination with the nature of the media's information sources, were conducive to legitimizing the administration's perspective on the crisis.

As the researchers concluded, these findings indicate that television news coverage of the conflict in the Persian Gulf significantly affected Americans' political concerns and the criteria by which they evaluated their leader, George Bush. Prior to the crisis, Americans were preoccupied with economic problems and crime, and their feelings toward George Bush were colored primarily by economic considerations. Following the Iraqi invasion of Kuwait, the Gulf crisis became the public's paramount concern, and evaluations of Bush became more dependent on foreign policy considerations.

The priming effect was also studied by Pan and Kosicki (1997), who related media coverage to the public's evaluation of the president's performance. They found that the period between August 1990 and early November 1992 was characterized by two "issue regimes": the Gulf War and an economic recession. Analysis of aggregate media content and opinion poll data found that George Bush's job approval ratings were closely tied to the changes in the salience of these two issues. The results showed that the pattern of forming approval ratings was related to these two different issue regimes.

As the researchers argued, no American president so far has shared George Bush's experience of bouncing between the ceiling and floor of the public opinion ratings within such a short period of time (less than a year). These studies explained this unique bouncing by the priming effect. The studies were able to show that it is possible to identify issue regimes by using the relative amount of media coverage on one issue and the public's nomination of the most important issue facing the nation. The issue regime concept helps us to interpret the priming effect in terms of the reality of political communication.

Another important element in structuring public opinion was the media's silencing of dissent, not only by framing protestors in a negative way but also by promoting a limited set of patriotic themes. Gulf War coverage gave primary emphasis to views that supported patriotism, militarism, and nationalism. Media framing augmented the Spiral of Silence and sustained the positive evaluation of war by invoking symbolic patriotic values that equated attachment to country, national unity, and collective interests with conformity to majority sentiment. Dissenters in media reports were framed symbolically as untrustworthy, disheveled, nonconforming "others" who personify a threatening strangeness. The attitudes primed include negative stereotypes of people who could not fit in, contributing to the viewer's fear of social isolation as a consequence of identification with an unpopular cause. Other possible frames for these activities were available, including the portrayal of these people as caring individuals standing up for their convictions, or as thoughtful people able to engage in mature political judgment through critical reflection. If these frames had been emphasized, it seems plausible that different attitudes toward dissent would have been primed. The framing and priming found in this segment triggered the fear of isolation, contributing to a Spiral of Silence.

We should also relate the technical jargon to the framing of the war. As the literature about priming and framing suggests, frequent repetition and redundancy increased the probability that citizens would access and use particular attitude structures related to technology in evaluating the war. As we demonstrated earlier, euphemism and metaphors of technological precision, although first used by military experts, soon permeated the speech of CNN and NBC correspondents. The use of this jargon by experts, its adoption and repetition by media, and its recurrence in the broadcasts created a specialized abstract language. The reporters adopted this ubiquitous technological discourse and described the war using the framing provided by the U.S. military. The use of this technical language defined the frame through which the public understood and evaluated the war effort. As Carol Cohn (1991) concludes, this "language of war" supplanted any other political or moral discourse, leading military briefings to act "as a diversion that filled our minds with slick high-tech imagery; . . . as a conjurer's trick that made dead bodies vanish and hid human suffering; and finally, as a selective medium, which allowed certain kinds of discussion but not others" (pp. 14-15). The language of clean technology directs us to evaluate the war's success in terms of the technological precision of weapons, rather than in terms of other values, including loss of life, environmental damage, or even U.S. policy objectives.

Thus, the social mechanisms of agenda setting, framing, and priming enhance a Spiral of Silence, inducing the climate of sustained, consensual support for the administration's policy in the war. Taken together, framing, priming, and the Spiral of Silence offer an explanation for the increase in public support for Operation Desert Storm and for the endurance of overall support, long after most rally effects would have dissipated. In this war, argue Allen, Oloughlin, Jasperson, and Sullivan (1994), media provided the public with ubiquitous, redundant, repetitious messages of support. More than serving simply as conduits for military information, media also framed and primed views of dissent, patriotism, technology, and elite consensus to construct a reality that stifled dissent and influenced citizens' evaluations of military actions. The framing of U.S. technological superiority, the language of technology and military jargon, and the priming of a limited understanding of patriotic values also contributed to the Spiral of Silence. Television news coverage, such as CNN's, with its emphasis on simplification through quick, easy-to-digest video clips and sound bites, stereotyping, and repetition, is an ideal vehicle for the transmission of symbols capable of promoting a Spiral of Silence.

NOTES

1. As in other parts of this book, one should not overlook the political and ideological dimensions of research in this area. The Gulf War was "decoded" in various ways, ranging from anti-American perspectives to patriotic, pro-American views, using only one scale as an example. This chapter describes the manipulation of the media images of the war. Such analyses were performed mainly after the war, mostly by critical scholars, and were not "balanced" by less critical research.

2. For evidence of American and world exposure to CNN during the Gulf War, see Gustadt (1993).

3. An indication of the joy of the CNN staff with the war and their role is the books published by CNN men, expressing their pride and contentment. See, for example, Wiener (1992) and Smith (1991).

4. These figures were found in "The People, the Press, and the War in the Gulf," Times Mirror Center for People and the Press, releases of January 10, January 31, and March 25, 1991.

5. The need for such identification was suggested by one of the book's reviewers. The author is grateful for the helpful suggestion.

PART III

Conclusions

CHAPTER TWELVE

Virtual Reality: Virtual or Real?

A computer was something on TV,
From a science fiction show.
A window was something you hated to clean.
And ram was the cousin of a goat.

Meg was the name of my girlfriend,
And gig was your middle finger upright.
Now they all mean different things.
And that really mega bytes.

An application was for employment.
A program was a TV show.
A cursor used profanity.
A keyboard was a piano.

Memory was something that you lost with age.
A CD was a bank account.
And if you had a $3\frac{1}{4}$ floppy,
You hoped nobody found out.

Compress was something you did to the garbage,
Not something you did to a file.
And if you unzipped anything in public,
You'd be in jail for a while.

Log on was adding wood to the fire.
Hard drive was a long trip on the road.
A mouse pad was where a mouse lived.
And a backup happened to your commode.

Cut you did with a pocket knife.
Paste you did with glue.
A web was a spider's home.
And a virus was the flu.

I guess I'll stick to my pad and paper.
And the memory in my head.
I hear nobody's been killed in a computer crash.
But when it happens they wish they were dead.

—Unknown writer, disseminated on the Internet

The notion of cultivation and mainstreaming emerged with the age of television. However, the end of the 20th century and the beginning of the 21st century mark the age of new media technologies. The 1990s saw an explosion in computer communication. One scholar coined the word *compucation* to describe this new process, combining computers and communication. Every day, millions of messages of electronic mail (e-mail) are carried by the Internet and other commercial services. Companies specializing in providing on-line information and entertainment have millions of subscribers. Every day or night, millions of individuals all over the world log on to computerized chat lines, check bulletin boards, shop, read the news, play games, engage in on-line conferences, and transfer information files. This chapter examines the new realities created by these technologies, from computer games to virtual communities, and the effects these new media have on their users. Is the reconstruction of reality magnified by our new media environment?

Cyberspace and the Internet

It started in the early 1970s, during the heat of the Cold War, when the U.S. Department of Defense was concerned about the vulnerability of its computer network to nuclear attack. The alternative idea was to decentralize the whole system by creating an interconnected web of computer networks. The net was designed so that every computer could talk to every other computer. Information was bundled in a packet, called an *Internet Protocol Packet,* which contained the destination address of the target computer. The computers themselves then figured out how to send the packet. Thus, if one portion of the network happened to be disabled, the rest of the network could still function normally. The system that the Pentagon eventually developed was called ARPANET. At about the same time, companies developed software that allowed computers to be linked to local networks (LANs) that also contained the Internet Protocol programs.

The users of this early network were primarily scientists, academics, and computer experts. In the late 1980s, however, the National Science Foundation, whose own network was already connected to the net, created five centers at U.S. universities. This was the birth of the Internet. The Internet is a network of computer networks, a system that combines computers from all over the world into one big computer that can operate from a single PC (for detailed information on the Internet, see Kent, 1994; Krol, 1994). Some computers are run by government agencies, some are run by universities, some by libraries, some by school systems, some by businesses, and so on. The connections between these networks can be ordinary phone lines, microwaves, optical fibers, or wires built specially for this purpose. Now that students, scientists, government officials, and in fact everyone can have access to the information superhighway, to worldwide databases and to the cyberspace network, the number of users, the amount of information exchanges, and the time spent surfing in cyberspace have increased tremendously. In the mid-1990s, the Internet connected more than 18,000

networks, with the number increasing daily. Hooked into those networks were about 3.2 million host computers (experts estimate that
about 1,000 host computers are added to the net every day) and maybe
50 to 60 million users spread across all seven continents. The estimated
number of users in the early years of the 21st century is over a billion.

Computer-Mediated Communication (CMC)

The new mode of communication, namely, communication mediated by
computers, includes various means. Among them are:

E-mail: Instead of regular mail, using paper, envelopes, and stamps,
millions of people are exchanging messages, from recipes to scientific
data, through the electronic mail. It is fast, cheap, and pretty reliable.
Data for this book reached me through e-mail, and most of the exchange
with contributors or publishers was done through this channel. This new
and popular mode of communication is very different from the conventional modes. It is not as direct as a personal call or conversation, not
as formal as a printed letter, and not as private as a letter in an envelope.
Its special language and use of various icons and symbols produces a
very different text (where, for example, some may be blamed for being
"noisy" or "loud" if they use capital letters in their messages).

Telnet: Telnet is used for remote log-in to access computers at other
locations. Once "in," the user can access his library, scan databases, be
updated with recent news (or gossip), or get the latest sports scores.
Again, using Telnet, one can access numerous sources of information at
remote locations and scan them for any topic or issue. Telnet is indeed
the experience of enjoying "being there" while away.

Newsgroups: The newsgroups are electronic bulletin boards arranged according to topic. People interested in this topic can join the
newsgroup and read or post messages. There are thousands of different
newsgroups with topics ranging from scientific and intellectual issues
to pornography. Each newsgroup is made up of messages about the
topic. If one or more people reply to a message, those messages are

grouped into a thread. The newsgroups are uncensored. Some commercial companies that offer access to the Internet, such as America Online, may restrict the groups available to their subscribers, and some offensive messages might be posted in a code, but for the most part anything goes. After subscribing to a certain newsgroup, subscribers automatically receive a copy of all the messages posted to that particular group.

World Wide Web (WWW): The WWW is part of the Internet that contains multimedia items and hypertext, a means of instantly accessing related information. Many big companies have web sites that are used for marketing and advertising functions. Using the WWW, it is possible to transfer whole files of information from one distant computer to another, chat with other people on-line, and navigate around the Internet.

On-line information systems: These are private systems that provide information and entertainment to their subscribers. There are several major systems, some owned by large organizations, that provide basically the same services to their subscribers. They include America Online (with 1.25 million subscribers), CompuServe, Prodigy, GEnie, and Delphi.

The number of subscribers to these services has been steadily rising. Fees include about $5 to $10 per month for basic uses, with extra charges for some premium services (such as searching some specialized databases). All of the above services provide chat lines, libraries of software that can be downloaded, online magazines and newspapers, financial databases, games, e-mail, educational databases, on-line press conferences, reference services, and access to at least some parts of the Internet, to name just a few of the features available.

Virtual Reality

The information superhighways are not the only way the computer is emerging as a mass communication medium. Another exciting development is virtual reality (or VR). There are several definitions of this new medium, but it is usually defined as electronic simulations of environments experienced via head-mounted eye goggles and wired clothing, enabling the end user to interact in realistic three-dimensional situations (for a review of the various definitions, see Steuer, 1995). VR seeks to achieve an illusion of presence by placing the operator in front of a wall screen, or wrap-around room screen, or by using head-mounted displays (HMDs) in which the operator has two tiny (spectacles-sized) television screens placed in front of his or her eyes to simulate three-dimensional stereoscopic vision. Yet, virtual reality is more than an upgraded version of cinerama or a theme park ride, as it achieves not only a greater sense of presence, but through the use of computer technology, the capacity to direct one's gaze and movements so that one can explore and move around *inside* the illusory flow of images. Presence can be thought of as the experience of one's physical environment; it refers not to one's surroundings as they exist in the physical world, but to the perception of those surroundings as mediated by both automatic and controlled mental processes (Gibson, 1979). *Presence* is defined as the sense of being in an environment. The use of *telepresence* to refer to any medium-induced sense of presence describes the experience common to both teleoperation and the experience of virtual environments. Newer VR systems also include a pair of pressure-sensitive gloves that mimic the movement of human hands as they move in front of the eyes. The VR system has been in development for about two decades. NASA and the U.S. Defense Department used similar systems to train astronauts and pilots. Later, some VR hardware and software appeared in the marketplace (used mainly for design, architecture, medicine, education, and entertainment). Thus, VR can be used by real surgeons to practice on virtual patients. VR could easily revolutionize education: It permits students to walk around with wild animals or dinosaurs or even virtually become a dinosaur.

There are two major dimensions across which the VR communication technologies vary. The first, *vividness,* refers to the ability of a technology to produce a sensorially rich mediated environment. The second, *interactivity,* refers to the degree to which users of a medium can influence the form or content of the mediated environment. Steuer (1995) argues that when considering these dimensions, one should remember that Virtual Realities reside in an individual's consciousness; therefore, the relative contribution of each of these dimensions to creating a sense of environmental presence will vary across individuals. Similarly, differences in the content of the mediated environment, that is, in the kinds of entities represented and in the interactions among them, will also affect the perception of presence. However, the variables vividness and interactivity refer only to the representational powers of the technology, rather than to the individual; that is, they determine properties of the stimulus that will have similar but not identical ramifications across a range of perceivers.

Media scholars are interested in particular in how people are influenced by media presentations, how people incorporate information from the media into their judgments about the "real" world. Shapiro and Lang (1991) suggest that mediated experiences that closely mimic nonmediated ones cause difficulties for the reality-monitoring process so that when memories are retrieved, mediated and nonmediated experiences are confused. Biocca (1997) considers how VR interfaces are evolving to embody the user progressively. He highlights the effect of embodiment on the sensation of physical presence, social presence, and self presence in virtual environments. This pattern of progressive embodiment is most evident in the discourse, research, and development of advanced immersive VR. Embodiment, he argues, plays an important role in the design of virtual environments, especially collaborative virtual environments. In immersive virtual environments the environment surrounds the body, often engulfing the senses, and, therefore, the mind. Embodiment of the user is a critical dimension of the program for intelligence augmentation that motivates the advancement of VR systems. The phrase *intelligence augmentation* describes how communication technologies can be cognitive prostheses amplifying or assisting cognitive processes or developing cognitive skills.

This leads us to the question: If embodiment contributes to intelligence augmentation, what does it mean to be embodied? In other words, what are the psychological effects of goals of embodiment in virtual environments? Most commonly, the psychological effects or goals of progressive embodiment can be expressed as various forms of what is called presence. Lombard and Ditton (1997) argue that communication technologies such as VR are designed to provide media users with an illusion that a mediated experience is not mediated, a perception defined as presence. Traditional media such as the telephone, radio, television, film, and many others offer a lesser degree of presence as well. They examined the key concept of presence by applying six conceptualizations of presence found in a diverse set of literatures:

1. *Presence as social richness* (the extent to which a medium is perceived as sociable, warm, sensitive, personal, or intimate when it is used to interact with other people)

2. *Presence as realism* (the degree to which a medium can produce seemingly accurate representations of objects, events, and people—representations that look, sound, and/or feel like the "real" thing)

3. *Presence as transportation* (involves the idea of "You are there," in which the user is transported to another place; "It is here," in which another place and the objects within it are transported to the user; and "We are together," in which two or more communicators are transported together to a place that they share)

4. *Presence as immersion* (the idea of perceptual and psychological immersion, or the degree to which a virtual environment submerges the perceptual system of the user. In most compelling VR experiences, the senses are immersed in the virtual world; the body is entrusted to a reality engine)

5. *Presence as social actor within medium* (in parasocial interaction, media users respond to social cues presented by people they encounter within a medium)

6. *Presence as medium as social actor* (social responses of media users not to entities—people or computer characters—within a medium, but to cues provided by the medium itself. For example, because computers use natural language and interact in real time, even experienced computer users tend to respond to them as social entities)

Each of these six elements represents one or more aspects of what is defined as presence: the perceptual illusion of nonmediation, most powerful in the case of VR.

VR: Virtual or Reality?

The phrase *virtual reality* is an oxymoron, a contradiction in terms. *Virtual* means not in fact; *reality* means in fact. VR, then, means not in fact fact. The semantic confusion is related to the problematic social implications: Does it make us accept the virtual as real? In defining synthetic experience, Robinett (1992) differentiated four sources of VR models:

1. *Models can be scanned from the real world.* Teleoperation uses video cameras (one for each eye) to scan the real world at a remote site. Binaural sound recordings (one microphone for each ear) scan an audio model of the real world. Remote sensing data scan the real world using different senses.

2. *Models can be computed mathematically.* One of NASA's VR experiments represents air flow around the wing of a jet with visible moving patterns that are generated by a mathematical formula. In some cases, a thing rather than a place is modeled, such as an individual molecule.

3. *Models can be constructed by artists.* Polygonal CAD models are created with complete coordinate structures, allowing new views to be computed dynamically. These models can be based on actual or imaginary spaces (e.g., an exact replica of a real laboratory or an imaginary kitchen). The models are not necessarily 3-D. BattleTech, FighterTown, and other VR games show participants 2-D displays of the 3-D worlds they are flying or driving through.

4. *Models can be edited from a combination of scanned, computed, and constructed content.* Several versions of second-person VR combine 3-D motion video scanned from the real world with live motion video of the participant and computer-generated models of other entities to interact with. VR worlds may add mathematical forces such as gravity, force feedback, or magnetism to constructed or scanned models.

How real can these VRs be? Mark Slouka (1995), a lecturer in literature and culture at the University of California, San Diego, has written a book with the provocative and carefully chosen title *The War of the Worlds* in recognition of the H. G. Wells classic novel. In the original version, an alien invasion threatens the existence of Earth's people; in Slouka's book, an alien world, roughly comparable to VR, threatens our world, the real reality. The threat, argues Slouka, is pervasive, increasing, and supported by several promoters:

> My quarrel is with the relatively small but disproportionately influen-
> tial group of self-described "Net religionists" and "wannabe gods"

who believe that the physical world can (and should) be "downloaded" into a computer, who believe that the future of mankind is not in RL (real life) but in some form of VR (virtual reality); who are working very hard (and spending enormous amounts of both federal and private money) to engineer their very own version of the apocalypse. (p. 10)

Slouka (1995) is not particularly concerned with the Information or Postindustrialist Society. It is rather the "post-flesh, post-touching, post-human" one that he fears. To trivialize human existence and its many thousands of years of development, he argues, is to make mockery of everything that makes us human. Shapiro and McDonald (1995) expressed concern about people being unable to distinguish virtual experiences from reality: "Virtual reality (VR) has the potential to involve users in sensory worlds that are indistinguishable or nearly indistinguishable from the real world" (p. 324). In addition, VR environments may even merge with the real world: According to Krueger (1990),

A computer presence will permeate the workplace and the home, available whenever a need is felt. . . . Such interfaces may resemble the real world or include devices . . . that have no antecedents in the real world. . . . Artificial realities . . . need not conform to physical reality any more than our homes mirror the outside environment. (p. 422)

How can VR influence reality judgments? Based on their survey of communication literature, Shapiro and McDonald (1995) argue that whenever a new medium emerged in the past, people largely applied the judgment processes they already used: "Mass media with elements of virtual reality are at least as likely to shape our attitudes, beliefs, and behaviors as other forms of mass media. Those judgments are likely to be continuous, not dichotomous and, with experience, relatively sophisticated" (p. 331). Moreover, they argue that just as with other mass media, there is likely to be a media dependency effect. People are most likely to be influenced by media information when they have little other experience that enables them to evaluate the new information. Thus, VR can serve as the only source of information on experiences, places, situations, and actions one can share only by this medium. The additional sensory experience and feeling of being immersed in a virtual environment are likely to have even stronger effects, particularly on involuntary emotional responses. For example, there is some evidence that seeing certain events on television (e.g., a car crash or violence) produces some physiological and emotional responses similar to responses to the real thing. It seems likely that the more VR can make a car crash look and feel like a car crash, the bigger the physiological and emotional response. Another possibility suggested by Shapiro and McDonald is that the more detailed familiar contexts and the more trivial detail in a VR presentation, the more likely it will influence reality judgments. For example, it is easy to imagine that a hoax presented as a VR news story could be very convincing, indeed, especially about an unfamiliar topic. In addition, the abundance of detail may make event memories more vivid and thus more likely to influence reconstruction as media experiences accumulate over time. This led Shapiro and McDonald to conclude their suggestions with the following statement:

> VR has the potential to create an extremely rich perceptual and cognitive environment. Interacting with such an environment may sometimes tax mental capacities. Under such perceptual and cognitive stress people may be more likely to accept precepts and statements as real because they don't have the capacity to check for veracity, and the default value is real. (p. 334)

Some Concerns About VR

Few scientists and researchers of VR and its uses and applications have considered this medium's potential effects on our minds. However, Cartwright (1994) raised several questions regarding these effects: What happens to the normal mind when we enter the virtual world? What happens when a VR user loses contact with the "real world"? What happens when we find out that we cannot go back to the real world after experiencing the virtual one? Answers, he argues, are hard to find:

> Strangely, the developers of virtual reality seem largely unconcerned by the possible dangers inherent in launching individuals into another reality. Few of them have given any thought as to whether or not all cybernauts will return safely, unscathed by their experience. (p. 22)

The more senses that are involved at once and the more "real" the experience is, the more immersed one may become in VR and the harder it may become to distinguish the real from the artificial worlds. Immersion, as we will see later in the case of playing virtual games of violence, is a key predictor of impact. How will such immersion affect people with mental or emotional problems? Even people with minor neuroses or perceptual problems, argues Cartwright (1994), may find that their sensations and reactions are exaggerated in VR. Their residual memories and learning may even become distorted on returning to the real world. But in addition to affecting more fragile individuals, VR may affect people not considered at risk, making it difficult for them to adjust to a new psychology in VR. Ordinary psychological principles, ones that we take for granted in the real world, either do not exist or operate quite differently in the virtual world. Let us examine some of these problematic aspects:

Reality contact: Reality contact is often used by psychiatrists as a measure of successful adjustment to the world around us and as an indicator of mental health. In fact, a lack of reality contact is often associated with poor adjustment or even mental illness. Paradoxically, however, it is precisely this loss of at least some reality contact that is the main attribute of experiencing VR. In the real world, major disturbances in perception, such as hallucinations, can affect all of the senses and our ability to adjust to our surroundings. Yet, VR is the deliberate manipulation of the senses to produce a kind of hallucinatory state. The difference, of course, is that the VR voyager is presumably a willing traveler and that the experience is well controlled. Unwilling or unsuspecting participants of VR might be led to the experiences of certain schizophrenia-like states.

Embodiment and disembodiment: One of the most remarkable attributes of VR is the potential not only to shed one's body but to gain a new and perhaps vastly different body. Disembodiment is necessary to leaving the real world. But disembodiment and the rematerialization into a virtual body is *not* required to visit all types of cyberspace. For example, electronically flitting about the current textual Internet and browsing through the virtual libraries of the world does not require a virtual body. Certain types of game-playing, acting, dancing, and simulated physical activities, however, will require virtual bodies, perhaps even different senses, strengths, and abilities. But "giving" people a new, and possibly superior body in VR raises potential problems. Given such a perfect virtual body, argues Cartwright (1994), a quadriplegic might resist returning to the real world. We are totally in the dark when it comes to such venues, when the virtual world might be more attractive than the real one. We know about many forms of addiction, including media addiction, but what will be the form and consequences of addiction to the unreal world of virtual realities?

Fake identities: In the virtual world, one is neither expected nor required to keep real-world attributes, such as age, appearance, profession, or gender. Consequently, the virtual world becomes a place of experimentation and exploration. It is possible to explore different aspects of oneself and to examine one's identity. One of the most popular phenomena is of gender crossing, the deliberate assumption of the opposite gender (see later in this chapter). One can be either gender in these on-line discussions, or any age, nationality, race, or profession. While experimenting with a fake identity, people may disappoint those communicating with them, establishing an unreal communication between unreal identities.

Decentered self: The prospect of electronically projecting the ego into a virtual body, or to any virtual space beyond the real body, is a totally new phenomenon. Cartwright (1994) argued that although this decentering can be illuminating and instructive, it can also be destabilizing and destructive.

> It is wonderful to imagine that virtual reality will facilitate the decentering process, thus fostering increased compassion and empathy. The problem is that for some individuals, it may produce weakened self-esteem and feelings of worthlessness and insignificance. Such a downward slide could be dangerous to the integrity of the real person and, in extreme cases, lead to self-destructive acts. (p. 25)

Multiple identities: If it is possible in the virtual world to fake identity, to become embodied, to swap genders, and to decenter the self and assume a different identity, then it may also be possible to assume more than one identity at the same time. Although, in the real world, multiple personality may be associated with mental disorders, we have no idea of the consequences of such multiple identities in the VR experience. There are numerous possible consequences, but some include psychotic breaks or emotional disturbances. Such hazards may lead the future operators of VR to use the warning: "Only travelers who are well equipped emotionally and understand the psychological terrain should venture here" (Cartwright, 1994, p. 26). Although some of these concerns are rather speculative, the following issue of virtual violence and its impact is far more realistic.

Playing Virtual Violence

Playing video and computer games, and recently VR games, is a valued leisure activity among young people, especially adolescents. These games often involve virtual violence in various forms, including killing, raping, bombing, burning, and injuring human targets. As we learned, research suggests that exposure to media violence may affect attitudes and behavior (see Chapter 5). Today's video and computer games are much more realistic and often more violent than their predecessors. As movie-quality images and VR technology enhance realism, game content must be evaluated from the participants' perspective. As with television, playing video and computer games provides opportunities for observational learning. In addition to the relatively passive influence of watching television, playing electronic games adds an active dimension that may intensify the impact of game playing (Chambers & Ascione, 1987). However, the antisocial behavior often required to win in these games rarely generates realistic consequences, and the true impact of violent actions is obscured. As Funk and Buchman (1996) noted, "there is insufficient research to support strong causal statements about the impact of playing violent electronic games. Past work suggests that the gender of the player, time spent, and location of play (home or arcade) are key predictor variables" (p. 20).

Some studies found that younger children became more aggressive after exposure to violent video games (e.g., Griffiths, 1991). Researchers noted increases in the aggressive free play of 5th-grade girls after playing or just observing another aggressive video game (e.g., Cooper & Mackie, 1986). Recent studies examined the impact of playing or observing a violent VR game. In VR, various special effects and peripheral equipment give the player a heightened sense of involvement, even immersion, in the game. Some propose that this perceptual absorption will increase the impact of game playing. In the Calvert and Tan (1994) study, college students either played, observed, or were led through the motions typical of the violent game. The purpose of this study was to compare the impact of participation versus observing an aggressive VR game on young adults' arousal levels, feelings of hostility, and aggressive thoughts. The major hypothesis was that physiological arousal and aggressive thoughts would increase more for those who participated directly in the VR experience than for those who observed it. The arousal and social cognitive theories were expected to provide the best fit for explaining how VR affects adults' aggressive behaviors.

As expected, subjects' heart rates increased after participation in the VR game. Physiological arousal was a function of the VR experience rather than of movement per se because the control condition moved in ways that paralleled the VR group. This finding provides support for the arousal theory. Those who played the VR game also reported more dizziness and nausea than did those in either the observation or control conditions. Most important, aggressive thoughts increased more for those who played than for those who observed the VR game or simulated game movements, providing support for the social cognitive theory over the arousal theory. More specifically, the aggressive content of thoughts separated VR game players from those in other conditions. This differs from regular video games: In video games, no differences were found between participants and observers of a violent video game. In the Silvern and Williamson (1987) study, young children who viewed a *Road Runner* cartoon or who played a *Space Invaders* video game increased their subsequent aggressive interpersonal behavior. Thus, participants and observers were affected similarly by exposure to a violent television program or video game. In the VR context, immersion may potentially be a more powerful perceptual experience than video game play, thus increasing the impact of interactive over observational experiences. In summary, young adults who played an aggressive VR game exhibited increased physiological arousal and increases in aggressive thoughts. These results suggest that increasing the realism of violent electronic games may increase the influence of game content.

However, the prevalence of computer games indicates that it is unlikely that playing these games causes severe psychopathology in the average player. But media research suggests, as we noted in Chapter 5, that frequent exposure to violent contents may have a subtle negative influence over the long term and may decrease empathy, disinhibit aggressive responses, and strengthen the general perception that the world is a dangerous place. Self-concept was seen as a key mediating variable. Harter (1986, 1987a, 1987b) has developed a multidimensional theory of self-concept that defines and measures various aspects of self-esteem. The notion of self-concept was related to the impact of playing VR and computer games. Thus, for example, if game playing supports self-esteem without further impairing key skills, the initial relationship between game playing and self-esteem could be positive. However, if competence in the key area drops below socially acceptable levels as a result of game playing, decreasing social support and acceptance, the overall relationship could be negative.

Funk and Buchman (1996) conducted a study relating adolescent electronic game-playing habits, preference for violent games, frequency and location of play, and self-concept. Multivariate analyses identify marked gender differences in game-playing habits and in scores on the Harter Self-Perception Profile for Adolescents. For girls, more time playing video or computer games is associated with lower Harter scores on six subscales, including self-esteem. Are there "high risk" players? At the present time, there is no indication that playing electronic games causes major adjustment problems for most players. Associations between game-playing habits and adjustment problems have been previously reported for subgroups of players. Dominick (1984) reported a positive association between low self-esteem and solitary arcade play for young adolescent boys. Funk and Buchman's results suggest that, for young adolescent girls, a persistent major time commitment to playing electronic games may be a marker for lower perceived self-competence in one or more key developmental areas. It is possible that, by examining participants with the most extreme playing habits, meaningful relationships between game preference and self-concept may be identified for subgroups in future research. If so, concluded the researchers, then specific game-playing habits may eventually be another warning sign used to identify adolescents who are at high risk for adjustment problems.

Finally, living in VR may involve deviant behavior. The best illustration of this risk is the case of rape in cyberspace. The incident known as the first widely publicized rape in cyberspace occurred in the virtual place or MUD called LambdaMOO. In front of witnesses, the alleged rapist, Mr. Bungle, sexually assaulted several people until he was captured (Dibbell, 1993). MacKinnon (1998) analyzed this rape as a social construction and, using the "Bungle Affair" as a case study, recommended a course of action for reducing or eliminating instances of rape in VR. The facts of the case as reported by Dibbell are that (a) Mr. Bungle used a voodoo doll to (b) force legba, a person of indeterminate gender, to sexually service him in a variety of ways, and to force legba into unwanted liaisons with other individuals present in the room.

Aside from the fact that rape, with or without the use of a voodoo doll, was not explicitly prohibited in LambdaMOO at the time of the incident, the question to be answered is if a rape occurred. The given in the problem is that the reality of the parties involved is mediated via the computer that hosts LambdaMOO, that the textual narrative generated by the mediation constitutes the reality of the parties, and that the parties influence the generation of the narrative by interacting with the host computer. Although there was no law proscribing rape, it was generally understood to be antisocial behavior, and the members of LambdaMOO society had relied on the traditional methods of social control to curtail it. Since this case, an arbitration system has been set up in LambdaMOO so that individuals can bring suit against one another, the range of possible judgments notably including virtual death. The fact that LambdaMOO is a text-based VR should lead not only to asking if a rape has occurred, but also, was it a rape or simply an inert description of the act? Reid writes (1995),

> Users treat the worlds depicted by MUD programs as if they were real.
> . . . The illusion of reality lies not in the machinery itself but in the
> user's willingness to treat the manifestations of his or her imaginings
> as if they were real. (pp. 165-166)

As MacKinnon concludes, perhaps the high degree of anonymity, mobility, and voluntary accountability among VR users exposes them to possibly greater consequences of social disorganization than is experienced in real life.

Cultivation Theory and VR

Heeter (1995) argues that the interaction of reality and virtual experiences is complex:

> Like movies and novels only far more so, enjoyment of virtual experience is higher if you feel like you have entered another world. Theorists speak of creating a suspension of disbelief in theater audiences that allows viewers to get involved in the drama. VR seems to require a more intense involvement—engagement of belief, perhaps. In part this feeling depends on technical and artistic aspects of the experience, and in part it depends on your ability and willingness to act and feel as if a virtual world is real. (p. 206)

VR is certainly giving new meaning to the idea of mediated realities and should be related to cultivation theory. Although the cultivation paradigm highlighted the role of television, the basic argument seems even more valid in the case of VR. According to the cultivation theory, instead of immediate change in viewer attitude or behavior as a result of viewing a specific program one time, the "massive long-term and common exposure of large and heterogeneous publics to centrally produced, mass-distributed, and repetitive systems of stories" (Gerbner et al., 1986, p. 18) will help form people's perceptions of what the world is like.

VR media have not yet reached the stage of mass consumption. The potential cultivation effects can be studied, however, and some argue that the VR experience is likely to have a stronger cultivation impact than TV shows. In the two VR centers studied by Heeter, entertainment VR is a repetitive experience. After 1 year of BattleTech Center operation, one of the frequent BattleTech players had played more than 800 times. He spent at least 130 hours inside the BattleTech world, blowing up other people's robots. FighterTown members fly once a month for at least a year. In addition to being a repeated experience, VR is much more of an active, direct experience than is being a passive audience member for traditional mass media. Cultivation analysis demonstrated its arguments by using the example of the Mean World Syndrome. They count acts of violence per hour in representative samples of TV shows every season. However, the world of VR entertainment is scarier: Acts of violence at BattleTech are reported on a computer printout at the end of the 10-minute game and can number in the hundreds.

Most entertainment VR centers that exist today are based on combat or military themes. Heeter argues that the designers of VR entertainment are cognizant of possible social and media backlash about the violence, and their language and world designs reflect that awareness. Humans never die in these games: At BattleTech, they eject to safety at the last minute and reappear in a new robot; at FighterTown, they parachute to safety. Players have more than one "life" in most games and thus can survive any victimization, violence, or death. System operators also carefully avoid associating the virtual enemy with a particular nationality or ethnicity (except when real humans are playing against real humans in real time); instead, the virtual enemies are futuristic robots, imaginary people, or aliens. It is interesting to note that the players themselves sometimes ask whether the enemy can represent some real-life foe (e.g., during the Persian Gulf War, people asked to have the enemy targets be Iraqi). The language used in these VR games indeed reminds us of the sterile Gulf War: Consistent with military speak, at FighterTown players do not "blow people up," they "engage enemy targets." These nameless, faceless, unreal enemies are different from action-adventure TV and movie antagonists, where the bad guys are human actors with visible physical and social characteristics.

This might be the reason for Heeter's (1995) finding that many VR users are engaged in virtual violence: Prospective VR players expressed a desire to shoot at attacking enemies an average of 5.5 out of 7 where 7 is *very much*. (Two thirds of males and 16% of females would like this very much—the average for males was 6.2 compared to 4.6 for females, significantly different by t test at $p < .001$.) Prospective players also expressed a desire to see explosions in realistic detail when ships are blown up (5.5 out of 7, where 7 is *very much*). According to Heeter, BattleTech players enjoy blowing people up—the average degree of enjoyment is 1.5 out of 7, where 1 is *very much*. This was significantly different by gender, but both sexes enjoyed blowing people up. Slightly more than one third (35%) find it more fun to blow up good friends(!) than strangers (only 5%), but the majority (57%) say it makes no difference. In open-ended responses to a question of what they would like to experience in VR, 47% of male and 13% of female prospective players volunteered that they would like to experience sex or violence. There was little overlap. One quarter of the males were interested in "war, combat, death, and destruction"; one quarter wanted sex. The percentages among females were lower (10% and 5%, respectively). These findings led Heeter (1995) to conclude,

> Following social learning theory, the less close to reality, the less likely violent behavior in VR will be replicated in real life. Rather than merely observing a violent behavior, in VR you engage in violent behavior. . . . At today's VR centers, no humans are shown being injured. So, there are reasons to postulate a more intense effect of violent VR than violent TV, and also reasons to postulate a less intense effect. Advances in VR technology may be accompanied by more hard-core VR violence, with stronger negative effects. (p. 207)

VR Users and Reality

In one of the first empirical attempts to measure VR's effect on perceptions of reality, Heeter (1995) collected data on five different VR experiences, ranging from games (virtual cockpit) to second-person experiences. There were a total of 787 respondents who offered their reactions to four different VR experiences. Two were entertainment VR experiences (BattleTech and FighterTown), two were second-person VR prototypes (CyberArts and SIGGRAPH), and one was a group of college students (Michigan State University) who had never experienced VR.

Heeter studied how much participants had been able to engage belief that VR is real. For the second-person survey, she used several survey questions: How real did the overall experience feel? How real did the 3-D feel? To what extent did you feel a physical response when your screen self touched other objects? To what extent did you feel an emotional response when your screen self touched other objects? Which felt like the real you—the being on the screen or the one the camera was pointed at? The first five questions used a 7-point response scale, with possible answers ranging from 1 = *not at all* to 7 = *very much*. The last question could be answered with "the being on the screen," "the being the camera was pointed at," or "both."

Then the responses were split at the median, putting the respondents who indicated stronger than neutral agreement with the "entered other world" statement into one group and the rest into a second group. *T* test comparisons of means between those two groups were significant for every variable in the group, even with a small sample size of 85 (see Table 12.1). The degree to which CyberArts participants reported feeling as if they had entered another world strongly related to every other measure of enjoyment of the virtual experience. The findings described in Table 12.1 inspired ongoing research into what factors contribute to a sense of presence in virtual worlds, reported in more detail by Heeter (1992).

Both studies of second-person VR found similar proportions of participants reporting three kinds of reactions: 29% to 31% of the people who tried it felt as if the "being on the screen" was their real self; 26% to 29% felt that the physical body the camera was pointing at was their real self; 40% to 42% felt as if both were real. The percentages were surprisingly consistent across different audiences and different virtual experiences. This may be a personality characteristic related to propensity to get involved in virtual experiences. To extend the reactions to second-person VR, it seems that about one quarter of the population is easily able to "engage belief" and get involved in a virtual experience. Second-person VR requires a rather outrageous leap of faith, to transfer your sense of self into a world on the screen. But perhaps that leap is a powerful first step to experiencing a virtual world; "like Peter Pan thinking a happy thought, once you make that initial leap, reality becomes plastic and you can fly" (Heeter, 1995, p. 193).

Virtual Communities or Pseudocommunities?

The use of the Internet as mail system became a growth industry and millions of Internet regulars belong now to many kinds of virtual communities. These communities are organized around a political, environmental, social, cultural, or leisure interest. The virtual commu-

TABLE 12.1 Heeter's (1995) Findings on Virtual Reality Experiences

	Entered other world?		
	yes	no	p <
How real did the overall experience feel?	5.4	3.4	.00
How real did the 3-D feel?	4.6	3.7	.00
To what extent did you feel a physical response when your screen self touched other objects?	5.5	4.2	.06
To what extent did you feel an emotional response when your screen self touched other objects?	4.8	3.4	.00
The being on the screen or both felt like the real one.	90%	50%	.00
On a scale of 0 to 10 where 10 is very much, how would you rate your enjoyment of the experience?	6.8	5.8	.06

nities are characterized by individuals trying to understand themselves by entering environments in which they have some degree of control over what information about themselves is presented to others. By playing with different and even contrasting personae, they hope to discover more about their interests, desires, and even sexuality. In these virtual communities, individuals may reach out to others to form lobbying groups, to exchange information and support for a host of medical and psychological problems, and to mount worldwide campaigns against political oppression, child exploitation, and looming environmental disasters. These virtual communities offer members a number of advantages, including instantaneous delivery of announcements, a communication channel that is less inhibiting than face-to-face confrontations, and a never-closing forum. Many groups use a communication structure called a *listserv,* which can be viewed as either a newsgroup limited to formally subscribed members or a mail group in which every message posted immediately is made available to all group members. Joining and quitting usually is done automatically by posting an appropriate message, thus making the virtual membership easy and not demanding.

Most of the virtual communities are using the Internet Relay Chat (IRC). IRC has enabled fast human discourse, crossing boundaries of time, distance, culture, and politics. IRC is a dynamic form of communication: New comments appear at the bottom of your screen as you watch, and older comments scroll off the top of your screen. Somewhere in the world, a human being has typed those words on a keyboard, no more than a couple of seconds ago; the conversation literally continues to move up your screen as you watch. Those thousands of people tuned into IRC at any one time are divided into hundreds of channels, which Internet users can join or leave at any time; like Ascend newsgroups, the channels operating at any one time include a rich variety of topics, from the scholarly to the obscene. You sense, even from a brief visit to IRC land, that many of these people have built a kind of community. IRC is for them the corner pub, the cafe, the common room, their community. By the early 1990s, there were hundreds of channels and many thousands of people chatting across the IRC net, 24 hours a day. Some scholars pointed to IRC's reversal of the role of social context in shaping conversation and community (e.g., Rheingold, 1994). In the real world, social conventions are built into houses and schools and offices, signaled by modes of dress and codes of etiquette, posture, accent, tone of voice, and hundreds of other symbolic codes.

Critical to the rhetoric surrounding the new modes of communication is the promise of a renewed sense of community and, in many instances, new types and formations of community. Computer-mediated communication, it seems, will do by way of electronic pathways what cement roads were unable to do, namely, connect us rather than atomize us, put us at the controls of a vehicle and yet not detach us from the rest of the world. This is particularly important as it relates, in Berger and Luckmann's (1967) terms, to the *social construction of reality*. That reality is not constituted by the networks CMC users use; it is constituted in the networks. VR, CMC, and cyberspace are commonly imagined in terms of reaction against, or opposition to, the real world. Generally, there is the belief or hope that the mediated interaction that takes place in the virtual world will represent an ideal and universal form of human association and collectivity. Michael Benedikt (1991) sets it in the historical context of projects undertaken in pursuit of realizing the dream of the Heavenly City:

> The Heavenly City stands for our state of wisdom, and knowledge; where Eden stands for our intimate contact with material nature, the Heavenly City stands for our transcendence of both materiality and

nature; where Eden stands for the world of unsymbolised, asocial reality, the Heavenly City stands for the world of enlightened human interaction, form and information. (p. 15)

This vision expresses the utopian aspirations in the VR project. Not all virtual realists are quite so unrealistic, however. There are others with a more pragmatic and political disposition who have more to contribute to our understanding of the relation between cyberspace and the real world. There is still the sense of VR as an alternative reality in a world gone wrong with VR seen as the basis for developing new and compensatory forms of community: A. R. Stone (1991) argued that virtual communities represent

> flexible, lively, and practical adaptations to the real circumstances that confront persons seeking community. They are part of a range of innovative solutions to the drive for sociality—a drive that can be frequently thwarted by the geographical and cultural realities of cities. . . . In this context, electronic virtual communities are complex and ingenious strategies for survival . . . virtual communities of cyberspace live in the borderlands of both physical and virtual culture. (pp. 111-112)

The most sustained attempt to develop this approach is that of Howard Rheingold (1994) in his book *The Virtual Community*. Like other virtual communitarians, Rheingold starts out from what he sees as the damaged or decayed state of modern democratic and community life. The use of computer-mediated communications, he argued, is driven by the hunger for community that grows in people around the world as more and more informal public spaces disappear from our real lives. Rheingold emphasizes the social importance of the places in which we gather together for conviviality, "the unacknowledged agora of modern life. . . . When the automobile-centric, suburban, fast-food, shopping mall way of life eliminated many of these 'third places' from traditional towns and cities around the world, the social fabric of existing communities started shredding" (p. 6). His hope is that virtual technologies may be used to staunch such developments. Rheingold's belief is that cyberspace can become one of the informal public places where people can rebuild the aspects of community that were lost. In cyberspace, he maintains, we shall be able to recapture the sense of a social commons, to recover the values and ideals that have been lost to the real world, and to construct new sorts of community, linked by commonality of interest and affinity rather than by accidents of location.

Rheingold's (1994) definition is extremely popular but also raises many debatable issues, especially with regard to the notion of community. This is due to the fact that Rheingold argues via a variety of analogies from the real world, such as homesteading, that virtual communities are indeed new forms of community. The debate over the validity of Rheingold's position has raised doubts about the existence of virtual communities and the appropriate use of the term. Weinreich (1997) argued that the idea of virtual communities "must be wrong" because "*community* is a collective of kinship networks which share a common geographic territory, a common history, and a shared value system, usually rooted in a common religion." In other words, Weinreich rejects the existence of virtual communities because group-CMC discussions cannot possibly meet his definition. Weinreich's view is similar to that presented by several authors who consider virtual communities to be pseudocommunities, most notably Beniger (1987), who describes

> the great societal transformations of the 19th century . . . a sharp drop in interpersonal control of individual behavior: from traditional communal relationships (Gemeinschaft) to impersonal, highly restricted association or Gesellschaft . . . from face-to-face to indirect or symbolic group relations. (p. 353)

Beniger borrows from Tonnies's distinctions between Gemeinschaft and Gesellschaft: For Beniger, a pseudocommunity is one in which impersonal associations constitute simulated personalized communication, what he calls "a hybrid of interpersonal and mass communication." This criticism of pseudocommunity centers on the insincerity (or inauthenticity) of communication that it represents and the goals toward which that communication may be directed. Is the pseudocommunity a "place" where people lack the genuine personal commitments to one another that form the bedrock of genuine community? (On this issue, see Q. Jones, 1997). Or is our notion of *genuine* changing in an age where more people every day live their lives in increasingly artificial environments?

Rheingold (1994) believes that we now have "access to a tool that could bring conviviality and understanding into our lives and might help revitalize the public sphere"; that, through the construction of an "electronic agora," we shall be in a position to "revitalize citizen-based democracy." It is envisaged that such communities will develop in ways that transcend national frontiers: Rheingold (1994) thinks of local networks as "gateways to a wider realm, a 'global civil society' and a new kind of international culture" (p. 110). Rheingold's vision is fundamentally conservative and nostalgic. He is essentially concerned with the restoration of a lost social entity, the community:

> The fact that we need computer networks to recapture the sense of cooperative spirit that so many people seemed to lose when we gained all this technology is a painful irony. . . . While we've been gaining new technologies, we've been losing our sense of community, in many places in the world, and in most cases the technologies have precipitated that loss. (p. 110)

The virtual community is seen as rekindling the sense of family, community, and town square, "communitarian places online." The electronic community is characterized by commonality of interests, by the sense of shared consciousness, consensus, and mutual understanding. Rheingold (1994) is intent on connecting virtual solutions to real-world problems. Nevertheless, as some scholars note, "Rheingold is a self-styled visionary. His ideas are projected as exercises in radical imagination. . . . There is, however, something deceptive in this sense of continuity and fulfillment" (Robins, 1995, pp. 149-150).

One of the main attributes of real, conventional face-to-face communication is interactivity. Some, like Rafaeli (1998), criticize the idealization of face-to-face interactivity:

> Interactivity is generally assumed to be a natural attribute of face-to-face conversation, but it has been proposed to occur in mediated communication settings as well. Interactivity is an expression of the extent that in a given series of communication exchanges, any third (or later) transmission (or message) is related to the degree to which previous exchanges referred to even earlier transmissions. . . . This complex and ambitious definition misrepresents the intuitive nature of interactivity. In fact, the power of the concept and its attraction are in the matter-of-factness of its nature. The common feeling is that

interactivity, like news, is something you know when you see it. (pp. 110-111)

Rafaeli (1998) goes on to ask the fundamental question: Why should face-to-face communication serve as an ideal? The most likely answer is that it is a form of communication that we identify and associate with community, with Gemeinschaft, and face-to-interface communication we associate with the impersonal community or the so-called "pseudocommunity." Rafaeli and Sudweeks (1998) argue that the most "real" part of the social phenomenon of communication is the text exchanged—more real even than the groups, people, and emotions involved. Thus, they believe the groups formed on the net are neither pseudo, nor imagined. Yet Schudson (1978) has noted that

> when we criticize the reality of the mass media, we do so by opposing it to an ideal of conversation which we are not inclined to examine. We are not really interested in what face-to-face communication is like; rather, we have developed a notion that all communication should be like a certain model of conversation, whether that model really exists or not. (p. 323)

Computer-mediated communication gives us the "feeling" that Rafaeli emphasizes, but, as Jones (1995) noted, "we are too media-savvy to be misled to believe that CMC has achieved the face-to-face ideal" (p. 10). We thus totter between the belief that CMC will, to borrow from Marshall McLuhan, "retribalize" us by engaging us in an ideal form of communication we have abandoned and the belief that our inter-action will become mechanized and lack the "richness" of face-to-face conversation. Creating software (and hardware) for CMC has become a race to provide the most "lifelike" interaction possible, a race charac-terized by extreme attentiveness to information richness and simulation. Each checkpoint in this race asks whether or not we have taken a step toward realizing the conversational ideal. According to the ideal, we are reassured by the belief that the reality our eyes perceive in face-to-face communication is more real (or less manipulable) than other media by which we perceive reality. That belief reasserts itself in the under-standing we have that what mediated reality lacks is sufficient richness to convey nonmediated reality. Yet, even in face-to-face interaction, much of what is most valuable is the absence of information, the silence and pauses between words and phrases. Cohen (1985) criticized the idyllic (and often romantic) view of face-to-face interaction, too:

> The idea that, in small-scale society, people interact with each other as "whole persons" is a simplification. They may well encounter each other more frequently, more intensively, and over a wider range of activities than is the case in more anonymous large-scale milieux. But this is not to say that people's knowledge of "the person" overrides their perception of the distinctive activities (or "roles") in which the person is engaged. (p. 29)

This leads us to another problem, that of identity or "real knowledge of the person": One of the main attributes of these communities is anonymity. In the real world, it is very difficult to conceal your identity, but the virtual communities allow their members to use virtual identities. This, of course, led many users to use false identities. Most common is the false sexual identity. Why do men want to be women in virtual worlds? A few suggestions are given by Rosenberg (1997):

- Due to the pressure of cultural stereotypes, it may be difficult for some men to explore within themselves what society labels as "feminine" characteristics. These men may rely on the anonymity of cyberspace to express their feminine side, which they feel they must otherwise hide.
- Adopting a feminine role in cyberspace may be a way to draw more attention to themselves. Getting noticed and responded to in cyberspace is not always easy, especially in such distracting, "noisy" environments as the visual chat habitats.
- Some men may adopt a feminine identity to investigate male/female relationships. They may be testing out various ways of interacting with men to learn, firsthand, what it's like being on the woman's side.
- Disguised as a woman, a man looking for intimacy, romance, and/or cybersex from another man may be acting on conscious or unconscious homosexual feelings.

Another criticism of virtual communities focuses on their entirely synthetic, false nature:

> There is the invocation of community, but not the production of a society. There is "groupmind," but not social encounter. There is

on-line communion, but there are no residents of hyperspace. This is
another synthetic world, and here, too, history is frozen. What we have
is the preservation through simulation of the old forms of solidarity
and community. In the end, not an alternative society, but an alternative to society. (Robins, 1995, p. 150)

Even Rheingold (1994) agrees that virtual communities could be luring
us into an attractively packaged substitute for democratic discourse.

Three different kinds of social criticisms are relevant to the notion
of virtual communities as a means of enhancing democracy. One school
of criticism emerges from the way electronic communications media
already have turned more and more of the content of the media into
advertisements for various commodities, a process these critics call
commodification. The "commodification of the public sphere" is what
social critics claim we are witnessing with the commercialization of the
public debate. This might happen to computer-mediated participation
in virtual communities. The second school of criticism focuses on the
fact that interactive networks could be used in conjunction with other
technologies as a means of surveillance, control, and disinformation as
well as a conduit for useful information. Along with all the person-to-
person communications exchanged on the networks are vast flows of
other kinds of personal information—credit information, transaction
processing, health information. The same channels of communication
that enable citizens around the world to communicate with one another
also allow government and private groups or individuals to gather
information about them. The spreading use of computer matching to
piece together the digital trails we all leave in cyberspace is one indication of privacy problems to come.

Finally, the third category of critical claims belong to the so-called
hyper-realist school. Hyper-realists see the use of communications technologies as a route to the total replacement of the natural world and the
social order with a technologically mediated hyper-reality, a "society of
the spectacle" in which we are not even aware that we work all day to
earn money to pay for entertainment media that tell us what to desire
and which brand to consume and which politician to believe. We don't
see our environment as an artificial construction that uses media to
extract our money and power. We take it as real reality, the way things

are. These critics believe that information technologies have already changed what used to pass for reality into a slicked-up electronic simulation. The first hyper-realists pointed out how politics had become a movie, how war became show business (see Chapter 10), and how violence turned into entertainment. To hyper-realists, CMC, like other communications technologies of the past, is doomed to become another powerful conduit for "disinfotainment." Although a few people will get better information via high-bandwidth supernetworks, the majority of the population is likely to become more precisely befuddled, more exactly manipulated. The illusion of democracy offered by CMC utopians, according to these reality critiques, is just another distraction from the real power play behind the scenes of the new technologies—the replacement of democracy with a global mercantile state that exerts control through the media-assisted manipulation of desire rather than the more orthodox means of surveillance and control.

The virtual communities force us to rethink many of the ideas that we long held about social relationships, social groups, presentation of self, social identities, and social support. Ironically, this artificial medium, made possible only because of machines such as computers and telecommunications devices, has raised serious questions about human relationships. As several scholars have noted, the emergence of these virtual communities may have some harmful impact: "Dangers do exist, in that dependency on artificial worlds for human relationships may be destructive of real relationships in the real world, which after all is not just another chat room, another MUD, or another window on a computer screen" (Rosenberg, 1997, p. 436). Even Rheingold (1994), the most influential virtual community utopian, warned,

> Virtual communitarians, because of the nature of our medium, must pay for our access to each other by forever questioning the reality of our online culture. The land of the hyper-real begins when people forget that a telephone only conveys the illusion of being within speaking distance of another person and a computer conference only conveys the illusion of a town hall meeting. It's when we forget about the illusion that the trouble begins. When the technology itself grows powerful enough to make the illusions increasingly realistic, as the Net promises to do within the next ten to twenty years, the necessity for continuing to question reality grows even more acute. (p. 286)

The Future: New Media, New Cultivation

As this chapter has documented, the computer has become the modern mass medium. The new mode of communication, namely, computer-mediated communication or CMC, includes various means, ranging from the Internet and the World Wide Web to VR. The rapid changes in our communication environment have many social implications. First, the conventional media are no longer the sole source of information, the sole agents of surveillance: Computer owners do not have to depend only on the traditional mass media for information; they can download press releases, scientific reports, personal observations, and even photographs or footage posted on the Internet and other information services.

Whereas, in the mass media, the flow of information and entertainment is monitored by gatekeepers, computer networks like the Internet have no gatekeepers. This may have several implications, some of which are very important to our perspective here, the role of media in reconstructing reality. Gatekeepers also function as evaluators of information. Newspaper editors and television news directors consider the authenticity and credibility of potential news sources. If the system works properly, rumors and false information are filtered out before they are published or broadcast. Information obtained on the Internet, however, comes without a guarantee. Some of it might be accurate; some of it you must use at your own risk. And, of course, no gatekeeper means no censorship. The Internet is like a huge city. There are streets where violence, threat, hate, and victimization are the messages, the pictures, and the language used.

Another aspect of CMC is its vividness and speed, easy access to everywhere in cyberspace with no time or distance limits. What happens when VR becomes more appealing than real reality? Will large numbers of us abandon socially relevant pursuits for a virtual travel in the media world? As computers' capabilities to develop increasingly complex and realistic images advance, the illusion will become even more convincing. Moreover, in the future, elements of VR are likely to find their way into a variety of mass media. For Biocca and Levy (1995), the age of VR has begun:

The elements of the new dominant medium are in place: a paradig-
matically different communication interface design, new channels of
sensory information, and new modes of mediated communication. Is
this a new communication system emerging? We believe that the
answer is most likely yes. . . . It is clear that radically different
communication capabilities are being designed for an emerging communication system and VR interfaces are an example of these capabilities. . . . Virtual reality may be the ship that helps us sail the vast oceans
of cyberspace. (pp. 30-31)

Shapiro and McDonald (1995) share the same vision: They argue
that VR is likely to fundamentally change the audience's experience.
Viewers of documentaries and news may be able to feel as if they are on
the streets of Beirut as militia shell each other or as if they are on an
African plain in the middle of a herd of elephants. Fiction viewers may
feel like they are in the midst of the action. Fantasy games may evolve
to the point where members of VR audiences will have enough sensory
input to feel as if they really are the heroes trying to find their way
through the dungeon. Computer games and simulations will be far more
realistic and engaging. All of these may lead to more powerful effects
on perceptions of reality than those we know now.

VR appears to be different from conventional mass media in at least
two ways. First, the audience members' sensory experience can be much
more like the sensory experience of the real physical world. Second, and
related to that, is an effect we will call immersion. Audience members
can feel much more like they are part of, perhaps even actors in, events
rather than just observers. Current virtual environments are often
visually less like the natural environment than many computer games.
Even when it is possible to create VR systems that are more similar to
external reality, part of the attraction of VR may be its ability to create
convincing alternative worlds. Nonetheless, it may be useful to define
an "ideal" VR as a VR environment so sophisticated that no matter how
the user moves or interacts with the environment the user will not be
able to use sensory cues to determine whether his or her current
environment is real or virtual. Such an ideal VR is probably impossible,
but some future VR systems are likely to strive for this ideal. The
increased sensory richness of an ideal VR may still influence reality
construction and reconstruction. One possible influence on construction is that sensory richness will tend to tie up mental capacity, reducing

what is available for assessing the reality of an object or event. Given the biases discussed earlier, that may make it more likely that objects and events will be accepted as real. "Perhaps the most likely effect of increased sensory richness will be on the unconscious mechanisms that may use information accumulated over time to influence reconstruction," argue Shapiro and McDonald (1995, p. 339). Some investigators have suggested, for example, that television's sensory resemblance to real life may influence physiological and unconscious cognitive mechanisms and make it more likely that memories of television events will be judged as real events than less sensory-rich experiences (Shapiro & Lang, 1991). If so, an ideal VR, with its even greater sensory resemblance to natural reality, should be even more likely to lead to such "reality monitoring" errors.

When looking at the near future of VR, Krueger (1990) suggested that there will be two forms of computer-human interface. One possibility is a computer interface that merges with the environment so that actions the user performs are acted on to accomplish the user's intentions. The VR artifacts will have many of the characteristics usually associated with reality. As aspects of the virtual environment become part of our natural environment, the distinction between computer reality and "real" or conventional reality will become increasingly blurred. Humans may need to become even more sophisticated about reality judgments, making distinctions between physical reality, computer artifacts, and computer artifacts that allow manipulation of physical reality. The other kind of computer interface Krueger mentioned is what we generally think of as VR. Through various forms of sensory feedback, the user has, to some extent, the experience of entering an environment created by a computer. This highlights a potentially important difference between conventional mass media and VR. With conventional mass media, the receiver is distinct and separate. When a person watches a war on television or a videotape of surgery, it is clear that he or she is an observer, not a participant. An ideal VR has the potential to blur that distinction. The news, using VR, may give people the impression that they are actually in the war zone or in the operating room.

This, argued Shapiro and McDonald (1995), raises the possibility of a new form of experience substantially different from anything possible today. If all the usual perceptual cues indicate that what a person is experiencing is real and the person has the feeling of actually being part of events, just how does someone in an ideal VR environment distinguish what is real from what is not real? One possible answer offered by Shapiro and McDonald is that experience and thought cues are probably more important than perceptual richness and the vivid reality of VR. For example, the user's memory of entering the VR environment can serve as a cue that the VR experience is not real. In addition, events, even perceptually real ones that theoretically could happen in the real world, may be judged impossible or unlikely. No matter how "real" the experience seemed, most people would know that they weren't really in that reality, driving a fast car, operating on a patient, or fighting aliens. Another possible way to distinguish an ideal VR from reality is to test that VR either mentally or physically. The ultimate test would be to leave the virtual environment and see how real it is. A mental test will involve the user's asking himself or herself: Did I turn on this device and enter this virtual world?

However, many of these tests assume that the user has enough real experiences to allow him or her to make valid judgments about various aspects of the VR experience. But just as television fiction viewers sometimes forget that the actors they are watching aren't real, VR users may get lost in the VR environment. Thus, we may conclude that the "realness" of any VR-mediated experience can be ranked somewhere along a continuum from easy to reject as not real, to more difficult. The cultivation effect of these new modes of virtual realities may thus be a more complex process with multiple phases and levels of adapting these realities as real. As Rheingold (1992) argues,

> The effects of VR are so widespread, scattered over so many different scientific disciplines, potential commercial applications, and social roles, that the larger pattern that connects it all into something meaningful across all dimensions seems elusive. What is needed, . . . is a conceptual framework. One way to begin building such a framework is to look for a foundation in the past, to examine history in search of long-term patterns that might help make sense of tomorrow's complex mix of possibilities. (p. 377)

The badly needed framework may well be founded on the history of communication research in general, and on cultivation analysis in particular. The search for mediated realities, new meanings to perceived realities, and long-term impact, especially of a medium that puts the user in a VR, can certainly benefit from the theory, concepts, and methods of the cultivation paradigm. As Chayko (1993) claims,

> In modern everyday life, it is difficult (and becoming impossible) to definitively classify experience as "real" or "not real"; it is more helpful to determine the degree or "accent" of reality in an event. The frames we once used, conceptually, to set the real apart from the unreal are not as useful as they once were; they are not as sturdy; they betray us. As they become ever more fragile, we require new concepts and understandings. (p. 178)

CHAPTER **THIRTEEN**

Communicating Unreality

This book presents pictures of realities. It reviews the mass-mediated images of people and cultures; of various social groups according to age, gender, race, religion, and ethnicity; of places like emergency rooms and a city struck by smart missiles; of professions and occupations; of actions like war and sex; of identities and communities in cyberspace; of love and violence. Most of the images are reconstructed realities: They often distort the "true" reality, poorly represent it, focus only on certain dimensions of the "real" situation or redefine it for their audiences. The numerous comparisons between "reel reality" and "real reality," presented throughout this book, reveal the gap between reality and the reconstruction of realities as communicated by the mass media. The audiences, as many other studies have found, rely on the mediated unreality and often accept it as "the world out there."

Spies in the Virtual Promised Land

Who is to be blamed for communicating unreality: the media? the sociopolitical system? the public? the complexity of reality itself? the media production process? the hidden manipulators who own or run the media? The answers given by scholars and researchers lead in various directions. Before answering, let us look back, more than 33 centuries

359

ago, to the Biblical spies, sent by Moses to tour the Promised Land. In the 13th century B.C., in the desert of Sinai, the big Exodus of the Israelites from Egypt to the Promised Land, Israel, had lingered for 40 years. According to the book of Exodus, 600,000 people followed Moses into the desert, guided by God's message: "Depart, go up hence, thou and the people that thou hast brought up out of the land of Egypt, unto the land which I swore unto Abraham, to Isaac, and to Jacob, saying: Unto thy seed will I give it" (Exodus 33:1). The narrative depicts Moses facing an impossible challenge: He was ordered to command a collection of ex-slaves, a forming nation that lacked any political, religious, or social identity, across the desert into a land they had never seen. En route, the Israelites complained and rebelled. Pressured and unable to communicate with the masses, Moses turned to God. In response, he was instructed to select 70 elders who would be the mediators between him and the people, thus first introducing the Two-Step Flow model and the notion of opinion leaders.[1]

After having encamped at Mount Sinai for almost a year, the Israelites proceeded northward toward the Promised Land. Their next station was Kadesh in the wilderness of Paran. There, in Kadesh, Moses was ordered by God to send spies to tour the Promised Land: "Send men to spy out the land of Canaan, which I am giving to the children of Israel" (Numbers 12:2).[2] So Moses chose 12 men, one from each of the 12 tribes, and sent them to spy out the land: "See what the land is like; whether the people who dwell in it are strong or weak, few or many; whether the land they dwell in is good or bad; whether the cities they inhabit are like camps or strongholds; whether the land is rich or poor" (Numbers 13:17-20).

The 12 spies went and spied on the land, from the Wilderness of Zin in the south to Rehob in the north. After 40 days, they returned to Moses and the congregation of the Israelites, bringing with them not only the stories but also samples of the fruits of the Promised Land, the grapes, figs, and pomegranates. But the description of the land and its people varied across the spies' accounts. This may well be the first example of reconstructed mass-mediated realities in history and, in fact, a rather tragic case when one considers the consequences of the spies' stories. After 40 years of wandering in the desert, after suffering starvation, thirst, disasters, wars, crises, and disputes, the Israelites were more than eager to learn about their future home, the land promised to them by God, their future homeland. But the spies' stories were different, confusing and presenting different portrayals of that virtual land. Ten spies declared that conquest was impossible, describing the giants living there ("We were like grasshoppers in our own sight, and so we were in their sight"). Two other spies, Caleb and Joshua, presented a very different account: They confidently asserted that with divine aid conquest was possible.[3] Caleb said, "Let us go up at once and take possession, for we are well able to overcome it," while other spies said, "We are not able to go up against the people, for they are stronger than we" (Numbers 13:30-31).

The impact on the public was powerful: The Israelites, unwilling to believe that the God who had recently delivered them from Egypt would also enable them to conquer the Promised Land, became an insolent mob, bitterly arguing, "If only we had died in the land of Egypt! Or if we only had died in the wilderness! Why has the Lord brought us to this land to fall by the sword, that our wives and children should become victims? . . . Let us select a leader and return to Egypt" (Numbers 14: 2-4). Something was going very wrong if God in judgment contemplated annihilation of rebellious Israel. The mob threatened to stone the two spies (Joshua and Caleb) whose stories differed from the others and threatened to overthrow Moses, choose a new leader, and return to slavery in Egypt. Moses had to ask for God's pardon, but God's fury led to the death of the 10 spies in a plague, and all the other Israelites (except for Joshua and Caleb) were denied entrance to the Promised Land and had to die in the desert.

Whose fault was this tragedy? The spies who brought back conflicting versions of the "real" Promised Land? The people who focused on the pessimistic attributes of the land, disregarding the less gloomy version of the two other spies? The complex reality "out there" that combined a land of "milk and honey," "an exceedingly good land"[4] with numerous tribes, some hostile and some very strong, fortified castles, rivers and seas, making its portrayal in a short "story" to a mass audience (ratings of 100% among the 600,000 Israelites)—an impossible mission? Or was it Moses' guilt, because he was the one who selected the spies and sent them? And what about God's responsibility? After all, it was God's idea to send spies; it was God's plan that they would return with encouraging stories of the Promised Land. And God chose to reward only two of the spies whose stories matched the version desired by God. Liebes (1994), in her analysis of the spies affair, suggested three explanations of why the 10 spies were punished. The explanations are closely related to communication issues, namely: (a) the spies added their personal opinions and judgments to the facts they were supposed to report (editorializing and subjectivity), (b) they insinuated their opinions in the report itself (bias), and (c) they released the report to the public rather than funneling it through the leader (control).

Moses himself, in later accounts of the spies incident, gave different interpretations of the guilt issue. An older Moses told the younger generation, the sons of those who left Egypt, that it was the spies' distorted version that angered God: "For when they went up to the Valley of Eshcol and saw the land, they discouraged the heart of the children of Israel, so that they did not go into the land which the Lord had given them" (Numbers 32:9). The distressing outcome of the mission arose because its members did not act as explorers but rather as spies, giving military advice. In particular, they betrayed their task to praise the "good land" and thereby to improve public morale; instead, they were directly responsible for doing the exact opposite—demoralizing the people who had come out of Egypt, gone through the desert, and were now approaching the Promised Land.

But there is yet a third version of the same story, again told by Moses before he died. This time, the responsibility rested solely on the people. Moses argued that the spies were sent because the people demanded it: "And every one of you came near to me and said 'Let us send men before us, and let them search out the land for us, and bring back word to us of the way by which we should go up, and of the cities into which we shall come' " (Deuteronomy 1:22). Moses, in this version not the initiator but the follower ("the plan pleased me well," he argued), described the report of the spies as purely positive: "And they brought back word to us, saying, 'It is a good land which the Lord our God is giving us' " (Deuteronomy 1:25). The Israelites, however, argued Moses, were complaining, scared, and faithless. They "read" into the spies' report fearful and threatening facts, thus losing their trust in God. This time, God's anger is presented as directed only against the people, not the spies: "And the Lord heard the sound of your words, and was angry" (Deuteronomy 1:34). So the Bible gives us three different accounts, attributing the guilt to different actors, from the reporters to their audiences, from the confusing reports to their biased interpretations.

The empirical evidence of mass-mediated unrealities and their impact on the public led to various attempts to explain the cultivation effect by the contents, the media, the economic-political system, the mainstream social ideology, the media consumers and their needs and values, manipulative actors such as social elites, psychological processes invoked by exposure to mass media, and others. There are many ways of conceptualizing the actors behind the cultivation process. The numerous examples of reconstructed realities presented in this book, suggest various explanations that vary from one case to another: In the Gulf War, it was the manipulation by the Pentagon, the White House, the Saudis, and their PR agency that produced and fed the media with images of an unreal war; in the case of presenting violence and crime, some explanations lead to the commercial, ratings-oriented value of these contents whereas others (such as Gerbner himself) point to the ideological value (promoting reliance on authority, law and order, conformity); women's depiction in the media was explained by males' dominance in the media industry (thus blaming the production power structure), by the existing social "climate" supporting males' superiority, or by the political-economics of the advertising industry seeking to maximize profits by selective targeting; MTV's distorted images of sex and sexuality were explained by the audience's needs and expectations; the images of death and dying in the media were related to human fears and anxieties; and images of American life and society, varying across cultures and societies, were explained by political interests (e.g., "an enemy turned friend," in the case of China), and by cultural invasion in the form of U.S. dominance in the world flow of news and entertainment. Let us group and organize these various factors, starting with the contribution of the political-economic environment.

The Context: The Political-Economic Environment

Our communications systems are part of the cultural industries. However, media organizations are both similar to and different from other industries. On the one hand, they clearly have a range of features in common with other areas of production and are increasingly integrated into the general industrial structure. On the other hand, it is equally clear that the goods they manufacture—the newspapers, advertisements, television programs, and feature films—play a pivotal role in organizing the images and discourses through which people make sense of the world. A number of writers acknowledge this duality rhetorically but go on to examine only one side, focusing either on the construction and consumption of media meanings or on the economic organization of media industries. Golding and Murdock (1991) argue that what distinguishes the critical political economy perspective is its focus on the interplay between the symbolic and economic dimensions of mass communications. It sets out to show how different ways of financing and organizing cultural production have traceable consequences for the range of discourses and representations in the public domain and for audiences' access to them.

The political economy of communications is focused on three areas of analysis. The first is concerned with the production of cultural goods, to which political economy attaches particular importance in its presumption of the limiting impact of cultural production on the range of cultural consumption. A good example of such an argument is the heavy use of violence in TV and movies as related to its economic appeal: "Violence travels well around the world," argued Gerbner (1996). "The rationalization for the imbalance is that violence 'sells' " (p. 32). Similarly, the underrepresentation of the elderly in the media is explained by commercial considerations:

> The consistent pattern of omission revealed in these studies apparently reflects the sentiment within a market-based, productivity-obsessed culture, since the elderly are "past their prime" as productive employees and as consumers with substantial buying power, they are no longer important. (Powel & Williamson, 1985, p. 41)

Second, the political economy approach examines the political economy of texts to illustrate ways in which the representations present in media products are related to the political realities of power. The case of underrepresented minorities in the media serves as an example:

> Representation in the mediated reality of our mass media is in itself power; certainly it is the case that nonrepresentation maintains the powerless status of those groups that do not possess significant material or political power bases; this nonrepresentation we have referred to as symbolic annihilation, . . . those who are at the bottom of the

various power hierarchies will be kept in their places in part through their invisibility. (Gross, 1984, p. 345)

Finally, the political economy approach examines cultural consumption to illustrate the relation between material and cultural inequality that political economy is distinctively interested in addressing. The steadily increasing amount of cultural production accounted for by large corporations has long been a source of concern to scholars of communication and society. They saw a fundamental contradiction between the ideal that mass media should operate as a public sphere and the reality of concentrated private ownership. They feared that proprietors would use their property rights to restrict the flow of information and open debate on which the vitality of democracy depended. These long-standing worries have been reinforced in recent years by the emergence of multimedia conglomerates with significant stakes across a range of central communications sectors. Cultural production is also strongly influenced by commercial strategies built around synergies or cross-ownerships that exploit the overlap between the company's different media interests. The company's newspapers may give free publicity to their television stations, or the record and book divisions may launch products related to a new movie released by the film division. The effect is to reduce the diversity of cultural goods in circulation: "Although in simple quantitative terms there may be more commodities in circulation, they are more likely to be variants of the same basic themes and images" Golding & Murdock, 1991, pp. 23-24).

Over recent decades, media systems in many countries have been substantially altered by privatization policies. Major public media have been sold to private investors. Liberalization policies have introduced private operators into markets that were previously closed to competition, such as the broadcasting systems, and regulatory regimes have been altered in favor of freedom of operations for owners and advertisers. The net effect of these changes has been a substantial increase in the potential reach and power of the major communications companies and in the threat that public culture may be commandeered by private interests. To examine these assumptions, we need to move on to the political economy of media output. As noted earlier, research in cultural studies has been particularly concerned with analyzing the structure of media texts and tracing their role in sustaining systems of domination.

This work decisively rejected the notion that the mass media act as a transmission belt for a dominant ideology and developed a model of the communications system as a mechanism for regulating public discourse. We can distinguish two dimensions of this process. The first has to do with the range of discourses that particular forms allow into play, whether they are organized exclusively around official discourses or whether they provide space for the articulation of counterdiscourses. The second concerns the way that the available discourses are handled within the text, whether they are arranged in a clearly marked hierarchy of credibility that urges the audience to prefer one over the others. In short, critical political economy is concerned with explaining how the economic dynamics of production can structure public discourse by promoting certain cultural forms rather than others.

The Audience: The Active Public

A central actor in the cultivation process is the audience. The audience is not passive in the process, as highlighted in the tradition of reception research (e.g., Livingstone, 1991). The active audience is the perspective's core concept. Activity is evident in many dimensions of the audience's interaction with the medium and messages (e.g., use, intention, selectivity, interpretation, and involvement with the medium and its contents). However, people exhibit varying amounts of activity when using the media, suggesting that media behavior is variably purposeful and goal directed. Bauer (1963) argued that we need to consider the initiative of the audience in "getting the information it wants and avoiding what it does not want" (p. 7). Thus, Kim and Rubin (1997) argued, it is reasonable to suggest that some activity inhibits effects, whereas other activity enhances effects. In short, not only is activity variable, but different ways of being active contribute to different outcomes. Examining the variable nature of activity, then, should help us better explain media effects such as cultivation.

Informed by a long history of theoretical debates, and taking into account some of the contradictions between active audiences and dominant messages, or directive texts and resourceful readers, empirical reception research offers an integrating, convergent approach to the television audience. This approach focuses on the audience's active interpretation—or meaning negotiation—of media contents, where these are increasingly analyzed within their everyday context. Empirical reception research regards the audience's interpretations as primary, seeking to relate these to ethnographic and to effects-related concerns at a later stage:

> Not only should we ask what readers do to texts or how texts direct readers but also the dynamic between text and reader should be addressed. How do both reader and text embody a set of expectations of the other which inform this dynamic? How do actual, empirical readers differ from researchers' expectations of the ideal or model reader? How can theories of audience and text analysis be integrated without underestimating either the role of the reader or the complexity of program meanings, as has traditionally occurred when text and reader (or, roughly, critical and administrative mass communications research) are separated? (Livingstone, 1991, p. 286)

Umberto Eco (1979) uses the concept of code to analyze the "role of the reader," arguing that the existence of this role itself undermines structuralist theories of what he terms the *crystalline text:*

> The existence of various codes and subcodes, the variety of sociocultural circumstances in which a message is emitted (where the codes of the addressee can be different from those of the sender) and the rate of initiative displayed by the addressee in making presuppositions and abductions—all result in making a message . . . an empty form to which various possible senses can be attributed. . . . A well-organized text on the one hand presupposes a model of competence coming, so to speak, from outside the text, but on the other hand works to build up, by merely textual means, such a competence. (pp. 5-8)

Emphasis is shifted from an analysis of the meanings in the text, which are central to the text-based approaches to analysis of media contents (such as television programs), to an analysis of the process of reading a text. Thus, the meanings that are communicated depend on an interaction between the text and the reader. Arguing that texts are dynamic, that meanings are context-dependent, and that interpretations may be divergent, audience reception scholars study the activities of actual audiences to know how they interpret programs, within what contexts and with what interpretative resources they view television, and how and why they diverge in their readings.

Let me illustrate the notion of reception analysis with the empirical study of Liebes and Katz on the international reception of the popular prime-time drama, *Dallas*, by diverse cultural groups (Katz & Liebes, 1986; Liebes & Katz, 1986, 1990).

They analyzed focus group discussions held during and after viewing an episode of *Dallas* in people's own homes. Analysis of *Dallas* revealed basic cultural themes that structure the program (such as lineage, inheritance, sibling rivalry, property, sex, and marriage) and may account for the program's popularity. Although these may suggest a common reception by the audience, the empirical audience study found that viewers of different social and cultural backgrounds generated very divergent interpretations of the same episode. For example, Russian Jews were focused on ideological, moral, and political messages underlying the narratives, whereas Americans focused on personalities and motivations and Moroccan Arabs were concerned with event sequencing and narrative continuity. Each group's interpretation was clearly based on and constrained by the text, and yet, the interaction between cultural resources and textual openness permitted the negotiation of quite different readings on viewing the episode. Viewers' interpretations may differ not only from each other but also from critics' expectations when interpreting popular culture. This strengthens the case for empirical research and demands caution in making purely textual analyses. For example, Radway (1984, 1985) contrasts the readings of popular romance novels by ordinary women readers with those of literary critics: "Different readers read differently because they belong to what are known as various interpretive communities, each of which acts upon print differently and for different purposes" (Radway, 1985, p. 341). Livingstone (1990a, 1990b), revealed the complex relationship between genre, involvement, interpretation, and pleasure in the reception process (in which romantic and cynical viewers diverged in their readings of a *Coronation Street* soap opera).

For several decades, media theorists have struggled to specify properly the sense in which audiences are active. Audience activity may have various forms: People are "active" in various ways in response to the flood of media information that must be balanced with other commitments. The antecedents of these forms of activity and their effects, we should note, are not reducible to social status or any other set of variables. They tend to reflect a combination of modest influences of many structural, cultural, and political variables.

A long tradition in social psychology addresses the role of audience activity before, during, and after exposure in understanding media effects. Ball-Rokeach, Rokeach, and Grube (1984) argued that media system dependencies stemming from individual goals, motivation, and media expectations "have consequences for an individual's selective exposure decisions and, then, for the effects of such exposure on cognition and behavior" (p. 94). People must first select and attend to messages if these messages are to have the opportunity to affect them. Facilitative activity includes the selection of, attention to, and interest in messages, thus enabling messages to affect responses. Audience members are potentially more affected by media content when they intentionally and selectively seek, attend to, and are involved with that content. Selectivity, attention, and involvement are forms of activity that may facilitate media effects. There are also inhibitory activities that deter media effects. Communicators have difficulty influencing audience members who avoid, discount, or are not interested in messages. Owing to such influences as personal interests, prior dispositions, social categories, and group norms, such messages are unlikely to alter perceptions, images, and attitudes. Avoidance, distraction, and media skepticism are forms of audience activity that may deter media effects. A review of these efforts suggests several dimensions of audience activity (McLeod, Kosicki, & Pan, 1991).

Gratifications: The idea that individuals are motivated to use media in various ways to meet their needs, often called the "uses and gratifications" approach, replaced message-driven effects (what media do to people) with an audience-driven perspective (what people do with media). However, it is possible, and even potentially constructive, to see uses and gratifications research as an important complement to media effects research. Numerous studies found evidence of the relationships between the audience's motives for exposure and the subsequent effects of the exposure (Rubin, 1969, 1994). Thus, we could hypothesize, for example, that different cultivation impacts would be found among viewers of the same program, if their motives for exposure were different.

Selectivity: The notion of selectivity suggests that people selectively seek out information that is consonant with their pre-existing attitudes and beliefs and avoid information that is discrepant with their views. Selectivity was found to operate at various junctures in the reception process: exposure, attention, perception or interpretation, and retention. Selectivity would thus interact with media messages enhancing effects of consonant material and reducing or eliminating the impact of discrepant content. This certainly supports the resonance and mainstreaming effects in the cultivation process. When media messages are supported by the dominant views (mainstreaming) or by occurrences (resonance), the potential of powerful impact is enhanced.

Attention: Perhaps the most obvious form of audience activity is attention, the focusing of increased mental effort. Commonsense assumptions tell us that learning from media should be enhanced at higher levels of attention. Attention has effects independent of the level of exposure. Chaffee and Choe (1980) found that attention paid to television news accounted for much more of the gains in campaign knowledge than did the frequency of news viewing. In certain situations, the influences of news exposure and attention may interact to produce a combined effect beyond their additive effects. We may hypothesize that cultivation impact levels will vary according to the audience's level of attention.

Media images: Audiences have conceptions or commonsense theories about the media. To the extent that people do have such lay theories or images, it is reasonable to consider them as a form of audience activity potentially affecting how people use media and what they get from their content. One such dimension of image, credibility, is vital to media effects. McLeod (1986) and his colleagues identified four other dimensions of audience media images that have been replicated several times: (a) patterning of news, the idea that news constitutes a comprehensive picture of the world; (b) negative aspects of content, the view that news is dull despite being sensational and dominated by bad news and reporters' biases; (c) dependency and control, a tendency to see media institutions as hegemonic in being consonant, controlling, and overly relied on; and (d) special interests, a tendency to see media as representing special interests and being special interests themselves. Even after controlling for a host of social structural and media use variables, images of news have shown a consistent pattern of enhancing learning from news. Beyond learning of factual information, all five dimensions of media images are connected in various ways to other effects: media use, choice of strategies for processing information, community involvement, cognitive complexity, and the framing of major news stories.

Motivation: Motivation is a crucial contributor to models of media effects, including uses and gratifications, media dependency, and cultivation. According to personality theories of motivation, needs are driving forces behind behavior. Some researchers have argued different needs signify different degrees of purpose and of motivation and differences in behavior and outcomes. Variations in needs, purpose, and motivation are reflected in instrumental and ritualized orientations to media motivation and use (Rubin, 1984, 1994). An instrumental orientation reflects purposive and active media behavior. It suggests selecting and using media content to gratify goal-directed needs or wants, such as information seeking or arousal. In contrast, a ritualized orientation is less purposive and less active. It suggests using a medium, irrespective of content, to fill time, to escape, or to provide company.

Information-processing strategies: Audience activity is evident in the strategies people use to cope with the flood of information that threatens to overwhelm them (Graber, 1988). Several forms of processing activity were related to enhancing gratifications and influence from news programs: (a) selective scanning, involving skimming and tuning out items as a response to the volume of news and limited time available; (b) active processing, or going beyond a given story to interpret or reinterpret the information according to the person's needs; and (c) reflective integration, representing the often fragmented nature of news and the salience of certain information such that it is replayed in the person's mind and becomes the topic of discussion with other people. Each of these dimensions has been shown to have a connection with various types of media effects. All three processing strategies may be related to the cultivation process, as they focus on different conceptual frames that people use to interpret and understand media messages. Processing strategies not only vary across individuals and over different phases of media exposure but also are associated with variations in cognitive responses.

As described in Chapter 4, several researchers suggested that the process of cultivation is in fact a two-step process involving the subprocesses of learning and construction. Learning is the relationship between amount of television viewing and storing images of reality. The more people view, the more information they learn from television. Construction is the process of using that incidental information to form beliefs about social reality.

Interpersonal communication: Interpersonal relations, once seen as an alternative to media influence and diminishing its effects, are now viewed as varying patterns potentially either enhancing or limiting effects. For example, presidential debates increased interpersonal discussion, which in turn influenced outcomes such as information gain and voter turnout. Although it has never been explored, one potential contribution of interpersonal communication with regard to cultivation is resonance: If, for example, people not only are viewing television violence but also hear personal stories of the "mean world" out there, the combined effect of the two sources may be stronger.

The various dimensions of audience activity may function to promote or to deter media effects. Facilitative activity includes selectivity, attention, and involvement. Inhibitory activity includes avoidance, distraction, and skepticism. A study by Kim and Rubin (1997) suggests instrumental media motivation, selectivity, attention, and involvement as positive predictors of cultivation effects from watching daytime television serials. They expected avoidance, distraction, and skepticism to be negative predictors of those effects. The results largely supported their expectations: They observed direct links between instrumental motivation and media effects and indirect links that operated through audience activity. Thus, for example, content involvement and selective perception of program content directly and positively influenced cultivation. Exciting entertainment motivation was indirectly linked to cultivation through involvement activity. Information-voyeurism and social utility motives were indirectly linked to cultivation through selective perception and involvement.

The Individual: Personal Traits

As described in Chapter 4, there have been several research attempts to identify cognitive trait variables affecting cultivation. That is, if cultivation occurs in the presence of some enduring cognitive trait or habit, then that trait may be an important condition for the process. Potential intervening variables include IQ level, processing abilities, cognitive orientations, accessibility of information in memory, or construct accessibility.

One of the central psychological subprocesses involved in cultivation is the storage of information in the memory and then the access and retrieval of this information from the memory. Several studies have highlighted memory access, or *construct accessibility,* as a key factor affecting the influence of television viewing on perceptions of social reality. Memory accessibility can be generally viewed as the ease with which information is retrieved, and information that is more easily retrieved is considered more accessible. Several studies have demonstrated that this accessibility increased the probability that the accessible construct would be used as a basis for judgment. When the notion of construct accessibility was applied to the process of cultivation (see Chapter 4), significant and consistent individual differences were found, reflecting the intervening role of memory accessibility. "These results," argued the researchers, "are consistent with the hypothesis that the cultivation effect is related to the accessibility of information in memory" (Shrum & O'Guinn, 1993, p. 460). Relevant images of reality, "cultivated" from television viewing, are more accessible in memory for heavier viewers.

Another individual trait that may affect cultivation is a critical attitude toward media contents and messages. The researchers in this area suggested the term *critical consumption,* by which they meant evaluation of information during reception and greater retention of information provided by the media. This process of weighing and balancing may affect the likelihood of cultivation: When individuals attempt to construct a social reality estimate, they first retrieve relevant information to form the judgment and then weigh and balance the information with respect to its veracity. This relates, of course, to the reliability of the source as well as to the individual's general acceptance of media credibility.

Motivation and involvement are two additional dimensions of individual traits that may affect or interact with the cultivation process. Involvement is a motivated state of anticipation and of felt importance of messages. It reflects active participation in message processing and mediates how we acquire, process, and share information. In this sense, involvement influences how we interpret, attach meaning to, and respond to messages. For example, emotionally involved viewers may identify and parasocially interact with media characters. Involvement reflects instrumental media motivation, such as seeking exciting and entertaining news information (Rubin & Perse, 1987a, 1987b). The studies in this area found that involved individuals process information more deeply. Besides critical consumption, discussed earlier, which prevents many social reality effects, it is equally appropriate to suggest that uninvolved or passive reception can enhance some media effects. Perse (1990), who applied the notion of involvement to cultivation analysis, suggested that involvement has two dimensions: orientation and intensity. Orientation marks the direction of the cognitive-emotional processing. People may become involved with any aspect of the message: information about issues, personalities, plot, music, or audience. Intensity marks the depth of the processing. As people become more involved, they follow the path of paying attention to the information, categorizing it as familiar or unfamiliar, relating the information to prior knowledge, and reacting to it emotionally.

Mental imagery was another personal trait suggested to enhance media impact. Mental imagery has often been defined as the mental invention or recreation of an experience that in at least some respects resembles the experience of actually perceiving an object or event, either in conjunction with, or in the absence of, direct sensory simulation. A study of media impact on fright reactions and belief in the paranormal revealed the relevance of individual differences in mental imagery (Sparks, Sparks, & Gray, 1995).

Finally, differences in personal experiences may form conditions for media influence in at least three ways. First, some degree of confirmation from real-world experience, other sources, or even pre-existing beliefs about social reality may be necessary to validate the media message (Sparks, Nelson, & Campbell, 1997). Second, messages from other sources that are heavily used or relied on could provide sufficient disconfirmation of the media messages. Third, media portrayals both form and match the mainstream of beliefs but only among certain subgroups who share these beliefs.

There is, of course, a close association between the notion of personal experience and the process of critical consumption or the weighing and balancing and the two-step cultivation. First, the individual acquires from the media various bits of information about actions and characterization and associations between these bits of information; this may be best explained as the learning stage. Second, the individual may use these bits of information to construct more general and integrated conceptions of the world, and it is probably here, in the construction stage, that processes such as weighing television against other sources of information occur. At this stage, personal experience may be used for the evaluation of the information and the reconstruction of meanings.

Although this line of research, namely, relating individual traits to the media's impact on perceptions and beliefs, is relatively new, there are encouraging findings from these first attempts. Future cultivation researchers may adopt additional personality traits and test their potential contribution. Among the five personality traits that were recently related to general media consumption: extroversion, neuroticism, openness to experience, agreeableness, and consciousness (Finn, 1997). The significance of these traits when predicting media use and exposure should encourage future researchers to try to relate them to media effects, too.

The Media: Production and Processing in the Media

The production process in the media is often regarded as a social process of constructing the news, of making news, and of the social construction of reality. The reality does not seem as important as what the media processing does with this reality. "News is what newspapermen make it," concluded one study (Gieber, 1964, p. 173). "News is the result of the methods newsworkers employ," according to another (Fishman, 1980, p. 14), and "News is manufactured by journalists," in the words of a third (Cohen & Young, 1973, p. 93). The "making of the story," according to Tuchman (1980), always involves reconstruction:

> To say that a news report is a story, no more, but no less, is not to demean news, nor to accuse it of being fictitious. Rather, it alerts us that news, like all public documents, is a constructed reality possessing its own internal validity. (p. 97)

As Schudson (1991) pointed out, journalists write the words that turn up in the papers or on the screen as stories: "Not government officials, not cultural forces, not 'reality' magically transforming itself into alphabetic signs, but flesh-and-blood journalists literally compose the stories we call news" (p. 142). The sociology of the production of news goes back some years. In the 1920s, Max Weber (1921/1946) wrote of the social standing of the journalist as a political person, and Robert Park (1923), an ex-journalist himself, wrote about the generation of news and news itself as a form of knowledge. But the formal study of how news organizations produce and process news products emerged later, with the notion of the gatekeepers. Social psychologist Kurt Lewin coined the term *gatekeeper* and several social scientists applied it to journalism. The term is still in use and provides a handy metaphor for the relation between news organizations and news products. However, as Schudson (1991) noted,

> The problem with the metaphor is that it leaves "information" sociologically untouched. It minimizes the complexity of news making. News items are not simply selected but "constructed." The gatekeeper metaphor describes neither this nor the feedback loops in which the agencies that generate information for the press anticipate the criteria of the gatekeepers in their efforts to get through the gate. (p. 141)

Three perspectives on news making are now commonly used, replacing the somewhat oversimplified concept of gatekeeping. The first is the view of political economy (see above), which relates the outcome of the news process to the economic structure of the news organization. The second approach is that of mainstream sociology, the study of social organization and the sociology of occupations and occupational ideology; unlike the standard political economy perspective, this takes the journalists' professed autonomy and decision-making power as the central problem for understanding journalism in liberal societies. This perspective tries to understand how journalists' efforts on the job are constrained by organizational and occupational routines. Third, there is a "culturological" or anthropological approach that emphasizes the constraining force of broad cultural symbol systems regardless of the details of organizational and occupational routines. The sociological perspective is highly relevant to the issue of reconstructing realities. For example, Molotch and Lester (1974) created a typology of news stories according to whether the news "occurrence" is planned or unplanned and whether the planners of the occurrence are or are not also the promoters of it as news. If an event is planned and then promoted as news by its planners, this is a routine news item (or, as some may argue, public relations routine). If the event is planned but promoted by someone different from the agent of the occurrence, it is a scandal. If the event is unplanned and then promoted as news by someone other than its hapless instigator, it is an accident. This typology defines news by the way it comes to the awareness of a news organization. In none of the three news types is the occurrence a spontaneous event in the world that the news media discover on their own by surveying the world scene (thus, their typology fails to recognize the concept of investigative journalism). For Molotch and Lester, it is a mistake to try to compare news accounts to reality, labeling the discrepancy bias. Instead, they seek out the purposes that create one reality instead of another. Molotch and Lester reject what they call the "objectivity assumption" in journalism— not that the media are objective but that there is a real world to be objective about. For Molotch and Lester, the mass media reflect not a world "out there" but "the practices of those who have the power to determine the experience of others" (p. 104).

Numerous studies came up with essentially the same observation: News making is a social process, an interaction of reporters and officials, of reporters and editors, of reporters and their perceived audiences (see, e.g., Winch, 1997). If one theoretical source for the sociology of news has been symbolic interactionism or social constructionist views of society, a complementary source has been organizational or bureaucratic theory. If, on the one hand, the creation of news is seen as the social production of reality, on the other hand, it is taken as the social manufacture of an organizational product, one that can be studied like other manufactured goods. What is fundamental in the organizational approach as opposed to the social constructionist is the emphasis on (a) constraints imposed by organizations despite the private intentions of the individual actors and (b) the inevitability of social construction of reality in any social system: Many analysts from a social organizational perspective abandon any strong claim that there is a reality out there that journalists or journalistic organizations distort. News is not a report on a factual world; news is "a depletable consumer product that must be made fresh daily" (Tuchman, 1980, p. 179). It is not a gathering of facts that already exist; indeed, as Tuchman has argued, facts are defined organizationally.

Finally, there is the culturological approach, which suggests that there are aspects of news processing and production that go beyond what sociological analysis of news organizations is normally prepared to handle. This approach suggests that the most important filter through which news is constructed is "the cultural air we breathe, the whole ideological atmosphere of our society, which tells us that some things can be said and that others had best not be said" (Bennett, 1982, p. 303). That cultural air is created in part by ruling groups and institutions, but also in part by the social context in which it takes place. Gans (1979) proposed a list of such cultural values for American journalism; it included ethnocentrism, altruistic democracy, responsible capitalism, small-town pastoralism, individualism, and moderatism. They are the unquestioned and generally unnoticed background assumptions through which the news is gathered and within which it is framed.

Schudson (1991) claimed that if there is a general cultural air journalists breathe along with others in their society, there is also a specifically journalistic cultural air tied to the occupational practices of journalists. The routines of journalists are not only social, emerging from interactions among officials, reporters, and editors, but emerging out of interactions of professionals with their clients. Journalists at work operate to maintain and improve not only their social relations with sources and colleagues but also their cultural image as journalists in a wider world. Zelizer (1990), for example, has demonstrated the ways in which reporters in American broadcast news visually and verbally establish their own authority by suggesting their personal proximity to the events they cover. Regardless of how the news was in fact gathered, it is presented in a style that promotes an illusion of the journalist's adherence to the journalistic norm of proximity. Thus, "the reality journalists manufacture provides not only a version and vision of 'the world' but of 'journalism' itself" (Schudson, 1991, p. 155).

The Message: Text, Narrative, Genres

All media effects studies, and especially those on reconstructed realities, carry implicit or explicit assumptions about media content and their contribution. A major distinction pertinent to media input is the one between diffuse-general and content-specific influences. Diffuse-general effects are those stemming largely from the activity of media use. One example of this is the time spent watching television displacing other things people might be doing, such as reading books or participating in community life. Another type of diffuse-general effect centers on the form rather than the content of the medium. McLuhan was a major proponent of this view when he insisted that the medium was the message, not its content. Whereas some content-specific approaches imply that "we become what we see," diffuse-general approaches make less of a connection between the specifics of content and the outcomes manifested.

Content-specific formulations continue to dominate conceptions of media effects. The ways of looking at content, however, have changed considerably. Expanding beyond the confines of quantifiable manifest content analysis conducted in the early 1950s, researchers have conceived content as a holistic message system, as a textual structure, as a symbolic representation of reality with various embodiments of meanings, and as a system of organized conceptual frames that shape how audiences understand and interpret reality. The wide range of conceptual work on media content moves much beyond the simple dichotomy of diffuse-general versus content-specific to allow for a much wider range of possible content-related media effects and for a much closer fit between the subtle content characteristics analyzed and the effects examined.

A good example of the content-reality reconstruction relationship is the micro-social approach of Bennett (1988). He specifies four information content elements in the news that combine to prevent the audience from developing a real understanding or a basis for political participation: personalization, dramatization, fragmentation, and normalization. The first of these elements, personalization, is a tendency for the news media to concentrate on people engaged in political struggles rather than on the power structures and processes behind the issues. Dramatization, the second element, refers to the tendency of journalists to select those events that are most easily portrayed in short, capsule stories with actors at their center. The third tendency, fragmentation, fed by the first two tendencies, isolates stories and facts such that events become self-contained happenings but have no past or future. Finally, journalists tend to use official sources who provide soothing normalized interpretations of crises and problems without going into their deeper meanings. Each of Bennett's content elements contains explicit or implicit hypotheses about various audience outcomes. For example, together these information problems would lead audiences to adopt passive attitudes, to blame individuals rather than the system for problems, and to lack understandings characterized by complexity, historicity, and connectedness.

The categorization according to genre is an important one for cultivation research. As Corner (1988) noted, "Genre is a principal factor in the directing of audience choice and of audience expectations" (p. 270). For Dubrow (1982), genre "functions much like a code of behavior established between the author and his reader" (p. 2). It sets up expectations; it bears complex and possibly contradictory relations to other genres or codes; its conventions are historically and socially located. Dubrow argues that reader-response criticism may profitably reveal the expectations that specific, located readers apply to different genres, thus undermining the critic's tendency to see genres as absolute, consistent, and deterministic. The analysis of readers' expectations of genres is important not only for our understanding of genre but also for understanding the role of the reader in interpreting texts and this interpretation's impact on the readers. Genre knowledge is one resource on which readers draw. It frames their general approach to the text, determines the types of inferential connections to be made, and establishes the paradigms of possibilities at each narrative choice point. Viewers' retelling of the soap opera narrative discussed above reveals the use of genre knowledge. For example, viewers drew inferences about the characters' motivations to lend coherence to their narratives, using frameworks that, whether construed as romantic or cynical, are typical of this genre and that provide an account of characters' actions, intentions, and moral position.

Genre is a crucial factor in understanding the impact of mediated realities. Without recognition by the researcher that television, both as a formal system and as a social process, is constituted from often very different genres, the danger is that an essentialistic tendency will, by default, assert itself (leading to generalizations such as "television is," "television portrays," etc.). The most consequential division across the television genres is that between fictional and nonfictional programming. Although this is not always a clean division in formal systems—certain principles of television grammar, for instance, apply to both—the levels of reference, modes of address, forms of propositional or more associative symbolic discourse, and the presence or absence of television's own representatives (i.e., the reporter, the host) serve to mark the two areas into distinctive communicative realms.

The characteristic properties of text-viewer relations in fictional contents primarily have to do with imaginative pleasure, particularly the pleasures of dramatic circumstance and character. In the last few years, there has been a shift away from news and current affairs as the paradigm for British and American reception studies and toward popular domestic drama series or soaps, particularly the more successful U.S. series. The result of this emphasis has been an intensive linking of work on reception with questions of realism, pleasure, gender, and viewing context. Livingstone (1991) argues that

> not only may genre expectations help account for the approach that audiences take to texts from particular genres, and indeed, for the different approaches they take to different genres, but they also account for discrepancies between actual readings and predicted or "correct" readings, as identified by text analysis. (p. 296)

The distinction of genres according to the fiction/nonfiction categorization has been seen to exemplify textual closure. In the case of the news genre, this closure may be construed as either ideological or didactic in motive, and so reception issues concern whether or not people's readings match those intended, and if not, how the different readings are to be explained. In the case of fictional contents such as romance and soap opera, this genre has been seen as ideologically closed, in that it is concerned to indulge fantasy, to redirect attention from the political to the personal, to legitimate normative or conservative judgments and expectations, and so forth. More recently, however, to account for its immense appeal, especially to women, some authors have argued for the openness of the genre and, in addition, for the subversive or alternative feminist subtext of the genre. The soap opera genre has been considered open insofar as its narratives are unbounded, weaving in and out of each other over time, and multiple, with no single hero and hence no prioritized moral perspective. As a consequence, reception research in both the news and romance genres has been concerned with revealing multiple or alternative readings of supposedly normative texts. The research has focused on issues of narrative structure, openness and closure, identification and the subject position, active and passive constructions of meaning, realist and romantic conventions, social contexts of viewing, pleasure, and, implicitly at least, effects.

The analysis of genre inevitably draws on psychological assumptions about the reader or viewer. Beer (1970) writes of the romance:

> It absorbs the reader into experience which is otherwise unattainable. It frees us from our inhibitions and preoccupations by drawing us entirely into its own world—a world which is never fully equivalent to our own although it must remind us of it if we are to understand it at all. (p. 3)

Fiction and soap opera bear a close relation to the forms of everyday life: "The rhythms of the interwoven stories in the typical romance construction correspond to the way we interpret our own experiences as multiple, endlessly interpreting stories, rather than simply as a procession of banal happenings" (Beer, 1970, p. 9). It is this parallel between real reality and reel reality that accounts for the popularity of certain genres and their impact, and this parallel is revealed through analysis both of the viewers' needs and motives and the structure of the genre (an example for such analysis is Livingstone's 1990 study of viewers' romantic and cynical readings of soap operas and the genre's narrative).

Finally, there are two major content elements that may affect the cultivation process: vividness, which refers to the ability to produce a sensory-rich mediated environment; and interactivity, which refers to the degree to which users of a medium can influence the form or content of the mediated environment. As discussed in Chapter 12, the new media, namely, computer-mediated communication, or CMC, are more vivid, interactive, and faster than conventional communication technologies. As computers' capabilities to develop increasingly complex and realistic images advance, the illusion will become even more convincing and effective. The cultivation effect of these new modes of Virtual Realities may thus be a more complex process with multiple phases and levels of adapting these realities as real.

The Need for a Dynamic-Transactional Model

The biblical spies' affair attributes the guilt to many actors and factors: the reports, the editing, the audience, the complex reality, the interpretations, and so on. These numerous factors, active in the process of reconstruction of reality by the modern mass media, require a multivariate model. The dynamic-transactional approach, developed originally by German researchers as a new approach to the study of mass communication effect, is especially suitable to serve as the theoretical framework for the cultivation process (see, e.g., Fruh, 1992; Fruh & Schonbach, 1982; Schonbach & Fruh, 1984).

The dynamic-transactional approach (DTA) was conceptualized as an integration of the old stimulus-response approach to media effects and the uses and gratifications approach. Thus, the concept of audience stimulation by the media and the concept of audience activity are integrated. The DTA claims that the media stimulus cannot determine completely what the recipients experience or how they react, nor are the recipients completely free in their interpretation or selection of the stimulus. Recipients and stimuli have both active and passive properties. The recipients are active in using their interpretative abilities, by which they re-create the stimulus in their individual way according to various cognitive and emotional states, cognitive abilities, cognitive and emotional dispositions, and circumstantial influences. However, the recipients can also be passive, as the stimulus may contain elements that offer little room for individual interpretation and more or less forces them to perceive it and react to it in a particular way. Due to common socialization, common physiological and psychological properties, and a shared symbolic environment, some stimuli may influence all individuals in more or less the same way without much room for interpretation. Furthermore, individuals have developed patterns of habitual or ritualized media use, patterns that reduce the range of possible active media choices. Then, the media stimuli themselves may be passive in that they are acted on by the viewers' interpretations, selection, and attention.

Thus, the DTA conceptualizes media stimuli and audiences as interdependent phenomena. They are both independent and dependent variables at the same time. They transact. The second main concept of the DTA is the dynamic aspect of communication and media reception. The DTA is a process-oriented view of communication. The idea of transactional relationships directs attention not to static outcomes of causation but to the dynamic interplay among many factors. A first attempt to employ the DTA model was reported by Sander (1997), who applied the model to the impact of TV violence on German viewers' perceptions of violence.

Applying the DTA conceptualization—namely, the idea of dynamic transaction between the media and the audiences—to the case of cultivation results in a complex model (DTC model). The DTC model is considered to be the most updated combination of all the variables, interactions, and subprocesses in the dynamic process of cultivation. It assumes a continuous transaction between the individuals' inner states (e.g., emotional and cognitive) and qualities of the media messages programs (e.g., content characteristics), as well as "environmental" elements (e.g., cultural and social settings). The stimuli sent out from the media transact with the audience's mental states, needs, expectations, traits, and psychological processing, producing different effects on beliefs, images, perceptions, and "pictures of reality." Thus, the model contains five major groups of variables: content variables; the individual's personal traits and characteristics; the context or social, cultural, and political setting; the media production and processing; and the social processing of the messages by the audiences. The effects themselves may be a sixth dimension as they can be short- or long-term effects, and on one or more of the dimensions of reconstruction of reality (various domains or areas, such as violence, gender, etc.). The five groups (with some illustrative variables for each group) are listed in Table 13.1.

TABLE 13.1. Five Major Groups of Variables in the Dynamic-Transactional Approach

Contextual Factors	Media Production	The Message	Individual Traits	Reception and Processing
cultural	gatekeeping	genre	personal experiences	uses and gratifications
political	professional routines	narrative	critical consumption	processing strategies
economic	pressures	vividness	involvement	selectivity
media systems	professional socialization	interactivity	mental imagery	memory accessibility

Using Facet Theory to Conceptualize the DTC Model

The complexity of the multivariate relationships between these five groups of variables, each containing various aspects and variations, calls for the use of the facet approach.[5] The value of the facet approach is that it provides a metatheoretical framework for empirical research. Louis Guttman (1979), a major advocate of and my teacher for this approach, summarized its promise as follows:

> Facet theory is proving to provide an effective approach for fruitful design of content, leading to appropriate data analysis techniques, and producing laws of human behavior in a cumulative fashion. One by-product is the establishment of more solid bases for policy decisions. (p. 3)

Facet theory, as an approach to the design of research projects, measuring instruments, and data analysis, developed out of the work of Guttman and his colleagues. Facet theory is actually a bottom-up approach, starting with substance and aiming, above all, at establishing empirical laws. They help to specify and differentiate the conditions under which certain observations are expected to occur, provided certain side constraints are satisfied. If found true consequently, such hypotheses become laws. A facet may be, in essence, any way of categorizing observations as long as the elements of the category scheme are mutually exclusive.

My own interest in the use of facet theory grew out of the realization of the complexity of the cultivation process and the futility of conventional approaches to apply only certain variables in the study of this multivariate phenomenon. The ability to formalize the numerous elements and relationships, which is provided by the facet theory, appears to make it an ideal approach to present the cultivation process and its complex nature. The idea of setting up the variables and the relationships in terms of a mapping sentence, developed by the facet approach users, was especially appealing. As Guttman (1994) suggested, "To ensure that a set of facets be properly designed, both for theory construction and for practical selection of items for fieldwork, it is useful to write it out in the form of a mapping sentence" (p. 596). Mapping sentences prove particularly useful for constructing complex models and for combining elements (i.e., the facets) and relationships (connecting the facets). Mapping sentences, therefore, often contain many facets and allow for thousands of different ways to read them, thus implying thousands of possible question types. A simple, starting mapping sentence for the cultivation process will involve only the five elements of the DTC model. This would yield the mapping sentence found in Figure 13.1 (for the sake of clarity, only examples or suggested principles of categories for each facet are given).

This relatively simple mapping sentence helps to clarify the process of cultivation. However, this is a rather oversimplified presentation as the "facets" are not really facets but groups of facets. Facets are not fixed once and for all: If there are alternatives that are clearer in their semantics, simpler to use, associated with fewer exceptions, or better suited to constructing a particular theory, then such definitions will be adopted. Thus, the facets presented above can be further refined by a better division and classification. This will result in a more complex mapping sentence (see Figure 13.2).

The second mapping sentence, although more complex, richer in variables, and providing more combinations of contributing factors—is rather simple. We can easily add more facets, more categories, and thus more complex combinations describing the process. However, even at this stage, we should note how this second mapping sentence provides thousands of potential hypotheses: The present 15 facets with their

A=setting   B=individual traits   C=the message
              (cultural)   (personal experiences)   (genre)
Person in the........(political).......with the....(source confusion)......processes....(medium)
              (economic)   (critical consumption)   (interactivity)
                                 (motivation)   (vividness)
                                 (involvement)   (narrative)
                                 (mental imagery)
                                 (construct accessibility)

                    D=Media production   E=personal processing
                    (gatekeeping)   (uses and gratifications)
...produced and shaped by...(ideology)....using his/her...   (selectivity)
                    (ownership)   (attention)
                    (competition)   (processing strategies)
                    (pressures)   (personal communication)
                    (occupational routines)

              F=Realities   Accuracy
              (violence)   very low
....will perceive....(personal victimization) --------with------->
              (gender roles)
              (sub-groups)   to
              (professions)
              (war and conflicts)
              (sex and sexuality)
              (other societies)
              (politics)   very high

Figure 13.1   The DTC Model: Mapping Sentence 1

numerous categories yield a total of 1,074,954,240 combinations. Some of these are redundant, and yet there are millions of combinations that may serve as potential hypotheses. For example, the comparison of the same combination A1, B1, C1 . . . once with $N = 1$ and once with $N = 3$ may tell us whether the contribution of interactivity, when all other factors are controlled, is crucial. Only the use of a systematic, multivariate, and dynamic model like the DTC will explore the complex nature of the process of reconstruction of reality by the mass media. It conceptualizes media stimuli and audiences as interdependent phenomena, it allows for various causal relationships like simple causation or sequential interactions, and it attempts to combine all the factors revealed to be involved in the process—from media characteristics to individual traits and preferences.

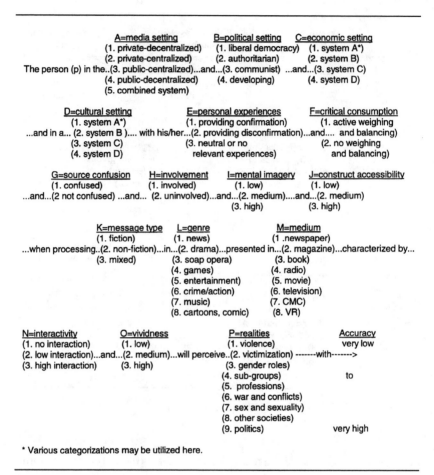

Figure 13.2   The DTC Model: Mapping Sentence 2

The chained men in Plato's cave, the Israelites confused by the biblical spies returning from the Promised Land, and the audiences of modern mass media are all consumers of reconstructed images and realities. This book explored the numerous areas in which evidence of the media's impact on the audience's perceptions of reality were found. And yet, despite the accumulating evidence, the process of communicating unrealities remains complex and involving multistep, multivariate relationships. Future research should further investigate the contribution of these many subprocesses and actors. It appears that the introduction and spread of modern communication technologies such as computer-mediated communication will only enhance the necessity of studying the role of the media in communicating and cultivating unrealities. Whereas Plato's cavemen looked at dark shadows on a wall and the Israelites listened to oral descriptions of the Promised Land, today's audience is exposed to modern technologies of communication with their speed, vividness, interactivity, and multisensual totality—which may provide a more powerful impact on our virtual realities.

NOTES

1. On the "opinion leaders in the wilderness," see Weimann (1995b, pp. 3-8).

2. The Hebrew word for spy (*meragel*), and its root *r-g-l,* is not found at all in this story, but rather the verb *tour,* which means "to travel with a purpose, explore, make a reconnaissance." The men sent by Moses should therefore be called explorers (or reporters!) and not spies; the two terms are not identical.

3. In a later mission, Joshua also sends "two men, spies, in secret, saying, 'Go, see the land' " (Joshua 2:1), and they come back and report, "and also all the inhabitants of the land melt away before us" (v. 24).

4. The phrase "good land" (*eretz tova*) is found in many places in Scripture, as in "The land is very, very good" (Numbers 17:7); "To a good and broad land" (Exodus 3:8); "And they said, The land is good" (Deuteronomy 1:2); or "For we saw the land, and behold it was very good" (Judah 8:9). The meanings of *good land* can be many and different, thus adding to the confusion created by the spies' reports.

5. On facet theory and its potential contribution to social research, see Levy (1994), Borg (1994), and Canter (1996).

References

Abernathy-Lear, G. (1994). African Americans' criticisms concerning African American representations on daytime serials. *Journalism Quarterly, 71,* 830-839.

Adler, R. (1976, January 12). Sex and suffering in the afternoon. *Time,* pp. 46-53.

Albert, W. G. (1978). Dimensionality of perceived violence in rock music: Musical intensity and lyrical violence content. *Popular Music & Society, 6,* 27-38.

Allen, B., Oloughlin, P., Jasperson, A., & Sullivan, J. L. (1994). The media and the Gulf War: Framing, priming, and the Spiral of Silence. *Polity, 27,* 255-284.

American Psychiatric Association. (1994). *Diagnostic and statistical manual of mental disorders* (4th ed.). Washington, DC: Author.

Amos, D. (1991, Winter). Seeing is not believing. *Nieman Reports,* p. 61.

Andersen, A. E., & DiDomenico, L. (1992). Diet vs. shape content in popular magazines: A dose-response relationship to the incidence of eating disorders? *International Journal of Eating Disorders, 11,* 283-287.

Andison, F. S. (1977). TV violence and viewer aggression: A cumulation of study results, 1956-1976. *Public Opinion Quarterly, 41,* 314-331.

Aries, P. (1974). *Western attitudes towards death: From the Middle Ages to the present.* Baltimore, MD: Johns Hopkins University Press.

Aries, P. (1981). *The hour of our death.* London: Allen Lane.

Armstrong, G. B., Neuendorf, K. A., & Brentar, I. E. (1992). TV entertainment, news, and racial perceptions of college students. *Journal of Communication, 42,* 153-176.

Aronoff, C. (1974). Old age in prime time. *Journal of Communication, 24,* 86-87.

Asch, S. E. (1958). Effects of group pressure upon the modification and distortion of judgments. In E. Maccoby, T. Newcomb, & P. Hurtley (Eds.), *Readings in social psychology* (3rd ed.). New York: Holt.

Asu, A., & Robins, K. (1992). Exterminating angels: Morality, violence, and technology in the Gulf War. In H. Mowlana, G. Gerbner, & H. Schiller (Eds.), *Triumph of the image* (pp. 202-212). Boulder, CO: Westview.

Atkin, C. K. (1983). Effects of realistic TV violence vs. fictional violence on aggression. *Journalism Quarterly, 60,* 615-621.

Atkin, C., Greenberg, B., & McDermott, S. (1983). Television and race role socialization. *Journalism Quarterly, 60*(3), 407-414.

Atkin, C., & Miller, M. (1975). *The effects of television advertising on children: Experimental evidence.* Paper presented to the Mass Communication Division, International Communication Association.

Aufderheide, P. (1986). Music videos: The look of the sound. *Journal of Communication, 36*(1), 57-78.

Baer, N. A. (1996). Cardiopulmonary resuscitation on television: Exaggerations and accusations. *The New England Journal of Medicine, 334*(24), 1604-1605.

Bagdikian, B. H. (1984, June 12). The lords of the global village. *The Nation,* p. 2.

Baily, M. (1969). The women's magazine short-story heroine in 1957 and 1967. *Journalism Quarterly, 46,* 364-366.

Ball-Rokeach, S. J., Rokeach, M., & Grube, J. W. (1984). *The great American value test: Influencing behavior and belief through television.* New York: Free Press.

Bandura, A. (1977). *Social learning theory.* Englewood Cliffs, NJ: Prentice Hall.

Bandura, A., Ross, D., & Ross, S. (1963a). Imitation of film-mediated aggressive models. *Journal of Abnormal and Social Psychology, 66,* 3-11.

Bandura, A., Ross, D., & Ross, S. (1963b). Vicarious reenforcement and imitative learning. *Journal of Abnormal and Social Psychology, 67*(6), 601-607.

Banks, J. (1996). *Monopoly television: MTV's quest to control the music.* Boulder, CO: Westview.

Banks, J. (1997). MTV and the globalization of popular culture. *Gazette, 59,* 43-60.

Baran, S. J. (1976a). How TV and film portrayals affect sexual satisfaction in college students. *Journalism Quarterly, 53*(3), 468-473.

Baran, S. J. (1976b). Sex on TV and adolescent sexual self-image. *Journal of Broadcasting, 20,* 61-68.

Barcus, F. E. (1983). *Images of life on children's television: Sex roles, minorities, and families.* New York: Praeger.

Basow, S. A. (1992). *Gender: Stereotypes and roles* (3rd ed.). Pacific Grove, CA: Brooks/Cole.

Bauer, R. A. (1963). The initiative of the audience. *Journal of Advertising Research, 3,* 2-7.

Bauman, Z. (1990). Effacing the face: On the social management of moral proximity. *Theory, Culture, and Society, 7,* 5-14.

Baxter, R. L., De Riemer, C., Landini, A., Leslie, L., & Singletary, M. (1985). A content analysis of music videos. *Journal of Broadcasting and Electronic Media, 29,* 333-341.

Becker, L. B., & Dunwoody, S. (1982). Media use, public affairs knowledge, and voting in a local election. *Journalism Quarterly, 59,* 212-218.

Beer, G. (1970). *The romance.* London: Methuen.

Bell, J. (1992). In search of a discourse on aging: The elderly on television. *The Gerontologist, 32,* 305-311.

Belson, W. A. (1967). *The impact of television: Methods and findings in program research.* London: Crosby Lockwood.

Benedikt, M. (1991). Introduction. In M. Benedikt (Ed.), *Cyberspace: First space* (pp. 1-25). Cambridge: MIT Press.

Beniger, J. (1987). Personalization of mass media and the growth of pseudocommunity. *Communication Research, 14,* 352-371.

Bennett, T. (1982). Media, reality, signification. In M. Gurevitch, T. Bennett, J. Curran, & J. Woollacott (Eds.), *Culture, society, and the media* (pp. 287-308). London: Methuen.

Bennett, W. L. (1988). *News: The politics of illusion* (2nd ed.). New York: Longman.

Berelson, B., & Steiner, G. A. (1964). *Human behavior: An inventory of scientific findings.* New York: Harcourt, Brace & World.

Berger, P., & Luckmann, T. (1967). *The social construction of reality.* New York: Anchor Books.

Berkowitz, L. (1965). Some aspects of observed aggression. *Journal of Personality and Social Psychology, 2,* 359-369.

Berman, L. (1988). Fictional depiction of suicide in television films and imitation effects. *American Journal of Psychiatry, 145,* 982-986.

Beuf, A. (1974). Doctor, lawyer, household drudge. *Journal of Communication, 24,* 142-145.

Biocca, F. (1997). The cyborg's dilemma: Progressive embodiment in virtual environments. *Journal of Computer Mediated Communication, 3*(2).

Biocca, F., & Levy, M. R. (1995). Virtual reality as a communication system. In F. Biocca & M. R. Levy (Eds.), *Communication in the age of virtual reality* (pp. 15-31). Hillsdale, NJ: Lawrence Erlbaum.

Bodenhausen, G. J. (1997). Advertising's effects on men's gender role attitudes. *Sex Roles, 36,* 551-572.

Borg, I. (1994). Evolving notions of facet theory. In I. Borg & P. Mohler (Eds.), *Trends and perspectives in empirical social research* (pp. 178-200). Berlin: de Gruyter.

Brabant, S., & Mooney, L. (1986). Sex role stereotyping in the Sunday comics: Ten years later. *Sex Roles, 14,* 141-148.

Bradley, D. (1987, July 11). For a young Black revelation and anger: How TV drew our family together—in spite of its messages. *TV Guide,* pp. 8-11.

Brake, M. (1985). *Comparative youth culture: The sociology of youth cultures and youth subcultures in America, Britain, and Canada.* London: Routledge & Kegan Paul.

Brody, R. A. (1991). *Assessing the president; The media, elite opinion, and public support.* Stanford, CA: Stanford University Press.

Brosius, H. B., Weaver, J. B., & Staab, J. F. (1993). Exploring the social and sexual "reality" of contemporary pornography. *Journal of Sex Research, 30,* 161-170.

Brown, J. D., & Campbell, K. (1986). Race and gender in music videos: The same beat but a different drummer. *Journal of Communication, 36,* 9-106.

Brown, J. D., Campbell, K., & Fisher, L. (1986). American adolescents and music videos: Why do they watch? *Gazette, 37,* 19-32.

Brown, J. D., & Newcomer, S. F. (1991). Television viewing and adolescents' sexual behavior. *Journal of Homosexuality, 21,* 77-91.

Brown, J., & Schulze, L. (1990). The effects of race, gender, and fandom on audience interpretations of Madonna's music videos. *Journal of Communication, 40,* 88-102.

Brownmiller, S. (1975). *Against our will: Men, women, and rape.* New York: Simon & Schuster.

Bryant, J. (1986). The road most traveled: Yet another cultivation critique. *Journal of Broadcasting & Electronic Media, 30,* 231-235.

Bryant, J., Carveth, R. A., & Brown, D. (1981). Television viewing and anxiety: An experimental examination. *Journal of Communication, 31,* 106-119.

Buerkel-Rothfuss, N. D., & Mayes, S. (1981). Soap opera viewing: The cultivation effect. *Journal of Communication, 31,* 108-115.

Busby, L. J. (1975). Sex-role research in the mass media. *Journal of Communication, 25,* 107-131.

Busby, L. J. (1985). The mass media and sex-role socialization. In J. R. Dominick & J. E. Fletcher (Eds.), *Broadcasting research methods* (pp. 267-295). Boston: Allyn & Bacon.

Buss, E., & Malamuth, N. (Eds.). (1996). *Sex, power, conflict.* New York: Oxford University Press.

Butler, M., & Paisley, W. (1980). *Women and the mass media.* New York: Human Sciences Press.

Byrd, E. K. (1989). A study of depiction of specific characteristics of characters with disability in film. *Journal of Applied Rehabilitation Counseling, 20,* 43-45.

Calvert, S. L., & Tan, S. L. (1994). Impact of virtual reality on young adults' physiological arousal and aggressive thoughts: Interaction versus observation. *Journal of Applied Developmental Psychology, 15,* 125-139.

Cantor, D. (1996). The potential of facet theory for applied social psychology. In D. Cantor (Ed.), *Psychology in action* (pp. 39-70). Aldershot, UK: Dortmouth.

Cantor, J., & Hoffner, C. (1990). Children's fear reactions to a televised film as a function of perceived immediacy of depicted threat. *Journal of Broadcasting & Electronic Media, 34,* 421-442.

Cantor, J., & Reilly, S. (1982). Adolescents' fright reactions to television and films. *Journal of Communication, 32,* 87-108.

Cantor, J., & Sparks, G. G. (1984). Children's fear responses to mass media: Testing some Piagetian predictions. *Journal of Communication, 34,* 90-103.

Cantor, J., & Wilson, B. J. (1984). Modifying fear responses to mass media in preschool and elementary school children. *Journal of Broadcasting, 28,* 431-443.

Cantor, M. G., & Pingree, S. (1983). *The soap opera.* Beverly Hills, CA: Sage.

Cantril, H., Gaudet, H., & Hertzog, H. (1940). *The invasion from Mars.* Princeton, NJ: Princeton University Press.

Caplan, R. E. (1985). Violent program content in music video. *Journalism Quarterly, 62,* 146.

Carter, B. (1991, May 1). Children's TV, where boys are king. *New York Times,* p. C18.

Cartwright, G. F. (1994). Virtual or real? The mind in cyberspace. *The Futurist, 24,* 22-26.

Carveth, R., & Alexander, A. (1985). Soap opera viewing motivations and the cultivation process. *Journal of Broadcasting and Electronic Media, 29,* 259-273.

Cassata, B., Anderson, P., & Skill, T. (1980). The older adult in daytime serial drama. *Journal of Communication, 30,* 48-49.

Cassata, M. B., Skill, T. D., & Boadu, S. O. (1983). Life and death in the daytime television serial: A content analysis. In M. Cassata & T. Skill (Eds.), *Life on daytime television: Tuning in American serial drama* (pp. 47-70). Norwood, NJ: Ablex.

Centerwall, B. S. (1989a). Exposure to television as a cause of violence. In G. Comstock (Ed.), *Public communication and behavior* (Vol. 2, pp. 1-58). New York: Academic Press.

Centerwall, B. S. (1989b). Exposure to television as a risk factor for violence. *American Journal of Epidemiology, 129*(4), 643-652.

Chaffe, S. H., & Choe, S. Y. (1980). Time of decision and media use during the Ford-Carter campaign. *Public Opinion Quarterly, 44,* 53-59.

Chambers, J. H., & Ascione, F. R. (1987). The effects of prosocial and aggressive video games on children's donating and helping. *Journal of Genetic Psychology, 149,* 499-505.

Chaudhary, A. J. (1980). Press portrayal of black officials. *Journalism Quarterly, 57,* 636-641.

Chayko, M. (1993). What is real in the age of virtual reality? "Reframing" frame analysis for a technological world. *Symbolic Interaction, 16,* 171-181.

Cheney, G. (1993). We're talking war: Symbols, strategies, and images. In B. S. Greenberg, & W. Gantz (Eds.), *Desert Storm and the mass media* (pp. 61-73). Cresskill, NJ: Hampton Press.

Chirocos, T., Eschholz, S., & Gertz, M. (1997). Crime, news, and fear of crime: Toward an identification of audience effects. *Social Problems, 44,* 342-357.

Chomsky, N. (1992). The media and the war: What war? In H. Mowlana, G. Gerbner, & H. Schiller (Eds.), *Triumph of the image* (pp. 51-63). Boulder, CO: Westview.

Clark, C. (1969). Television and social control: Some observations on the portrayal of ethnic minorities. *Television Quarterly, 8,* 18-22.

Clark, D. G., & Blankenberg, W. B. (1972). Trends in violent content in selected mass media. In G. A. Comstock & E. A. Rubinstein (Eds.), *Television and social behavior: Vol. 1. Media content and control* (pp. 188-243). Washington, DC: Government Printing Office.

Cobb, N., Stevens-Long, J., & Goldstein, S. (1982). The influence of televised models on toy preference in children. *Sex Roles, 8,* 1075-1080.

Cohen, A. (1985). *The symbolic construction of community.* London: Tavistock.

Cohen, B. (1963). *The press and foreign policy.* Princeton, NJ: Princeton University Press.

Cohen, J., & Weimann, G. (1998, May). *Cultivation revisited: Some genres have some effects on some viewers.* Paper presented at the Annual Conference of the International Communication Association (ICA), Jerusalem, Israel.

Cohen, S., & Young, J. (1973). *The manufacture of news: A reader.* Beverly Hills, CA: Sage.

Cohn, C. (1991). *The language of the Gulf War* (publication of the Center for Psychological Studies in the Nuclear Age). Cambridge, MA: Harvard Medical School.

Coleman, W. (1983). Another view: Twenty years later. *NBMC Media Line, 3,* 5-6.

Combs, B., & Slovic, P. (1979). Newspaper coverage of causes of death. *Journalism Quarterly, 56,* 837-843.

Comstock, G. (1972). New research on media content and control (Overview). In G. A. Comstock & E. A. Rubenstein (Eds.), *Television and social behavior, Vol. 1: Media content.* Washington, DC: Government Printing Office.

Comstock, G., & Cobbey, R. E. (1982). Television and children of ethnic minorities: Perspectives from research. In G. L. Berry & C. Mitchell-Kernan (Eds.), *Television and the socialization of the minority child* (pp. 245-269). New York: Academic Press.

Cooper, J., & Mackie, D. (1986). Video games and aggression in children. *Journal of Applied Social Psychology, 16,* 726-744.

Cooper, M. (1991, January 28). The very nervy win of CNN. *U.S. News & World Report,* p. 44.

Copeland, G. A. (1989). Face-ism and primetime television. *Journal of Broadcasting and Electronic Media, 33,* 209-214.

Corner, J. (1988). Meaning, genre, and context: The problematics of "public knowledge" in the new audience studies. In J. Curran & M. Gurevitch (Eds.), *Mass media and society* (pp. 267-284). London: Edward Arnold.

Courtney, A. E., & Whipple, T. W. (1974). Women in TV commercials. *Journal of Communication, 24,* 110-118.

Cowan, G., Lee, C., Levy, D., & Snyder, D. (1988). Dominance and inequality in X-rated video cassettes. *Psychology of Women Quarterly, 12,* 299-311.

Cowgill, D. O., & Baulch, N. (1969). The use of leisure time by older people. *The Gerontologist, 2,* 47-50.

Cumberbatch, G., & Negrine, R. (1992). *Images of disability on television.* London: Routledge.

Daddario, G., Kang, J. G., Morgan, M., & Wu, Y. K. (1988). Les programmes Americains de television et les transformations culturelles en Coree et a Taiwan (U.S. TV programs and cultural transformations in Korea and Taiwan). *Tiers-Monde, 3,* 65-74.

Dates, J. L., & Barlow, W. (Eds.). (1990). *Split image: African Americans in the mass media.* Washington, DC: Howard University Press.

Davis, R. H. (1983). Television health messages: What are they telling us? *Generations, 3,* 43-45.

Davis, R. H., & Davis, D. (1985). *TV's images of the elderly.* Lexington, MA: Lexington Books.

Davis, T. (1991, June). Blue collar auteur. *American Film,* pp. 19-23.

De Charms, R. (1968). *Personal causation.* New York: Academic Press.

DeFleur, M. L. (1970). *Theories of mass communication* (2nd ed.). New York: David McKay.

DeFleur, M. L., & Ball-Rokeach, S. (1982). *Theories of mass communication* (4th ed.). New York: Longman.

DeFleur, M., & Ball-Rokeach, S. (1989). *Theories of mass communication.* New York: Longman.

DeFleur, M., & DeFleur, L. (1967). The relative contribution of television as a learning source for children's occupational knowledge. *American Sociological Review, 32,* 777-789.

DeFleur, M., & Dennis, E. (1991). *Understanding mass communication* (4th edition). Boston: Houghton Mifflin.

Dennis, E. E., Stebenne, D., Pavlik, J., Thalhimer, M., LaMay, C., Smillie, D., FitsSimon, M., Gazsi, S., & Rachlin, S. (1991). Public perceptions of war coverage. In Denis, E. E. et al. (Eds.) *The media at war: The press and the Persian Gulf conflict* (pp. 86-95), New York: Gannett Foundation.

Diamond, E. (1991, January 28). CNN's triumph. *New York,* p. A36.

Diamond, S. (1985). Pornography: Image and reality. In V. Burstyn (Ed.), *Women against censorship* (pp. 40-57). Vancouver, BC: Douglas & McIntyre.

Dibbell, J. (1993). *A rape in cyberspace or how an evil clown, a Haitian trickster spirit, two wizards, and a cast of dozens turned a database into a society.* Electronic document available from *julian@panix.com.*

Diem, S. J., Lantos, J. D., & Tulsky, J. A. (1996). Cardiopulmonary resuscitation on television: Miracles and misinformation. *The New England Journal of Medicine, 334*(24), 1578-1582.

Dietz, P. E., & Evans, B. (1982). Pornographic imagery and the prevalence of paraphilia. *American Journal of Psychiatry, 139,* 1493-1495.

Dobkin, B. A. (1992). Constructing new narratives: ABC and CNN cover the Gulf War. In R. E. Denton (Ed.), *The media and the Persian Gulf War* (pp. 107-122). Westport, CT: Praeger.

Dominick, J. R. (1984). Videogames, television violence, and aggression in teenagers. *Journal of Communication, 34,* 136-147.

Dominick, J. R. (1990). *The dynamics of mass communication* (3rd ed.). New York: McGraw-Hill.

Dominick, J. R., & Rauch, G. E. (1972). The image of women in network TV commercials. *Journal of Broadcasting, 16,* 259-265.

Donaldson, J. (1981). The visibility and image of handicapped people on television. *Exceptional Children, 47*(6), 413-416.

Donnerstein, E., Linz, D., & Penrod, S. (1987). *The question of pornography.* New York: Free Press.

Doob, A. N., & Macdonald, G. E. (1979). Television viewing and fear of victimization: Is the relationship causal? *Journal of Personality and Social Psychology, 37,* 170-179.

Dorr, A. (1986). *Television and children: A special medium for a special audience.* Beverly Hills, CA: Sage.

Dorr, A., & Kovaric, P. (1980). Some of the people some of the time—but which people? Televised violence and its effects. In E. L. Palmer & A. Dorr (Eds.), *Children and the faces of television: Teaching, violence, selling* (pp. 183-200). New York: Academic Press.

Dorr, A., & Kunkel, D. (1990). Children and the media environment: Change and constancy amid change. *Communication Research, 17,* 5-25.

Downing, M. (1975). *The world of daytime television serial drama.* Unpublished dissertation, University of Pennsylvania.

Downs, A. C. (1981). Sex-role stereotyping on prime-time television. *Journal of Genetic Psychology, 138*(2), 253-258.

Drabman, R. S., & Thomas, M. H. (1974). Does media violence increase children's toleration of real-life aggression? *Developmental Psychology, 10*, 418-442.

Drabman, R. S., & Thomas, M. H. (1976). Does watching violence on television cause apathy? *Pediatrics, 57*, 329-331.

Dubrow, H. (1982). *Genre.* London: Methuen.

Durkin, K. (1985). Television and sex-role acquisition 1: Content. *British Journal of Social Psychology, 24*, 101-113.

Dworkin, A. (1981). *Pornography: Men possessing women.* New York: Perigree.

Ebert, R. (1993). *Roger Ebert's movie home companion.* Kansas City, MO: Andrews & McMeel.

Eco, U. (1979). Introduction: The role of the reader. In *The role of the reader: Explorations in the semeiotics of texts.* Bloomington: Indiana University Press.

Elliot, T. R., & Byrd, E. K. (1982). Media and disability. *Rehabilitation Literature, 43*, 11-12.

Elliot, T. R., & Byrd, E. K. (1983). Attitude change toward disability through television portrayal. *Journal of Applied Rehabilitation Counseling, 14*, 35-37.

Elliot, T. R., & Byrd, E. K. (1984). Attitude change toward disability through television portrayal with male college students. *International Journal of Rehabilitation Research, 7*, 124-131.

Ellis, G. T., & Sekyra, F. (1972). The effects of aggressive cartoons on the behavior of first grade children. *Journal of Psychology, 81*, 37-43.

Entman, R. M. (1990). Modern racism and the images of blacks in local television news. *Critical Studies in Mass Communication, 7*, 332-345.

Entman, R. M. (1992). Blacks in the news: Television, modern racism, and cultural change. *Journalism Quarterly, 69*, 341-361.

Entman, R. M. (1994). Representation and reality in the portrayal of blacks on network television news. *Journalism Quarterly, 71*, 509-520.

Enzensberger, H. M. (1991, February 9). The second coming of Adolf Hitler. *Guardian*, p. 13.

Eron, L. D. (1982). Parent-child interaction, television violence, and aggression of children. *American Psychologist, 37*, 197-211.

Eron, L. D. (1986). Interventions to mitigate the psychological effects of media violence on aggressive behavior. *Journal of Social Issues, 42*, 155-169.

Eron, L. D., & Huesmann, L. R. (1987). Television as a source of maltreatment of children. *School Psychology Review, 6*, 195-202.

Eveland, W. P., McLeod, D. M., & Signorielli, N. (1995). Actual and perceived U.S. public opinion: The spiral of silence during the Persian Gulf War. *International Journal of Public Opinion Research 7*, 91-109.

Eysenck, H. J., & Nias, D. K. B. (1978). *Sex, violence, and the media.* New York: Harper.

Fabes, R. A., & Strouse, J. S. (1984). Youth's perceptions of models of sexuality: Implications for sexuality education. *Journal of Sex Education Therapy, 10*, 33-37.

Fabes, R. A., & Strouse, J. S. (1987). Perceptions of responsible and irresponsible models of sexuality: A correlational study. *Journal of Sex Research, 23*, 70-84.

Farberow, N. L. (1989). Attitudes toward suicide. In R. Dickstra, R. Mris, S. Platt, A. Schidtke, & G. Sonneck (Eds.), *Suicide and its prevention: The role of attitude and information* (pp. 280-298). New York: E. J. Brill.

Featherstone, M. (1995). Post-bodies, aging, and virtual reality. In M. Featherstone & A. Wernick (Eds.), *Images of aging: Cultural representations of later life* (pp. 227-244). London: Routledge.

Fejes, F. J. (1992). Masculinity as a fact: A review of the empirical mass communication research on masculinity. In S. Craig (Ed.), *Men, masculinity, and the media* (pp. 9-22). Newbury Park, CA: Sage.

Ferrante, C., Haynes, A., & Kingsley, S. (1988). Image of women in television advertising. *Journal of Broadcasting & Electronic Media, 32,* 231-237.

Feshbach, S. (1976). The role of fantasy in the response to television. *Journal of Social Issues, 32,* 71-85.

Feshbach, S., & Singer, R. (1971). *Television and aggression.* San Francisco: Jossey-Bass.

Finkielkraut, A. (1991, March 1). The gulf of backwardness. *Guardian,* p. 24.

Finn, S. (1997). Origins of media exposure: Linking personality traits to TV, radio, print, and film use. *Communication Research, 24,* 432-456.

Fishman, G., & Weimann, G. (1997). Motives to commit suicide: Statistical versus mass-mediated reality. *Archives of Suicide Research, 3,* 1-14.

Fishman, M. (1980). *Manufacturing the news.* Austin: University of Texas Press.

Fiske, J. (1978). *Reading television.* London: Methuen.

Fiske, J. (1987). *Television culture.* London: Routledge.

Freud, S. (1963). Reflections upon war and death. In *Character and culture* (E. C. Mayne, Trans.). New York: Collier Books. (Original work published in 1915)

Frueh, T., & McGhee, P. E. (1975). Traditional sex-role development and amount of time spent watching television. *Developmental Psychology, 11,* 109.

Fruh, W. (1992). *Medienwirkungen: Das dynamisch-transaktionale modell.* Opladen: Westdeutscher Verlag.

Fruh, W., & Schonbach, K. (1982). Der dynamisch-transaktionale ansatz: Ein neues paradigma der medienwirkungsforschung. *Publizistik, 27,* 74-88.

Funk, J. B., & Buchman, D. D. (1996). Playing violent video and computer games and adolescent self-concept. *Journal of Communication, 6,* 19-32.

Furnham, A., & Schofield, S. (1986). Sex-role stereotyping in British radio advertisements. *British Journal of Social Psychology, 25,* 165-171.

Furnham, A., & Voli, V. (1989). Gender stereotypes in Italian television advertisements. *Journal of Broadcasting & Electronic Media, 33,* 175-185.

Furstenberg, F. F., Jr., Moore, K. A., & Peterson, J. L. (1985). Sex education and sexual experience among adolescents. *American Journal of Public Health, 75*(11), 1331-1332.

Gadow, K. D., & Sprafkin, J. (1989). Field experiments of television violence with children: Evidence for an environmental hazard? *Pediatrics, 83*(3), 399-405.

Gagnard, A. (1986). From feast to famine: Depiction of ideal body type in magazine advertising: 1950-1984. *Proceedings of the American Academy of Advertising, 27,* 461-470.

Gans, H. (1980). *Deciding what's news.* New York: Vintage Books.

Garay, R. (1988). *Cable television: A reference guide to information.* New York: Greenwood.

Gardner, J., & Radel, M. S. (1978). Portrait of the disabled in the media. *Journal of Community Psychology, 6,* 269-274.

Garfinkel, P. E., & Garner, D. M. (1982). *Anorexia nervosa: A multidimensional perspective.* New York: Brunner-Mazel.

Garner, D. M., Garfinkel, P. E., Schwartz, D., & Thompson, M. (1980). Cultural expectations of thinness in women. *Psychological Reports, 47,* 483-491.

Gerbner, G. (1969). Dimensions of violence in television drama. In R. K. Baker & S. J. Ball (Eds.), *Violence in the media* (Staff report to the National Commission on the Causes and Prevention of Violence) (pp. 311-340). Washington, DC: Government Printing Office.

Gerbner, G. (1972). Violence and television drama: Trends and symbolic functions. In G. A. Comstock & E. Rubinstein (Eds.), *Television and social behavior: Vol. 1. Content and control* (pp. 28-187). Washington, DC: Government Printing Office.

Gerbner, G. (1977, September-October). Proliferating violence. *Society,* pp. 8-14.

Gerbner, G. (1980). Death in prime time: Notes on the symbolic functions of dying in the mass media. *Annals, 447,* 64-70.

Gerbner, G. (1990). Epilogue: Advancing on the path of righteousness (maybe). In N. Signorielli & M. Morgan (Eds.), *Cultivation analysis: New directions in media effects research* (pp. 249-262). Newbury Park, CA: Sage.

Gerbner, G. (1992). Persian Gulf War: The movie. In G. Mowlana, G. Gerbner, & H. Schiller (Eds.), *Triumph of the image: The media's war in the Persian Gulf—a global perspective* (pp. 243-266). Boulder, CO: Westview.

Gerbner, G. (1993a). Learning productive aging as a social role: The lessons of television. In S. A. Bass, F. G. Caro, & Y. Che (Eds.), *Achieving a productive aging society* (pp. 207-220). Westport, CT: Auburn House.

Gerbner, G. (1993b). *Women and minorities on television* (a report to the Screen Actors Guild and the American Federation of Radio and Television Artists). Philadelphia: Annenberg School, University of Pennsylvania.

Gerbner, G. (1996). The hidden side of television violence. In G. Gerbner, H. Mowlana, & H. Schiller (Eds.), *Invisible crises* (pp. 27-34). Boulder, CO: Westview.

Gerbner, G., & Gross, L. (1976). Living with television: The Violence Profile. *Journal of Communication, 26,* 172-199.

Gerbner, G., & Gross, L. (1980). The violent face of television and its lessons. In E. Palmer & A. Dorr (Eds.), *Children and the faces of television: Teaching, violence, selling* (pp. 149-162). New York: Academic Press.

Gerbner, G., Gross, L., Eley, M., Jackson-Beck, M., Jeffries-Fox, S., & Signorielli, N. (1977). TV violence profile No. 8: The highlights. *Journal of Communication, 27,* 171-180.

Gerbner, G., Gross, L., Hoover, S., Morgan, M., Signorielli, N., & Wuthnow, R. (1984). *Religion and television.* Philadelphia: The Annenberg School of Communications, University of Pennsylvania.

Gerbner, G., Gross, L., Jackson-Beeck, M., Jeffries-Fox, S., & Signorielli, N. (1978).
Cultural indicators: Violence profile No. 9. *Journal of Communication, 28,*
176-207.

Gerbner, G., Gross, L., Morgan, M., & Signorielli, N. (1979). On Wober's "Televised violence and paranoid perception: The view from Great Britain." *Public
Opinion Quarterly, 43,* 123-124.

Gerbner, G., Gross, L., Morgan, M., & Signorielli, N. (1980a). The "mainstreaming" of America: Violence profile No. 11. *Journal of Communication, 30,*
10-29.

Gerbner, G., Gross, L., Morgan, M., & Signorielli, N. (1980b). *Media and the
family: Images and impact.* Paper for the National Research Forum on Family
Issues, White House Conference on Families.

Gerbner, G., Gross, L., Morgan, M., & Signorielli, N. (1981a). Final reply to Hirsch.
Communication Research, 8, 259-280.

Gerbner, G., Gross, L., Morgan, M., & Signorielli, N. (1981b, May/June). Scientists
on the TV screen. *Society,* pp. 41-44.

Gerbner, G., Gross, L., Morgan, M., & Signorielli, N. (1981c). Special report:
Health and medicine on television. *The New England Journal of Medicine,
305,* 901-904.

Gerbner, G., Gross, L., Morgan, M., & Signorielli, N. (1982). Charting the
mainstream: Television's contribution to political orientations. *Journal of
Communication, 32,* 100-127.

Gerbner, G., Gross, L., Morgan, M., & Signorielli, N. (1984). Political correlates
of television viewing. *Public Opinion Quarterly, 48,* 283-300.

Gerbner, G., Gross L., Morgan, M., & Signorielli, N. (1986). Living with television:
The dynamics of the cultivation process. In J. Bryant & D. Zillmann (Eds.),
Perspectives on media effects (pp. 17-40). Hillsdale, NJ: Lawrence Erlbaum.

Gerbner, G., Gross, L., Signorielli, N., & Morgan, M. (1979). The demonstration
of power: Violence profile No. 10. *Journal of Communication, 29,* 177-196.

Gerbner, G., Gross, L., Signorielli, N., & Morgan, M. (1980). Aging with television:
Images on television drama and conceptions of social reality. *Journal of
Communication, 30,* 37-47.

Gerbner, G., Morgan, M., & Signorielli, N. (1982). Programming health portrayals:
What viewers see, say, and do. In D. Pearl, L. Bouthilet, & J. Lazar (Eds.),
*Television and behavior: Ten years of scientific progress and implications for
the 80's: Vol. 2. Technical reviews* (pp. 291-307). Rockville, MD: National
Institute of Mental Health.

Gerbner, G., & Signorielli, N. (1979). *Women and minorities in television drama,
1969-1978.* Philadelphia: The Annenberg School of Communications, University of Pennsylvania.

Gerbner, G., & Signorielli, N. (1990). *Violence profile 1967 through 1988-89:
Enduring patterns.* Unpublished manuscript, University of Delaware, Newark.

Gibson, J. J. (1979). *The ecological approach to visual perception.* Boston: Houghton
Mifflin.

Gieber, W. (1964). News is what newspapermen make it. In L. A. Dexter & D.
Manning (Eds.), *White people, society, and mass communications* (pp. 164-
176). New York: Free Press.

Gilens, M. (1996). Race and poverty in America: Public misperceptions and the American news media. *Public Opinion Quarterly, 60*, 515-541.

Gilly, M. C. (1988). Sex role in advertising: A comparison of television advertisements in Australia, Mexico, and the United States. *Journal of Marketing, 52*, 75-85.

Goe, J. (1996). Reconsidering gender roles on MTV: Depictions in the most popular music videos of the early 1990s. *Communication Reports, 9*, 151-161.

Goffman, E. (1979). *Gender advertisements.* New York: Harper & Row. (Original work published 1976).

Golding, P., & Murdock, G. (1991). Culture, communications, and political economy. In J. Curran & M. Gurevitch (Eds.), *Mass media and society* (pp. 15-32). London: Edward Arnold.

Gorer, G. (1965). *Death, grief, and mourning.* New York: Doubleday Anchor Books.

Gosselin, A., DeGuise, J., & Paquette, G. (1997). Violence on Canadian television and some of its cognitive effects. *Canadian Journal of Communication, 22*, 143-160.

Gould, J. (1991, March). Is technology outstripping understanding? *RTNDA Communicator.*

Gould, M. S., & Shaffer, D. (1986). The impact of suicide in television movies: Evidence of imitation. *The New England Journal of Medicine, 315*, 690-694.

Graber, D. (1988). *Processing the news: How people tame the information tide* (2nd ed.). New York: Longman.

Gray, H. (1989). Television, black Americans, and the American dream. *Critical Studies in Mass Communication, 6*, 376-386.

Greenberg, B. S. (1972). Children's reactions to TV blacks. *Journalism Quarterly, 49*(1), 5-14

Greenberg, B. S. (1980). *Life on television: Content analysis of U.S. television drama.* Norwood, NJ: Ablex.

Greenberg, B. S. (1986). Minorities and the mass media. In J. Bryant & D. Zillmann (Eds.), *Perspectives on media effects* (pp. 165-188). Hillsdale, NJ: Lawrence Erlbaum.

Greenberg, B. S., Abelman, R., & Neuendorf, K. (1981). Sex on the soap operas: An afternoon delight. *Journal of Communication, 31*, 83-89.

Greenberg, B. S., & Atkin, C. (1982). Learning about minorities from television: A research agenda. In G. Berry & C. Mitchell-Kernan (Eds.), *Television and the socialization of the minority child* (pp. 215-243). New York: Academic Press.

Greenberg, B. S., & Brand, J. E. (1994). Minorities and the mass media: 1970s to 1990s. In J. Bryant & D. Zillmann (Eds.), *Media effects* (pp. 273-314). Hillsdale, NJ: Lawrence Erlbaum.

Greenberg, B. S., Linsangan, R. L., Soderman, A., Dorfman, S., Heeter, C., & Stanley, C. (1987). *Adolescents and their exposure to television and movies sex* (Project CAST Report No. 4, Department of Telecommunication). East Lansing: Michigan State University.

Greenberg, B., Richards, M., & Henderson, L. (1980). Trends in sex-role portrayal on television. In B. Greenberg (Ed.), *Life on television: Content analysis of U.S. television drama* (pp. 65-88). Norwood, NJ: Ablex.

Greenberg, B. S., Siemich, M., Dortman, S., Heeter, C., Stanley, C., Soderman, A., & Linsangan, R. (1986). *Sex content in X-rated films viewed by adolescents* (Project CAST Report No. 3, Department of Telecommunication). East Lansing: Michigan State University.

Greenberg, B., Simmons, K., Hogan, L., & Atkin, C. (1980). The demographics of fictional TV characters. In B. Greenberg (Ed.), *Life on television: Content analysis of U.S. television drama* (pp. 35-46). Norwood, NJ: Ablex.

Greeson, L. E., & Williams, R. A. (1986). Social implications of music videos for youth: An analysis of the content and effects of MTV. *Youth & Society, 18,* 177-189.

Griffin, M., & Lee, J. (1995). Picturing the Gulf War: Constructing an image of war in *Time, Newsweek,* and *U.S. News and World Report. Journalism and Mass Communication Quarterly, 72,* 813-825.

Griffin, S. (1981). *Pornography and silence: Culture's revenge against nature.* New York: Harper & Row.

Griffiths, M. D. (1991). Amusement machine playing in childhood and adolescence: A comparative analysis of video games and fruit machines. *Journal of Adolescence, 14,* 53-73.

Gross, L. (1984). The cultivation of intolerance: Television, blacks, and gays. In G. Melischek, K. E. Rosengren, & J. Stappers (Eds.), *Cultural indicators* (pp. 345-364). Wien: Osterreichische Akademie der Wissenschaften.

Gross, L. S. (1992). *Telecommunications: An introduction to the electronic media* (4th ed.). Dubuque, IA: C. Brown.

Gross, L., & Jeffries-Fox, S. (1978). What do you want to be when you grow up, little girl? In G. Tuchman, A. K. Daniels, & J. Benet (Eds.), *Hearth and home: Images of women in the mass media.* New York: Oxford University Press.

Guback, T. H. (1974). Film as international business. *Journal of Communication, 24,* 90-101.

Gunter, B. (1986). *Television and sex role stereotyping.* London: John Libbey.

Gustadt, L. E. (1993). Taking the pulse of the CNN audience: A case study of the Gulf War. *Political Communication, 10,* 389-409.

Guttman, L. (1979, October). *New development in integrating test design and analysis.* Paper presented to the 40th International Conference on Testing Problems, New York.

Guttman, L. (1994). The mapping sentence for assessing values. In S. Levy (Ed.), *Louis Guttman on theory and methodology: Selected writings* (pp. 595-602). Aldershot, UK: Dortmouth.

Hall, S. (1981). Encoding/decoding in television discourse. In S. Hall et al. (Eds.), *Culture, media, language* (pp. 24-38). London: Hutchinson.

Hallin, D. C., & Gitlin, T. (1993). Agon and ritual: The Gulf War as popular culture and as television drama. *Political Communication, 10,* 411-424.

Hall-Preston, E. (1990). Pornography and the construction of gender. In M. Morgan & N. Signorielli (Eds.), *Cultivation analysis* (pp. 107-122). Newbury Park, CA: Sage.

Harris, A., & Feinberg, J. (1977). Television and aging: Is what you see what you get? *The Gerontologist, 17,* 464-468.

Harris, J. H. (1994). *A cognitive psychology of mass communication* (2nd ed.). Hillsdale, NJ: Lawrence Erlbaum.

Harris, P. R., & Stobart, J. (1986). Sex role-stereotyping in British television advertisements at different times of the day: An extension and refinement of Manstead & McCulloch. *British Journal of Social Psychology, 25,* 155-164.

Harrison, K. (1997). Does interpersonal attraction to thin media personalities promote eating disorders? *Journal of Broadcasting and Electronic Media, 41,* 478-500.

Harrison, K., & Cantor, J. (1997). The relationship between media consumption and eating disorders. *Journal of Communication, 47,* 40-67.

Harter, S. (1986). Processes underlying the construction, maintenance, and enhancement of the self-concept in children. In J. Suls & A. G. Greenwald (Eds.), *Psychological perspectives on the self* (Vol. 3, pp. 137-181). Hillsdale, NJ: Lawrence Erlbaum.

Harter, S. (1987a). The determinants and educational role of global self-worth in children. In N. Eisenberg (Ed.), *Contemporary topics in developmental psychology* (pp. 219-242). New York: John Wiley.

Harter, S. (1987b). Developmental and dynamic changes in the nature of the self-concept: Implications for child psychotherapy. In S. R. Shirk (Ed.), *Cognitive development and child psychotherapy* (pp.119-160). New York: Plenum.

Hartmann, D. P. (1969). Influence of symbolically modeled instrumental aggression and pain cues on aggressive behavior. *Journal of Personality and Social Psychology, 11,* 280-288.

Harwood, J., & Giles, H. (1992). "Don't make me laugh": Age representations in a humorous context. *Discourse & Society, 3,* 403-436.

Hawkins, R. P., & Pingree, S. (1980). Some processes in the cultivation effect. *Communication Research, 7,* 193-226.

Hawkins, R. P., & Pingree, S. (1981a). Uniform content and habitual viewing: Unnecessary assumptions in social reality effects. *Human Communication Research, 7,* 219-301.

Hawkins, R. P., & Pingree, S. (1981b). Using television to construct social reality. *Journal of Broadcasting, 25,* 347-364.

Hawkins, R. P., & Pingree, S. (1982). Television's influence on social reality. In D. Pearl, L. Bouthilet, & J. Lazar (Eds.), *Television and behavior: Ten years of scientific progress and implications for the eighties: Vol. 2. Technical reviews* (pp. 224-247). Rockville, MD: National Institute of Mental Health.

Hawkins, R. P., & Pingree, S. (1990). Divergent psychological processes in constructing social reality from mass media content. In N. Signorielli & M. Morgan (Eds.), *Cultivation analysis* (pp. 35-50). Newbury Park, CA: Sage.

Hawkins, R. P., Pingree, S., & Adler, I. (1987). Searching for cognitive processes in the cultivation effect. *Human Communication Research, 13,* 553-577.

Head, S. (1954). Content analysis of televised drama programs. *Quarterly of Film, Radio, and Television, 9,* 175-194.

Hearold, S. (1986). A synthesis of 1,043 effects of television on social behavior. In G. Comstock (Ed.), *Public communication and behavior* (Vol. 1, pp. 65-133). New York: Academic Press.

Heath, L., Bresolin, L. B., & Rinaldi, R. C. (1989). Effects of media violence on children: A review of the literature. *Archives General Psychiatry, 46,* 376-379.

Heath, L., & Gilbert, K. (1996). Mass media and fear of crime. *American Behavioral Scientist, 39,* 379-386.

Heath, L., & Petraitis, J. (1987). Television viewing and fear of crime: Where is the mean world? *Basic and Applied Social Psychology, 8,* 97-123.

Hebditch, D., & Anning, N. (1988). *Porn gold: Inside the pornography business.* London: Faber & Faber.

Heeter, C. (1992). Being there: The subjective experience of presence. *Presence, 1*(2), 262-271.

Heeter, C. (1995). Communication research on consumer VR. In F. Biocca & M. R. Levy (Eds.), *Communication in the age of virtual reality* (pp. 191-218). Hillsdale, NJ: Lawrence Erlbaum.

Heinberg, L. J., & Thompson, J. K. (1995). Body images of thinness and attractiveness: A controlled laboratory investigation. *Journal of Social and Clinical Psychology, 14*(4), 325-338.

Heller, M. S., & Polsky, S. (1975). *Studies in violence and television.* New York: American Broadcasting Companies.

Herold, E. S., & Foster, M. E. (1975). Changing sexual references in mass circulation magazines. *The Family Coordinator, 24,* 21-25.

Hess, R. B. (1974). Stereotypes of the aged. *Journal of Communication, 24,* 76-85.

Himmelweit, H. T., & Swift, B. (1976). Continuities and discontinuities in media usage and taste: A longitudinal analysis. *Journal of Social Issues, 32*(4), 133-156.

Hirsch, P. M. (1980). The "scary world" of the nonviewer and other anomalies: A reanalysis of Gerbner et al.'s findings of cultivation analysis, part 1. *Communication Research, 7,* 403-456.

Hirsch, P. M. (1981a). Distinguishing good speculation from bad theory: Rejoinder to Gerbner et al. *Communication Research, 8,* 73-95.

Hirsch, P. M. (1981b). On not learning from one's own mistakes: A reanalysis of Gerbner et al.'s findings on cultivation analysis. *Communication Research, 8,* 3-37.

Hodges, K. K., Brandt, D. A., & Kline, J. (1981). Competence, guilt, and victimization: Sex differences in attribution of responsibility, *Sex Roles, 7,* 537-546.

Holden, S. (1986, June 29). Madonna goes heavy on heart. *New York Times,* p. H22.

Holden, S. (1993, May 26). Teenagers living under the gun. *New York Times,* p. C13.

Holding, T. A. (1975). The B.B.C. "Befrienders" series and its effects. *British Journal of Psychiatry, 124,* 470-472.

Hollenbeck, A. R., & Slaby, R. G. (1979). Infant visual and vocal responses to television. *Child Development, 50,* 41-55.

Huang, S. (1992). *An empirical analysis of Chinese advertising.* Beijing: Beijing Broadcast Institute Press.

Huesmann, L. R., Eron, L. D., Berkowitz, L., & Chaffee, S. (1987). *Effects of television violence on aggression: A reply to Freedman.* Unpublished manuscript, Department of Psychology, University of Illinois, Chicago.

Huesmann, L. R., Lagerspetz, K., & Eron, L. D. (1984). Intervening variables in the TV violence-aggression relation: Evidence from two countries. *Developmental Psychology, 20*, 746-775.

Hughes, M. (1980). The fruits of cultivation analysis: A re-examination of the effects of television watching on fear of victimization, alienation, and the approval of violence. *Public Opinion Quarterly, 44*, 287-302.

Humphrey, R., & Schumann, H. (1984). The portrayal of blacks in magazine advertisements: 1950-1982. *Public Opinion Quarterly, 48*, 551-563.

Huston, A. C., Donnerstein, E., Fairchild, H., Feshbach, N. D., Katz, P. A., Murray, J. P., Rubinstein, E. A., Wilcox, B. L., & Zuckerman, D. (1992). *Big world, small screen: The role of television in American society*. Omaha: University of Nebraska Press.

Huston, A. C., Watkins, B. A., & Kunkel, D. (1989). Public policy and children's television. *American Psychologist, 44*, 424-433.

Intons-Peterson, M. J., & Reskos-Ewoldsen, B. (1989). Mitigating the effects of violent pornography. In S. Grubar & J. Hoff-Wilson (Eds.), *For adult users only: The dilemma of violent pornography* (pp. 234-245). Bloomington: Indiana University Press.

Iyengar, S. (1991). *Is anyone responsible? How television frames political issues*. Chicago: University of Chicago Press.

Iyengar, S., & Kinder, D. R. (1987). *News that matters*. Chicago: University of Chicago Press.

Iyengar, S., Peters, M. D., & Kinder, D. R. (1982). Experimental demonstrations of the "not-so-minimal" consequences of television news programs. *American Political Science Review, 76*, 848-858.

Iyengar, S., & Simon, A. (1993). News coverage of the Gulf Crisis and public opinion: A study of agenda-setting, priming, and framing. *Communication Research, 20*, 365-383.

Jackson, L. A., & Ervin, K. S. (1991). The frequency and portrayal of black families in fashion advertisements. *Journal of Black Psychology, 18*, 67-70.

Jamieson, K. H. (1992). *Dirty politics*. New York: Oxford University Press.

Jeffries-Fox, S., & Signorielli, N. (1978). Television and children's conceptions of occupations. In H. S. Dordick (Ed.), *Proceedings of the sixth annual telecommunication policy research conference* (pp. 21-38). Lexington, MA: Lexington Books.

Jhally, S., & Lewis, J. (1992). *Enlightened racism*. Boulder, CO: Westview.

Johnstone, J. W. C., Hawkins, D. F., & Michener, A. (1994). Homicide reporting in Chicago dailies. *Journalism Quarterly, 71*(4), 860-872.

Jones, E. F. (1985). Teenage pregnancy in developed countries: Determinants and policy implications. *Family Planning Perspectives, 17*, 53-63.

Jones, K. (1997). Are rap videos more violent? Style differences and the prevalence of sex and violence in the age of MTV. *Howard-Journal-of-Communications, 8*, 343-356.

Jones, Q. (1997). Virtual-Communities, virtual settlements & cyber-archaeology: A theoretical outline. *Journal of Computer Mediated Communication, 3*(3).

Jones, S. G. (1995). *CyberSociety: Computer-mediated communication*. Thousand Oaks, CA: Sage.

Joy, L. A., Kimball, M. M., & Zabrack, M. L. (1986). Television and children's aggressive behavior. In T. M. Williams (Ed.), *The impact of television: A natural experiment in three communities* (pp. 303-360). Orlando, FL: Academic Press.

Kalis, P., & Neuendorf, K. A. (1989). Aggressive cue prominence and gender participation in MTV. *Journalism Quarterly, 66,* 148-154.

Kalof, L. (1990, September). *Images of gender and sexuality: A study of the adolescent's interpretation of media messages.* Paper presented at the 10th Annual Conference on Youth, Center for Population Options, Arlington, VA.

Kalof, K. (1993). Dilemmas of femininity: Gender and the social construction of sexual imagery. *The Sociological Quarterly, 34,* 639-651.

Kaminsky, S. M., & Mahan, J. H. (1988). *American television genres.* Chicago: Nelson-Hall.

Kang, J. G., & Morgan, M. (1988). Culture clash: U.S. television programs in Korea. *Journalism Quarterly, 65,* 431-438.

Katz, E. (1983). Publicity and pluralistic ignorance: Notes on "The Spiral of Silence." In *Mass communication yearbook* (Vol. 4, pp. 89-99). Beverly Hills, CA: Sage.

Katz, E. (1992). The end of journalism? Notes on watching the war. *Journal of Communication, 42,* 5-13.

Katz, E., & Liebes, T. (1986). Mutual aid in the decoding of *Dallas:* Preliminary notes from a cross-cultural study. In P. Drummond & R. Paterson (Eds.), *Television in transition.* London: British Film Institute.

Kearl, M. C. (1989). *Endings: A sociology of death and dying.* New York: Oxford University Press.

Keller, C. E., Hallahan, D. P., McShane, E. A., Crowley, E. P., & Blandford, B. J. (1990). The coverage of persons with disabilities in American newspapers. *Journal of Special Education, 24,* 271-282.

Kellner, D. (1992). *The Persian Gulf TV war.* Boulder, CO: Westview.

Kellner, D. (1993). The crisis in the Gulf and the lack of critical media discourse. In B. S. Greenberg & W. Gantz (Eds.), *Desert Storm and the mass media* (pp. 237-247). Cresskill, NJ: Hampton Press.

Kelman, H. (1993). The reaction of mass public to the Gulf War. In S. A. Renshon (Ed.), *The political psychology of the Gulf War.* Pittsburgh, PA: University of Pittsburgh Press.

Kendrick, D. T., & Gutierres, S. E. (1980). Contrast effects and judgments of physical attractiveness: When beauty becomes a social problem. *Journal of Personality and Social Psychology, 38,* 131-140.

Kent, P. (1994). *The complete idiot's guide to the Internet.* Indianapolis, IN: Alpha Books.

Kessler, R., Downey, G., Stipp, H., & Milavsky, R. J. (1989). Network television news stories about suicide and short-term changes in total U.S. suicides. *The Journal of Nervous and Mental Disease, 177*(9), 551-555.

Kessler, R., & Stipp, H. (1984). The impact of fictional television suicide stories on U.S. fatalities: A replication. *American Journal of Sociology, 90,* 151-167.

Kim, J., & Rubin, A. M. (1997). The variable influence of audience activity on media effects. *Communication Research, 24,* 107-135.

Kimball, M. M. (1986). Television and sex-role attitudes. In T. M. Williams (Ed.), *The impact of television: A natural experiment in three communities* (pp. 265-301). Orlando, FL: Academic Press.

Kinder, M. (1984). Music video and the spectator: Television, ideology, and dream. *Film Quarterly, 34,* 2-15.

Klassen, M. L., Wauer, S. M., & Cassel, S. (1990). Increases in health and weight loss in food advertising in the eighties. *Journal of Advertising Research, 30*(6), 32-37.

Korzenny, F., & Neuendorf, K. (1980). Television viewing and self-concept of the elderly. *Journal of Communication, 30,* 71-80.

Kovaric, P. M. (1993). Television, the portrayal of the elderly, and children's attitudes. In G. L. Berry & J. K. Samen (Eds.), *Children and television* (pp. 243-254). Newbury Park, CA: Sage.

Krantzler, N. (1986). Media images of physicians and nurses in the United States. *Social Science & Medicine, 22*(9), 933-952.

Krech, D., Crutchfild, R. S., & Ballachey, E. L. (1972). *Individual in society.* New York: McGraw-Hill.

Krol, E. (1994). *The whole Internet.* Sebastopol, CA: O'Reilly and Associates.

Krueger, M .W. (1990). Videoplace and the interface of the future. In B. Laurel (Ed.), *The art of human-computer interface design* (pp. 417-422). Reading, MA: Addison-Wesley.

Kubey, R. (1980). Television and aging: Past, present, and future, *Communication Research, 15*(1), 71-92.

Kubey, R., & Csikszentmihalyi, M. (1990). *Television and the quality of life: How viewing shapes everyday experiences.* Hillsdale, NJ: Lawrence Erlbaum.

Lambert, W. E., & Klineberg, O. (1967). *Children's views of foreign people: A cross-national study.* New York: Appleton-Century-Crofts.

Lang, K., & Engel Lang, G. (1953). The unique perspective of television and its effects: A pilot study. *American Sociological Review, 17,* 3-12.

Lang, K., & Lang, G. (1959). The mass media and voting. In E. Burdick & A. J. Brodbeck (Eds.), *American voting behavior* (pp. 217-235). Glencoe, IL: Free Press.

Laquey, T. (1993). *Internet plus companion.* Reading, MA: Addison-Wesley.

Lazar, B. (1994). Why social work should care: Television violence and children. *Child and Adolescent Social Work Journal, 11,* 3-19.

Lazarsfeld, P., Berelson, B., & Gaudet, H. (1944). *The people's choice.* New York: Duell, Sloan and Pearce.

Lazier, L., & Gagnard-Kendrick, A. (1993). Women in advertisements: Sizing up the images, roles, and functions. In P. J. Creedon (Ed.), *Women in mass communication* (pp. 199-219). Newbury Park, CA: Sage.

Lazier-Smith, L. (1988). *The effect of changes in women's social status on images of women in magazine advertising: The Pingree-Hawkins sexism scale reapplied, Goffman reconsidered, Kilbourne revisited.* Unpublished doctoral dissertation, Indiana University.

Lee, M. A., & Solomon, N. (1991). *Unreliable sources.* New York: Lyle Stuart.

Lefkowitz, E., Eron, D., Walder, L. O., & Huesmann, L. R. (1977). *Growing up to be violent: A longitudinal study of the development of aggression.* New York: Pergamon.

Lefkowitz. M. M., et al. (1971). Television violence and child aggression: A follow-up study. In G. A. Comstock & E. Rubinsten (Eds.), *Television and social behavior: Vol. 3. Television and adolescent aggression* (pp. 198-225). Washington DC: Government Printing Office.

Lemert, J. B. (1981). *Does mass communication affect public opinion after all?* Chicago: Nelson-Hall.

Levinson, R. (1975). From Olive Oil to sweet Polly Purebread: Sex role stereotypes and televised cartoons. *Journal of Popular Culture, 9,* 561-572.

Levy, M. R., & Windahl, S. (1985). The concept of audience activity. In K. E. Rosengren, L. A. Wenner, & P. Palmgreen (Eds.), *Media gratifications research: Current perspectives* (pp. 109-122). Beverley Hills, CA: Sage.

Levy, S. (Ed.). (1994). *Louis Guttman on theory and methodology: Selected writings.* Aldershot, UK: Dortmouth.

Lewis, L. A. (1987). Form and female authorship in music video. *Communication, 9,* 355-377.

Lewis, L. A. (1990). *Gender politics and MTV: Voicing the difference.* Philadelphia: Temple University Press.

Li, D., & Gallup, A. M. (1995, September-October). In search of the Chinese consumer. *The China Business Review,* pp. 19-22.

Liebert, R. M., & Sprafkin, J. (1988). *The early window: Effects of television on children and youth* (3rd ed.). New York: Pergamon.

Liebes, T. (1994). Crimes of reporting: The unhappy end of a fact-finding mission in the Bible. *Journal of Narrative and Life History, 41,* 135-150.

Liebes, T., & Katz, E. (1986). Patterns of involvement in television fiction: A comparative analysis. *European Journal of Communication, 1,* 151-171.

Liebes, T., & Katz, E. (1990). *The export of meaning.* Oxford, UK: Oxford University Press.

Linsley, W. A. (1989). The case against censorship of pornography. In D. Zillmann & J. Bryant (Eds.), *Pornography: Research advances and policy considerations* (pp. 343-350). Hillsdale, NJ: Lawrence Erlbaum.

Linz, D. (1989). Exposure to sexually explicit materials and attitudes toward rape: A comparison of study results. *The Journal of Sex Research, 26,* 50-84.

Linz, D., Donnerstein, E., & Penrod, S. (1984). The effects of multiple exposures to filmed violence against women. *Journal of Communication, 34,* 130-147.

Linz, D., Donnerstein, E., & Penrod, S. (1988). The effects of long-term exposure to violent and sexually degrading depictions of women. *Journal of Personality and Social Psychology, 55,* 758-768.

Linz, D., & Malamuth, N. (1993). *Pornography.* Newbury Park, CA: Sage.

Lippmann, W. (1922). *Public opinion.* New York: Macmillan.

Liqun, L. (1991). The images of the United States in present-day China. In E. E. Dennis, G. Gerbner, & Y. N. Zassoursky (Eds.), *Beyond the cold war* (pp. 116-125). Newbury Park, CA: Sage.

Liska, A., & Baccaglini, W. (1990). Feeling safe by comparison: Crime in the newspapers. *Social Problems, 37,* 360-374.

Livingstone, S. (1990a). Divergent interpretations of a television narrative. *Journal of Communication, 16,* 25-57.

Livingstone, S. (1990b). *Making sense of television: The psychology of audience interpretation*. Oxford: Pergamon.

Livingstone, S. (1991). Audience reception: The role of the viewer in retelling romantic drama. In J. Curran & M. Gurevitch (Eds.), *Mass media and society* (pp. 285-306). London: Edward Arnold.

Livingstone, S., & Green, G. (1986). Television advertisements and the portrayal of gender. *British Journal of Social Psychology, 25,* 149-154.

Lombard, M., & Ditton, T. (1997). At the heart of it all: The concept of presence. *Journal of Computer Mediated Communication, 3*(2).

Long, M., & Simon, R. (1974). The roles and statuses of women on children's and family TV programs. *Journalism Quarterly, 51,* 107-110.

Longino, H. E. (1980). Pornography, oppression, and freedom: A closer look. In L. Lederer (Ed.), *Take back the night: Women on pornography* (pp. 40-54). New York: William Morrow.

Lott, B. (1989). Sexist discrimination as distancing behavior: Prime-time television. *Psychology of Women Quarterly, 13,* 341-355.

Lovaas, I. O. (1961). Effect of exposure to symbolic aggression on aggressive behavior. *Child Development, 32,* 37-44.

Lovdal, L. T. (1989). Sex role messages in television commercials: An update. *Sex Roles, 21,* 715-724.

Lowery, S., & DeFleur, M. L. (1983). *Milestones in mass communication research*. New York: Longman.

Lowry, D. T., Love, G., & Kirby, M. (1981). Sex on the soap operas: Patterns of intimacy. *Journal of Communication, 31,* 90-96.

Lowry, D. T., & Towles, D. E. (1989a). Prime-time TV portrayals of sex, contraception, and venereal diseases. *Journalism Quarterly, 66,* 347-352.

Lowry, D. T., & Towles, D. E. (1989b). Soap opera portrayals of sex, contraception, and sexually transmitted diseases. *Journal of Communication, 39,* 76-83.

Luebke, B. (1989). Out of focus: Images of women and men in newspaper photographs. *Sex Roles, 20,* 121-133.

Lukosiunas, M. A. (1991). Enemy, friend, or competitor? A content analysis of the *Christian Science Monitor* and *Izvestia*. In E. E. Dennis, G. Gerbner, & Y. N. Zassoursky (Eds.), *Beyond the cold war* (pp. 100-110). Newbury Park, CA: Sage.

Lysonski, S. (1985). Role portrayals in British magazine advertisements. *European Journal of Marketing, 19,* 37-55.

MacKinnon, R. (1998). The social construction of rape in virtual reality. In F. Sudweeks, M. McLaughlin, & S. Rafaeli (Eds.), *Network & netplay: Virtual groups on the Internet* (pp. 147-172). Menlo Park, CA: AAAI Press.

Macklin, M. C., & Kolbe, R. H. (1983). Sex role stereotyping in children's advertising: Current and past trends. *Journal of Advertising, 13,* 34-42.

Malamuth, N. M., & Check, J. V. P. (1985). The effects of aggressive pornography on beliefs of rape myths: Individual differences. *Journal of Research in Personality, 19,* 299-320.

Malamuth, N. M., Reisin, I., & Spinner, B. (1979, September). *Exposure to pornography and reactions to rape*. Paper presented at the 87th Annual Convention of the American Psychological Association, New York.

Malamuth, N., & Spinner, B. (1980). A longitudinal content analysis of sexual violence in the best-selling erotic magazines. *Journal of Sex Research, 16,* 226-237.

Malmsheimer, R. (1988). *Doctors only: The evolving image of the American physician.* New York: Greenwood.

Manstead, A., & McCulloch, C. (1981). Sex-role stereotyping in British television advertisements. *British Journal of Social Psychology, 20,* 171-180.

Mares, M. L. (1996). The role of source confusions in television's cultivation of social reality judgements. *Human Communication Research, 23,* 278-297.

Masland, T. (1991, September 1). Book review. *Philadelphia Inquirer,* p. 2F.

Masse, M., & Rosenblum, K. (1988). Male and female created they them: The depiction of gender in the advertising of traditional women's and men's magazines. *Women's Studies International Forum, 11,* 127-144.

Mast, G. (1986). *A short history of the movies* (4th ed.). New York: Macmillan.

McCombs, M. E., & Shaw, D. L. (1976). Structuring the "Unseen Environment." *Journal of Communication, 26,* 14-28.

McDermott, S., & Greenberg, B. (1984). Parents, peers, and television as determinants of black children's esteem. In R. Bostrom (Ed.), *Communication yearbook* (Vol. 8, pp. 164-177). Beverly Hills, CA: Sage.

McKee, K. B., & Purdun, C. J. (1996). Mixed messages: The relationship between sexual and religious imagery in rock, country and Christian videos. *Communication Reports, 9,* 163-171.

McLaughlin, J. (1975). The doctor shows. *Journal of Communication, 25,* 182-184.

McLeod, J., Kosicki, G. M., & Pan, Z. (1991). On understanding and misunderstanding media effects. In J. Curran & M. Gurevitch (Eds.), *Mass media and society* (pp. 235-266). London: Edward Arnold.

McLeod, J. M. (1986). *Public images of mass media news: What are they and does it matter?* Paper presented at the Association for Education in Journalism and Mass Communication, Norman, OK.

McNair, B. (1996). *Mediated sex: Pornography & postmodern culture.* London: Arnold.

Medrich, E. A. (1979). Constant television: A background to daily life. *Journal of Communication, 29,* 173-176.

Mehta, M. D., & Plaza, D. E. (1997). Pornography in cyberspace: An exploration of what's in Usenet. In S. Kiesler (Ed.), *Culture of the Internet* (pp. 53-67). Mahwah, NJ: Lawrence Erlbaum.

Mellen, J. (1977). *Big bad wolves: Masculinity in the American film.* New York: Pantheon.

Mellor, P. (1993). Death in high modernity. In D. Clark (Ed.), *The sociology of death* (pp. 24-54). Oxford, UK: Blackwell.

Michaelson, J. (1987, September 9). Black image: We're not there yet. *Los Angeles Times,* part VI.

Milavsky, J. R., Kessler, R., Stipp, H., & Rubens, W. S. (1982). Television and aggression: Results of a panel study. In D. Pearl, L. Bouthilet, & J. Lazar (Eds.), *Television and behavior: Ten years of scientific progress and implications for the 80s* (Vol. 2, pp. 138-157). Washington, DC: Government Printing Office.

Miller, M. M., & Reeves, B. (1976). Dramatic TV content and children's sex-role stereotypes. *Journal of Broadcasting, 20,* 35-50.

Mills, C. W. (1967). The cultural apparatus. In I. L. Horowitz (Ed.), *Power, politics, and people: The collected essays of C. Wright Mills* (pp. 404-420). New York: Oxford University Press.

Modleski, T. (1982). *Loving with a vengeance: Mass produced fantasies for women.* New York: Methuen.

Molotch, H., & Lester, M. (1974). News as purposive behavior: On the strategic use of routine events, accidents, and scandals. *American Sociological Review, 39,* 101-112.

Mooney, L., & Barbant, S. (1987). Two martinis and a rested woman: "Liberation" in the *Sunday Times* comics. *Sex Roles, 17,* 409-420.

Morgan, M. (1982). Television and adolescent's sex-role stereotypes: A longitudinal study. *Journal of Personality and Social Psychology, 43*(5), 947-955.

Morgan, M. (1983). Symbolic victimization and real world fear. *Human Communication Research, 9,* 146-157.

Morgan, M. (1984). Heavy television viewing and perceived quality of life. *Journalism Quarterly, 61,* 499-504.

Morgan, M. (1987). Television, sex-role attitudes, and sex-role behavior. *The Journal of Early Adolescence, 7,* 269-282.

Morgan, M. (1989). Television and democracy. In I. Angus & S. Jhally (Eds.), *Cultural politics in contemporary America* (pp. 240-253). New York: Routledge.

Morgan, M. (1990). International cultivation analysis. In M. Morgan & N. Signorielli (Eds.), *Cultivation analysis: New directions in media effects research* (pp. 225-247). Newbury Park, CA: Sage.

Morgan, M., Alexander, A., Shanahan, J., & Harris, C. (1990). Adolescents, VCRs, and the family environment. *Communication Research, 17,* 83-106.

Morgan, M., & Gross, L. (1982). Television and educational achievement and aspiration. In D. Pearl, L. Bouthilet, & J. Lazar (Eds.), *Television and behavior: Ten years of scientific progress and implications for the 80s: Vol. 2. Technical reviews* (pp. 78-90). Rockville, MD: National Institute of Mental Health.

Morgan, M., Lewis, J., & Jhally, S. (1992). More viewing, less knowledge. In H. Mowlana, G. Gerbner, & H. Schiller (Eds.), *Triumph of the image* (pp. 216-235). Boulder, CO: Westview.

Morgan, M., & Rothschild, N. (1983). Impact of the new television technology: Cable TV, peers, and sex-role cultivation in the electronic environment. *Youth and Society, 15,* 33-50.

Morgan, M., & Shanahan, J. (1991). Do VCRs change the TV picture? VCRs and the cultivation process. *American Behavioral Scientist, 35,* 122-135.

Morgan, M., & Shanahan, J. (1997). Two decades of cultivation research: An appraisal and meta-analysis. In B. Berelson (Ed.), *Communication yearbook* (Vol. 20, pp. 1-45). Thousand Oaks, CA: Sage.

Morgan, M., &. Signorielli, N. (1990). Cultivation analysis: Conceptualization and methodology. In N. Signorielli & M. Morgan (Eds.), *Cultivation analysis* (pp. 13-34). Newbury Park, CA: Sage.

Morley, D. (1992). *Television, audiences, and cultural studies.* London: Routledge.

Morrison, D. E. (1992). *Television and the Gulf War.* London: John Libbey.

Morse, M. (1985). Rock video: Synchronizing rock music and television. *Fabula, 5,* 13-32.

Mossberg, W. S. (1991, February 28). U.S. used press as weapon. *Wall Street Journal.*

Mowlana, H., Gerbner, G., & Schiller, H. I. (Eds.). (1992). *Triumph of the image: The media's war in the Persian Gulf.* Boulder, CO: Westview.

MTV Research. (1991). *Marketing report.* New York: Time Warner.

Mueller, J. E. (1994). *Policy and opinion in the Gulf War.* Chicago: Chicago University Press.

Murphy, D. J., Burrows, D., Santilli, S., Kemp, A. W., Tenner, S., Kreling, B., & Tenno, J. (1994). The influence of the probability of survival on patients' preference regarding cardiopulmonary resuscitation. *The New England Journal of Medicine, 330,* 545-549.

Mussen, P., & Rutherford, E. (1961). Effects of aggressive cartoons on children's aggressive play. *Journal of Abnormal and Social Psychology, 62,* 461-464.

Muzzio, D. (1996). "Decent people shouldn't live here": The American city in cinema. *Journal of Urban Affairs, 18,* 189-215.

Myers, P. N., & Biocca, F. A. (1992). The elastic body image: The effects of television advertising and programming on body image distortions in young women. *Journal of Communication, 42,* 108-133.

National Coalition on Television Violence. (1984). *MCTV Music video monitoring project.* Unpublished report.

National television violence study (3 vols.). (1997). Thousand Oaks, CA: Sage.

Neville, T. J. (1980). More on Wober's "televised violence." *Public Opinion Quarterly, 44,* 116-117.

Newcomb, H. (1978). Assessing the violence profile of Gerbner and Gross: A humanistic critique and suggestion. *Communication Research, 5,* 264-282.

Newcomb, T. (1950). *Social psychology.* New York: Dryden.

Nikken, P., & Peeters, A. L. (1988). Children's perception of reality. *Journal of Broadcasting & Electronic Media, 32,* 441-452.

Noelle-Neumann, E. (1973). Return to the concept of powerful mass media. In H. Eguchi & K. Sata (Eds.), *Studies of broadcasting* (pp. 102-123). Tokyo: Nippon Hoso Kyokai.

Noelle-Neumann, E. (1974). Spiral of silence: A theory of public opinion. *Journal of Communication, 24,* 43-51.

Noelle-Neumann, E. (1984). *The spiral of silence: Public opinion—our social skin.* Chicago: University of Chicago Press.

Noelle-Neumann, E. (1989). Advances in spiral of silence research. *Communication Review, 10,* 3-34.

Noelle-Neumann, E. (1991). The theory of public opinion: The concept of the spiral of silence. *Communication Yearbook, 14,* 256-287.

Northcott, H. C. (1975). Too young, too old: Aging in the world of television. *Gerontologist, 15,* 184-186.

O'Donnell, W. J., & O'Donnell, K. J. (1978). Update: Sex-role messages in TV commercials. *Journal of Communication, 28,* 156-158.

Oliver, M. B. (1994). Portrayals of crime, race, and aggression in "reality-based" police shows: A content analysis. *Journal of Broadcasting and Electronic Media, 38,* 180-192.

Page, H. (1997). Black male imagery and media containment of African American men. *American Anthropologist, 99,* 99-111.

Palys, T. S. (1986). Testing the common wisdom: The social content of video pornography. *Canadian Psychology, 27,* 22-35.

Pan, Z., & Kosicki, G. M. (1997). Priming and media impact on the evaluations of the president's performance. *Communication Research, 24*(1), 3-30.

Park, R. E. (1923). The natural history of the newspaper. *American Journal of Sociology, 29,* 273-289.

Parke, R. D., Berkowitz, L., Leyens, J. P., West, S., & Sebastian, R. J. (1977). Some effects of violent and nonviolent movies on the behavior of juvenile delinquents. In L. Berkowitz (Ed.), *Advances in social psychology* (Vol. 10). New York: Academic Press.

Payne, D. E., & Peake, C. A. (1977). Cultural diffusion: The role of U.S. TV in Iceland, *Journalism Quarterly, 54,* 523-531.

Peirce, K. (1989). Sex-role stereotyping of children and television: A content analysis of the roles and attributes of child characters. *Sociological Spectrum, 9,* 321-328.

Peirce, K. (1990). A feminist theoretical perspective on the socialization of teenage girls through *Seventeen* magazine. *Sex Roles, 23,* 491-500.

Perse, E. M. (1986). Soap opera viewing patterns of college students and cultivation. *Journal of Broadcasting and Electronic Media, 30,* 75-193.

Perse, E. M. (1990). Cultivation and involvement with local television news. In N. Signorielli & M. Morgan (Eds.), *Cultivation analysis* (pp. 51-70). Newbury Park, CA: Sage.

Perse, E. M., Ferguson, D. A., & McLeod, D. M. (1994). Cultivation in the newer media environment. *Communication Research, 21,* 79-104.

Pettegrew, J. (1995). A post-modernist moment: The 1980s commercial culture and the founding of MTV. In G. Dines & J. M. Humez (Eds.), *Gender, race, and class in media* (pp. 474-496), Newbury Park, CA: Sage.

Petty, R. E., & Cacioppo, J. T. (1984). The effects of involvement on responses to argument quantity and quality: Central and peripheral routes to persuasion. *Journal of Personality and Social Psychology, 46,* 69-81.

Petty, R. E., Cacioppo, J. T., & Kasmer, J. A. (1987). The role of affect in the elaboration likelihood model of persuasion. In L. Donohue, H. E. Sypher, & E. T. Higgins (Eds.), *Communication, social cognition, and affect* (pp. 117-146). Hillsdale, NJ: Lawrence Erlbaum.

Pfau, M., Mullen, L. J., Diedrich, T., & Garrow, K. (1995). Television viewing and public perceptions of attorneys. *Human Communication Research, 21,* 307-330.

Pfau, M., Mullen, L. J., & Garrow, K. (1995). The influence of television viewing on public perceptions of physicians. *Journal of Broadcasting & Electronic Media, 39,* 441-458.

Phillips, D. P. (1979). Suicide, motor vehicle fatalities, and the mass media: Evidence toward a theory of suggestion. *American Journal of Sociology, 84,* 1150-1174.

Phillips, D. P. (1980). Airplane accidents, murder, and the mass media: Toward a theory of imitation and suggestion. *Social Forces, 58,* 1001-1024.

Phillips, D. P. (1982). The impact of fiction television stories on American adult fatalities: New evidence on the effect of the mass media on violence. *American Journal of Sociology, 87,* 1340-1359.

Phillips, D. P., & Carstensen, L. L. (1986). Clustering of teenage suicides after television news stories about suicide. *New England Journal of Medicine, 315,* 685-689.

Phillips, D. P., & Carstensen, L. L. (1988). The effect of suicide stories on various demographic groups: 1968-1985. *Suicide and Life-Threatening Behavior, 18,* 100-114.

Phillips, D. P., Lesyna, K., & Paight, D. (1991). Suicide and the media. In R. W. Morris, A. L. Berman, J. T. Maltsberger, & R. I. Yufit (Eds.), *Assessment and prediction of suicide* (pp. 87-99). New York: Guilford.

Phillips, D. P., & Paight, D. J. (1987). The impact of televised movies about suicide. *New England Journal of Medicine, 317,* 809-811.

Pingree, S. (1978). The effects of nonsexist television commercials and perceptions of reality on children's attitudes about women. *Psychology of Women Quarterly, 2,* 262-277.

Pingree, S. (1983). Children's cognitive processes in constructing social reality. *Journalism Quarterly, 60,* 415-422.

Pingree, S., & Hawkins, R. P. (1981). U.S. programs on Australian television: The cultivation effect. *Journal of Communication, 31,* 97-105.

Pingree, S., Hawkins, R. P., Butler, M., & Paisley, W. (1976). A scale of sexism. *Journal of Communication, 26,* 193-200.

Pingree, S., Starrett, S., & Hawkins, P. (1979). *Soap opera viewers and social reality.* Unpublished manuscript, Women's Studies program, University of Wisconsin-Madison.

Platt, S. (1987). The aftermath of Angie's overdose: Is soap (opera) damaging to your health? *British Medical Journal, 294,* 954-957.

Poindexter, P. M., & Stroman, C. (1981). Blacks and television: A review of the research literature. *Journal of Broadcasting, 25,* 103-122.

Polivka, J. S. (1988). Is America aging successfully? A message from media cartoons. *Communication & Cognition, 21,* 97-106.

Pollay, R. W., Tse, D. K., & Wang, Z. (1990). Advertising, propaganda, and value change in economic development: The new cultural revolution in China and attitudes toward advertising. *Journal of Business Research, 20,* 83-95.

Postol, T. A. (1992). Lessons of the Gulf War experience with Patriot. *International Security, 16,* 119-171.

Potter, W. J. (1986). Perceived reality and the cultivation hypothesis. *Journal of Broadcasting and Electronic Media, 30,* 159-174.

Potter, W. J. (1989). Three strategies for elaborating the cultivation hypothesis. *Journalism Quarterly, 65,* 930-939.

Potter, W. J. (1991a). Examining cultivation from the psychological perspective. *Communication Research, 18,* 77-102.

Potter, W. J. (1991b). The linearity assumption in cultivation research. *Human Communication Research, 17,* 562-583.

Potter, W. J. (1991c). The relationships between first- and second-order measures of cultivation. *Human Communication Research, 19,* 92-113.

Potter, W. J. (1994). Cultivation theory and research: A methodological critique. *Journalism Monographs, 147,* 1-35.

Potter, W. J., Vaughan, M. W., Warren, R., Howley, K., Land, A., & Hagenmeyer, J. C. (1995). How real is the portrayal of aggression in television entertainment programming? *Journal of Broadcasting and Electronic Media, 39,* 496-516.

Powel, L. A., & Williamson, J. B. (1985). The mass media and the aged. *Social Policy, 16,* 38-49.

Preston, E. H. (1990). Pornography and the construction of gender. In N. Signorielli & M. Morgan (Eds.), *Cultivation analysis* (pp. 107-122). Newbury Park, CA: Sage.

Prince, S. (1990). Power and pain: Content analysis and the ideology of pornography. *Journal of Film and Video, 42,* 31-41.

Purdun, C. J., & McKee, K. B. (1995). Strange bedfellows: Symbols of sexuality and religion on MTV. *Youth and Society, 26,* 38-49.

Rabinovitz, L. (1994). Soap opera woes: Genre, gender, and the Persian Gulf War. In S. Jeffords & L. Rabinovitz (Eds.), *Seeing through the media: The Persian Gulf war* (pp. 189-204). New Brunswick, NJ: Rutgers University Press.

Radway, J. (1984). *Reading the romance: Women, patriarchy, and popular literature.* Chapel Hill: University of North Carolina Press.

Radway, J. (1985). Interpretive communities and variable literacies: The functions of romance reading. In M. Gurevitch & M. R. Levy (Eds.), *Mass communication review yearbook* (Vol. 5). Beverly Hills, CA: Sage.

Rafaeli, S. (1998). Interactivity: From new media to communication. In R. R Hawkins, J. M. Wiesmann, & S. Pingree (Eds.), *Advancing communication science: Merging mass and interpersonal processes* (Sage Annual Reviews of Communication Research, Vol. 16, pp. 110-134). Newbury Park, CA: Sage.

Rafaeli, S., & Sudweeks, F. (1998). Interactivity on the nets. In F. Sudweeks, M. McLaughlin, & S. Rafaeli (Eds.), *Network & netplay: Virtual groups on the Internet* (pp. 173-189). Menlo Park, CA: AAAI Press.

Range, L. M., Goggin, W. C., & Steede, K. K. (1988). Perception of behavioral contagion of adolescent suicide. *Suicide and Life-Threatening Behavior, 18,* 334-341.

Rapping, E. (1995). Daytime inquiries. In G. Dines & J. M. Humez, *Gender, race, and class in media.* Thousand Oaks, CA: Sage.

Reeves, B., & Miller, M. M. (1978). A multidimensional measure of children's identification with television characters. *Journal of Broadcasting, 22,* 71-86.

Reid, E. (1995). Virtual worlds: Culture and imagination. In S. Jones (Ed.), *Cyber-Society: Computer-mediated communication and community* (pp. 162-178). Thousand Oaks, CA: Sage.

Reid, L. N., Whitehill King, K., & Kreshel, P. J. (1995). Black and white models and their activities in modern cigarette and alcohol ads. *Journalism Quarterly, 71,* 873-886.

Reid, P. T. (1979). Racial stereotyping on television: A comparison of the behavior of both black and white television characters. *Journal of Applied Psychology, 64*(5), 465-489.

Rheingold, H. (1992). *Virtual reality.* London: Mandarin.

Rheingold, H. (1994). *The virtual community.* London: Secker and Warburg.

Richter, A. (1991). Enemy turned partner: A content analysis of *Newsweek* and *Novoye Vremya.* In E. E. Dennis, G. Gerbner, & Y. N. Zassoursky (Eds.), *Beyond the cold war* (pp. 91-99). Newbury Park, CA: Sage.

Ridley-Johnson, R., Chance, J. E., & Cooper, H. (1984). Correlates of children's television viewing: Expectancies, age, and sex. *Journal of Applied Developmental Psychology, 5,* 225-235.

Rimmer, R. H. (1986). *The X-rated videotape guide.* New York: Harmony.

Roberts, C. (1975). The presentation of blacks in network television newscasts. *Journalism Quarterly, 52,* 50-55.

Robinett, W. (1992). Synthetic experience: A proposed taxonomy. *Presence, 1,* 229-247.

Robins, K. (1995). Cyberspace and the world we live in. In M. Featherstone & R. Burrows (Eds.), *Cyberspace, cyberbodies, cyberpunk* (pp. 135-155). London: Sage.

Robinson, J. D. (1989). Mass media and the elderly: A uses and dependency interpretation. In J. F. Nussbaum (Ed.), *Life-span communication* (pp. 319-337). Hillsdale, NJ: Lawrence Erlbaum.

Robinson, J. P. (1974). The press as kingmaker. *Journalism Quarterly, 51,* 587-594.

Rodwin, L., & Hollister, R. (Eds.). (1984). *Cities of the mind: Images and themes of the city in social sciences.* New York: Plenum.

Rogers, E. M., & Dearing, J. W. (1988). Agenda-setting research: Where has it been, where is it going? In J. A. Anderson (Ed.), *Communication yearbook* (Vol. 11, pp. 555-594). Newbury Park, CA: Sage.

Rokeach, M. (1968). *Beliefs, attitudes, and values: A theory of organization and change.* San Francisco: Jossey-Bass.

Rosenberg, R. S. (1997). *The social impact of computers* (2nd ed.). San Diego, CA: Academic Press.

Ross, L., Anderson, D. R., & Wisocki, P. A. (1982). Television viewing and adult sex-role attitudes. *Sex Roles, 8,* 589-592.

Rubin, A. M. (1969). Uses, gratifications, and media effects research. In J. Bryant & D. Zillmann (Eds.), *Perspectives on media effects* (pp. 281-301). Hillsdale, NJ: Lawrence Erlbaum.

Rubin, A. M. (1984). Ritualized and instrumental television viewing. *Journal of Communication, 34,* 66-77.

Rubin, A. M. (1994). Media uses and effects: A uses-and-gratifications perspective. In J. Bryant & D. Zillmann (Eds.), *Media effects: Advances in theory and research* (pp. 417-436). Hillsdale, NJ: Lawrence Erlbaum.

Rubin, A., & Perse, A. M. (1987a). Audience activity and soap opera involvement: A uses and effects investigation. *Human Communication Research, 14,* 246-268.

Rubin, A., & Perse, A. M. (1987b). Audience activity and television news gratifications. *Communication Research, 14,* 58-84.

Rubin, A. M., Perse, E. M., & Taylor, D. S. (1988). A methodological investigation of cultivation. *Communication Research, 15,* 107-134.

Ruffini, G. (1991, March). Press fails to challenge the rush to war. *Washington Journalism Review,* pp. 21-23.

Russel, C. (1995). *Narrative mortality: Death, closure, and New Wave cinemas.* Minneapolis: Minnesota University Press.

Said, E. (1993). *Culture and imperialism.* London: Chatto and Windus.

Said, E. (1997). *Covering Islam.* New York: Vintage Books.

Sander, I. (1997). An empirical investigation of factors influencing viewers' perceptions of TV violence. *European Journal of Communication, 12,* 43-98.

Sanoff, A. P., & Thomton, J. (1987, July). TV's disappearing color line. *U.S. News & World Report, 13,* 57.

Sapolsky, B. S., & Tabarlet, J. O. (1991). Sex in primetime television 1979 versus 1989. *Journal of Broadcasting and Electronic Media, 35,* 505-516.

Schickel, R. (1989). *Schickel on film.* New York: William Morrow.

Schiller, H. (1969). *Mass communication and American empire.* New York: Augustus M. Kelley.

Schiller, H. (1973). Authentic national development versus the free flow of information and the new communications technology. In G. Gerbner, L. Gross, & W. Melody (Eds.), *Communication, technology, and social policy* (pp. 234-248). New York: John Wiley.

Schiller, H. (1977). The free flow of information—For whom? In G. Gerbner (Ed.), *Mass media policies in changing cultures* (pp. 124-139). New York: John Wiley.

Schmidtke, A., & Hafner, H. (1988). The Werther Effect after television films: New evidence for an old hypothesis. *Psychological Medicine, 18,* 665-676.

Schonbach, K., & Fruh, W. (1984). Der dynamisch-transaktionale ansatz II: Konsequenzen. *Rundfunk & Fernsehen, 32,* 315-329.

Schonwetter, R. S., Teasdale, T. A., Taffet, G., Robinson, B. E., & Luchi, R. J. (1991). Educating the elderly: Cardiopulmonary resuscitation decisions before and after intervention. *Journal of American Geriatric Society, 39,* 372-377.

Schonwetter, R. S., Walker, R. M., Kramer, D. R., & Robinson, B. E. (1993). Resuscitation decision making in the elderly: The value of outcome data. *Journal of General Internal Medicine, 8,* 295-300.

Schudson, M. (1978). The ideal of conversation in the study of mass media. *Communication Research, 12,* 320-329.

Schudson, M. (1982). The politics of narrative form: The emergence of news conventions in print and television. *Daedalus, 111,* 97-112.

Schudson, M. (1991). The sociology of news production revisited. In J. Curran & M. Gurevitch (Eds.), *Mass media and society* (pp. 141-159). London: Edward Arnold.

Seefeldt, C. (1977). Young and old together. *Children Today, 6,* 22.

Seggar, J. F., Hafen, J., & Hannonen-Gladden, H. (1981). Television's portrayals of minorities and women in drama and comedy drama, 1971-80. *Journal of Broadcasting, 25,* 277-288.

Seidman, S. A. (1992). An investigation of sex-role stereotyping in music videos. *Journal of Broadcasting & Electronic Media, 36,* 209-216.

Shagrin, C. (1990, Spring). On the trail of the elusive '90s viewer. *Nielsen Newscast,* pp. 2-3.

Shah, D. (1997, May). *Civic participation, interpersonal trust, and television use: A motivational approach to social capital.* Paper presented to the Political Communication Division of the International Communication Association, Montreal, Canada.

Shaheen, J. (1979). The American media and the stereotyped Arab. In *The Arab image in Western mass media* (pp. 21-28). London: Morris International.

Shaheen, J. (1984a, March-April). Arabs—TV's villains of choice. *Channels,* pp. 52-53.

Shaheen, J. (1984b). *The TV Arab.* Bowling Green, OH: Bowling Green University Popular Press.

Shaheen, J. (1994). Arab images in American comic books. *Journal of Popular Culture, 28,* 123-133.

Shapiro, M. A. (1987). *The influence of communication-source coded memory traces on world view.* Unpublished doctoral dissertation, University of Wisconsin, Madison.

Shapiro, M. A. (1991). Memory and decision processes in the construction of social reality. *Communication Research, 18,* 3-24.

Shapiro, M. A., & Lang, A. (1991). Making television reality: Unconscious processes in the construction of social reality. *Communication Research, 18,* 685-705.

Shapiro, M. A., & McDonald, D. G. (1995). I'm not a real doctor, but I play one in virtual reality: Implications of virtual reality for judgments about reality. In F. Biocca & M. R. Levy (Eds.), *Communication in the age of virtual reality* (pp. 323-345). Hillsdale, NJ: Lawrence Erlbaum.

Shayon, R. L. (1977). Television international. In G. Gerbner (Ed.), *Mass media policies in changing culture.* New York: John Wiley.

Sheridan, P. J. (1991, July). FCC report concedes TV's future to cable. *Broadcasting,* pp. 19-20.

Sherman, B. L., & Dominick, J. R. (1986). Violence and sex in music videos, TV, and rock-n-roll. *Journal of Communication, 36,* 79-93.

Shinar, D., Tolner, A., & Biber, A. (1980). Images of old age in television drama imported to Israel. *Journal of communication, 30,* 50-55.

Shrum, L. J. (1996). Psychological processes underlying cultivation effects: Further tests of construct accessibility. *Human Communication Research, 22*(4), 482-509.

Shrum, L. J., & O'Guinn, T. C. (1993). Processes and effects in the construction of social reality: Construct accessibility as an explanatory variable. *Communication Research, 20,* 436-471.

Signorielli, N. (1985). *Role portrayal and stereotyping on television: An annotated bibliography of studies relating to women, minorities, aging, sexual behavior, health, and handicaps.* Westport, CT: Greenwood.

Signorielli, N. (1987). Drinking, sex, and violence on television: The cultural indicators perspective. *Journal of Drug Education, 17*(3), 245-260.

Signorielli, N. (1989). Television and conceptions about sex-roles: Maintaining conventionality and the status quo. *Sex Roles, 21*(5/6), 337-356.

Signorielli, N. (1990). Television's mean and dangerous world: A continuation of the cultural indicators perspective. In N. Signorielli & M. Morgan (Eds.),

Cultivation analysis: New directions in media effects research (pp. 85-105). Newbury Park, CA: Sage.

Signorielli, N. (1993a). Death and the media. In N. Signorielli (Ed.), *Mass media images and impact on health* (pp. 102-113). Westport, CT: Greenwood.

Signorielli, N. (1993b). *Mass media images and impact on health: A sourcebook.* Westport, CT: Greenwood.

Signorielli, N. (1993c). Sex and sexuality. In N. Signorielli (Ed.), *Mass media images and impact on health* (pp. 51-70). Westport, CT: Greenwood.

Signorielli, N. (1993d). Television and adolescents' perceptions about work. *Youth & Society, 24,* 314-341.

Signorielli, N., & Lears, M. (1992). Children, television, and conceptions about chores: Atittudes and behaviors. *Sex Roles, 27,* 157-170.

Signorielli, N., McLeod, D., & Healy, E. (1994). Gender stereotypes in MTV commercials: The beat goes on. *Journal of Broadcasting and Electronic Media, 38,* 91-101.

Silk, C., & Silk, J. (1990). *Racism and anti-racism in American popular culture.* Manchester, U.K.: Manchester University Press.

Silvern, S. B., & Williamson, P. A. (1987). The effects of video game play on young children's aggression. *Journal of Applied Developmental Psychology, 8,* 453-462.

Silverstein, B., Perdue, L., Peterson, B., & Kelly, E. (1986). The role of the mass media in promoting a thin standard of attractiveness for women. *Sex Roles, 14,* 519-532.

Simpson, C. (1996). Elisabeth Noelle-Neumann's "Spiral of Silence" and the historical context of communication theory. *Journal of Communication, 46,* 149-173.

Singer, D. G., & Singer, J. L. (1988). Some hazards of growing up in a television environment: Children's aggression and restlessness. In S. Oskamp (Ed.), *Television as a social issue* (pp. 171-188). Newbury Park, CA: Sage.

Singer, J. L., & Singer, D. G. (1981). *Television, imagination, and aggression: A study of preschoolers.* Hillsdale, NJ: Lawrence Erlbaum.

Skelly, G., & Lundstrom, W. (1981). Male sex roles in magazine advertising, 1959-1979. *Journal of Communication, 31,* 52-57.

Skogan, W. G., & Maxfield, M. G. (1981). *Coping with crime.* Beverly Hills, CA: Sage.

Slater, D., & Elliott, W. R. (1982). Television's influence on social reality. *Quarterly Journal of Speech, 68,* 69-79.

Slouka, M. (1995). *War of the worlds: Cyberspace and the high-tech assault on reality.* New York: Basic Books.

Small, W. (1994). The Gulf war: Mass media coverage and restraints. In T. A. McCain & L. Shyles (Eds.), *The 1,000-hour war: Communication in the gulf* (pp. 3-18). Westport, CT: Greenwood.

Smith, D. D. (1976). The social content of pornography. *Journal of Communication, 26,* 16-24.

Smith, L. (1994). A content analysis of gender differences in children's advertising. *Journal of Broadcasting and Electronic Media, 38,* 323-337.

Smith, P. M. (1991). *How CNN fought the war: A view from the inside.* New York: Birch Lane Press.

Smith Hobson, S. (1974). The rise and fall of blacks in serious television. *Freedomways, 14,* 185.

Smythe, D. W. (1954). Reality as presented by television. *Public Opinion Quarterly, 18,* 143-156.

Soares, E. (1978). *The soap opera book.* New York: Harmony Books.

Sommers-Flanagan, R., Sommers-Flanagan, J., & Davis, B. (1993). What's happening on music television? A gender role content analysis. *Sex-Roles, 28,* 745-753.

Sparks, G. G., Nelson, L. C., & Campbell, R. G. (1997). The relationship between exposure to televised messages about paranormal phenomena and paranormal beliefs. *Journal of Broadcasting and Electronic Media, 41,* 345-359.

Sparks, G. G., & Ogles, R. M. (1990). The difference between fear of victimization and the probability of being victimized: Implications for cultivation. *Journal of Broadcasting and Electronic Media, 34,* 351-358.

Sparks, G. G., Sparks, C. W., & Gray, K. (1995). Media impact on fright reactions and belief in UFOs: The potential role of mental imagery. *Communication Research, 22,* 3-23.

St. Lawrence, J. S., & Joyner, D. J. (1991). The effects of sexually violent rock music on males' acceptance of violence against women. *Psychology of Women Quarterly, 15,* 49-63.

Stack, S. (1990). Media impacts on suicide. In R. Dester (Ed.), *Current concepts of suicide* (pp. 67-82). New York: Charles Press.

Stack, S., & Gundlach, J. (1992). The effect of country music on suicide. *Social Forces, 71,* 211-218.

Staples, R., & Jones, T. (1985). Culture, ideology, and black television images. *The Black Scholar, 16,* 10-20.

Steed, K. K., & Range, L. M. (1989). Does television induce suicidal contagion with adolescents? *Journal of Community Psychology, 17,* 166-172.

Sternglanz, S., & Serbin, L. (1974). Sex role stereotyping in children's television programs. *Developmental Psychology, 10,* 710-715.

Steuer, F. B., Applefield, J. M., & Smith, R. (1971). Televised aggression and the interpersonal aggression of preschool children. *Journal of Experimental Child Psychology, 11,* 442-447.

Steuer, J. (1995). Defining virtual reality: Dimensions determining telepresence. In F. Biocca & M. R. Levy (Eds.), *Communication in the age of virtual reality* (pp. 33-56). Hillsdale, NJ: Lawrence Erlbaum.

Stevenson, R. L. (1994). *Global communication in the twenty-first century.* New York: Longman.

Stevenson, T. H. (1992). A content analysis of the portrayal of blacks in trade publication advertising. *Journal of Current Issues and Research in Advertising, 14,* 67-74.

Stice, E. M., Schupak-Neuberg, E., Shaw, H. E., & Stein, R. I. (1994). Relation of media exposure to eating disorder symptomatology: An examination of mediating mechanisms. *Journal of Abnormal Psychology, 103,* 836-840.

Stice, E. M., & Shaw, H. E. (1994). Adverse effects of the media portrayed thin-ideal on and linkages to bulimic symptomatology. *Journal of Social and Clinical Psychology, 13,* 288-308.

Stone, A. R. (1991). Will the real body please stand up? Boundary stories about virtual culture. In M. Benedikt (Ed.), *Cyberspace: First space* (pp. 81-113). Cambridge: MIT Press.

Stone, E. (1991, March). News practices. *RTNDA Communicator.*

Strauss, A. (1968). *The American city: A sourcebook of urban imagery.* Chicago: Aldine.

Stroman, C. A. (1986). Television viewing and self-concept among black children. *Journal of Broadcasting and Electronic Media, 30,* 87-93.

Stross, R. (1990). *Bulls in the China shop and other Sino-American business encounters.* New York: Pantheon Books.

Strouse, J. S., & Buerkel-Rothfuss, N. L. (1987). Media exposure and the sexual attitudes and behaviors of college students. *Journal of Sex Education and Therapy, 13,* 43-51.

Sun, S. W., & Lull, J. (1986). The adolescent audience for music videos and why they watch. *Journal of Communication, 36,* 115-125.

Surgeon General's Scientific Advisory Committee on Television and Social Behavior. (1971a). *Television and growing up: The impact of televised violence.* Washington, DC: Government Printing Office.

Surgeon General's Scientific Advisory Committee on Television and Social Behavior. (1971b). *Television and social behavior* (5 vols.). Washington, DC: Government Printing Office.

Talk of the town. (1991, January 21). *New Yorker,* p. 21.

Tamborini, R., Zillmann, D., & Bryant, J. (1984). Fear and victimization: Exposure to television and perceptions of crime and fear. In R. N. Bostrom (Ed.), *Communication yearbook* (Vol. 8, pp. 492-513). Beverley Hills, CA: Sage.

Tan, A. (1979). TV beauty ads and role expectations of adolescent female viewers. *Journalism Quarterly, 56,* 283-288.

Tan, A. (1986). Social learning of aggression from television. In J. Bryant & D. Zillmann (Eds.), *Perspectives on media effects* (pp. 41-55). Hillsdale, NJ: Lawrence Erlbaum.

Tan, A. S. (1987). American TV and social stereotypes of Americans in Taiwan and Mexico. *Journalism Quarterly, 63,* 809-814.

Tan, A. S., Tan, G. K., & Tan, A. S. (1987). American television in the Philippines: A test of cultural impact. *Journalism Quarterly, 63,* 67-82.

Tannenbaum, P. H. (1971). *Emotional arousal as a mediator of communication effects* (Technical reports of the Commission on Obscenity and Pornography, Vol. 8). Washington DC: Government Printing Office.

Tannenbaum, P. H. (1980). Entertainment as vicarious experience. In P. H. Tannenbaum (Ed.), *The entertainment functions of television* (pp. 107-131). Hillsdale, NJ: Lawrence Erlbaum.

Taylor, H., & Dozier, C. (1983). Television violence, African Americans, and social control: 1950-1976. *Journal of Black Studies, 14,* 107-136.

Taylor, P. M. (1992). *War and the media: Propaganda and persuasion in the Gulf War.* Manchester, U.K.: Manchester University Press.

Thomas, S. (1986). Gender and social-class coding in popular photographic erotica. *Communication Quarterly, 34,* 103- 114.

Toro, J., Cervera, M., & Perez, P. (1988). Body shape, publicity, and anorexia nervosa. *Social Psychiatry and Psychiatric Epidemiology, 23,* 132-136.

Tuchman, G. (1980). *Making news: A study in the construction of reality.* New York: Free Press.

Tunstall, J. (1977). *The media are American.* London: Constable.

Turner, C. W., Hesse, B. W., & Petterson-Lewis, S. (1986). Naturalistic studies of the long-term effects of television violence. *Journal of Social Issues, 42,* 51-73.

U.S. Commission on Obscenity and Pornography. (1970). *The report of the Commission on Obscenity and Pornography.* New York: Bantam.

U.S. Department of Labor. (1992). *U.S. Department of Labor statistics.* New York: Author.

Van der Voort, T. H. A. (1986). *Television violence: A child's eye view.* Amsterdam: North Holland.

Van Tubergen, N. G., & Boyd, D. A. (1986). Third-world image of the U.S.: Media use by Jordanians. *Journalism Quarterly, 63,* 607-611.

Varis, T. (1974). Global traffic in television. *Journal of Communication, 24,* 102-109.

Varis, T. (1984). The international flow of television programs. *Journal of Communication, 34,* 143-152.

Vasil, L., & Wass, H. (1993). Portrayal of the elderly in the media: A literature review and implications for educational gerontologists. *Educational Gerontology, 19,* 71-85.

Vidmar, N., & Rokeach, M. (1974). Archie Bunker's bigotry: A study in selective perception and exposure. *Journal of Communication, 24,* 35-47.

Vincent, R. C. (1989). Clio's consciousness raised? Portrayal of women in rock videos, re-examined. *Journalism Quarterly, 66,* 155-160.

Vincent, R. C., Davis, D. K., & Boruszkowski, L. A. (1987). Sexism on MTV: The portrayal of women in rock videos. *Journalism Quarterly, 64,* 750-755.

Volgy, T., & Schwartz, J. (1980). Television entertainment programming and socio-political attitudes. *Journalism Quarterly, 57,* 150-155.

Walker, D. C., Wicks, R. H., & Pyle, R. (1991, August). *Differences in live coverage between CNN and the broadcast networks in the Persian Gulf War.* Paper presented at the Association for Journalism and Mass Communication Convention, Boston.

Walker, J. (1987). How viewing of MTV relates to exposure to other media violence. *Journalism Quarterly, 64,* 756-762.

Walter, T., Littlewood, J., & Pickering, M. (1995). Death in the news: The public invigilation of private emotion. *Sociology, 29,* 579-596.

Wang, J. (1997). Through the looking-glass of foreign ads in China. *Asian Journal of Communication, 7,* 19-42.

Wanta, W., & Leggett, D. (1989). Gender stereotypes in wire service sports photos. *Newspaper Research Journal, 10,* 105-114.

Ware, M., & Stuck, M. (1985). Sex role messages vis-à-vis microcomputer use: A look at the pictures. *Sex Roles, 13,* 205-214.

Waste, R. (1995). Urban poverty and the city as reservation. *Journal of Urban Affairs, 17,* 315-324.

Weaver, J. (1991). Responding to erotica: Perceptual and dispositional consequences. In J. Bryant & D. Zillmann (Eds.), *Responding to the screen: Reception and reaction processes* (pp. 329-354). Hillsdale, NJ: Lawrence Erlbaum.

Weaver, J. (1992). The perceptual and behavioral consequences of exposure to pornography: The social science and psychological research evidence. In C. Itain (Ed.), *Pornography: Women, violence, & civil liberties* (pp. 284-309). Oxford, UK: Oxford University Press.

Weaver, J., Masland, L., & Zillmann, D. (1984). Effect of erotica on young men's aesthetic perception of their female sexual partners. *Perceptual and Motor Skills, 58,* 929-930.

Weaver, J., & Wakshlag, J. (1986). Perceived vulnerability to crime, criminal victimization experience, and television viewing. *Journal of Broadcasting and Electronic Media, 30,* 141-158.

Weber, M. (1946). Politics as a vocation. In H. Gerth & C. W. Mills (Eds.), *From Max Weber: Essays in sociology* (pp. 77-128). London: Kegan Paul. (Original work published 1921)

Weimann, G. (1984). Images of life in America: The impact of American TV in Israel. *International Journal of Intercultural Relations, 8,* 185-197.

Weimann, G. (1995a). Zapping in the Holy Land: Coping with multichannel TV in Israel. *Journal of Communication, 45,* 97-103.

Weimann, G. (1995b). *The influentials: People who influence people.* New York: State University of New York Press.

Weimann, G. (1996). Cable comes to the Holy Land: The impact of cable TV on Israeli viewers. *Journal of Broadcasting and Electronic Media, 40,* 243-257.

Weimann, G. (1999). Gender images in Israeli TV commercials. *Megamot* (in Hebrew).

Weimann, G., Brosius, H. B., & Wober, M. (1992). TV diets: Toward a typology of TV viewership. *European Journal of Communication, 7,* 491-515.

Weimann, G., & Fishman, G. (1988). Attribution of responsibility: Sex-based bias in press reports on crime. *European Journal of Communication, 3,* 415-430.

Weimann, G., & Fishman, G. (1995). Reconstructing suicide: Reporting suicide in the Israeli press. *Journalism Quarterly, 72,* 551-558.

Weimann, G., & Winn, C. (1994). *The theater of terror: Mass media and international terrorism.* New York: Longman.

Weinreich, F. (1997). Establishing a point of view toward virtual communities. *Journal of Computer Mediated Communication, 3*(2).

Weitz, S. (1977). *Sex roles: Biological, psychological, and social foundations.* New York: Oxford University Press.

Welch, R., Huston-Stein, A., Wright, J., & Plehal, R. (1979). Subtle sex-role clues in children's commercials. *Journal of Communication, 29,* 202-209.

Wells, A. (1972). *Picture tube imperialism?* New York: Orbis Books.

Whetmore, E. J. (1991). *Mediamerica: Form, content, and consequence of mass communication* (4th ed.). Belmont, CA: Wadsworth.

Wicker, T. (1991, March 20). An unknown casualty. *New York Times,* p. A29.

Wiener, R. (1992). *Live from Baghdad: Gathering news at ground zero.* New York: Doubleday.

Wilson, B. (1997). "Good blacks" and "bad blacks" media: Constructions of African-American athletes in Canadian basketball. *International Review for the Sociology of Sport, 32,* 177-189.

Winch, S. P. (1997). *Mapping the cultural space of journalism.* Westport, CT: Praeger.

Winick, C. (1985). A content analysis of sexually explicit magazines sold in an adult bookstore. *Journal of Sex Research, 21,* 206-210.

Wiseman, C. V., Gray, J. J., Mosimann, J. E., & Ahrens, A. H. (1990). Cultural expectations of thinness in women: An update. *International Journal of Eating Disorders, 11,* 85-89.

Wober, J. M. (1978). Televised violence and paranoid perception: The view from Great Britain. *Public Opinion Quarterly, 42,* 315-321.

Wober, J. M. (1979). Televised violence and viewers' perceptions of reality: A reply to criticisms of some British research. *Public Opinion Quarterly, 43,* 271-273.

Wober, M., & Gunter, B. (1982). Impressions of old people on TV and in real life. *British Journal of Social Psychology, 21,* 335-336.

Wroblewski, R., & Huston, A. C. (1987). Televised occupational stereotypes and their effects on early adolescents: Are they changing? *Journal of Early Adolescence, 7,* 283-297.

Wyer, R. S., & Srull, T. K. (1989). *Memory and cognition in its social context.* Hillsdale, NJ: Lawrence Erlbaum.

Zelizer, B. (1990). Where is the author in American TV news? On the construction and presentation of proximity, authorship, and journalistic authority. *Semiotica, 80,* 45-57.

Zelizer, B. (1992). CNN, the Gulf War, and journalistic practice. *Journal of Communication, 42,* 66-81.

Zillmann, D. (1979). *Hostility and aggression.* Hillsdale, NJ: Lawrence Erlbaum.

Zillmann, D. (1989). Pornography research and public policy. In D. Zillmann & J. Bryant (Eds.), *Pornography: Research advances and policy considerations* (pp. 387-403). Hillsdale, NJ: Lawrence Erlbaum.

Zillmann, D., & Bryant, J. (1982). Effects of massive exposure to pornography. In N. Malamuth & E. Donnerstein (Eds.), *Pornography and sexual aggression* (pp. 115-138). New York: Academic Press.

Zillmann, D., & Bryant, J. (1984). Pornography, sexual callousness, and the trivialization of rape. *Journal of Communication, 32*(4), 10-21.

Zillmann, D., & Bryant, J. (1988a). Effects of prolonged consumption of pornography on family values. *Journal of Family Issues, 9,* 518-544.

Zillmann, D., & Bryant, J. (1988b). Pornography's impact on sexual satisfaction. *Journal of Applied Social Psychology, 18,* 438-453.

Zillmann, D., & Bryant, J. (Eds.). (1989). *Pornography: Research advances and policy considerations.* Hillsdale, NJ: Lawrence Erlbaum.

Zillmann, D., & Wakshlag, J. (1985). Fear of victimization and the appeal of crime drama. In D. Zillmann & J. Bryant (Eds.), *Selective exposure to communication* (pp. 141-156). Hillsdale, NJ: Lawrence Erlbaum.

Zinkhan, G. M., Qualls, W. J., & Biswas, A. (1990). The use of blacks in magazine and television advertising. *Journalism Quarterly, 67,* 547-553.

Zuckerman, D., Singer, D., & Singer, J. (1980). Children's television viewing, racial and sex-role attitudes. *Journal of Applied Social Psychology, 10,* 281-294.

Author Index

Subject Index

About the Author

Gabriel Weimann is a full professor of communication at Haifa University, Israel. His research interests include the study of media effects, personal influence, modern terrorism and the media, and public opinion. He has published three books: *The Influentials: People Who Influence People* (1995), *The Theater of Terror* (1994), and *Hate on Trial* (1986). His numerous research reports have been published in journals such as *Journal of Communication, Public Opinion Quarterly, Communication Research, Journal of Broadcasting and Electronic Media, American Sociological Review,* and others. He has received numerous grants and awards from international foundations, including the Fulbright Foundation, the Canadian-Israel Foundation, Alexander von Humboldt-Stiftung, the German National Research Foundation (DFG), and the Sasakawa Foundation.

DATE DUE

APR 2 6 2001		

HIGHSMITH #45115